Poverty and Pacification

PRAISE FOR *POVERTY AND PACIFICATION: THE CHINESE STATE ABANDONS THE OLD WORKING CLASS*

"Dorothy Solinger has produced a remarkable sequel to her classic account of China's rural migrant workers (*Contesting Citizenship in Urban China*, 1999). In *Poverty and Pacification,* Solinger shifts her attention to the tens of millions of veteran urban workers who have lost their jobs as China's factories have been privatized, restructured, and closed. Based on more than two decades of research in nine Chinese cities, she provides a disturbing portrayal of how industrial restructuring has dismantled the lives of men and women who had once been promised lifetime employment. While her earlier book documented the severe difficulties encountered by rural migrants, it also reflected their hopes of upward mobility; her new book, in contrast, treats the downward trajectory of once proud workers who have been cast aside."
—**Joel Andreas, Johns Hopkins University; author of *Rise of the Red Engineers* and *Disenfranchised***

"In this interesting book, Dorothy Solinger crystallizes her long-standing research on China's urban poor, exposing the government's miserable treatment of a huge number of former workers who had once been loyal stalwarts of Maoist socialism. Drawing from a vast amount of field notes and documentation, she analyzes the manipulative mechanisms by which different levels of the government have been able to relegate this sector of the populace to marginal oblivion."
—**Anita Chan, editor of *The China Journal***

"Solinger's study of China's forgotten and invisible urban residents—often living in desperate conditions at odds with the dominant narrative of China's miracle of economic growth and development—is the culmination of two decades of research. It is a work of meticulous detail, drawing on multiple methods and sources of information presented alongside a commanding knowledge of the literature that explains the emergence of China's social assistance in the economic and political context of the last thirty years. What marks this as a standout study of China's management of the urban poor and the development of the social assistance system is Solinger's empathy for those in poverty, receiving what help the state deems adequate. They are not forgotten or ignored; rather, they are central to the analysis, and it is all the stronger for it."
—**Dr. Daniel R. Hammond, University of Edinburgh**

"Dorothy Solinger is one of the most eminent social scientists who specializes in modern China. This admirable study of China's inadequate welfare system for the urban poor, based on in-depth documentary research and insightful interviews, reveals the callous underside of the Chinese leadership's social policies. It is one of Solinger's best books."
—**Jonathan Unger, emeritus, Australian National University**

Poverty and Pacification

The Chinese State Abandons the Old Working Class

Dorothy J. Solinger

ROWMAN & LITTLEFIELD
Lanham • Boulder • New York • London

Published by Rowman & Littlefield
An imprint of The Rowman & Littlefield Publishing Group, Inc.
4501 Forbes Boulevard, Suite 200, Lanham, Maryland 20706
www.rowman.com

86-90 Paul Street, London EC2A 4NE

British Library Cataloguing in Publication Information Available

Library of Congress Cataloging-in-Publication Data

Names: Solinger, Dorothy J, author.
Title: Poverty and pacification : the Chinese state abandons the old
    working class / Dorothy J. Solinger.
Description: Lanham : Rowman & Littlefield, 2021. | Includes
    bibliographical references and index.
Identifiers: LCCN 2021037770 (print) | LCCN 2021037771 (ebook) | ISBN
    9781538154953 (cloth) | ISBN 9781538154960 (epub)
Subjects: LCSH: Government business enterprises—China. | Government
    business enterprises—Government policy—China. | Minimum wage—Law and
    legislation—China. | Employees—Dismissal of—China. |
    Unemployment—Law and legislation—China. | Unemployment insurance—Law
    and legislation—China.
Classification: LCC HD4318 .S65 2021 (print) | LCC HD4318 (ebook) | DDC
    338.7/490951—dc23
LC record available at https://lccn.loc.gov/2021037770
LC ebook record available at https://lccn.loc.gov/2021037771

To all of those whose lives were wrenched,
'Twas not their fault; they were retrenched.
This is their story.

Contents

Tables and Figure

TABLES

FIGURE

Preface

In the late 1990s, soon after completing my book on rural migrants in Chinese cities and the serious issues and many facets of their lack of citizenship there (*Contesting Citizenship in Urban China*, 1999), I learned about something occurring then that I found even more disturbing. This was the predicament of possibly as many as sixty million urban-registered, lifetime-employed, welfare-entitled, considered "older" (i.e., over the age of thirty-five), and undereducated former workers being summarily sacked from their positions.

Where the migrants experienced upward mobility, leaving the farms for the municipalities, the dislocated laborers went downward. A Chinese adage captures this disparity in the alteration in life circumstances and status the two collectivities experienced: 由 俭入奢易，由奢入俭難 (*yu jian ru she yi, yu she ru jian nan*, which translates to "It's easy to go from frugality to extravagance, hard to go from extravagance to frugality"). The retrenched individuals were, plainly put (and as acknowledged by the regime), sacrificed on the altar of China's reach for modernity, for a version of market reform, and for prominence in the global economy. I was anxious to hear from them.

Walking along the streets of Wuhan, where thousands of these people—many with no income and no welfare benefits, struggling to earn by the *mao* (毛, which was then worth just about twelve US cents)—I found them friendly and open, sympathetic and pitiable, easy to meet and talk with. Besides those out in the open, help from friends and fellow scholars in China allowed me to gain entry into the homes of many more of these suddenly redundant persons, both in Wuhan and, as the years went by, in another five large Chinese cities (Lanzhou, Xi'an, Shanghai, Guangzhou, Zigong [in Sichuan]), and in three prefecture-level Hubei cities (Qianjiang, Xiantao, and Jingzhou). In addition, in the first few years, the Wuhan city government graciously arranged interviews for me with urban officials who could explain the *dibao*, the Minimum

Livelihood Guarantee program. The program is a kind of social assistance devised to silence the protests of those laid-off and offer them some measure of succor, with the stated goal of keeping them from interfering with the ongoing program of enterprise restructuring. Through my networks, I also connected with scholars and officials in China who were researching this subject. I extend heartfelt thanks first of all to the Wuhan Foreign Affairs Bureau, and then to all the many informants—redundant laborers, *dibao* recipients, and administrators and researchers who conversed with me in China, of which there were well over one hundred. That this project went on for over twenty years (somewhat on and off) turned out to be a blessing: I feel fortunate that I spent this time that yielded so much, and so many different kinds of, data.

Because the study stretched over more than two decades, I was privileged to present portions of this book at numerous conferences and in a large number of seminar settings. These gatherings were held at the following locations or with the following associations: the Graduate School of International Studies, University of Denver; Centre d'Études et de Récherches Internationales, Paris; Cortona, Italy; the British Association for Chinese Studies; the Centre for Social Policy Studies, Hong Kong Polytechnic University; the Woodrow Wilson International Center for Scholars; the College of Social Sciences, National Taiwan University; The Hoover Institution, Stanford University; the Fairbank Center, Harvard University; the Asia Center, University of Kentucky; The Maureen and Mike Mansfield Center, University of Montana; Beijing University; POSRI International Forum, Seoul, Korea; Monash University; the Copenhagen Business School; the Asian Studies Centre, St. Antony's College, Oxford University; the Urban China Research Centre, Cardiff University; Nankai University; Hong Kong University of Science and Technology; the Centre for East Asian Studies, University of Turku, Finland; City University of Hong Kong; China Studies Centre, University of Sydney; Central China Normal University, Wuhan; J-China Korea Forum, Seoul, Korea; Fudan Institute for Advanced Study in the Social Sciences; Rutgers University; Chinese University of Hong Kong; the Centre for Contemporary China Studies, University of Melbourne; Made in China Summer School, Venice; China Center for Social Policy, Columbia University; the University of South Wales, Sydney.

Additionally, I very much appreciate having been invited to present parts of this work in lectures at these institutions, again going back twenty years: the Weatherhead East Asian Institute, Columbia University; the Universities Service Center, Chinese University, Hong Kong; École des Hautes Études en Sciences Sociales, Paris; the University of British Columbia; the Center for Chinese Studies, Stanford University; the Asian Studies Center, University of Pittsburgh; Murdoch University, Australia; University of Western Australia;

the East Asian Institute, National University of Singapore; China Research Centre, University of Technology, Sydney; the China Institute, Australian National University; the Center for Chinese Studies, University of Michigan; Chatham House, London; Academic Sinica, Taipei; The New England China Seminar, Harvard University; Wuhan University; Graduate School of International Studies and Institute for China Studies, Seoul National University; the China Institute, University of Alberta, Edmonton; the 21st China Research Institute, University of California, San Diego; Shanghai Academy of Social Sciences; Hong Kong University; Hong Kong University of Science and Technology; Nanjing University of Finance & Economics; Kennedy School Social Policy, Harvard University; Brown University; Department of Government and Public Administration, Chinese University of Hong Kong; Shandong University; Columbia School of Social Work; and David M. Kennedy Center for International Studies, Brigham Young University. In all of these venues, I was fortunate to receive beneficial questions and advice.

I am especially grateful to fellow scholars who shared my journey through these materials and sometimes offered more of them, namely, Joel Andreas (who helpfully read several chapters), Mun Young Cho, Ding Jianding (for several interviews over the years), Qin Gao (who was always quick and extremely helpful in replying to my many questions through email and in keeping me abreast of her ever-expanding portfolio of relevant papers), Daniel Hammond, Jennifer Pan (who read a chapter), and Tang Jun (for many warm and fruitful discussions). Their own impressive and stimulating work has been a wonderful inspiration and foundation for my own. Xian Huang, Ruan Yandong (who carefully and fully replied to numerous emails), and Li Bingqin helped me understand issues connected with health care and pensions.

Wang Feng provided assistance with my calculations, Michael Fuller helped organize the list of references and was available for computer assistance on more than one occasion, and Maureen Graves checked for repetition. Thomas Rawski read Chapter Two and provided astute queries that led me to clarify and qualify and Martin Whyte gave encouraging comments on another early chapter. Shenjing He, Bill Hurst, and Fulong Wu, all of whose work relates to mine, have graciously replied to questions. I also extend my gratitude to John Osburg and two anonymous reviewers, who offered excellent advice, which I tried to follow, on my initial proposal, and who all supported publication. Among scholars in China, Ke Huibing sent me valuable statistical data. Ding Jianding and Liu Xitang each met with me (on several occasions), as did Han Keqing, Shi Li, Wang Zhenyao, and Lu Hanlong (once each). Xiong Yihan arranged interviews for me in Shanghai.

In China, a number of colleagues and students aided me with interviews, either coming with me or meeting with informants by themselves, especially in cities where the dialect or even the language (as in Guangzhou) was unfamiliar to me. I have probably lost the names of some of the large number of people who worked with me in this way. But I will use this occasion to thank those whose names I still retain for arranging interviews in various cities: Ding Yi, Jiao Ruoshui, Le Zhang, Sun Lin, Sun Feixue, Huang Fei, Chi Li, Ying Chang, Huang Xiangchun, Huang Lingjun, Xiong Yihan, Ding Jianding, and Shenjing He. Yi Wenfan (then an undergraduate) helped with translating some of the interviews in which the speakers spoke in local dialect.

Graduate students who were involved in the interviews included He Lingyun, Huang Wenjie, Huang Xi, Li Dengke, Liu Jingwen, Lu Xue, and Wu Tianshi. In Irvine, Tian Li helped me enormously in translating transcripts of difficult and totally ungrammatical interviews done in local Beijing and Changsha slang that appeared in the book, Han Keqing, et al., eds. *Zhongguo chengshi dibao fangtanlu* [Interviews with Minimum Livelihood Guarantee Recipients in Urban China]. Jinan: Shandong renmin chubanshe [Shanghai people's publishing], 2012. Also in Irvine, Liu Ying, Yidi Wu, and Michelle Zhang (then an undergraduate) located articles for me in Chinese journals. Not everyone who worked with me wants his or her name listed.

I also extend appreciation to Elizabeth Knup at the Ford Foundation in Beijing for providing a small grant that enabled me to visit four cities in autumn 2014, in each of which I interviewed scholars and *dibao* recipients, and to the Center for the Study of Democracy and the Center for Asian Studies, University of California, Irvine, for travel grants over many summers for my research in China. I also owe a large debt of gratitude to Susan McEachern for her early confidence in and enthusiasm and support for this project over the past several years. It was wonderful to have her backing and, at several points, valuable advice. Katelyn Turner at the press also made a big contribution with her unfailing attention to my many questions. Big thanks to Chris Fischer as well for gracious and laborious work at the production end.

Above all, without the specific input of five people, this book would not have been written or would not have been written as well. In the beginning and on several occasions afterward, Katherine Carlitz urged me in no uncertain terms to write the book. She has also been so graciously interested in and supportive of this project and, to my surprise, as a Ming literature specialist, even read the whole manuscript, providing very welcome encouragement at the end.

All along the way, Ying Zhang, our East Asian librarian at UC Irvine, found multitudes of citations and original articles for pieces I had lost in our 2003 house fire and invariably replied to my incessant queries unbelievably rapidly and accurately. Kathryn Ragsdale skillfully and sensitively read over the whole manuscript, suggesting many emendations of diction and word usage. Haotian Chen expertly and graciously prepared all the tables, my requirements for which frequently underwent alterations. And finally, and by no means least, my husband, Thomas P. Bernstein, lived through these years and came on some of the trips to China with me; later, he read most of the chapters and offered insightful comments. His constant support and companionship are heartily acknowledged!

At this time, the plaintive, long-ago words of a chemical-fiber worker, already laid-off from his state-owned enterprise job six years earlier, come back to mind: "The Party, the government, and the trade union didn't ask us about our situation. So thank you for asking and caring."[1] My hope is that those reading these lines and the text that follows will also care.

Chapter Four, now updated and revised, was originally published as a book chapter as: "The New Crowd of the Dispossessed: The Shift of the Urban Proletariat from Master to Mendicant," in Peter Hays Gries and Stanley Rosen, eds., *State and Society in 21st Century China* (New York and London: Routledge Curzon, 2004), 50–66. I gratefully acknowledge permission to include this piece in the present work. I also thank the journal *China Perspectives* for allowing me to include an updated and somewhat revised version of my article, "Manipulating China's Minimum Livelihood Guarantee: Political Shifts in a Program for the Poor in the Period of Xi Jinping," which appeared in the journal number 2 of 2017 on pages 47 through 57. It is now part of Chapter Nine. And Chapter Eight in the present book is a slightly revised version of my article in *The China Quarterly*, written with Yiyang Hu, under the title "Welfare, Wealth and Poverty in Urban China: The Dibao and its Differential Disbursement," and published there in issue Number 211 (September 2012), on pages 741 through 764. I very much appreciate that journal's agreement that I use that paper here.

The cover design is to illustrate the huge disparity between how the regime intended to portray the proletariat before about 1995: high in status, performing important jobs in production, deserving of respect, and working cooperatively, in the drawing at the top, and the solitary labor and low-ranking position of the dismissed worker of yore, now consigned to the role of street sweeper, at the bottom. The poster of Mao-era workers is from the IISH/ Stefan R. Landsberger/Private Collection. The photo of the street sweeper, which many laid-off workers came to be, is from Alamy.

Irvine, California
April 2021

---

1. Interview, August 18, 2002, Wuhan.

Section I

BACKGROUND

Chapter One

Three Shifts in State Mission

Creation of the Xiagang

The home is very small and narrow, the wife's complexion is yellowish white; she's always lying on the small, short bamboo bed, the daughter is sitting at the bedside chatting with the mother, and the father is cooking food. The kitchen has no ventilator, so the air throughout the whole home is filled with the mist of oil soot.

First, the husband speaks:

> My wife [aged forty-four] got uremia [urine poison illness] in 2002; she's from the countryside and has never worked; for her medical funds, she's completely dependent on me. Before, when she wasn't sick, she could do household chores, now she can only lie on the bed, can't do anything. The medical fees are very high; she sometimes gets dialysis. We basically despise this illness, every day she stays home, takes a little medicine, and in this way drags on.

Soon the wife chimes in:

> The doctors in the hospital would let you stay for treatment, but we haven't so much money; basically, we can't afford it. Each day, I can take some medicine to control the illness, and that's very good; I can't hope to cure the illness, can just live a day and write it off [*huo yitian, suan yitian*, 活 一天, 算 一天]; sometimes I think if I can only lie on the bed all day like this, unable to do anything, it's the family's burden, it's not as good as dying earlier.

As she speaks, there's a tear in her eye, and the daughter quietly goes away.[1]

This is the scene in August 2007 in Wuhan in the home of a steelworker laid-off from a state-owned plant, who once performed a specialized line of

---

1. Li Jingwen, then a graduate student in Wuhan, conducted this interview and wrote the description of the scene in Chinese.

work. But after his firm went bankrupt in 2005, he was relegated to street-sweeping at a salary of 500 yuan a month.

Other cases involved the impossibility of financing children's education after jobs ended, as this interview illustrates: A father of a sixteen-year-old boy is determined to put him through higher education: "There's no question that he'll go on, but when I think about college, I get so worried my scalp tingles. When the time comes, if I can come up with a solution to this problem, that'll be good. . . . I'm considering making him study at a free teachers' college, relying on the *dibao* [*zuidi shenghuo baozhang* 最低生活保障, for short, *dibao* 低保], but that little money is far, far from being enough."[2]

How did this happen?

Biting poverty in China's cities is the direct product not of the workings of the market, nor did it arise from the country's subjection to the vagaries of the global economy. Instead, it emerged from the programmatic choices of the rulers perched at the helm of the polity: its existence is derived from the developmental imaginary these leaders have envisioned for thrusting the nation onto the pathway of "modernity"—a drama in which the cast-aside workers (those pushed out of their jobs in the 1990s and early 2000s who became the new urban poor) seemed, to these leaders, to be not up to performing even bit parts. These now impoverished people deserve our attention. And they, and their treatment, can serve as a laser beam to light up the trajectory Chinese society has traversed from the time of Mao Zedong to the era of Xi Jinping.

Clearly the presence of urban penury, its modalities, and its meanings are not simply a social or even just an economic phenomenon, though they are those as well. For my purpose here, however, these phenomena are pregnant with political significance; they are the artifact of the enactment over a generation of a set of politicians' preferences for the better bred and more highly talented over the ordinary among the Chinese populace. Throughout the past quarter-century, the appearance of hardship and of its partakers, the lately impoverished in the metropolises, has not been accidental, I contend. These new paupers are situated as they are because they were purposively discarded and placed in the shadows; they have become invisible.

Indeed, when speaking of China in recent years, quite a different narrative is rife: reports of miracles of accomplishment abound. Commentators marvel over the country's "rise," not just in its steadily inflating power abroad but also particularly in its having "pulled millions up from poverty" at home. Such stories of success generally have one of two foci: if the narrative is about "rise," the locus of attention is the burgeoning urban middle and rich classes; if the point is to look at poverty, it is only the peasants—the rural people-in-the-countryside—who are addressed. Still another issue: most in-

---

2. Interviews, late August 2007, Wuhan.

vestigation of Chinese privation has focused on the phenomenon of poverty itself, or else on the efficacy of particular efforts at reducing or eliminating indigence.[3] Thus, all we get, in the main, is about positive, upward trajectories. But there is much more to the tale, though it is rarely told.

Perhaps the regime has willed it so. For this has been a government—much like its predecessors going back some 150 years—that aims for progress, prosperity, and productivity, not just to impress its own populace, but also to present to the world-at-large. Indeed, much of the legitimacy of the current, post-Mao political order over the past four-plus decades (since 1978) has been tethered to achievements in amassing wealth, stimulating national pride, and fabricating a new, "high-quality" citizenry, all aimed at permitting China to be conceived, finally, as fully "modern." What does not—most likely cannot—be forced into that mold is best chucked aside, pitched out of the range of watching gazes and robbed of agency. China is proud, but it is also self-conscious; its dreams must be glorious and its path seen as ever pushing onward, toward modernity.

In such a context, poverty in the cities is simply out of place. It is not to be available for viewing, nor is it even to be mentioned. And yet, the poverty-stricken and urban-registered in the cities cannot be merely left to expire in situ immediately, the nation's leaders know. So, the Communist Party devised a mode of maintaining these indigents, if barely, by means of a system of a sort of social assistance. In doing so, sadly, it employs a method that—whether intentionally or not (there is no way to be sure)—more or less confines the cities' poor into a space of exclusion from which they cannot escape. Fashioned, then, as the "other" side of the "modern," these unfortunates thus are as if shucked away.[4]

This book is the product of over twenty years of (sometimes intermittent) research. The work involved talks with some one hundred informants of several types. Most were in-home and street, in-depth, open-ended interviews with recipients of the *dibao* (in probably every case a household in which at least one member had been laid off [*xiagang*, 下岗]) in nine Chinese cities (five large cities—Wuhan, Guangzhou, Lanzhou, Xi'an, Shanghai; Zigong

---

3. Albert Park, Sangui Wang, and Guobao Wu, "Regional Poverty Targeting in China," *Journal of Public Economics* 86, no. 1 (2002): 123–53; Cheng Fang, Xiaobo Zhang, and Shenggen Fan, "Emergence of Urban Poverty and Inequality in China: Evidence from a Household Survey," *China Economic Review* 13 (2002): 430–43; Azizur Rahman Khan and Carl Riskin, *Inequality and Poverty in China in the Age of Globalization* (New York: Oxford University Press, 2001); and Xin Meng, Robert Gregory, and Youjuan Wang, "Inequality and Growth in Urban China, 1986–2000," IZA Discussion paper series, no. 1452, 2005. Qin Gao has written extensively on the *dibao*; her many publications are cited throughout this book.

4. See Lisa Rofel, *Other Modernities: Gendered Yearnings in China after Socialism* (Berkeley: University of California Press, 1999), xiii, 3; and Ann Anagnost, *National Past-Times: Narrative, Representation, and Power in Modern China* (Durham, NC: Duke University Press, 1997), 77.

(in Sichuan); and in three smaller, prefectural-level Hubei cities—Xiantao, Jingzhou, and Qianjiang). There were also conversations with Chinese scholars, community *dibao* workers, and urban officials. Additionally, I did research in documentary and secondary sources (much of it in Chinese journals). All of my subjects (or their spouses) were urban-registered, NOT rural migrants living in the cities.

I consider the topic from a range of angles, addressing especially this question: Just why, and through what historical events and processes, was the once-proud proletariat[5] so suddenly appraised as passé, and why, when they were made into paupers, were they managed, by the very minimal *dibao*, so meagerly, and in some ways increasingly so, with time? I will make the case that China's municipally situated and registered needy (holding *chengshi hukou*, 城市户口), once they had been viewed as useless in the late 1990s, were thrust away for three principal reasons: first, because of the state's obsession with forging stability (which, after their firing, they were deemed capable of disrupting), and second and third, its authorities' passion for forging a "modern" workforce and for sustaining the appearances they judge necessary for attaining their own vision of modernity. This form of modernity is a site of aspiration regarded by the powerful as uniquely suitable for realizing their imaginary and their designs of national rejuvenation, regeneration, and renovation.

The crux of my claim lies in a distressing appraisal of the state's "Minimum Livelihood Guarantee" (the *dibao*) and its use often more against than for the poor. The *dibao* is a scheme initiated formally in 1999, at a time of crisis for the old, urban working class, when tens of millions of its cohorts were summarily thrown from their once-lifetime, entitlement-laden work posts. Then, following rampant worker protests against loss of their livelihood and their welfare—disturbances that aroused alarm among the country's leadership about instability threatening enterprise reform and foreign investment—the *dibao* was institutionalized nationwide.

Many of the laid-off later became its recipients or "targets" (*duixiang*, 对象), or the *dibaohu* (低保户, *dibao* households). This "guarantee" is a program whose urban component is inadequate, belittling, debasing, and impoverishing. So, this book intermixes information and analysis about the laid-off staff and workers (*xiagang zhigong*, 下岗职工, for short, the 下岗) and the *dibaohu*, many of whom are the same individuals. I clarify in the individual chapters which of these two sets of people I am discussing there.

In the present chapter, I unravel the macro-level Party policies that, at three critical junctures, led gradually—and perhaps without explicit official inten-

---

5. Andrew G. Walder, *Communist Neo-Traditionalism* (Berkeley: University of California Press, 1986); Joel Andreas, *Disenfranchised: The Rise and Fall of Industrial Citizenship in China* (New York: Oxford University Press, 2020).

tion—to the production of this weighty portion of the present Chinese urban poor. My purpose is to trace the large political-economic context in which this collectivity was created. I do this by relating this transformation of the old proletariat to decisions taken at three key Communist Party conclaves that transpired between 1978 and 2002, by which time those who had been the "masters of the nation" had been largely obliterated as actors.

I position the genesis of this abjection within the history of China's transition away from its socialist past. The impoverishment of the former working class thereby becomes a shorthand emblem that, writ large, can stand for the transformation the country has experienced to date. I accomplish this by pointing to three junctures at which the eventual fate of the members of the old, socialist urban workforce was gradually sealed, their customary standing unraveled. These times were 1978, 1997, and 2002, each the moment of a critical convocation of the Chinese Communist Party. In succession at these occasions, first an economic, then a political, and, finally, a social blow was dealt to the wallets, the dignity, and the habitus of China's socialist-era, state-enterprise employed urban laborers.

THREE SHIFTS IN STATE MISSION

The death of strongman Party chief and ideologue Mao Zedong in 1976 set into motion an historic metamorphosis of the Chinese nation's identity and of the emphases and direction set for it by its top politicians. Those who had succeeded Mao in power by 1978 and thereafter were ones who had been attacked, purged, or, at best, sidelined in the upheavals of Mao's 1966–1976 Cultural Revolution, and who were "rehabilitated" or otherwise resurfaced after its demise. These officials, who were born-again, as it were, set forth an altered state project, or "mission," involving, in sequence over the subsequent quarter-century, a set of three huge transformations in the once-socialist state's economy, its political-ideological foundations, and its class structure.[6]

These momentous changes involved recrafting the state's economic mechanism and its ancillary components; rewriting the ideology of the Chinese Communist Party (or what may more aptly be characterized as revamping the enactment of the official ideology); and upending the class order. Each of these had major implications for the formerly hallowed "leading class" or "master" of Chinese society, those whose status had been that of lofty laboring masses, the human motor force in Marx's envisioned

---

6. I use "mission" as in Alfred Stepan, "State Power and the Strength of Civil Society in the Southern Cone of Latin America," in *Bringing the State Back In*, ed. Peter B. Evans, Dietrich Rueschemeyer, and Theda Skocpol (Cambridge, MA: Cambridge University Press, 1985), 317–43.

march from capitalism to socialism. In truth, the three sets of decisions and transformations were overlapping and mutually reinforcing in their imprint on society and in their cumulative impact on the working class.[7] For analytical purposes, however, I separate them here.

Where Mao had castigated capitalism and all of its apparatuses (including profits and their seeking; bonuses; commerce and markets; prices; inequality; consumerism; and private ownership), the new approach inserted into economic life one after another of these very mechanisms and incentives. So, with that towering leader departed, what I perceive as three critical crossroads over the following two decades and a half together worked to transfigure the world, the lives, and the prospects of the workers of the Maoist past.

The First Shift, 1978: Economics

This first transformation—what I term the *economic* conversion—was instigated at the end of 1978 with the ascension to leadership of the crafty and visionary Deng Xiaoping, who, along with other members of the purged, pre-Cultural Revolution political elite, recharted the course of the country. Their regime was marked by cautious and mostly steady steps away from powering production by means of plans and commands to introducing and then championing the play of market forces and the institution of private enterprise. This journey from planning constituted the first of three major turning points in manufacturing the marginality of the urban proletariat.

In the early 1980s, when Deng Xiaoping took over the helm of state from Mao-appointed Hua Guofeng, he uttered an aphorism allowing—or even encouraging—"some [to] get rich first." This maxim served to glorify the pursuit of wealth for those positioned to participate in that venture and set the tone for a public stance ennobling money-making in the years to come.[8] In so announcing, Deng legitimized at the popular level practices that had been anathema, even criminal, for most of three decades under Mao Zedong and his followers.

In addition to that adage, from the early 1980s onward, there were other origins to the plunge into profit-seeking. One of these was the Communist Party Politburo members' consensus that the economy was seriously stagnating, which they attributed to two sets of factors.[9] The first was the long-term

---

7. Thank you to Joel Andreas for this insight.

8. Ezra F. Vogel, *Deng Xiaoping and the Transformation of China* (Cambridge, MA: Belknap Press of Harvard University Press, 2011), 391. "邓小平：让一部分人先富起来" (Deng Xiaoping: First allow one group of people to get rich), 中国共产党新闻网 (News of the Communist Party of China), http://cpc.people.com.cn/GB/34136/2569304.html, accessed June 25, 2016. Thanks to Karl Gerth for this reference.

9. For the political elite's consensus view of the national economy in the late 1970s and early 1980s: Ma Hong and Sun Shangqing, eds., *Zhongguo jingji jiegou wenti yanjiu* [Investigations into problems of China's economic structure] (Beijing: Renmin chubanshe [People's publishing com-

rigidities that were part and parcel of the state planning system copied from the Soviet Union; the obsolete machinery long used in the factories of that system contributed mightily too. The second cause was the more recent assault the economy had endured in the destruction, battles, and work stoppages of the just-concluded Cultural Revolution.[10] These problems became starkly salient as the country began, at Deng's and his colleagues' initiation, to engage with the world economy and what would eventually be realized as its threatening force of competition. Though this involvement had begun, if hesitantly, in the early 1970s, it took on growing intensity and depth as the years passed. Another crucial factor in that early drive toward affluence was the Communist Party's urgent need to justify its rule to a populace that had sustained a yearning for commodities for decades.

The decisions the leadership made at first in the interest of promoting nationwide prosperity were not meant specifically to induce "market" practices. They instead constituted practical steps: First, the rulers shifted the weight of state investment from heavy to light industry (i.e., from big machinery, chemicals, metals, and the like to items of daily use) in order to meet domestic consumers' desires and the world market's demands. Their second move was to stimulate the output and the productivity of the economy. The political elite understood that in industry, for instance, by allowing enterprises to retain a small portion of their earnings and by permitting them to take responsibility for their own profits and losses, productivity would increase.

In agriculture, too, it was not really a preference for markets that spurred reforms. Rather, local cadres, in conjunction with daring peasants, of their own volition, returned to practices authorized briefly by the Party nearly twenty years earlier in the wake of the catastrophe of the 1957–1960 Great Leap Forward but which Mao Zedong soon afterward rescinded. In both cases—in industry and in agriculture—the idea was to incentivize and thereby enhance production. Firms were empowered to sell surpluses above their output quotas, and rural market fairs were sanctioned for the first time since the early 1960s, all in the interest of improving economic achievement.

As the 1980s wore on, however, bit by bit, these steps did lead to markets. A critical mechanism in this process was what was called "dual-track pricing." This system encouraged officials who managed scarce resources and goods to use prices set by supply and demand to deal in items in short supply, even as state plan-dictated prices remained in effect for those without this

---

pany], n.d.); and Ma Hong, *Jingji jiegou yu jingji guanli* [Economic structure and economic management] (Beijing: Renmin chubanshe [People's publishing company], 1982).

10. Barry Naughton, *Growing Out of the Plan: Chinese Economic Reform, 1978–1995* (New York: Cambridge University Press, 1995); and Dorothy J. Solinger, *From Lathes to Looms: China's Industrial Policy in Comparative Perspective, 1979–1982* (Stanford, CA: Stanford University Press, 1991), Chapters 3 and 4.

power.[11] By the late 1980s, farmers, along with enterprise managers, were willy-nilly deeply involved in markets, and "collectively" (not state-owned) firms were proliferating. These developments happened more or less spontaneously, outside of specific official orders.

Other pivotal alterations included a nod to private commerce, which began in the early 1980s by letting small traders carry out marketing for profit, at first just at short distances and in small amounts.[12] Over time, this seemingly innocuous move eventuated in longer distance and larger bulk business, and with officials and those with linkages to officials setting up enormously lucrative companies, as well as in an unstoppable flood of corruption.[13]

In foreign trade, joint ventures were sanctioned, yet they were closely circumscribed at the outset. But again, gradually, the monopoly over commodities held by state-owned companies was relaxed considerably, and foreign investment exploded.[14] Nonetheless, the political elite as a whole was not fully unified as to the extent and depth of all these changes. So, the process became prolonged, with fits and starts, both throughout the 1980s and again after the protests and bloody showdown at Tiananmen Square in 1989.[15] For the workers, this set of economic decisions began to scrape away at the dominance and the budgets of the state-owned firms, from which so many of the members of the proletariat would, with time, be forced to depart.

The Second Shift, 1997: Political

The second shift, the political conversion, was slow in arriving. As foundational modifications to the economic structure and its workings progressed—if with some tortuousness—certainly the course toward undoing the socialist framework was charted and pursued. But as this transpired, the regime

11. Naughton, *Growing Out*, 181ff; Joseph Fewsmith, *Rethinking Chinese Politics* (New York: Cambridge University Press, 2021), 51–52.

12. Dorothy J. Solinger, "Commercial Reform and State Control: Structural Changes in Chinese Trade, 1981-1983." *Pacific Affairs* (Summer 1985): 197–215.

13. *Idem.*, "Urban Entrepreneurs and the State: The Merger of State and Society," in *State and Society in China: The Consequences of Reform*, ed. Arthur Lewis Rosenbaum (Boulder, CO: Westview Press, 1992), 121–41; David L. Wank, *Commodifying Communism: Business, Trust, and Politics in a Chinese City* (New York: Cambridge University Press, 1999); Susan Young, *Private Business and Economic Reform in China* (Armonk, NY: M.E. Sharpe, 1995); and Bruce J. Dickson, *Wealth into Power; The Communist Party's Embrace of China's Private Sector* (New York: Cambridge University Press, 2008).

14. Margaret Pearson, *Joint Ventures in the People's Republic of China* (Princeton, NJ: Princeton University Press, 1991); Nicholas R. Lardy, *Foreign Trade and Economic Reform in China, 1978–1990* (New York: Cambridge University Press, 1992); *idem., China in the World Economy* (Washington, DC: Institute for International Economics, 1994); and Barry Naughton, "China's Emergence and Prospects as a Trading Nation," *Brookings Papers on Economic Activity*, The Brookings Institute, no. 2 (1996): 273–344.

15. Joseph Fewsmith, *Dilemmas of Reform in China: Political Conflict and Economic Debate* (Armonk, NY: M.E. Sharpe, 1994).

remained reluctant for years to relinquish altogether the social order of old, with its accustomed beneficiaries in the cities: the workers. The Party was cautious, too, about repudiating its discomfort with the bourgeoisie and, at first, even with petty marketers.[16] Those who had long been on the receiving end of China's old socialism, the members of the working class, were, for the most part, permitted to continue in their work posts, despite the passage in 1986 of laws approving both bankruptcy and contract (i.e., time-limited) labor, neither of which had existed before.[17] A few years later, in 1992, a State Council document also granted new rights for firms in the state sector to recruit and release workers on their own.[18]

All the same, for the extended period from 1979 to the late 1990s, the policy was for firms to keep on their original workers via an array of disparate strategies over the years. At first, this was achieved by retirements that permitted their own offspring to take their spots; then, it entailed the formation of "labor service companies" meant to provide job training and job creation. Later, it was insisted that firms "redeploy" or channel elsewhere (*fenliu*, 分流), their redundant workers, retraining them and/or creating new affiliated enterprises, or compel them to take "early retirement." In short, restrictions were announced against dismissing workers, even if there was no work for them and little or no pay.[19] Up to around 1995, however, many workers and their families were still being served by their old work units.[20] (More in Chapter Two.)

Thereafter, layoffs changed all that. With the uptick in employee shedding around and after 1995, a national reemployment program (given new force in 1997 with the Fifteenth Party Congress) was launched that offered enter-

---

16. Dorothy J. Solinger, *Chinese Business Under Socialism: The Politics of Domestic Commerce* (Berkeley: University of California Press, 1984).

17. Lin Lean Lim and Gyorgy Sziraczki, "Employment, Social Security, and Enterprise Reforms in China," in *Changes in China's Labor Market: Implications for the Future*, ed. Gregory K. Schoepfle (Washington, DC: U.S. Department of Labor, Bureau of International Labor Affairs, 1996), 50; *U.S. Foreign Broadcast Information Service*, July 19, 1994, 18–26, from Xinhua (XH), July 5, 1994; James V. Feinerman, "The Past—and Future—of Labor Law in China," in Schoepfle, *Changes in China*, 119–34. A draft bankruptcy law was passed at the end of 1986, but into the 1990s the central government continued authorizing loans and bailouts for, and allocating energy and raw materials to, failing firms to prevent them from going under (Dorothy J. Solinger, *China's Transition from Socialism* [Armonk, NY: M.E. Sharpe, 1993], 278).

18. Naughton, *Growing Out*, 294–97.

19. According to the *South China Morning Post* (*SCMP*), March 9, 1997, the Ministry of Labor admitted at the annual session of the National People's Congress that about ten million state firm workers had not been paid or were being underpaid. But one delegate put the total at twenty-five million, including nineteen million surviving on a low income. Antoine Kernen, "Surviving Reform in Shenyang—New Poverty in Pioneer City," *China Rights Forum* (*CRF*) (Summer 1997), 9, states that in 1997, in Shenyang, only 5 percent of the firms were paying workers' salaries on a regular basis! Also, Liu Binyan, "The Working Class Speaks Out," *China Focus* 5, no. 8 (August 1997), 1.

20. Lowell Dittmer and Lu Xiaobo, "Personal Politics in the Chinese Danwei under Reform," *Asian Survey* 36, no. 3 (March 1996): 246–67; and email from Joel Andreas, January 19, 2019.

prises tax and loan incentives for developing new avenues of work for surplus labor.[21] That program also called on firms to set up "reemployment centers" that were to attempt to find new placements for their discharged workers, provide them with "basic livelihood stipends" (基本生活费, *jiben shenghuofei*), and contribute to their pension and medical insurance funds.

This shift also eventuated as, over the course of the first half of the 1990s, China experienced two harsh austerity programs (both instituted by the leadership to slow down the economy) that eventually set into motion radical change in firms' handling of their employees. Both were the products of leadership decisions on domestic political grounds, not—as in France, for instance, at the time—of troubles induced by participation in international trade.[22] The first was installed under the reform-shy, conservative, pro-planning faction in the wake of the Tiananmen outbursts of 1989, which these politicians understood as having largely been sparked by popular dissatisfaction with a sudden hike in prices produced by the previous decade of market reforms.[23] The second spate of austerity was launched by then-Vice Premier Zhu Rongji in mid-1993. His motive was to halt what post-1949 China deemed runaway inflation, the result of stepped-up reform and economic growth given impetus by Deng Xiaoping in early 1992.[24] Because of stiff curtailment of access to guaranteed loans for state firms on both occasions, losses in these enterprises rose significantly.

During the first run of austerity, total state enterprise losses doubled each year;[25] then, after a 1991 relaxation, followed by 1992's pro-growth stimulus policy, the second program led to almost half the state firms showing operating losses in 1994 and 1995. By 1996, 45 percent of the state sector was operating at a loss; for the first time, state firms collectively lost more money than they took in. Industrial operating losses in state-owned firms amounted then to 53 billion *yuan*, up more than one-third over the year before, with 12,000 enterprises running long-standing deficits. At that point, about one-fifth of

21. Leonard J. Hausman and Barry J. Friedman, "Employment Creation: New and Old Methods," unpublished ms. (n.p., n.d. [1996 or 1997]); Barry L. Friedman, "Employment and Social Protection Policies in China: Big Reforms and Limited Outcomes," in Gregory K. Schoepfle, *Changes*, 151–66; Lim and Sziraczki, "Employment"; Feinerman, "The Past"; Hilary K. Josephs, "Labor Law Reflects New Realities," *CRF* (Fall 1996), 25; Christine P. W. Wong, Christopher Heady, and Wing T. Woo, *Fiscal Management and Economic Reform in the People's Republic of China* (Hong Kong: Oxford University Press, 1995), 14; Dorothy J. Solinger, "Labor Market Reform and the Plight of the Laid-Off Proletariat," *The China Quarterly* (*CQ*), no. 170 (June 2002), 304–26.
22. Dorothy J. Solinger, *States' Gains, Labor's Losses: China, France and Mexico Choose Global Liaisons* (Ithaca, NY: Cornell University Press, 2009).
23. Naughton, *Growing Out*, 284.
24. Naughton, "China's Emergence," 294; Wing Thye Woo, "Crises and Institutional Evolution in China's Industrial Sector," in *China's Economic Future: Challenges to U.S. Policy*, ed., Joint Economic Committee, Congress of the United States (Armonk, NY: M.E. Sharpe, 1997), 164–65; Naughton, *Growing Out*, 274–300.
25. Ibid., 286–87.

the assets of banks consisted of uncollectible loans, the effect of the vulner-ability of state bankers to continual requests from failing firms for operating capital.[26] But unlike in Western Europe, where an intensified reliance on the market and an affiliated flexibility in the use of labor were the outcomes just of economically induced losses, in China, these outcomes came not only from reasonable apprehension about future forays into the world market but also, significantly, from political judgments and choices about the future visage of the nation.

A partial act along the way to a more drastic ruling on the management of manual labor—and perhaps a sign that the economy was to become yet more marketized—was a pivotal pronouncement at the 1992 Fourteenth Chinese Communist Party Congress. This was a declaration that, though the economy was yet a "socialist" one, it should henceforth be understood as a "socialist *market* economy." Nonetheless, up until 1997, at the Party's Fif-teenth Congress, caution continued: there were over that five-year span still no fundamental authoritative alterations in the actual treatment accorded the workforce, with its lifetime job security and welfare, nor in the established framework for and governance of the state's sociopolitical economy.[27]

But by the latter years of the 1990s, as noted above, something major was in the air: China's imminent acceptance into the World Trade Organization (for which it had applied more than a decade earlier) seemed on the horizon. This prospect spelled the denouement of central policy makers' long-standing coddling of loss-making enterprises. The approaching accession was consid-ered certain to expose industry to global competition for Chinese firms, so many of which were still operating with antiquated technology and ill-trained workers and turning out inferior products.[28] It appeared certain to policy mak-ers that such plants—and people—would be overwhelmed and destroyed in the global market—and that the nation would stand at a disadvantage were they to remain in place.

Thus, as the specter of WTO entry advanced, the Fifteenth Party Con-gress laid down another critical milestone, this one best characterized as a *political* turn (even as the economic pressures from enterprise losses were a reality): an announcement that enterprises in trouble were to be discontin-ued in one way or another and their workers—especially those individuals

26. Loraine A. West, "The Changing Effects of Economic Reform on Rural and Urban Employ-ment," paper [to be] presented at "Unintended Social Consequences of Chinese Economic Reform" conference, Harvard School of Public Health and The Fairbank Center for East Asian Studies, Har-vard University, May 23–24, 1997 (draft), 6.

27. The 1995 Labor Law made some alterations, but in practice, little changed. http://english.mofcom.gov.cn/aarticle/policyrelease/internationalpolicy/200703/20070304475283.html, accessed January 25, 2021.

28. Mo Rong, "Jiaru WTO yu woguo de jiuye" [Entering the WTO and Our Country's Employ-ment], *Laodong baozhang tongxun* [Labor security bulletin], no. 4 (2000): 18–21.

viewed to be impeding growth, efficiency and, by extension, modernization—shucked off in huge proportions.[29] This maneuver was at its core political in that in one stroke it meant that at last the leadership was jettisoning
de facto what had for the prior four dozen years been its power base and its
doctrinal claim to legitimacy.

The Party was, in practice (if not in its open discourse), tossing away what
had long been its rhetorical obeisance to Marxist ideology, a creed that took
the working class as the master of society, the segment situated at society's
peak. Ordinary workers, whom the state constitution nonetheless continued
for some time to dignify with the label "masters of the country,"[30] suffered an
immediate and fatal drop in their status—a shocking plunge into downward
mobility—as their sociopolitical place (at least in its public image) plummeted
from commanding the highest of respect in society to languishing at practically the lowest. Indeed, on a massive scale, plants across the country were
enjoined to throw off their less-productive workers; local officials also were
to push these firms toward bankruptcies, shutdowns, mergers, and takeovers.[31]
These various measures ultimately propelled a spree in which plants dispensed
with their unwanted employees; according to several sources, some sixty million state and collective firm workers were dismissed almost at one shot.[32]

Granted, this was a move that was in part in tune with the pure play of market forces. Certainly, a range of economic factors sparked this bloodletting,
including the mounting losses in state firms; a decline in the employment elas-

---

29. This order came with the slogan *jianyuan, zengxiao* (减员曾效, "reduce staff, increase
efficiency").

30. For the version of the Constitution then-current, see www.socialism.org/systems/thelawsof
china/amendments.htm or english.peopledaily.com.cn/constitution/constitution.html.

31. Into the 1990s, only a scant number of bankruptcies were permitted (Hausman and Friedman,
"Employment Creation," 36). But a sharp increase took place in 1996 and 1997, with over 9,000
firms reportedly applying for bankruptcy in the month of September 1997 (Hang-Sheng Cheng, "A
Mid-Course Assessment of China's Economic Reform," in Joint Economic Committee, *China's Economic Future*, 29–30). An official source claimed that 675 state enterprises were declared bankrupt
and closed in 1997 (*Summary of World Broadcasts* [*SWB*], FE/3168 [3/6/98], S2/1, from XH, 3/4/98).

32. Deng Quheng and Bjorn Gustafsson, "A New Episode of Increased Urban Income Inequality
in China," in *Rising Inequality in China: Challenges to a Harmonious Society*, ed. Li Shi, Hiroshi
Sato, and Terry Sicular (Cambridge, MA: Cambridge University Press, 2015), 257. The bulk of
the layoffs took place between 1997 and 2002. See also Wang Depei, "'San min' yu 'erci gaige'"
['Three people' and 'The Second Reform'], *Gaige neican* [Reform Internal Reference], no. 7
(2001), 25. Tang Jun, "Dibao zhiduzhong de shehui paichi" [Social discrimination in the minimum
living guarantee system], paper presented at the Conference on Social Exclusion and Marginality in
Chinese Societies, sponsored by the Centre for Social Policy Studies of the Department of Applied
Social Sciences, the Hong Kong Polytechnic University and the Social Policy Research Centre,
Institute of Sociology, the Chinese Academy of Social Sciences, Hong Kong, November 16–17,
2001, 1, held that working-age city residents without full-time formal work numbered not less than
sixty million, amounting to an unemployment rate of 12 to 15 percent. According to economic ad-
viser Hu Angang, between 1995 and 2001, fifty-four million jobs were terminated (*SCMP*, August
10, 2002); and that China laid off fifty-five million people from 1995 to mid-2002 (*China News
Digest*, July 9, 2002). More on this in Chapter Two.

ticity of economic growth;[33] a drop in the tariffs on many imports in preparation to enter the World Trade Organization (which pushed Chinese producers into an unaccustomed competition which they had no capacity to join); and a growing and glaring mismatch between the type of jobs becoming available, on the one hand, and the wanting skills of the old proletariat, on the other.[34]

And, to some extent, modifications in the global economy, and in China's relation to it, did have a role to play. Tracing these changes requires a quick review of the course the country had traversed in the decades before this juncture. After the Communist Party victory in 1949, during its first decade in power, its leaders shunned or were shunned by much of the Western world, and its chief economic foreign partners were just the Soviet Union and other state-socialist economies. With the split with the Soviets after 1960, China's principal ties were with the Third World and with a few individual capitalist countries. Its continuing isolation from the core of international economic activity into the early 1970s enabled it to escape the early onslaught of the processes of globalization. For China was involved neither in the breakdown of Bretton Woods (never having been party to that agreement) nor in the two oil price shocks of the decade.

Even at the end of 1978, when its own oil production reached a plateau, China did not suffer from the price rises affecting the rest of the world. The leadership simply and suddenly discontinued a quite sizable planned and contracted importation of large-scale foreign plant projects, mainly because of the huge amounts of energy their operation would have demanded.[35] Peaking oil production was one factor in China's shift to an outward-oriented market-driven strategy after 1978. And, related to this, the country embarked then upon a massive manufacture of light industrial goods for export,[36] which conveniently required less energy to produce.[37]

---

33. In the 1990s, the elasticity coefficient of employment growth was just 0.106, meaning that for each percentage point of economic growth there was only 0.106 of a percentage point of employment growth. This represented a decrease of two-thirds since the 1980s, when a percentage point of growth in GDP pushed up job numbers by about one-third of a percentage point (Hu Angang, "Employment and Development: China's Employment Problem and Employment Strategy," *National Conditions Report*, no. 6 [30 April 1998], 3); *idem.*, "Shishi jiuye youxian zhanlue, wei renmin tigong gengduode gongzuo gangwei" [Realize the employment preferential strategy and supply more jobs for people], Zhongguo kexueyuan, Qinghua daxue, guoqing yanjiu zhongxin (Chinese Academy of Science and Tsinghua University National Conditions Research Centre), Report no. 78. Speech delivered at a specialists' forum directed by State Planning Commission Vice-Chairman Wang Chunzheng, September 29, 2000, 6).
34. Dorothy J. Solinger, "China's Urban Workers and the WTO," *The China Journal*, no. 49 (January 2003): 61–87.
35. Shigeru Ishikawa, "Sino-Japanese Economic Cooperation," *CQ*, no. 109 (1987): 12.
36. Bruce Cumings, "The Political Economy of China's Turn Outward," in *China and the World*, ed. Samuel S. Kim (Boulder, CO: Westview Press, 1984), 242; Solinger, *From Lathes.*
37. Dwight H. Perkins, *China: Asia's Next Economic Giant?* (Seattle: University of Washington Press, 1986), 50–1.

Thus, within two years after the 1976 death of the fiercely ideological Mao Zedong, Deng Xiaoping and his colleagues had ushered in China's much-publicized "opening up" of its national economy. Nonetheless, in several important respects, this economy long afterward remained less "globalized" than those of other countries with comparably developed economies. Even in the midst of the Asian financial crisis of the late 1990s, China was less at the mercy of threatening international economic pressures than nations elsewhere in East Asia. This relative safety owed much to the continuing non-convertibility of its currency on the capital account (the current account having become convertible in 1996).

Besides, China's foreign debt at the time—though by no means negligible—was quite manageable and surely not by itself a spur to revamping domestic economic arrangements (as distinct, for instance, from Mexico's and those elsewhere in Latin America). A contemporaneous World Bank Development Report spoke of China's "improved creditworthiness," which had by then made it "the main beneficiary of syndicated lending to developing countries." The report did note a steady increase in the country's external debt (at about US$130 billion at year's end in 1996). But, its authors reasoned, the country's strong macroeconomic performance nonetheless afforded it excellent debt indicators, which, at the time, stood at less than half the average among developing countries and, indeed, among the lowest in the entire East Asian region at the time.[38] Besides its huge foreign exchange reserves, amounting to about US$140 billion at the end of 1997, and its favorable international balance of payments secured it further.[39]

Perhaps most importantly, China's long-time, low-cost domestic consumer economy and its relatively stable, low-wage structure meant that ever since the leadership invited in foreign firms starting in 1979 up to the late 1990s, there had been negligible competition from cheap foreign labor or from foreign consumer products priced below those available from China. In fact, on the eve of the financial crisis, China had already taken over the labor-intensive market for manufactured exports from South Korea, Taiwan, and Hong Kong.[40] Thus, in its current economic circumstances, it would seem that, except as incentive, ideology, and paradigm for modernity, globalization per se—that is, in its material incarnation—had little to do with China's major shifts.

---

38. The World Bank, *China 2020: China Engaged, Integration with the Global Economy* (Washington, DC: The World Bank, 1997), 25. As a Chinese source explained, contrasting China's debts with those in Southeast Asia, "China's debts are domestic loans . . . and its foreign debts are mainly long-term loans granted by international financial institutes, including the World Bank," in SWB, FE/3170 (March 9, 1998), S1/3, from *Sing Tao Jih Pao* (Hong Kong), March 7, 1998, A3.

39. SWB, FE/3168 (March 6, 1998), S2/1, from XH, March 4, 1998.

40. Dwight Perkins, "Prospects for China's Integration into the Global Economy," in Joint Economic Committee, *China's Economic Future*, 35.

Therefore, unlike the member states of the European Union or a major Latin American player such as Mexico, which all were at the center of the stage of global activity and vulnerable to its vacillations and caprices for nearly two decades, as of 1997, China was a nation only partially—if increasingly—a participant in the world economy. And yet its story demonstrates that the tenets of globalization and its seeming promise were so enticing, and also so ineluctable, that a country not yet wholly subject to its *actual* dynamics and pressures could still fall *virtually* captive to its consequences by virtue of its own leadership's will. As chief WTO negotiator Long Yongtu stated in a 1999 interview on the eve of the nation's accession, "China . . . must secure its place in this economic united nations. . . . The days when China was chronically excluded from the mainstream of the world economy must come to an end."[41]

In short, regardless of the absence of any severe foreign economic threat as of the late 1990s, from the end of 1997 onward, the industrial portion of the economy was thenceforth to be managed such that firms in the red should see their operations transformed, their obsolete machines ground to a halt, their business either bought out or merged with that of another more successful firm, or they were to be shuttered altogether (a process nicknamed "*guanting bingzhuan*" [关停 并转, close, stop, merge, transform]).

So, this huge dismissal of manufacturing labor, first initiated very gingerly in the late 1980s and at that point chiefly just in the northeast, suddenly became massive and nationwide, as more than an effect of economic forces. It was also, I argue, mainly, a step both triggered and orchestrated by political fiat. Indeed, that a specific "project," or mission, of the state lay behind the layoffs is evident in their simultaneity, their precipitateness, and in the sheer massiveness of the numbers affected, as well as in the fact that they got underway not in a time of recession or retrenchment but instead in a period of rapid and successful double-digit growth. Thus, this was the product of a politically devised state mission that had been gathering force for nearly two decades following Deng Xiaoping's reentry into the top Chinese leadership in 1978. I maintain that this was so even if the move did not lead to a programmatic alteration targeting the workers in the state-owned plants until 1997.[42]

While this shift in state mission did contribute to the nation's economic miracle and modernity, at the same time, it was at the very root of China's new urban poverty. Official concession that this was the case was sometimes articulated openly, if euphemistically, as in this statement from 1998, near the start of the process: "Following the prosperous development of the socialist

---

41. SWB, FE/3695, November 18, 1999, G/2, from Central Chinese TV, November 16, 1999.
42. Yang Yiyong et al., *Shiye chongji bo* [The shock wave of unemployment] (Beijing: Jinri Zhongguo chubanshe [China today publishing], 1997).

market economy, urban residents' rice bowl [metaphor for guaranteed life-time employment] is no longer iron; adding on other unforeseen events, some staff and workers' basic livelihood has met with difficulty."[43]

Another admission is a somewhat later one, announced in the aftermath of a serious spate of worker protests. This acknowledgment expressed rather more concern with the effects of the move's outcome for the nation's tranquility than with laborers' livelihood:

> In China, we allow some people to become rich first through their own efforts, but an excessive income gap will destabilize social order, and is something that needs government attention. . . . The side effects of this huge gap are mainly seen in the following . . . aspects. First, as earnings increase, living standards have been generally raised, but low-income groups are slow to reap the rewards of this prosperity for a number of reasons. In the long term, this will trigger emotional dissatisfaction and affect social stability.[44]

My main point here is that urban indigence shot sharply upward once multitudes of state and collective enterprises were officially enjoined to cut back drastically on their workforces after the mid-1990s. And the poverty that ensued immediately thereafter is directly traceable to this showdown.

At the same time, with the total overhaul of the socialist economy and its institutions, traditional welfare entitlements were also taken away from the proletariat,[45] leaving these losers at a total loss. These targeted persons came to constitute a category comprised of a never-before so sizable segment of the city populace: they became the newly minted, state-policy-engendered, dirt-poor urbanites living in the midst of what still calls itself "socialist China." They became "the new urban poor."

The Third Shift, 2003: Social

The third milestone, which was put into place at first in 2000, just a few years after the Fifteenth Party Congress, marked, at base, a *social* transmutation. The project—or, one could say, the state mission—of national modernization

---

43. Yuan Lanhua and Lin Chengmei, "Ai ru chao yong—Qingdaoshi chengxiang zuidi shenghuo baozhang zhidu shishi jishi" [Love like a rising tide—a true reporting of the Qingdao city urban and rural minimum livelihood guarantee system], *Zhongguo minzheng* (China civil affairs), no. 7 (1998), 10.

44. D. Wang, "Director General of Economics Faculty at the Party School of the Chinese Communist Party Central Committee," Comments at the invitation of the "21st Century Business Herald," November 19, 2007, www.wsichina.org/morningchina/archive/20071120.html.

45. From an official website, "Zhongguo chengshi jumin zuidi shenghuo baozhang biaozhun de xiangguan fenxi, jingji qita xiangguan lunwen" [Relevant analysis of Chinese urban residents' dibao norm; economic and other related treatises], unpaged, http://www.ynexam.cn/html/jingjixue/jingjixiangguan/2006/1105/zhonggochengshijimin, accessed August 18, 2007; Ya Ping Wang, *Urban Poverty, Housing and Social Change in China* (London and New York: Routledge, 2004), 60, 71–87.

at that point had come to entail not just a transition from a state-run, Party-planned, socialist-style economic system (after 1978) to what is, even if still state-dominated, a capitalist, market economy. Neither was it only a matter of expropriating the old Chinese proletariat's political standing (after 1997). As the project unfolded, it also signaled an elemental transformation in the social order, that is, in the class basis of the ruling Party and, thus, in the underlying distribution of social power.

Over the first few years of the new century, there was much talk of the concept of the "Three Represents." This was an idiom dictating what social forces the Party was thenceforth to stand for in "society," perhaps in ranked order: the "advanced productive forces," "advanced culture," and "the people." The term was propagated by then-outgoing Party General Secretary and state President Jiang Zemin in early 2000 (probably invented by his theorist, Wang Huning, and other official political thinkers) and first announced during a trip to Guangdong Province. This "theory" also featured in Jiang's speech on the occasion of the eightieth anniversary of the founding of the Communist Party of China in July of the next year; at the Sixteenth Party Congress in the fall of 2002, it was engraved in the Party Constitution. Whereas following the 1989 Tiananmen crackdown a decision had been reached to bar entrepreneurs from the Party, Jiang's affirmation of this slogan constituted what Bruce Dickson called a "dramatic breakthrough in the party's relationship with the private sector." The motto became a catchword for Jiang's political platform and, indeed, for "correct" policy, especially in the two or three years thereafter while he remained at the helm of power.[46]

With the delivery of Jiang's political report to the Sixteenth Congress, rich in its references to the "Three Represents," a brand-new canonical imprimatur was implanted upon the official conception of Chinese society, amounting to a proclamation of the Party's foundational switch in its own social base. Not only that, but the now-sanctioned configuration of the social structure translated into abdicating entirely any reference to class. This was the first officially sanctioned reordering of elements in society since the time when Mao's obsessive emphasis on classes and class struggle was discarded over twenty years before—but at that time, this was done without altering either the place or the standing of the proletariat or those of the bourgeoisie.

The three categories that make up the "Three Represents" were clearly stand-ins for three specific social segments—those with the superior marketing

---

46. Joseph Fewsmith, *China Since Tiananmen* (New York: Cambridge University Press, 2001), 229–31; Bruce J. Dickson, *Red Capitalists in China: The Party, Private Entrepreneurs, and Prospects for Political Change* (New York: Cambridge University Press, 2003), 102–3, 161–62; Susan V. Lawrence, "Three Cheers for the Party," *Far Eastern Economic Review* (October 26, 2000), 32ff; and Andrew J. Nathan and Bruce Gilley, *China's New Rulers: The Secret Files* (New York: New York Review Books, 2002), 116, 167–68.

know-how to develop highly profitable business ventures; those possessed of the scientific and managerial knowledge and expertise needed to participate in a cosmopolitan, globally affiliated society; and the masses of ordinary, undistinguished people, respectively.

At some points in the speech, it almost appeared as if a fourth, lowlier segment of society (i.e., the old proletariat, the subject of this book, whose unmaking was now sealed) had been relegated to a place outside "the people" for the foreseeable future. That is, whether the poverty-stricken, the new urban poor, those who were suddenly without steady jobs, were to be part of the third group, the "people"—or whether they instead were to constitute a residual, more or less forgotten fragment of society—remained rhetorically uncertain. As I am arguing in this book, however, their treatment indicated that they were indeed to be seen as separate from the mainstream of society as that stream surged along into the future.

Thus, Jiang's new codification amounted to a trifurcation of the citizenry that exhibited a not-so-subtle preference for the members of its first two target groupings. Accordingly, the posture of the Party in its prior incarnation as Marx's vanguard of the proletariat was to be scrapped, replaced by a brand-new bearing: the Party as a conglomeration fit to command and speak for a competitive, modern, and sophisticated constituency, a society prepared to merge into and contend with superior members of the global economy.

The new centrality of the envisioned linkage between China's "best" citizens and the world beyond is evident elsewhere in Jiang's address. His bias grew directly out of his vision of the country's new place in the global market, which appeared early in his speech and also graced the talk's parting words. In his opening statement, Jiang paid homage to the "new phase of development" where the nation then found itself, an era in which, he stated, "Science and technology are advancing rapidly. Competition in overall national strength is becoming increasingly fierce. Given this pressing situation, we must move forward or we will fall behind."[47] In this same vein, the oration terminated with this evocation of the intimidating, if alluring, universe abroad: "We must be keenly aware of the rigorous challenges brought about by the ever-sharpening international competition as well as risks and difficulties that may arise on our road ahead."[48]

The leadership's fixation with China joining the global economic race, and its concomitant need to match or even to surpass rivals outside, had been coming into evidence already over the previous years, an up-to-date version

---

47. Jiang Zemin's "Report at 16th Party Congress," http://english.peopledaily.com.cn/200211/18/eng20021118_106983.shtml.
48. Ibid.

of long-held dreams for Chinese leaders. And this view of the country's altered relation to the world, surely magnified once China acceded to the World
Trade Organization in late 2001, unquestionably elevated the significance of
the sectors among the populace who could contribute to the nation's victory
in this endeavor.[49] At the same time, it relegated the undereducated and the
unskilled—those just then in the course of being dismissed from the arena of
the working world—to the margins of society.

True, "the people" (i.e., those not part of the "advanced" public) were not
neglected altogether in Jiang Zemin's vision. This third group, referred to as
"the overwhelming majority of the people"—whose "fundamental interests"
were to be safeguarded—seems to constitute the selfsame segment of the
population as those whose "fundamental interests" Jiang claims the major
policy decisions taken by the Central Committee at and after 2002's Sixteenth
Party Congress had been in accord. Jiang used the identical Chinese words
both times that he discussed the conglomeration he termed "the people."

If by this designation Jiang was indeed referring to the same set of people,
then he may have been implicitly, if discursively, abandoning—or at any
rate, omitting from his Three Represents—the victims of what he conceded
were the "difficulties" of recent years. For those victims were decidedly not
among those whose "fundamental interests" were being served. That they
belonged to a separate grouping altogether is evident in opinion surveys on
livelihood conducted around the time of Jiang's address, in which nearly one-
quarter of those questioned had recently seen a drop in their condition.[50] Jiang
himself was well aware of those left behind, as he explicitly made reference
to incomes increasing "only slowly"; to the new fact of unemployment; to
people "still badly off"; and to those suffering because "things have yet to be
straightened out in the matter of income distribution."[51]

Another hint of there being a distinct, disadvantaged segment of society appeared just after one of Jiang's mentions of the "fundamental interests" of the
"overwhelming majority." This was his admonition that, "More importantly,
we must pay great attention to less developed areas and the industries and
people in straitened circumstances and show concern for them," as if such
people constituted an altogether separate portion of the people, possibly one

---

49. Lu Xueyi, *Dangdai zhongguo shehui jieceng yanjiu baogao* [A research report on China's current social structure] (Beijing: shehui kexue wenxian chubanshe [Social science documents publisher],
2002), 142–43.

50. A mid-2001 probability survey under the auspices of the Chinese Academy of Social Sciences, targeting 6,000 urbanites in twelve provinces and seventy-two cities, counties, and districts,
found that 23.8 percent declared that their standard of living had changed for the worse (12.6
percent said somewhat worse, and 11.2 percent very much worse) compared with 1995 (Lu Xueyi,
Dangdai, 3, 39).

51. Jiang Zemin, "Report."

that was *not* a part of the Three Represents. And when Jiang enumerated the "main tasks for economic development and reform in the first two decades of this century," the charge "steadily [to] uplift the people's living standards" was only number seven out of seven, a listing order that had to have been intentional. One more example: in enumerating eight rather more concrete assignments, Jiang ranked the first one as to "take a new road to industrialization and implement the strategy of rejuvenating the country through science and education and sustainable development," while the mission of reforming the system of income distribution and improving the social security system was only sixth in line. Meanwhile, doing "everything possible to create more jobs and improve the people's lives" came last of all.

Finally, in the section of the speech concerning economic development, when Jiang turned to income distribution, he explicitly favored "efficiency" over "fairness," through "bringing market forces into play and encouraging part of the people to become rich first."[52] In short, China, under the rule of Jiang, progressively subjected itself to pressures for excellence and international competition. And, it appears here, for Jiang Zemin himself, this spelled a contraction of what had, under Mao, been the relevant political community. As a laid-off worker, perhaps convinced by the state's propaganda, is quoted as having said: "Our generation is just the sacrificial victims of reform and opening! The leaders said so."[53]

So, the fall in the fate of the once-exalted working class of China, and its transmutation from master to marginal, unfolded through a progression of three momentous decisions—one on the economy, one (even if basically economically driven) with fundamental political ramifications, and one with profound social implications. All of these were largely choices taken by a political elite goaded onward by an ideal of a China set to switch from backward to modern. This monumental movement these men accomplished on the backs of the proletariat, I contend, or, put differently, by turning their backs on these workers. That China's urban poverty is an outcome that was manufactured mainly in this fashion—and primarily in the service of fears about, and visions for, the country's immediate economic future—that is, that it was not simply an offshoot of changing economic circumstances—sets it apart from impoverishment elsewhere, I argue. I will revisit the issue of this disparity, and the intentionality that forged it, in Chapter Seven, when I compare China's social assistance with what exists in many other places.

---

52. Ibid.
53. Han Keqing, ed., *Zhongguo chengshi dibao fangtanlu* [Interviews with Minimum Livelihood Guarantee Recipients in Urban China] (Jinan: Shandong renmin chubanshe [Shanghai people's publishing], 2012), 95.

CHAPTERS OVERVIEW

I divide my ten chapters into four sections. The first section is on background, with the present chapter being the introduction and presenting the political-economic provenance of the laid-off proletariat. The second chapter in this section, "Urban Poverty and its Paltry Palliatives," reviews the issue of urban poverty and how it was handled by the polity before and after the mid-1990s. The chapter also grapples with a range of statistical approximations of the extent of impoverishment in the cities and how that indigence was produced by state policies, especially from the mid-1990s onward. The end of the chapter discusses the initiation of the *dibao*. Chapter Three, "The *Dibao* and the *Dibaohu*," examines the *dibao*'s official goals and procedures and its early history. The chapter goes on to summarize data on the recipients' demographic features and their well-being. It closes with an interrogation and assessment of the instability that the political leadership and much of society associate with the program's beneficiaries.

Section Two is entitled "Experiences of Layoff (xiagang) and Livelihood Guarantee (*dibao*)"; it contains the fourth, fifth, and sixth chapters. The first of these, Chapter Four, is entitled "*Xiagang*: From Master to Mendicant." It uses the image of the crowd to portray the seething anger of the laid-off at the time of their disposal, as their status plummeted from the peak of society to its nadir. It relates how, by the turn of the century, the workers—once considered the "masters of the factory" and the beneficiary of a relationship in which the state served as their benefactor and guardian—were turned into marginals. Both that chapter and the two following feed off my interviews with *xiagang* workers and *dibaohu*, with program administrators at a number of levels, as well as with social policy scholars.

Chapter Five, "the *Dibao:* Management and Missteps," lays out the administrative procedures and funding that comprise the *dibao* scheme in its actual, quotidian practices, noting how practices depart from regulations; detailing the subsidies that are supposed to (at least often are said to) accompany it; discussing the exclusions of eligible individuals and households and the failures of targeting; and demonstrating the campaign-like style of promoting the program in the years of its peak. Chapter Six, "*Dibao*: Survival and Perspectives," presents information about how individuals manage to subsist under its aegis. It shows the failures of the recipients to get paying work and the government's often lacking role in providing training and public-sector employment for them. I follow this with reflections from interviews with grantees about their problems in attempting to rely on their children and extended family members for financial assistance and their modes of survival; I also offer quotations from these people that reveal their despair and their hopes, their sense of shame and isolation, and the rebelliousness of a few. The chapter concludes with a view of the perspectives adopted by community-level officials who manage the program and within society, generally, along with insights into the official justification for the treatment of its targets.

Section Three, "Comparisons and Variations," consists of two chapters, the first of which, Chapter Seven, "'Social Assistance?': A Comparative Perspective," offers a typology of three ideal-typical models of welfare provision. I refer to these as "productivist," "partisan," and "pacifying/policing," respectively. The models highlight the aims that underlie features of and stances toward "social assistance" in China's *dibao* platform and compares these with what goes under that heading in other countries. Chapter Eight, entitled, "*Dibao:* Differential Disbursement," uses statistical tests to distinguish the variable treatment that *dibaohu* are accorded in wealthier and poorer cities. It argues that prime recipients of the funds—flexible laborers, the unemployed, and the disabled, respectively—are each disparately allocated the allowance in different municipalities as a function of whether a city is prosperous or poor.

The fourth section, "Harsh Changes," containing Chapters Nine and Ten, exposes that both in rewrites to the initial policy on the *dibao* and in dramatic cutbacks of the numbers of its beneficiaries, the regime has reimagined and repurposed the fundamental nature of the program. Chapter Nine, "Policy Manipulations," traces chronologically how, in the past decade, leaders in Beijing (and also locally) have demanded that the able-bodied poor go to work and not be succored. Decision makers also decreed that the program's allowances target the physically desperate, not laid-off workers (as it had at its inception just after retrenchments were occurring). Also, it documents how since the rise of Xi Jinping to Party leadership in 2012, there has been a heavy emphasis on fighting graft and corruption in the program; the chapter also shows a turn to relatively favoring the rural areas over cities in recent years. The big message here is that the regime has repeatedly reshaped this initiative to match the changing, broader political agenda of the Party.

The objective of Chapter Ten, "Denouement: Drastic Cut in the *Dibao* Rolls—Did Pensions Replace the *Dibao*?" is to determine whether it is possible that the number of *dibao* recipients was cut drastically in the years between 2009 and 2019 because former recipients became eligible for, and were given, their pensions. The chapter rejects that view, often officially propagated. I use various approaches to refute this argument and set forth a different understanding behind this downsizing. The final chapter, Conclusion, brings together the overall analysis and themes.

Chapter Two

Urban Poverty and
Its Paltry Palliatives

As noted in Chapter One, a familiar story that has won China much acclaim internationally asserts that the regime has managed to deliver hundreds of millions of poor people from poverty between 1978 and 2015.[1] But, impressive as those results were, particularly in the years long before the current leaders came on board,[2] the publicists fail to note that what they are telling is wholly a rural tale. So, in recent announcements, it was the impoverished population in the *countryside* that was "lifted up," whose numbers declined from 94.2 million at year-end 2000 down to thirty-six million in 2009, a rapid drop, such that the national poverty rate—but, again, only in the rural areas—fell from 10.2 percent to 3.8 percent over those years. In 2011, the government set forth a ten-year project to cut back poverty in the *rural* regions even more, with the result that by mid-2020 a claim was put forth that 850 million people had been "raised out of extreme poverty."[3]

In the years since he came to the helm, clearly President and Party head Xi Jinping and his regime have been especially preoccupied with the fate of the countryside. In their assertions, there is absolutely no mention of the cities and the sizable poverty that remains there, which the government largely ignores. Markedly, still with a focus exclusively on the rural parts of the coun-

1. Dou Ding, "China's Ambitious Path to Poverty Eradication," *Global Asia* 11, no. 2 (Summer 2016): 22, citing the World Bank; Yuan Yang and Nian Liu, "Inside China's race to beat poverty," *Financial Times,* June 25, 2020. The claim is that over 700 million were "delivered."
2. For instance, see Thomas G. Rawski, "Is China's success transferable?" in Ho-Mou Wu and Yang Yao, eds., *Reform and Development in China: What Can China Offer the Developing World?* (London: Routledge, 2011), 320–48.
3. Ding, "China's Ambitious Path," 24; and "Mr. Xi's antipoverty drive is focused on around five million people who earn less than 92 cents a day, down from nearly fifty-six million five years ago," Javier C. Hernandez, "'We Couldn't Be Poorer': Pandemic Hinders China's Antipoverty Efforts," *New York Times*, October 26, 2020.

try was Xi's early 2016 pledge that, "We should make sure the entire poor population in the *rural* [emphasis added] regions can rise out of poverty on schedule." In that same New Year's message, Xi set forth the goal of reaching a *xiaokang* (moderately well off, 小康) society by the year 2020, a mission he implied was limited at that point only by destitution in the countryside.[4] And yet, the ongoing situation in the cities belies the sincerity of that mission if the objective truly is to transform the lives of all the people of China so that they are all existing in reasonably comfortable circumstances, in city and countryside alike.[5]

In this chapter, I look at urban poverty and how it was handled before the mid-1990s, but then, in more detail than in the previous chapter, I consider how a significant new incidence of impoverishment was politically produced thereafter. The earlier effort at relief, the *sanwu* (three withouts, 三无), targeted a relatively small portion of the urban populace. The term referred to those without any of these three livelihood props: legal supporters; the ability to labor; and a source of income; in short, those who were impoverished owing to natural causes, such as orphans, the aged, and the disabled; the same label also was used to apply to the program itself. I draw several comparisons between the *sanwu* and the *dibao*, which was created in 1999 to replace the *sanwu*. The *dibao* was devised as the *sanwu* clearly became inadequate to meet the massive needs for relief that emerged once huge numbers—in the tens of millions—of additional urban poor appeared. These newly indigent people were a by-product of the progress of China's economic reforms and of the country's more pronounced entry into the global market as its membership in the World Trade Organization became imminent. Finally, I review the mounting of the *dibao* in 1999.

HISTORICAL POVERTY RELIEF IN THE CITIES (THE *SANWU*)

In the discussion that follows, I draw on the work of numerous scholars, most of whom come to disparate conclusions about the incidence of urban poverty, using varying standards and, for the most part, not specifying regional variations. Some do not indicate whether they are including rural migrants who

---

4. Ding, "China's Ambitious Path," 26.

5. Carl Minzner, *End of an Era: How China's Authoritarian Revival is Undermining its Rise* (New York: Oxford University Press, 2018), caption for photo following p. 141, referring to urban inequality, it states that it obtains [only] "between disadvantaged migrant workers and established urban residents." Terry Sicular, "Will China Eliminate Poverty in 2020?" *China Leadership Monitor*, November 2020, states that, "In 2018 relative poverty nationwide was estimated at 280 million, or 20 percent of the national population. Among all poor, about 40 million were urban and the rest were rural. The urban poverty rate was 5 percent." https://www.prcleader.org/sicular?utm_source=so&cid=181f57b0-7589-4ba6-b97c-2032dc9bab59, accessed December 8, 2018.

are resident in cities; nor do they state if they are counting just those with an urban household registration (*hukou*, 戶口). Nonetheless, the claims of all of them are of a rapid increase in the numbers of the urban poor after the late 1990s, when enterprises of all sizes and types were enjoined to dismiss all or much of their workforces.[6]

In the years before 1999, when the *dibao* program became mandatory in cities nationwide (actually, before about 1994, when the work unit [*danwei,* 单位] system with its generous welfare was mostly phased out),[7] the scheme that tended to the urban poor was entitled the *sanwu*. When the *dibao* was inaugurated, it was presented as a major improvement on what had been available to the very poor under the *sanwu* scheme, which was criticized as excessively stingy.[8]

Certainly, the apportionments for the *sanwu* were tiny. For instance, in 1979, recipients, of whom there were then just 240,000, were given a mere 75 yuan per year per person.[9] But, in fact, in *relative* material terms, the *dibao* did not really constitute a major improvement. For as of 1979, the average urban disposable income was also quite low, at 387 yuan per capita per annum.[10] So the *sanwu* targets collected an amount that was 19.4 percent of the wage of the average city citizen.

Jumping ahead thirteen years, things had improved, but just by a bit. In 1992, the average disposable annual urban income per capita was 2,026.6 yuan (168.88 yuan per month). At the time, the support for an especially poor urban citizen was 38 yuan per person per month, according to scholar Song Xiaowu, former president of the China Economic System Reform Research Association. This sum amounted to 22.5 percent of the average city income per capita, less than one-third of average food expenditure.[11] Two years later, in 1994, the average annual grant per person for *sanwu* beneficiaries was 585

---

6. Thank you to Thomas Rawski for alerting me to the need to explain this issue.

7. Lowell Dittmer and Xiaobo Lu, "Personal Politics in the Chinese Danwei under Reform," *Asian Survey*, no. 3 (1996): 246–67.

8. See reference to Zhong Renyao in footnote 13.

9. Yang Lixiong, "The Social Assistance Reform in China; Towards a Fair and Inclusive Social Safety Net," prepared for "Addressing Inequalities and Challenges to Social Inclusion through Fiscal, Wage and Social Protection Policies," United National Headquarters, New York, June 25–27, 2018 (unpaginated), http://www.un.org/development/.../The-Social-Assistance-Reform-in-China .pdf. By way of comparison, the average consumption expenditure of urban people was 383 yuan in 1978 and 468 yuan in 1980 (Guojia tongjiju, shehui tongjisi, bian [National Bureau of Statistics, Office of Social Statistics, ed.], 1990 *Zhongguo shehui tongji ziliao* [1990 Chinese social statistics materials] [Beijing: Zhongguo tongji chubanshe [China Statistics Press], 1990], 82). Thanks to Thomas Rawski for this data.

10. This figure for disposable income is in *2001 Zhongguo tongji nianjian* [2001 China Statistical Yearbook] (Beijing: Zhongguo tongji chubanshe [China Statistics Press], 2001), 304. The figures that follow for urban average disposable income come from the same table.

11. Song Xiaowu, *Zhongguo shehui baozhang zhidu gaige* [The reform of China's social security system] (Beijing: *Qinghua daxue chubanshe* [Qinghua University Press], 2001), 139. Song states that the 38 yuan represented 25 percent of an urban resident's average livelihood expenses.

yuan, according to social policy specialist Linda Wong. This would have come to 48.75 yuan per month, an amount that she deemed "not enough for subsistence." That sum represented a decline to 16.7 percent of the average per capita disposable urban income, which, for the average urban resident that year, came to 3,496.2 yuan.[12]

These kinds of data do make the *sanwu* grant seem quite parsimonious. Probably such figures are what led Zhong Renyao of East China Normal University to judge that, "the *sanwu* program was irrational"; its "relief standard . . . was obviously too low." In fact, he appraised the fund as serving only as "a symbolic, moral kind of support."[13] And yet, when the *sanwu* and the *dibao* allowances are compared, a surprising result emerges: the *dibao* recipients did not actually fare much better in terms of the *relative* size of their allowance (in relation to the contemporaneous average urban disposable income), when compared with what the *sanwu* got before them.[14]

Turning to the numbers of recipients, it is the case that far more people have been assisted by the *dibao* than by the old *sanwu* program. The Civil Affairs handbook for 2008 shows that, in 1992, a mere 192,000 people were being served by the *sanwu*,[15] amounting to 0.06 percent of the urban-registered population, which, in that year, was 323.72 million;[16] Song Xiaowu offers the same percentage of 0.06 of the city populace for 1992. But Song also writes that, according to a 1993 sample investigation of urban residents' living expenses, about fifteen million people were subsisting in poverty,[17] or 4.5 percent of the cities' population (333.51 million that year[18]). This, of course, was far beyond the number of those who were being helped. Song notes that social relief was covering just 1 percent of the official city populace, substantially better than the coverage the year before

---

12. Linda Wong, *Marginalization and Social Welfare in China* (London: Routledge, 1998), 123; Zhihong Qian and Tai-chee Wong, "The Rising Urban Poverty: A Dilemma of Market Reforms in China," *Journal of Contemporary China* 9, no. 23 (2000): 119, found that in the same year (1995), the per capita yearly income of poor households, who, they say, were 5 percent of all (presumably urban-registered) households, equaled less than Wong says, at just 1,360 yuan, which, they allege, was 35 percent of the average urban households' income. It could have been that the subsidy was increased in light of the already mounting numbers of sloughed-off workers.

13. Zhong Renyao, *Shehui jiuzhu yu shehui fuli* [Social assistance and social welfare] (Shanghai: Shanghai University of Finance and Economics Press, 2005), 66. Thanks to Daniel Hammond for sending me a copy of this page.

14. Jennifer Pan noted that *sanwu* targets had somehow to pay for their housing and benefits, while neither other contemporaneous urban citizens nor, later, many *dibao* recipients had to do so (email, January 3, 2020).

15. Zhongguo renmin gongheguo minzhengbu, bian [Chinese People's Republic Ministry of Civil Affairs, ed.], *2008 Zhongguo minzheng tongji nianjian* [2008 China Civil Affairs Yearbook] (Beijing: Zhongguo tongji chubanshe [China Statistics Press], 2008), 76.

16. *2001 Zhongguo tongji nianjian* [2001 China Statistical Yearbook] (Beijing: Zhongguo tongji chubanshe [China Statistics Press], 2001), 91.

17. Song, *Zhongguo shehui*, 137.

18. Ibid.

Table 2.1. Urban and Rural *Dibao* Expenditures as Percentage of GDP and of Total Government Expenditure, 2001–2018

Year	Urban Dibao Expenditures as % of GDP	Urban Dibao Expenditures as % of Total Govt. Expenditures	Rural Dibao Expenditures as % of GDP	Rural Dibao Expenditures as % of Total Govt. Expenditures
2001	0.0417	0.2443	0.0042	0.0248
2002	0.0893	0.4927	0.0058	0.0322
2003	0.1096	0.6107	0.0019	0.0105
2004	0.1067	0.6064	0.0100	0.0570
2005	0.1025	0.5657	0.0135	0.0746
2006	0.1022	0.5546	0.0198	0.1076
2007	0.1026	0.5572	0.0404	0.2191
2008	0.1231	0.6285	0.0716	0.3654
2009	0.1381	0.6319	0.1040	0.4757
2010	0.1270	0.5838	0.1077	0.4952
2011	0.1349	0.6041	0.1365	0.6112
2012	0.1248	0.5354	0.1329	0.5700
2013	0.1271	0.5397	0.1456	0.6183
2014	0.1121	0.4755	0.1351	0.5733
2015	0.1044	0.4090	0.1352	0.5296
2016	0.0924	0.3664	0.1363	0.5403
2017	0.0780	0.3150	0.1282	0.5173
2018	0.0639	0.2604	0.1174	0.4784

Sources: For *dibao* expenditures: *Zhongguo minzheng tongji nianjian, 2002–2019* [China Civil Affairs' Statistical Yearbook, 2002–2019]. For GDP and total government expenditures: *Zhongguo tongji nianjian, 2002–2019* [China Statistical Yearbook, 2002–2019].

but still a tiny proportion. By contrast, by 2002, the *dibao* was serving over twenty million indigents.

Also widely divergent was the proportion of GDP that *sanwu* relief occupied. In the reckoning of Zhong Renyao, the total expenditure for urban social relief (which included that for the *sanwu*) in 1992 came to 120 million yuan, or 0.005 percent of GDP.[19] In 2002, however, *dibao* expenditure represented nearly 0.1 percent of GDP. See Table 2.1. Thus, it would appear that the *dibao* radically boosted the government's outlays to the poor.

These positive comparisons, though, are in an important sense inapt. A critical bit of information is that, while poverty relief using the *dibao* has surely taken up a larger share of the GDP and reached more recipients, it remains sorely deficient, as is apparent in recipients' descriptions of their existence, quoted in Chapters Five, Six, and Ten. For one thing, the national regulations granted cities the authority to design the details of their own programs. Accordingly, as an investigation in five cities in 1998–1999 found,

---

19. Zhong, *Shehui jiuzhu*, 67.

Table 2.2.   Average *Dibao* Norm, Average Wage, and Average *Dibao* Norm as Percentage of Average Wage, 1998, Nineteen Large Cities

City	Avg. Dibao *Norm* (Yuan/Mon.)	Norm x 12 (A)	Avg.wage (B) (Yuan/Yr.)	A/B (%)
Beijing	200	2,400	12,285	19.5
Tianjin	185	2,220	9,946	22.3
Shenyang	150	1,800	7,811	23.0
Dalian	165	1,980	9,275	21.4
Changchun	130	1,560	7,869	19.8
Harbin	140	1,680	6,603	25.4
Jinan	140	1,680	8,326	20.2
Qingdao	160	1,920	8,125	23.6
Shanghai	205	2,460	12,059	20.4
Hangzhou	165	1,980	10,194	19.4
Nanjing	140	1,680	10,661	15.8
Wuhan	120	1,440	8,255	17.4
Chongqing	130	1,560	5,710	27.3
Chengdu	120	1,440	8,248	17.5
Xi'an	105	1,260	6,922	18.2
Lanzhou	100	1,200	7,736	15.5
Fuzhou	170	2,040	8,772	23.3
Shenzhen	245	2,940	18,381	16.0
Xiamen	250	3,000	12,799	23.4

Average: 20.5

Sources: For the *dibao* line, *"Xiao ziliao: Quanguo ge chengshi juimin zuidi shenghuo baozhang biaojun"* [Small material: Nationwide various cities' residents' minimum livelihood guarantee lines], *Shehui* [Society], 6 (1999): 26; for the average wage, Wuxi Statistical Yearbook 1999, from China data online, accessed May 29, 2008.

there were conspicuous variations in the approaches taken by the different municipalities the researchers investigated. See Tables 2.2 and 2.3. This study of 2,354 poor families discovered that the *dibao* line, also termed the *"dibao norm"* (*dibao biaozhun* 低保 标准) was respectively 31, 21, 21, 27, and 28 percent of the average local income in these cities at that time.[20] After an elevation of the norm in autumn 1999, Shanghai's rate went up to 40 percent, but in Wuhan, it remained low, at 27 percent.

But there were many other issues with the *dibao* when examined closely. For instance, by 2008, the *dibao* line tended to be set at just one-third of the minimum wage in a given city and two-thirds of the level of unemployment benefits.[21] Even in wealthy Shanghai that same year, the city's Bureau of Civil

---

20. Tang Jun, "The New Situation of Poverty and Antipoverty," in *2002 nian: Zhongguo shehui xingshi yu yuce (shehui lanpishu)* [2002: Analysis and Forecast of China's Social Situation (Blue Book on Chinese Society)], eds. Ru Xin, Lu Xueyi, Li Peilin, et al., January 1, 2002. [FBIS Translated Text].

21. Daniel Hammond, "Social Assistance in China, 1993–2002: Institutions, Feedback, and Policy Actors in the Chinese Policy Process," *Asian Politics & Policy* 3, no. 1 (2011): 72, citing Anthony Saich, *Providing Public Goods in Transitional China* (London: Palgrave Macmillan, 2008).

Table 2.3. *Dibao* Norm, Average Disposable Income, and *Dibao* Norm as a Percentage of Average Disposable Income, Various Cities, July 2002 (Unit: Yuan/Month)

City	Dibao *Line (A)*	Avg. Disp. Inc. (B)	A/B (%)
Beijing	290	1038.67	27.92
Tianjin	241	778.17	30.97
Shenyang	205	587.50	34.89
Dalian	221	683.33	32.34
Changchun	169	575.00	29.39
Harbin	200	583.67	34.27
Taiyuan	156	614.67	25.38
Jinan	208	748.42	27.79
Qingdao	205*	726.75	28.21
Shanghai	280	1104.17	25.36
Hangzhou	285*	981.5	29.04
Nanjing	220	763.08	28.83
Wuhan	210	651.67	32.23
Changsha	190*	751.75	25.27
Chongqing	185	603.17	30.67
Chengdu	178	747.67	23.81
Xi'an	156	598.67	26.06
Lanzhou	172	n.a.	n.a.
Shenzhen	317*	2078.42	15.25
Xiamen	290*	980.67	29.57
Guangzhou	300	1115.00	26.91

Average: 28.2

*Indicates that figure is average of upper and lower figures for *dibao* line for city for that year.

Sources: For the *dibao* line, "*Quanguo 36ge chengshi zuidi baozhang biaozhun yilan*" [General survey of 36 cities' minimum livelihood guarantee line], http://china.com.cn/city/txt/2006-11/25/content_740675\hich \af0\dbch\af13\loch\f08_2.htm, accessed August 17, 2007 (link no longer available); for urban residents' average disposable income, Chengdu Statistical Yearbook 2003, China data online, accessed May 29, 2008.

Affairs commissioned a household survey of 1,182 *dibao* recipients in which it discovered that 82.5 percent of the 400 households queried could not afford basic necessities despite the allowance.[22] A later piece of research noted that, as of 2013, the national average level of the *dibao* norm (or poverty line) was a mere 9.4 percent of the average wage,[23] according to one study.[24] See Table 2.4.

And, crucially, the *dibao* dropped over time as a percentage of average urban per capita income. In its early years, in 2002, for instance, the norm (or poverty line) across twenty-one large cities amounted, on average, to 28

---

22. Haimiao Zhang, "China's Social Assistance Policy: Experiences and Future Directions," *China Journal of Social Work* (*CJSW*) 7, no. 3 (2014): 227.

23. Jinxian Wang and Yanfeng Bai, "Development of Minimum Livelihood Guarantee Programmes in Urban China: An Empirical Analysis Based On 31 Regions Over 2003–2013," *CJSW* 9, nos. 1–3 (2016): 168.

24. Data in the Civil Affairs Statistical Yearbook, which was used to create Table 2.3, has slightly different figures from those in this study.

Table 2.4. Average Urban *Dibao* Norm as Percentage of National Average Disposable Income/Average Wage, 2006–2019 (Unit: CNY/Year)

Year	National Avg. Urban Disposable Income	Urban Dibao Norm as % of National Avg. Disposable Income	National Avg. Wage	Urban Dibao Norm as % of National Avg. Wage
2006	11,760	17.31	21,001	9.69
2007	13,786	15.88	24,932	8.78
2008	15,781	15.61	29,229	8.43
2009	17,175	15.92	32,735	8.35
2010	19,109	15.77	37,147	8.11
2011	21,810	15.82	42,452	8.13
2012	24,565	16.13	47,593	8.32
2013	26,955	16.62	52,388	8.55
2014	29,381	16.77	57,361	8.59
2015	31,195	17.35	63,241	8.56
2016	33,616	17.66	68,993	8.60
2017	36,396	17.82	76,121	8.52
2018	39,251	17.72	84,744	8.21
2019	42,359	17.68	93,383	8.02

Sources: For *dibao* norm: *Zhongguo minzheng tongji nianjian*, 2007–2020 [China Civil Affairs' Statistical Yearbook, 2007–2020]. For average disposable income and average wage: *Zhongguo tongji nianjian*, 2007–2020 [China Statistical Yearbook, 2007–2020].

percent of average per capita disposable income in those cities.[25] (This norm is not the amount a recipient receives; recipients get what is called a "subsidy" [*buzhu* 补助], calculated as the difference between a household's per capita income and the *dibao* norm in that person's city.) But that percentage subsequently dropped and then fluctuated after 2005 in the range of 15 to 18 percent—not so different from the *sanwu*'s 16.7 percent in 1994—just as demonstrating terminated workers became passive.[26] See Table 2.4.

And another noteworthy comparison is this: It is true that the *sanwu* beneficiaries' 38 yuan or 48.75 yuan per month (in 1994) sounds terribly measly. Yet the fact is that, in 2001, while the average *dibao* norm (i.e., the poverty line) was 147 yuan per capita per month nationally, the actual average subsidy (i.e., what was given out) came to just 29.6 yuan per person per month that year—at a time when the cost of living was certainly higher than it had been five and seven years earlier.[27] In what follows, I trace the path from *sanwu* assistance to the installation of the *dibao*. See Tables 2.5 and 2.6.

---

25. Dorothy J. Solinger, "Dibaohu in Distress: The Meager Minimum Livelihood Guarantee System in Wuhan," in *China's Changing Welfare Mix: Local Perspectives*, eds. Jane Duckett and Beatriz Carillo (London: Routledge, 2011), 45. Chapter Three specifies how the *dibao* works.

26. Dorothy J. Solinger, "Banish the Impoverished Past: The Predicament of the Abandoned Urban Poor," in *Polarized Cities: Portraits of Rich and Poor in Urban China*, ed. Dorothy J. Solinger (Lanham, MD: Rowman & Littlefield, 2019), 68 (sources given there).

27. 2008 Civil Affairs Yearbook, 78.

Table 2.5. National Average Urban and Rural *Dibao* Norms (poverty lines), 2001–2019 (Unit: CNY/Person*Month)

Year	National Avg. Urban Dibao *Standards*	National Avg. Rural Dibao *Standards*
2001	147.0	n.a.
2002	148.0	n.a.
2003	149.0	n.a.
2004	152.0	n.a.
2005	156.0	n.a.
2006	169.6	70.9
2007	182.4	70.0
2008	205.3	82.3
2009	227.8	100.8
2010	251.2	117.0
2011	287.6	143.2
2012	330.1	172.3
2013	373.3	202.8
2014	410.5	231.4
2015	451.1	264.8
2016	494.6	312.0
2017	540.6	358.4
2018	579.7	402.8
2019	624.0	444.6

Note: The "standards" [*biaozhun*] are the local poverty lines.

Source: *Zhongguo minzheng tongji nianjian*, 2002–2020 [China Civil Affairs' Statistical Yearbook, 2002–2020].

Table 2.6. National Average Urban *Dibao* Subsidies, 2001–2019 (Unit: CNY/Person*Month)

Year	National Average Urban Dibao *Subsidies*
2001	29.6
2002	43.9
2003	58.0
2004	65.0
2005	72.3
2006	83.6
2007	102.7
2008	143.7
2009	172.0
2010	189.0
2011	240.3
2012	239.1
2013	264.2
2014	285.6
2015	316.6
2016	n.a.
2017	n.a.
2018	n.a.
2019	n.a.

Note: The "subsidies" [*buzhu*] are the amount actually given to recipients.

Source: *Zhongguo minzheng tongji nianjian*, 2002–2020 [China Civil Affairs' Statistical Yearbook, 2002–2020].

URBAN POVERTY AND ITS NEW
PRODUCTION BEFORE THE *DIBAO*

Urban Poverty, 1990s

Back in the 1980s, the total of the exceptionally destitute urban poor was be-low one million.[28] But low incomes and a fairly spartan lifestyle were the lot for nearly everyone in the urban populace before the early 1990s. By 1995, however, the National Bureau of Statistics announced that some 12.4 million families were living in poverty (those households subsisting on an income be-low 5,000 yuan per year or 416 yuan per month, around US$1.50 per day[29]).[30] But Linda Wong termed even the Bureau's figure "definitely an undercount." She reached this conclusion by adding in what she calculated were ten million workers owed back wages, 1.5 million retired people whose pensions had been cut or stopped altogether, and 5.2 million registered unemployed, along with their dependents. Combining all of these categories of indigent people, she argued, meant that, by 1995, there were likely to have been some thirty million urban citizens, about 8.5 percent of the urban registered population, living in dire poverty.[31]

Feng Chen and Mengxiao Tang quoted a 1997 survey implemented in ten cities claiming that as many as two-thirds (67 percent) of laid-off workers were then already in poverty, while a shocking 31 percent of them had no income at all.[32] Other approaches also figured that the numbers were high: based on a 1998 National Bureau of Statistics sample of 17,000 households in 146 cities and eighty rural county seats, Athar Hussain found that if one were to use an expenditure per head count rather than income per head, the number of the poor would have more than doubled, from 14.7 million to 37.1 million.[33] Jiwei Qian and Ka Ho Mok advanced the startling estimate that

---

28. Mo Rong, *"Jiuye: zai tiaozhanzong guanzhu kunnan qunti"* [Employment: Under challenge, pay close attention to the masses in difficulty], in *Shehui lanpishu: 2003 nian: Zhongguo shehui xing-shi fenxi yu yuce* [Social blue book: 2003 analysis and predictions of China's social situation], eds. Ru Xin, Lu Xueyi, and Li Peilin (Beijing: shehui kexue wenxian chubanshe [Social science documents publishing company], 2003), 39–40. Mo, then of the Labor Science Research Institute, states that the numbers were between 600,000 and 800,000.

29. Here and in what follows, this kind of comparison, of course, ignores the far higher cost of living in the United States and, thus, the purchasing power capacity of the same amount of dollars.

30. Wong, *Marginalization*, 124. She does not provide a citation for this statement. Fulong Wu, Chris Webster, Shenjing He, and Yuting Liu, *Urban Poverty in China* (Cheltenham, UK: Edward Elgar, 2010) examines urban poverty from the mid-1990s to the late 2000s.

31. Wong, *Marginalization*, 124.

32. Feng Chen and Mengxiao Tang, "Labor Conflicts in China: Typologies and Their Implica-tions," *Asian Survey* 53, no. 3 (2013): 568.

33. Athar Hussain, "Urban Poverty in China: Measurement, Patterns and Policies," ms. (Geneva: International Labour Office, January 2003), 16. Tang Jun, "Jiasu zuidi shenghuo baozhang zhidu de guanfanhua yunzuo" [Speed up the *dibao*'s normalized operation], in *2004 nian: Zhongguo shehui xingshi fenxi yu yuce* [2004: Analysis and forecast of China's social situation], eds. Ru Xin, Lu Xue-

seventy-two million residents of cities were poor as of 2003, citing a World Bank report of 2009.[34] Peter Townsend introduced a standard of a different sort: He remarked that had the poverty line been drawn "50 percent higher than the very stringent threshold in fact adopted, 20 percent or nearly 90 million urbanites" (perhaps—though he does not specify—including migrants, who are not eligible for the *dibao*) could have been considered destitute in 1998. The figure would have been higher yet, he figured, if the costs of subsistence were used as the basis for the line.[35]

Here I return to Mo Rong. In 2002, he explained that the term "the poor" was being employed to refer to households where the average per-person income was below what was then the urban residents' minimum livelihood guarantee (*dibao*) or poverty line in their city of habitation, a threshold that then ranged from 78 yuan to 319 yuan per month among cities.[36] Overall, he argued that—contrary to what the National Bureau of Statistics had alleged was the case in 1995—in 2002, nationwide, on average, the line fell below the United Nation's poverty norm of US$1 per day at that time.[37] Indeed, the average *dibao* norm (or poverty line) nationwide that year was 148 yuan per month, which would have been about US$18 to US$19, or about $0.62 per day.[38] See Table 2.5.

Similarly, sociologist Li Peilin discussed this period in an internal journal. "Up to 2002," he wrote, "there were 20 million urban citizens surviving on

jin, and Li Peilin (Beijing: shehui kexue wenxian chubanshe [Social science documents publishing company], 2004), 121. Tang surmised that the urban poor amounted in 2003 to fifteen to thirty million people. See also Wing Thye Woo, Li Shi, Yue Ximing, Harry Wu Xiaoying, and Xu Xingpeng, "The Poverty Challenge for China in the New Millenium," report to the Poverty Reduction Taskforce of the Millennium Development Goals Project of the United Nations, October 2, 2004, revised draft; and Martin Ravallion, "A Guaranteed Minimum Income? China's Di Bao Program," ppt. (n.p., n.d.).

34. Jiwei Qian and Ka Ho Mok, "Dual Decentralization and Fragmented Authoritarianism in Governance: Crowding Out Among Social Programmes in China," *Public Administration and Development* 36, no. 3 (2016): 185–97. The report is The World Bank, Poverty Reduction and Economic Management Department, East Asia and Pacific Region, "From poor areas to poor people: China's evolving poverty reduction agenda: an assessment of poverty and inequality in China," (Washington, DC: The World Bank, 2009). It is not clear whether migrants are included, but on page 39, the report states that, "Between 1994, when it was at its peak, and 2006, employment in state-owned enterprises and urban collectives fell by 73 million from 145 million workers to 72 million." These numbers would not have included migrants.

35. Peter Townsend, "Social Security in Developing Countries: a Brief Overview," in *Building Decent Societies: Rethinking the Role of Social Security in Development*, ed. Peter Townsend (Houndmills, UK: Palgrave Macmillan 2009), 250. Townsend does not name a year, but the context seems to be 1998.

36. Mo, "Jiuye," 39.

37. Chunni Zhang, Qi Xu, Xiang Zhou, Xiaobo Zhang, and Yu Xie, "Are Poverty Rates Underestimated in China? New Evidence from Four Recent Surveys," *China Economic Review (CER)*, no. 31 (2014): 411, notes that, "Government statistics, though useful for tracking trends, may suffer from biases due to political interference or procedural limitations." "The sampling frame is not transparent," they add. On 420–21, they also figure that official figures could contain a bias in that the surveys might have underreported poor households.

38. 2008 Civil Affairs yearbook, 78.

the *dibao*, with incomes between 150 and 300 yuan per month," 70 percent (fourteen million) of whom were laid-off staff and workers and other unemployed people. But "really," he went on, "if [one counts] . . . those among the urban population in serious difficulty, the figure should be 30 million."[39] One remarkable feature of Li's essay is that, at that time as severe privation was besetting so much of the retrenched proletariat, that group's future ability to participate in an imagined, distant, well-off society concerned Li—unlike publicists today, who have forgotten them. His worry was displayed in the title of his article, which championed "establishing a moderately well-off society." There he referenced furloughed workers as among the target groups at risk, a cohort forgotten soon after. At this same juncture, another scholar, Wang Yanzhong, stated that those considered "middle-income-level residents . . . constitute [only] four percent of the urban populace."[40] Such a remark suggests that the impoverished must have been quite numerous back then.

Researchers at the World Bank seconded these results that indicated high numbers of urban poor. Their approach was to triple the 2009 World Bank poverty line, which then was 1,124 yuan per person per year, or 93.66 yuan per month. Three times that line would still have amounted to just 281 yuan per month, then equal to about US$1.17 per day. With that reckoning, they reasoned, "The urban disadvantaged population (that is, those with incomes below 281 yuan per month), [would have amounted to] about 34 to 72 million people in 2003, or 10 to 20 percent of the urban population."[41] So, if one pits Wang Yanzhong's 2003 estimate about the very low proportion of the city populace that the middle class then represented alongside the World Bank's figures for the poor, it would appear that there were many more indigent people living in the cities around the turn of the millennium than there were members of the "middle class."

Going forward some years, the problem of the urban poor did not diminish. Surveys done between 2007 and 2011 by a group of sociologists challenge official data, maintaining that thirty to forty-two million people in cities were then still living in poverty,[42] some 4.5 to 6.25 percent of the urban population. But if those residing in towns were included, the authors estimated that the

39. Li Peilin, "Quanmian jianshe xiaokang shehui de sige guanjian wenti" [4 key issues in completely establishing a well-off society], *Lingdao canyue* (*LC*) [Leadership consultations], no. 10 (April 5, 2003): 10.

40. Wang Yanzhong, "Jiaru WTO hou wo guo jingji fazhan wenti yu zhanwang" [Looking back and forward at our country's economic development after entering WTO], *LDCY*, no. 3 (January 25, 2003): 3.

41. Ibid., 72. It would appear that the researchers are not counting migrants, but this is not clear. See footnotes 33 and 34.

42. Their measure for the urban poverty line was US$1.50, given without a date. They do not specify if they included rural migrants who were residents in cities, but the data sources they drew upon suggest that they were not.

size of the urban populace then surviving at a level under the *dibao* line (the minimum living standard or poverty line) in their cities would have come to seventy-one million, or as much as 10.6 percent of the urban population.[43] Further, they quote the China Household Finance Survey of 2011 as having found that as much as 16 percent of urban residents were living on incomes below US$1.25 per day; besides, probably as much as 20 percent were subsisting at an income level that fell below the official minimum livelihood norms in their places of residence.[44] Agreeing that the issue was persisting, Guan Xinping asserted in 2014 that, "About two decades ago, when the Chinese government and researchers began to pay attention to urban poverty, the most prominent cause . . . was mass unemployment caused by layoffs in urban state enterprises, caused mainly by the reform of state enterprises in the 1990s . . . [and] 2012 survey data demonstrate that unemployment is *still* [emphasis added] one of the main factors causing urban poverty."[45]

The work of Bjorn Gustafsson and Sai Ding documents that between the years 2007 and 2013, a rising trend of urban inequality emerged, in which steadily larger numbers of people fell below a relative poverty line in China's municipalities. This result is evident in their discovery that, in 1988, just 7 percent of city dwellers (excluding rural migrants) were living in a household having an income under 60 percent of the urban median income; by 1995, that figure had gone up to 15 percent. In 2002 and 2007, the percentage had climbed to 19, and in 2013, over one-fifth (21 percent) of city residents were surviving on an income beneath the national median. Additionally, while just 3 percent of the urban population had per capita incomes below 50 percent of the median income in 1988, that proportion rose to 12 percent in 2002 and then to 15 percent in 2013.[46]

In this same vein, Zhang Ruli and Peng Qing adduced that if those whose incomes qualified them for the *dibao* but who for one reason or another had not been given it, along with those living on the margin just above the *dibao* threshold—and so treated as ineligible for it—were both added in, the poor population in the cities in early 2013 would have been thirty-one million, as

43. Zhang et al., "Are poverty rates?" 420. In 2010, the urban population was 669.78 million. See https://www.google.com/search?q=china's+urban+population+2010&sxsrf=ACYBGNSYxCJd8zB 9s1WBWaICiuNaWUlGhg:1577939887121&tbm=isch&source=iu&ictx=1&fir=4fGPwus92zdfOM %253A%252Cpqi1wgQexzDRRM%252C_&vet=1&usg=AI4_-kRRwvt4A7GlLHdvpn5ssNUxoYl1 9g&sa=X&ved=2ahUKEwjlpMuTjOTmAhXYvp4KHZjcD0YQ9QEwAHoECAYQAw&biw=1536 &bih=601#imgrc=Ys3a4o_fsLCGQM:&vet=1, accessed January 1, 2020.

44. Zhang et al., "Are poverty rates?," 418.

45. Guan Xinping, "Poverty and Anti-Poverty Measures in China," *CJSW* 7, no. 3 (2014): 279. Zhang et al. and Guan did not indicate whether their statistics included urban migrants.

46. Bjorn Gustafsson and Sai Ding, "Unequal Growth: Long-Term Trends in Household Incomes and Poverty in Urban China," in *Changing Trends in China's Inequality: Evidence, Analysis, and Prospects,* eds. Terry Sicular, Shi Li, Ximing Yue, and Hiroshi Sato (New York: Oxford University Press, 2020), 243, 253, and 262.

a conservative estimate, about 8 percent of the urban population. The authors went on to profess that, "Overall, since reform began, China's poor population has expanded annually; this trend is an uncontested fact."[47]

Bolstering that evaluation is a paper using data from a longitudinal series of surveys conducted by the China Family Panel Studies at the Institute of Social Science Survey at Peking University. These studies spanned the period from 2010 through May 2015 and queried 16,000 households in twenty-five provinces. The findings from the paper, which, like the Zhang-Peng research just cited, focus on *dibao*-eligible urban residents (thus, urban *hukou* holders, not including migrants) contribute an unexpected result that undermines Xi Jinping's singular rural emphasis on poverty eradication. "In each province outside of Liaoning," the study reports, "the estimated poverty rate was higher in urban than in rural areas," despite that "the estimated rural poverty rates in 2014 were significantly higher for each province than those reported by China's National Bureau of Statistics for the same year."[48]

Most striking is the following: in 2018, writing in the 2018 Chinese society blue book of the analysis of the country's social situation, Li Zhengang, a researcher at the Chinese Academy of Social Sciences Social Policy Research Office, wrote that since the Eleventh Five Year Plan (2006--2010), the number of peasants living in extreme poverty exhibited a trend of decrease, while the number of urban residents in extreme poverty (*tekun renyuan*, 特困人员) demonstrated a trend of increase.[49]

So how did this new impoverishment come about?

New Production of Poverty Before the *Dibao*

The journey that led first to a colossal upswing in penury in the cities in the 1990s and thence onward to the 1999 nationwide institution of the *dibao*,

---

47. Zhang Ruli and Peng Qing, "Zhongguo chengshi gaigezhong pinkun qunti zhengce de zhuanxing ji qi tedian" [In China's urban reform, the transformation of policy for the poor masses and its characteristics], *Shehui kexue jikan* [Social science journal], no. 4 (2014): 44. The authors explicitly state that this figure does not include migrants.

48. Ben Westmore, "Do Government Transfers Reduce Poverty in China? Micro Evidence from Five Regions," OECD Economics Department Working Papers No. 1415 (Paris: OECD Publishing, 2017), 9–10. On August 27, 2019, Westmore emailed: "My estimates suggest that there are a greater share of people in poverty in urban than in rural areas [in these four provinces]." His judgment relies on this: "The poverty lines in urban areas and in each specific administrative region are adjusted for cost of living differences," based on poverty being defined differently depending on the cost of living in different places.

49. Li Zhengang, "2018 nian chengxiang shehui jiuzhu fazhan zhuangkuang fenxi baogao" [2018 report on analysis of the development of urban and rural social assistance], in *2019 nian Zhongguo shehui xingshi fenxi yu yuce* [2019 analysis and prediction of Chinese society], eds. Li Peilin, Chen Guangjin, and Zhang Yi (Beijing: shehui kexue wenxuan chubanshe [social science documents publishing company]), 77–90; 374.

the Minimum Livelihood Guarantee, was the result of several major prods, most of which emerged as by-products of the otherwise mostly successful program of economic reform. These prods were: the collapse of workers' benefits with the demise of the decades' old work unit system; ongoing and perhaps insurmountable losses to the central government's treasury; and the evident inadequacy of the then-current mode of ministering to the urban poor, the *sanwu*, then in place, in the face of spreading mounting levels of impoverishment. In addition, as China's leaders looked ahead to entering the global market, they aimed to cut firms' financial obligations (especially the welfare benefits enterprises had long disbursed) in order to raise the competitive power of the state sector.

The choice after 1978 for economic reform—that is, to loosen and gradually undo the socialist-era state planning system—involved invigorating markets (gingerly at first) in place of the commands of the state plan, in a bid to drive up economic growth. One major consequence, the appearance of market competition—between state enterprises and collective, rural, and foreign firms—by the mid-1990s had seriously undermined the state firms' ability to feed the state treasury.[50] Indeed, by 1996, along with the aging of the workforce (and thus a need to pay out steadily larger amounts of pensions over time, a relentlessly escalating cost), a sharp increase had occurred in the number of state-owned firms throughout the country that were losing money.[51] Propping them up with steady infusions of subsidies and free loans seemed no longer feasible as the Chinese state industry, for the first time ever, experienced an overall deficit.[52]

Thus, as Qin Gao has noted, the total cost of social insurance for workers, combined with all other welfare payments, had leaped from 13.7 percent of the total wage bill in 1978 up to 28.3 percent just ten years later.[53] Both of these factors—fallout from unfamiliar competition and mushrooming social expenditures—added up to what governors considered to be serious brakes on the momentum of the nation's (or, probably, the state sector's) productivity. By the end of the 1990s, in the words of John Giles and his co-authors, "widespread financial insolvency of the state-owned enterprises forced the central government to end a long-standing commitment to life-time

---

50. Barry Naughton, "Implications of the State Monopoly Over Industry and its Relaxation," *Modern China (MC)* 18, no. 1 (1992): 14–41.

51. Loraine A. West, "The Changing Effects of Economic Reform on Rural and Urban Employment," Paper presented at "Unintended Social Consequences of Chinese Economic Reform" conference, Harvard School of Public Health and The Fairbank Center for East Asian Studies, Harvard University, May 23–24, 1997 (Draft), 6.

52. Thomas G. Rawski, "Reforming China's Economy: What Have We Learned?" *The China Journal (CJ)*, no. 41 (January 1999): 144.

53. Qin Gao, "The Social Benefit System in Urban China: Reforms and Trends from 1988 to 2002," *Journal of East Asian Studies*, no. 6 (2006): 31–67.

state-sector employment for the vast majority of urban residents."[54] One could question the word "forced"; nonetheless, this appraisal matched that of those taking decisions at the top of the Chinese polity at the time. Eva Hung and Stephen Chiu, agreeing with the judgment of the leadership, similarly deduced that massive worker layoffs became "unavoidable," given the costs facing the firms.[55]

Newly induced poverty on a large scale, and ministering to it in the midst of the breakdown of the former urban social assistance program, would appear to have been lesser concerns in the judgment of decision makers than were financial issues. Indeed, relinquishing the firms' formerly accustomed welfare responsibilities was actually celebrated as a means of lightening what was suddenly perceived as, and referred to as, a "burden."[56] By contrast, the importance of upgrading China's economic competitiveness was for China's political elite particularly crucial at this point, in light of the imminent accession of the country into the World Trade Organization, a step achieved at the end of 2001.[57] Viewed from a somewhat different perspective, one could say that the choice for markets in the years after 1978, involving foundational institutional change in the economic structure of the country—though ushering in much new growth—at the same time propelled a set of unseemly externalities, certainly from the perspective of the old working class.[58] In value terms, the workings of the market would exchange the regime's wonted fixation on socialist principles, such as equity and collectivity, for efficiency and competitiveness.[59]

---

54. John Giles, Albert Park, and Feng Cai, "Reemployment of Dislocated Workers in Urban China: The Roles of Information and Incentives," *Journal of Comparative Economics*, no. 34 (2006): 587; Knight and Li, "Unemployment duration."

55. Eva P. W. Hung and Stephen W. K. Chiu, "The Lost Generation: Life Course Dynamics and *Xiagang* in China," *MC* 29, no. 2 (2003): 205.

56. Feng Chen, "Industrial Restructuring and Workers' Resistance in China," *MC* 29, no. 2 (2003): 237.

57. Yanjie Bian, "The Prevalence and the Increasing Significance of *Guanxi*," *The China Quarterly*, no. 235 (September 2018): 613; Dorothy J. Solinger, *States' Gains, Labor's Losses: China, France and Mexico Choose Global Liaisons, 1980–2000* (Ithaca, NY: Cornell University Press, 2009). In an interview in Beijing (August 22, 2008), Wang Zhenyao, previously in charge of social assistance at the Ministry of Civil Affairs, noted that Premier Zhu Rongji had been worried that entry would result in a massive increase in unemployment. See Dorothy J. Solinger, "China's Urban Workers and the WTO," *CJ*, no. 49 (January 2003): 61–87.

58. Fulong Wu, "Urban Poverty and Marginalization under Market Transition: The Case of Chinese Cities," *International Journal of Urban and Regional Research* 28, no. 2 (June 2004): 403–4; Bjorn A. Gustafsson and Deng Quheng, "Di Bao Receipt and Its Importance for Combating Poverty in Urban China," *Poverty & Public Policy* 3, no. 1 (2011): 1.

59. Wang Shaoguang, "Shunying minxin de bianhua: cong caizheng zijin liuxiang Zhongguo zhengfu jinqide zhengce tiaozheng" [A Change that complies with popular sentiments: a recent policy readjustment in the flow of financial funds toward the Chinese government], paper presented to the Center for Strategic and International Studies, Washington, DC, unpublished manuscript, January 16, 2004, 3.

Evidence for this switch appears in the speeches of leaders during this period. In March 1998, at the Ninth National People's Congress, for instance, then-Premier Li Peng announced: "The government will encourage the establishment of large enterprise groups in order to increase their *competitiveness* in both domestic and foreign markets. . . . We should continue to implement . . . preferential policies that support enterprises when they carry out mergers and bankruptcies and try to increase *efficiency* through reducing staff size"[60] (emphasis added). Another few years later, in his political report to the 2002 Sixteenth Party Congress, then outgoing-Party leader Jiang Zemin, considering income distribution, explicitly favored "efficiency" over "fairness" through "bringing market forces into play and encouraging part of the people to become rich first."[61]

Empirically, two pivotal steps embodying these values, "*qiye gaizao*" (enterprise restructuring, 企业 改造)[115] and "*zhuada, fangxiao*" (抓大, 放小, that the central government was to grasp the large, strategically significant firms while permitting the mostly locally owned, smaller, but also some medium-sized, enterprises to be released to the play of market forces). Despite its innocuous label, "*gaizao*" in fact meant that many thousands of mostly small- and medium-sized state-owned and collectively-owned firms were sold off in part or in whole (often enough to their own managers), leased to private businesspeople, merged according to official orders, converted into shareholding companies with mixed public and private ownership, or, frequently, made to fall into bankruptcy.[62] According to Zhiming Cheng, as of the end of the year 2001, as many as 86 percent of state firms had been closed, bankrupted, sold, or merged into joint ventures; their total number had fallen from 63,737 down to 27,477 within another four years.[63]

The policy of "grasping the large" was officially pronounced in September 1995 at a plenary session of the Party's Central Committee and was inserted into the Ninth Five-Year Plan.[64] In line with this decision, the central government retained the ownership of between five hundred and a thousand large

---

60. The text of Li Peng's speech is in Summary of World Broadcasts, FE/3168, March 6, 1998, from Xinhua, March 5, 1998.

61. The report is at http://english.peopledaily.com.cn/200211/18/eng20021118_106983.shtml.

62. Ross Garnaut, Ligang Song, and Yang Yao, "The Impact and Significance of State-owned Enterprise Restructuring in China," *CJ*, no. 55 (January 2006): 35, explains that the term *gaizhi* often involved privatization but can refer to structural change of any sort in a firm, such as publicly offering assets as shares; allowing employees to purchase shares; internal restructuring; bankruptcy and reorganization; open sales; leasing; and the creation from it of a joint venture.

63. Chen, "Industrial Restructuring," 237.

64. Cheng, "Poverty," 144. The figures come from the "China Labour Bulletin." Garnaut, Song, and Yao, "The Impact," 38, reports that at the end of 1998, over 80 percent of state and collectives at the level of the county and below had experienced *gaizao*.

state enterprises, while the less important firms became subject to all manner of state-enforced, market-simulating transformations.[65]

Loss-making firms, especially those locally owned and managed and that had no particular strategic significance to the larger economy, were the primary targets. Thus, in the course of realizing this project, the remaining firms—those not retained by Beijing—were tossed to the rigors and discipline of the market, suddenly compelled to employ management methods akin to those generally used by private companies.[66] This inevitably entailed driving, or, at a minimum, endorsing, local officials' elimination and privatization of companies, thereby removing from the rolls at one fell swoop untold tens of millions of members of the prior workforce.[67] As Ming Tsui found in interviews with laid-off workers in Wuhan in the summer of 2000, in forty-six of the forty-nine layoffs her informants experienced, they had been "forced" out.[68]

Not only did so many find that their source of livelihood vanished in a flash, but these people had also to confront leaps in prices for the goods and services on which their daily existence rested. This occurred in the first place as planned prices and arranged distribution were eliminated; not only that, but medical and educational costs leaped up exponentially, with firms no longer charged with providing welfare services. At the same time, often, housing had to be purchased instead of being nearly rent-free as it had been before, and pension contributions became the obligation of the workers themselves (rather than of the enterprises, as they had been in the past).[69]

On top of these hardships, as Hung and Chiu learned in meetings with eighty redundant workers in Beijing in the summer of 1999, a full quarter of their informants had not been paid any wages at all as their former firms went under. Worse, research from 2003 uncovered that at that point in Shenyang, one of the most affected cities, people who had been either laid off, were uncounted, or were otherwise unregistered unemployed came to nearly 29 percent of all enterprise staff and workers. In Shanghai, the number was 24 percent, and in Tianjin, it was 20 percent. Other places, such as Chongqing, Wuhan, Xi'an, and Nanjing, saw people without work at about the same rate as in Tianjin.[70]

---

65. Garnaut, Song, and Yao, "The Impact," 37–38.

66. See Dorothy J. Solinger, "Capitalist Measures with Chinese Characteristics," *Problems of Communism*, no. 38 (January–February 1989): 19–33.

67. Chak Kwan Chan, "Re-thinking the Incrementalist Thesis in China: A Reflection on the Development of the Minimum Standard of Living Scheme in Urban and Rural Areas," *JSP* 39, no. 4 (2010): 631.

68. Knight and Li, "Unemployment," 105. Joel Andreas writes, "Local officials were pushed to privatize tens of thousands of state-owned and collectively-owned enterprises." (Joel Andreas, *Disenfranchised: The Rise and Fall of Industrial Citizenship in China* [New York: Oxford University Press, 2019], 197.)

69. Ming Tsui, "Managing Transition: Unemployment and Job Hunting in Urban China," *Pacific Affairs* 75, no. 4 (Winter 2002–2003): 523.

70. Gustafsson and Deng, "Di Bao Receipt," 2; Zhiming Cheng, "Layoffs and Urban Poverty In the State-Owned Enterprise Communities in Shaanxi Province, China," University of Wollongong Research Outline, 2012. Presented at 13th Annual Global Development Conference 'Urbanization

On a countrywide scale, estimated figures diverge. John Giles and his co-authors refer to official statistics that claim that "more than 25 million workers were officially let go in the years 1998 to 2002." Barry Naughton, variously, calculated that the amount of layoffs was "just shy of 50 million between 1993 and 2003 from state-owned enterprises, urban collectives and public service offices."[71]

Yet several researchers, including Giles et al. themselves, dispute those numbers, figuring they were much higher, in the range of fifty million to over seventy million workers retrenched.[72] Three other sources put the figure at around sixty million.[73] And taking in a longer time span, the World Bank calculated that the number was greater yet: between 1994 and 2006, its researchers found, employment in state and urban collective firms fell by seventy-three million, with the total of those at work beginning at 145 million in the earlier year and dropping down to seventy-two million in the later one.[74] This rising destitution did not go unaddressed: massive protests in the cities accompanied the job loss and pension shortfalls,[75] and official anxieties over the upheaval was what most directly led to the institution of the *dibao*.

ESTABLISHMENT OF THE *DIBAO*

The official effort to resolve this disorder finally eventuated in the *dibao*, labeled "the third line of defense," one last shot as earlier attempts to alleviate the distresses of job loss failed.[76] The first of these attempts was a

---

and Development: Delving Deeper into the Nexus,' New Delhi, India: Global Development Network, 16. Jieyu Liu, "Life Goes On: Redundant Women Workers in Nanjing," in *China's Changing Welfare Mix*, eds. Beatriz Carrillo and Jane Duckett (London: Routledge, 2011), 87.

71. Liu Jing and Deng Jingyuan, "Gaishan woguo shiye xianzhuangde shixian fangshi" [A method to realize the improvement of our country's unemployment situation], *Juece cankao* [Policy reference], no. 11 (2005): 61.

72. Barry Naughton, *The Chinese Economy: Adaptation and Growth* (second edition) (Cambridge, MA: The MIT Press, 2018), 214.

73. Giles, Park, and Cai, "Reemployment," 587. A study of five large cities in the late 2001 China Urban Labor Survey led these researchers to determine that the state-sector workforce had declined by forty-one million just in the years between 1996 and 2002, with an uncounted drop in the collective sector they termed "even more dramatic."

74. Hu Angang, "China's Present Economic Situation," 9; private communication from Hu, September 23, 2004; Hu also stated that China had laid off fifty-five million people from 1995 to mid-2002 (*China News Digest*, July 9, 2002). Wang Depei, "San min yu erci gaige" [Three types of people and the second reform], *Gaige neican* [Reform internal reference] 7 (2001): 24 refers to "numbers as high as sixty million" in 2001. Wang Shaoguang, "Shunying," 3, states that from 1995 to 2002, the number of state-sector employees declined by 40.98 million people, a decrease of 36.4 percent, and the numbers working in urban collectives went down by 20.25 million, a drop of 64.3 percent. Together this was a decline of 61.23 million people suddenly out of work, or 42.5 percent among the total workforce.

75. World Bank, "From Poor Areas," 39.

76. On pensioners' protests, see William Hurst and Kevin O'Brien, "China's Contentious Pensioners," *CQ* no. 170 (2002): 345–60. On other workers protests, Feng Chen, "Subsistence Crises,

"Reemployment Project" (REP), launched in 1995. As early as 1994, this platform was piloted in thirty cities experimentally and then extended nationwide the following year. It comprised a monumental effort directed at a sadly overambitious aim: to somehow arrange for the settlement of all the laid-off workers.[77] The REP was designed as a set of transitional measures to ensure that the laid-offs' basic livelihood, their welfare, and their opportunities for work could be provided during the time when the country's nascent labor market was yet imperfect and the nation's social insurance system incomplete.[78] The project was initially billed as resting upon four pillars: a form of unemployment insurance, professional introduction services, retraining, and creation of "labor service enterprises."[79] Much of this work was entrusted to Reemployment Service Centers (RSCs), which firms that had dismissed workers were ordered to create.

But there were critical limitations besetting the entire endeavor from the start: a scarcity of funds; that the firms pushing out their workers had either gone bankrupt or were suffering serious losses and deeply in debt;[80] the inability of enterprises with losses to establish RSCs that could perform their assigned roles; incalculable levels of corruption among local cadres and firm managers, who intervened between policy makers and intended recipients, taking substantial cuts along the way; and, perhaps most serious, a vast insufficiency in the supply of potential work posts in the economy.[81] The project was quietly put to rest soon after 2000.

The second effort was unemployment insurance. Though first established in 1986, this support began to be allocated actively only in 1993, at which

---

Managerial Corruption and Labour Protests in China," *CJ*, no. 44 (July 2000): 41–63; and Ching Kwan Lee, "Pathways of Labor Insurgency," in *Chinese Society: Change, Conflict and Resistance*, eds. Elizabeth J. Perry and Mark Selden (London: Routledge, 2000), 41–61.

77. Dorothy J. Solinger, "Labor Market Reform and the Plight of the Laid-Off Proletariat," *CQ*, no. 170 (June 2002): 304–26.

78. Ru Xin, Lu Xueyi, and Shan Tianlun, eds., *1998 nian: Zhongguo shehui xingshi fenxi yu yuce* [1998: Analysis and prediction of China's social situation] (Beijing: shehui kexue wenxian chubanshe [Social science documents publishers], 1998), 86.

79. Wang Dongjin, "Jianchi zhengque fangxiang, fahui xuehui gongneng wei jianshe you Zhongguo tese de laodong he shehui baozhang shiye fuwu" [Persist in an accurate direction, foster competence in studying, to build a labor and social security service with Chinese characteristics], *Zhongguo laodong (ZGLD)* [Chinese labor], no. 4 (2000): 5; Shen Wenming and Ma Runlai, "Zaijiuyezhong de zhengfu xingwei" [The government's behavior in reemployment], *ZGLD*, no. 2 (1999): 19; Lei Peng, "Zhigong peixun yu jiuye cujin—chengshi fupin de zongyao" [Staff and workers' training and the promotion of reemployment—the important path in urban poverty], *Lingdao neican (LDNC)* [Leadership internal reference], no. 11 (1998): 30–31.

80. According to N.a., "1998 nian qiye xiagang zhigong jiben qingkuang" [The basic situation of laid-off enterprise staff and workers in 1998] *Laodong baozhang tongxun* [Labor and social security bulletin], no. 1 (1999): 10, laid-off workers let go by enterprises losing money represented 67 percent of all laid-off workers as of the end 1998.

81. According to Zhang Handong, "Dangqian zaijiuye gongchengde qi da wuqu" [Seven big misunderstandings in the present reemployment project], *LDNC* no. 7 (1998): 27, "We lack at least 30 million jobs to reemploy the unemployed, the laid-off, and surplus labor."

time it was aimed just at urban workers in state firms. In 1998, a State Council regulation decreed that the guarantee should be extended to the private and other non-state-sector firms. The funds were supposed to be granted, at the rate of about 60 to 70 percent of the previous salary for the first twelve months if the person had been steadily employed for at least five years, and at 50 percent of the former wage for the second year of unemployment.[82] But an internal report based on a survey by the State Planning Commission's Macroeconomic Research Institute disclosed that as of the end of 1999, 73 percent of households where the head was employed reported they were not participating in the program, and only 18 percent said they were, with the others not replying. In four major cities, just 11 percent were participating, while among the out-of-work, merely 2.89 percent were part of the program. Among those laboring in the private sector, a scant 4 percent of the employees had been entered into the system as of the end of 1999.[83]

With these two ventures unsuccessful, politicians settled on the *dibao*, a program first launched in Shanghai in 1993 in response to worker outbursts over dismissals.[84] That worry about instability was a critical factor seems clear from the timing of events: a sudden and major hike in the numbers of recipients admitted into the scheme took place just as worker strikes and laid-off workers' demonstrations were spreading geographically and climbing in count. Sociologist Joel Andreas reports that, "Resistance reached a climax in 2001 and 2002 as officials began restructuring larger factories, spurring bigger protests." Millions of workers across the country occupied factory compounds and blockaded highways, railroad lines, and government offices. He terms "particularly alarming" "the militant, coordinated protests of tens of thousands of workers in large factories in the northeastern cit[ies] of Liaoyang and . . . Daqing" [a model in industry in Mao's day] that occurred in those years.[85]

As commentators have reflected, the motives of decision makers amounted to addressing the symptoms, not the root causes, of the poverty (i.e., they were not concerned to raise the skills or the educational levels of those they chose to leave behind or in other ways to provide a pathway out of poverty).[86]

---

82. Michael Korzec, "Contract Labor, the 'Right to Work' and New Labor Laws in the People's Republic of China," *Comparative Economic Studies* 30, no. 2 (1988): 138.

83. Guojia jiwei hongguan jingji yanjiuyuan ketizu [State Planning Commission, Macroeconomic Research Institute Task Force], "Jianli shehui baohu tixi shi wo guo shehui wending de guanjian" [Establishing a social protection system is the key to our country's social stability], *Neibu canyue* [Internal reference] 511 (May 5, 2000): 10–11.

84. The best history of the *dibao*'s creation is Daniel R. Hammond, *Politics and Policy in China's Social Assistance Reform: Providing for the Poor?* (Edinburgh: Edinburgh University Press, 2019).

85. Andreas, *Disenfranchised*, 198.

86. Zhiming Cheng, "Poverty in China's Urban Communities: Profile and Correlates," *China Report* 46, no. 2 (2010): 168; S. Cook, N. Kabeer, and G. Suwannarat, eds., *Social Protection in Asia* (Delhi: Har-Anand Publications, 2003); Chen Honglin, Wong Yu-Cheung, Zeng Qun, and

As Daniel Hammond aptly expressed it, "Poverty was not a key motivation but concern about the political consequences of poverty [namely, political instability that was already disturbing the ongoing economic reform program] was."[87] So a fiscal concern—ensuring quietude to carry on with growth—was tightly linked to a determination to halt the disturbances.

Those most involved in the project to extend Shanghai's pilot venture nationally and create the *dibao*, namely, Minister of Civil Affairs Duoji Cairang, Premier Li Peng, and Vice Premier (later Premier) Zhu Rongji, each had his own motives. For Duoji, the issue was the urgency of putting into place a new assistance program in light of the inadequacy of the *sanwu*, which was never designed, and was totally unequipped, to handle the numbers in need. The premier's fear was that the ongoing plan to push on with the reform of state enterprises could otherwise be endangered. For Zhu, critically, it was largely a matter of preserving peace and stability as reforms went forward.[88]

So, from 2000, when only 3.24 million individuals received the *dibao* allowance, the number of recipients spiked until late 2002, when the total served reached 20.65 million (and continued rising until a decline began after 2009). See Table 2.7. It is likely that the increase was made under orders from then-Premier Zhu Rongji.[89] Examples of Zhu's activism on this issue was his August 2001 call during an inspection of Guangzhou for strengthening the urban *dibao* and his command to ensure that all the urban poor who "should be protected as much as possible be protected" (*ying bao jin bao*, 应保尽保), in order to maintain social stability;[90] the November 2001 issuance of Document No. 87 by the State Council (which he headed), demanding that local governments extend the coverage of the *dibao*; and his heedful attention at the 2002 Eleventh National Civil Affairs Congress to then-recently erupted demonstrations in Daqing and Liaoyang. These massive protests, he tellingly proclaimed, "should give us a warning that only through guaranteeing the basic living of the urban poor can society maintain stability."[91]

Juha Hamalainen, "Trapped in Poverty? A Study of the *Dibao* Programme in Shanghai," *CJSW* 6, no. 3 (2013): 327; Chan, "Re-thinking the Incrementalist Thesis," 631–32; Guan, "Poverty"; and John Knight and Shi Li, "Unemployment Duration and Earnings of Re-Employed Workers in Urban China," *China Economic Review* 17 (2006): 105. Short-term training was offered but rarely led to building abilities or skills, much less to landing jobs.

87. Daniel Robert Hammond, "Explaining Policy Making in the People's Republic of China: The Case of the Urban Resident Minimum Livelihood Guarantee System, 1992—2003" (PhD dissertation, Department of Politics, University of Glasgow, 2010), 33.

88. Hammond, "Explaining Policy Making," 32; *idem., Politics and Policy*, Chapter Two.

89. Sources: *Zhongguo minzheng tongji nianjian* [China Civil Affairs Statistical Yearbook] (Beijing: Zhongguo tongji chubanshe), various years.

90. Hammond, *Politics and Policy*, 76.

91. D. Y. Hong, *China's Social Assistance during the Period of Transition* (in Chinese) (Shenyang: Liaoning Educational Press, 2004), 10, as cited in an anonymous article, with no further information.

Table 2.7. Urban *Dibao* Recipients, Urban Population, Recipients as Percentage of Urban Population, 1999–2019 (Unit: 10,000 People)

Year	Urban Dibao Recipients	Urban Population	Urban Dibao Recipients as Percentage of Urban Population
1999	256.9	43,748	0.59
2000	402.6	45,906	0.88
2001	1,170.7	48,064	2.44
2002	2,064.7	50,212	4.11
2003	2,246.8	52,376	4.29
2004	2,205.0	54,283	4.06
2005	2,234.2	56,212	3.97
2006	2,240.1	58,288	3.84
2007	2,272.1	60,633	3.75
2008	2,334.8	62,403	3.74
2009	2,345.6	64,512	3.64
2010	2,310.5	66,978	3.45
2011	2,276.8	69,079	3.30
2012	2,143.5	71,182	3.01
2013	2,064.2	73,111	2.82
2014	1,877.0	74,916	2.51
2015	1,701.1	77,116	2.21
2016	1,480.2	79,298	1.87
2017	1,261.0	81,347	1.55
2018	1,007.0	83,137	1.21
2019	860.5	84,843	1.01

Sources: For *dibao* recipients: *Zhongguo minzheng tongji nianjian*, 2000–2020 [China Civil Affairs' Statistical Yearbook, 2000–2020]. For urban population: *Zhongguo tongji nianjian*, 2000–2020 [China Statistical Yearbook, 2000–2020].

CONCLUSION

The two Chinese programs of the past three-quarter-century geared toward ministering to the poor in the municipalities—the *sanwu* and the *dibao*—both fell seriously short of the mark, if they truly aimed to succor the especially needy. During the era of Mao Zedong and even into the mid-1990s, assistance was meted out only to those who—without firm bodies, legal supporters, or income source—simply could not have survived without the pittance that was delivered to them. Among its gamut of human externalities, both positive and negative, economic reform brought in its wake a novel type of indigence in the cities: the abrupt impoverishment of the suddenly state-spawned jobless.

While the *dibao* was touted as a major upgrade to the *sanwu*, by a number of measures, it did not fare particularly well, whether its treatment of recipients is compared with the *sanwu* or with the livelihood situation of other urban residents, and certainly not in any absolute sense. Even as the nation prospered in the years before about 2014, with GDP and state revenues mounting impressively, the outlays for the *dibao* beneficiaries remained relatively meager, as a good many of them experienced a desperation that often perched them not far from the verge of starvation, as Chapters Four, Five, and Six will detail.

What does the state's treatment of these two castaways (the *sanwu* and the *dibaohu*) suggest about the larger portrait that China's leaders have hoped to present to their own mainstream subjects and to the world? In the case of the *sanwu*, one can read the narrative as constituting a portion of the regime's obeisance to its old socialist image: those unequipped to participate in the spectacle of a populace engaged in daily, collective toil, who were viewed as unprepared to join those who were "paid according to their labor," as the socialist creed has it, and who had no kin to knit them into the community, were best left by the wayside, tended to but barely. They could not be and were not of "the people," properly speaking.

As for the *dibaohu*, the members of this generation of urban poor, targeted for what amounted to a sort of alms (if they managed to be privileged enough to be accepted into the scheme), were judged not fit for a new China-in-the-world market—despite the country's leaders' continuing to label the nation a "socialist" one. In the twenty-first century, they were to be sacrificed on the altar of modernity and largely left, as beyond a remake, behind and outside the pale.[92] This may be why its cohorts have been nearly forgotten (especially after the rowdy among them went silent after 2004), and also why it has been just the rural poor who have captured the state's attention in recent years.

If not fully forgetting them, just how did the regime set out to succor these indigents? And what are their traits, as a group? Chapter Three examines in some depth the stated early aims of the *dibao* program and its execution over its first decade, before the scheme began to shrink. It also turns to the recipients, detailing the steps they are required to follow in order to be admitted into the scheme and presents a picture of their demographic features. It closes with an assessment of the perception of threat that they engendered in policy makers.

---

92. As H. Zhang, "China's Social Assistance," 227, remarked, "Social assistance labeled recipients as impoverished, which excluded them from society."

Chapter Three

The *Dibao* and the *Dibaohu*

How was the *dibao* to deal with this abrupt, massive, and uncommon impoverishment in the cities following pervasive enterprise failures? In this chapter, I lay out the goals and procedures initially specified officially for executing the work of the *dibao*. I also follow the course of the *dibao*'s funding up through its heyday, in 2007, soon after which (by 2010) the program took on steadily declining significance for the leadership (see Chapters Nine and Ten). I go on to provide a brief demographic sketch of its subjects, with special focus on their problems of health, often a major contributor to their penury once the old *danwei* system expired, which had provided free medical care for the workers. I conclude by documenting the connection the leadership draws between bestowing the *dibao* allowance on laid-off workers (the old proletariat whom policy makers rejected), on the one hand, and achieving stability in the cities, on the other.

THE *DIBAO*: GOALS; EARLY YEARS

Stated Goals

The charge of the *dibao* was to provide for urban residents whose household's per capita income failed to reach a locally (city or district within a city) determined minimal threshold for bare subsistence (the *dibao* norm or standard, essentially a given city's poverty line), called the *dibao biaozhun* (低保 标准). The method was to supplement such families' income with a subsidy (*buzhu*, 补助) to the extent necessary to bring their per capita monthly wherewithal up to the level deemed requisite for basic survival in their city or district of residence.[1] At the time of its national promulgation in September 1999, the project was proudly labeled by its publicists a "standardized, legalized, social guarantee system,"[2] a characterization more aspirational than actual.[3] The idea behind the policy amounted to supplying impoverished individuals with funds that were "just enough to keep body and soul together," in the words of its leading scholar within China, Tang Jun.[4]

The history of the scheme began with a half dozen years of grassroots experimentation nationwide after 1993, when Shanghai pioneered the system. With time, in the place of the old, urban, work unit-grounded, relatively universal, automatic-security entitlements granted by the urban enterprises of the socialist era, the state inaugurated the *dibao* as a discretionary, means-tested cash transfer program.[5] As admitted then by the vice chairman of the government office of Wuhan's Qiaokou District, "Urban *dibao* work concerns social stability; it's not only economic work, *even more* [emphasis added] it's a political task."[6] At this early stage—as was to remain the case—a piece in the official journal of the Ministry of Civil Affairs, *Zhongguo minzheng* (中国 民政), unabashedly declared that the program's aims were "to help the enterprises throw off their worries and solve their difficulties" and "to lighten the enterprises' burdens,"[7] mentioning nothing at all about recipients' indigence or any plans for its alleviation.

Writing in Shenyang, one writer went so far as to refer to the *dibao* as a "tranquilizer" (*dingxinwan*, 定心丸), one that would permit the state enterprises in Shenyang's Tiexi district (a site of massive layoffs) to go forward

---

1. Athar Hussain, "Urban Poverty in China: Measurement, Patterns and Policies," ms. (Geneva: International Labour Office, January 2003).

2. Ding Langfu, "Cong danwei fuli dao shehui baozhang—ji zhongguo chengshi jumin zuidi shenghuo baozhang zhidu de dansheng" [From unit welfare to social security—recording the emergence of Chinese urban residents' minimum livelihood guarantee system], *Zhongguo minzheng (ZGMZ)* [Chinese civil affairs], no. 11 (1999): 6–7.

3. "Chengshi jumin zuidi shenghuo baozhang tiaoli" [Regulations on the urban residents' minimum livelihood guarantee], *ZGMZ*, no. 11 (1999): 16–17.

4. Tang Jun, "The Report of Poverty and Anti-Poverty in Urban China—The Poverty Problems in Urban China and the Program of Minimum Living Standard," ms. (n.p., 2002), 4.

5. Sarah Cook, "The Challenge of Informality: Perspectives on China's Changing Labour Market," paper for IDS Bulletin, 2008.

6. Benkan jizhe/xinwen, benkan tongxunyuan/Liu Jing, "Guanzhu chengshi dishouru qunti: Wuhanshi Qiaokouqu chengshi jumin zuidi shenghuo baozhang gongzuo toushi," [This paper's news, this paper's correspondent, Liu Jing, "Pay close attention to urban low-income masses: Perspective on the work of Wuhan's Qiaokou District's urban residents' minimum livelihood guarantee"], *Hubei caishui* [Hubei finance and taxes], 2, no. 4 (2002).

7. Meng Jiawu and Tan Zhilin, "Wuhan chengshi zuidi shenghuo baozhang zhidu de sige tedian" [Four characteristics of Wuhan city's minimum livelihood guarantee system], *ZGMZ*, no. 7 (1996): 19; Yang Zongchuan and Zhang Qilin, "Wuhanshi chengshi jumin zuidi shenghuo baozhang zhidu shishi zhuangkuang de diaocha fenxi" [Analysis of an investigation of the implementation situation of Wuhan's urban residents' minimum livelihood guarantee system], *Jingji pinglun* [Economic review], 4 (1999): 102.

without obstruction. Without it, this essayist brazenly penned, "These people must become a burden that the enterprises would find it hard to throw off . . . possibly arousing even larger social contradictions."[8] If not in intent certainly in fallout, it is much akin to Tony Judt's characterization of the "modern welfare reform" in Western settings. For both introduce "conditionality" into "social citizenship" by forcing the beneficiaries to "pass certain tests and demonstrate appropriate behavior."[9] Too, much like "reformed" Western welfare programs, it reeks of distrust of its objects. Unlike similar schemes in democracies, however, its administrators' qualms were to be quieted by the watchful attention of the recipients' co-residents in their community's (*shequ*, 社区, usually a merger of a couple old residents' committees) courtyards.

Early Years

Following local trials of Shanghai's pilot program, the next step—probably not coincidentally—was taken in September 1997, around the time of the Fifteenth Party Congress (where then-Party General Secretary Jiang Zemin emphasized it twice[10]); this was the meeting, after all, that accelerated layoffs and bankruptcies in money-losing firms.[11] At that point, the State Council issued a notice, "On Establishing the Urban Residents' Minimum Livelihood System in the Whole Country," and demanded the process be completed by the end of 1999. As instructed, by late 1999, 2,306 cities and towns had installed the program, with over two million poor people seeing their bare sustenance underwritten, a full 79 percent of whom had newly become poor.[12]

Then came the publication, over Premier Zhu Rongji's signature, of the State Council's October 1999 relevant regulation, Number 271. Following that, the project's trajectory appeared to be one of progressive generosity. In the first ten months of 1999, 1.5 billion yuan was extended to the target population. Later that year, perhaps in anticipation of the upcoming fiftieth anniversary of the birth of the People's Republic, plus China's then-likely impending entry into the World Trade Organization (WTO)—with the shock it was expected

---

8. Ding, "Cong danwei," 7.

9. Tony Judt, "The Wrecking Ball of Innovation," review of Robert B. Reich, *Supercapitalism: The Transformation of Business, Democracy and Everyday Life* (New York: Knopf, 2007); *The New York Review of Books,* December 6, 2007, 24.

10. Jiang put forward two critical chores: to adjust and improve the ownership structure and to accelerate state-owned enterprise reform.

11. Jiang Zemin, "Political report," *Summary of World Broadcasts* FE/3023 (September 13, 1997), S1/1-S1/10; Wang Yanzhong, "Jiaru WTO hou wo guo jingji fazhan wenti yu zhanwang" [Looking back and forward at our country's economic development after entering WTO], *Lingdao canyue* [Leadership consultations] no. 3 (January 25, 2003): 3–6; and Hussain, "Urban Poverty," 52–53, all draw an explicit connection between these reforms and increasing the scope of the *dibao*.

12. Tang, "The Report," 15–17.

to deliver to urban employment[13]—the Ministry of Finance arranged an extra four hundred million yuan for supplementary funds during the second half of 1999. In addition, recipients received a raise of 30 percent in their allocations, 80 percent of the financing coming from the central government.[14] This trajectory—in parallel with the intensification of China's market reform and globalization—suggests that the *dibao*'s escalation in funding and scope were markers of decision makers' heightening unease with the sensational worker protests that profit-chasing, modernization, and prospective global entry were promoting, in and after 1997. The final major upgrade of the program came in 2003—jacking the numbers of participants to over twenty-two million—after China had finally joined the WTO. The Tenth Five-Year Plan (2001 to 2005) projected the system's development "from being a random and temporary sort of relief toward becoming a systematic guarantee."[15]

But despite seemingly beneficent intentions, the outlays remained marginal. Even after the sizable increase in the number of recipients from 1999 to 2003, those served still accounted for under 5 percent of the urban-registered population. Yet, as I have indicated in Chapter Two, the truly indigent urban population might well have been more in the range of 8 to 10 percent. In the following years, cities usually raised the subsidies for each *dibao* household at least once every two years and sometimes more often, as the urban standard of living within the general population improved. At certain junctures, the central government ordered an increase nationwide, as in the midst of a bout of inflation in August 2007.[16] But up through 2007, the total covered never went much above the twenty-two million of 2003 (and declined steadily—and soon precipitously—from 2009 onward; see Chapter Ten), suggesting a fundamental stinginess in the system. See Table 2.7.

The year 2002 saw a major jump in the quantity of funds expended, totaling 10.53 billion yuan, with the center paying almost 44 percent.[17] But even

---

13. That fall, the United States signed its bilateral agreement with China, a necessary prelude to China's entry. Chinese labor economists prepared for the worst (Mo Rong, "Jiaru WTO yu woguo de jiuye" [Entering the WTO and our country's employment], *Laodong baozhang tongxun* [Labor and social security bulletin] no. 4 [2000]: 18–21).

14. Wei Wei, "Chengshi dibao: tashang xin zhengcheng" [The urban *dibao*: step onto a new journey] (2000), *ZGMZ*, no. 1 (2000): 24–25; Tang, "The Report," 17; Mao Jiansheng, "Liguo limin de ningjuli gongcheng—Fan Baojun fubuzhang jiu chengshi jumin zuidi shenghuo baozhang zhidu jianshe hui benkan jizhe wen" [A cohesive project benefiting the nation and the people—Vice Minister Fan Baojun answers this journal's reporter's questions about the minimum livelihood guarantee system's construction], *ZGMZ* no. 4 (1997): 4–6.

15. N. a., "Zhongguo jianli chengxiang shehui jiuzhu tixi, 7 qianwan kunnan qunzhong ganshou wennuan yangguang" [China constructs an urban-rural social relief system, 70 million masses in difficulty feel warm sunshine], http://china.com.cn/txt/2006-11/30/content_7429928.htm.

16. "Urban minimum living subsidy increased," Xinhua, August 7, 2007.

17. 4.6 billion yuan came from the central treasury, and 5.93 billion from local governments, according to Xinhuanet (Beijing), July 19, 2002. Thanks to Jane Duckett for this citation. Table 9.5 shows that other sources have the total at 10.68 billion.

after extra resources were allocated, an official report admitted that, as of early 2002, the national average urban poverty line (or *dibao* norm) was a mere 152 yuan per person per month, equal to only 29 percent of the 2001 national average urban per capita income.[18] The subsidies, the amount actually handed out, that is, the supplement allocated to each person to bring his/her income up to the local poverty line, were, of course, much lower, at 43.9 yuan per person per month on average nationally. See Table 2.6. In 2003, as much as 15 billion yuan was budgeted (with the center dispensing 9.2 billion), thus shifting the proportions paid out by the different administrative levels: over 60 percent came from the central treasury.

Still, regardless of what seems to have been a new generosity, that year, the average per-person subsidy in cities was just 56 yuan per month.[19] In 2005, that average rose to around 70 yuan, with a probable annual total expenditure in the range of 19 billion yuan. See Table 3.1. Even as disbursements multiplied in yuan, however, the average amount of the per capita subsidy nationwide amounted to a piddling 9.2 percent of average urban per capita income, according to this source.[20]

At the end of 2007, when about 22.7 million people (300,000 more than at the same point a year earlier) were enjoying the program's protection,[21] the average monthly *dibao* norm (poverty line) nationally had gone up to 182 yuan per person, a rise of 12.8 yuan over 2006 (see Table 2.5). At the same time, the average subsidy nationwide had increased to 102.7 yuan per person per month, 23 percent over 2006. But the funds allocated to the *dibao* nationwide each year rose from a minuscule 0.113 percent of government expenditures in 1999 to a high of only 0.62 percent in 2003. See Table 3.2.[22]

---

18. This was reported in "Zhongguo chengshi jumin zuidi shenghuo baozhang biaozhun de xiangguan fenxi, jingji qita xiangguan lunwen" [Relevant analysis of Chinese urban residents' dibao norm; economic and other related treatises], http://www.ynexam.cn/html/jingjixue/jingjixiangguan/2006/1105/zhonggochengshijimin, accessed August 18, 2007. Table 2.5 shows 148 yuan, according to the Civil Affairs yearbook.

19. This is the figure given in Tang Jun, "Jiasu zuidi shenghuo baozhang zhidu de guifanhua yunzuo" [Speed up the standardization of the minimum livelihood guarantee system], in *Shehui lanpishu: 2004 nian: Zhongguo shehui xingshi fenxi yu yuce* [Social blue book: 2004 analysis and predictions of China's social situation], eds. Ru Xin, Lu Xueyi, and Li Peilin (Beijing: shehui kexue wenxian chubanshe [Social science documents company], 117–18. N.a., "Zhongguo jianli" gives the average subsidy as 58 yuan per capita per month; Table 2.6, based on the Civil Affairs yearbook, also shows 58 yuan.

20. Tang Jun, "Tiaozhengzhong de chengxiang zuidi shenghuo baozhang zhidu" [The urban and rural minimum livelihood guarantee system in adjustment], in *Shehui lanpishu: 2006 nian: Zhongguo shehui xingshi fenxi yu yuce* [Social blue book: 2006 analysis and predictions of China's social situation], eds. Ru Xin, Lu Xueyi, and Li Peilin (Beijing: shehui kexue wenxian chubanshe [Social science documents company], 2006), 165–68.

21. "China's subsistence allowance system benefits urban, rural poor equally," http://english.people.com.con/90001/90776/6344770.html, accessed January 24, 2008.

22. These calculations are based upon the figures for governmental expenditure in Zhonghua renmin gongheguo guojia tongjiju [Chinese People's Republic State Statistical Bureau] bian (ed.), *2007 Zhongguo tongji nianjian* [*2007 China Statistical Yearbook*] (Beijing: *Zhongguo tongji chubanshe*,

Table 3.1.   National Annual *Dibao* Expenditures, 1999–2019 (Unit: Billion CNY)

Year	National Dibao *Expenditures*
1999	2.37
2000	3.45
2001	5.09
2002	11.58
2003	15.31
2004	18.90
2005	21.72
2006	26.77
2007	38.64
2008	62.21
2009	84.51
2010	96.98
2011	132.76
2012	139.23
2013	162.36
2014	159.20
2015	165.08
2016	170.24
2017	169.23
2018	163.21
2019	164.67

Sources: *Zhongguo minzheng tongji nianjian*, 2000–2020 [China Civil Affairs' Statistical Yearbook, 2000–2020].

Given the large increases in government revenue over these years, it is notable that the percentage of funding going to the *dibaohu* did not see a greater rise over time and that the numbers served remained more or less fixed after 2002 (with an uptick in 2009), until the great slide downward after 2009 (see Chapter Ten).

In 2007, the average monthly per capita subsidy (102.7 yuan) remained a bare 8.8 percent of the average monthly urban income nationwide (1,148.83 yuan), with the norm (poverty line) of 182 yuan per person, just under 16 percent of the average urban income, in the official reckoning.[23] (See Tables 2.5 and 2.6.) This average was pulled down by the many millions of urbanites residing in smaller and poorer cities, where allowances were lower. It is hard

2007), 279. Hussain, "Urban Poverty," 71 states that, in 1999, the expenditure on the *dibao* amounted to 0.15 percent of total government expenditure.

   23. According to Premier Wen Jiabao's annual government work report of March 5, 2008 (Wen Jiabao, "Report on the Work of the Government," delivered at the First Session of the Eleventh National People's Congress, March 5, 2008), the average annual per capita income for urbanites in 2007 was 13,786 yuan (or 1,148.33 yuan/month), (http://www.chinadaily.com.cn/china/2008npc/200803/19/content_6549177.htm, 2008, accessed May 26, 2008).

Table 3.2.   National *Dibao* Expenditures as Percentage of GDP and of Total Government Expenditures, 1999–2018

Year	National Dibao Expenditures as Percentages of GDP	National Dibao Expenditures as Percentages of Total Govt. Expenditures
1999	0.0160	0.1130
2000	0.0300	0.1880
2001	0.0459	0.2691
2002	0.0951	0.5249
2003	0.1114	0.6212
2004	0.1168	0.6634
2005	0.1160	0.6403
2006	0.1220	0.6622
2007	0.1430	0.7763
2008	0.1947	0.9939
2009	0.2421	1.1076
2010	0.2348	1.0790
2011	0.2713	1.2153
2012	0.2577	1.1054
2013	0.2728	1.1580
2014	0.2472	1.0488
2015	0.2396	0.9386
2016	0.2288	0.9067
2017	0.2062	0.8323
2018	0.1813	0.7388

Sources: For *dibao* expenditures: *Zhongguo minzheng tongji nianjian,* 2000–2019 [China Civil Affairs' Statistical Yearbook, 2000–2019]. For GDP and total government expenditures: *Zhongguo tongji nianjian,* 2000–2019 [China Statistical Yearbook, 2000–2019].

to imagine that the households so aided could have survived with even a minimal degree of satisfaction. It is also striking that the nutritional, educational, and health standards among recipients remained remarkably unchanged and essentially abysmal over a span of ten years; interviewers in the homes of *dibaohu* in 2007 and 2008 found conditions identical to those described in Tang Jun's team's fieldwork in five cities a decade earlier. Chapter Six documents these conditions.

PREPARATION, APPLICATION

Preparation

As the Chongqing Bureau of Civil Affairs vice director wrote about the city's 1996 trial initiation of the project, "thought work" preceded everything else. His explanation was that, "The urban *dibao* system is a wholly new [kind of] work, [people's] hidden income is hard to estimate, the situation is complex;

if the work isn't done properly, it will provoke new unstable elements and give birth to new social contradictions."[24] In other words, the program was considered likely to result in resentments, anger, and jealousies if control were not exercised over recipients' (and potential recipients') perception of the plan—not to mention disapproval in society at large. (Chapter Six documents the reactions in society.) Regardless of such cautionary measures, however, there have been wrinkles (of an unknowable amount) in the running of the program, whether because of dissatisfied recipients, dishonest disbursers, or the various people who have determined how to finesse the system. (Chapter Five discusses these further.)

Once the publicity campaign had been waged, additional preparatory work in a given locale typically entailed conducting in-depth, large-scale surveys, involving verifying family incomes, employment situations, and consumption patterns. Also necessary were training personnel, undertaking multiple censuses, pooling and analyzing statistics, and composing reports. In Chongqing, as many as 600,000 households were scrutinized in the process![25] Execution of the system—as for any new policy in China—was generally done first in a larger city in each province, to serve as an "experimental point" for the region. Concrete management of the program split decision-making among four urban levels: city, district, street, and community (*shequ*, 社区). All these jurisdictions were to share in reporting, registering, investigating, approving, issuing forms, making modifications, and filing cases.[26] In large cities, *dibao* norms were set not just at the city level but also by districts, given variation in prices, occupational structure, and income levels within such municipalities.

Application

An applicant's journey toward becoming a recipient begins with a written entreaty accompanied by documentary proof of penury, to be submitted to one's community office. After filing the request, community officials have a certain amount of time (set locally, from five to ten days) to assess the candidate's

24. Yuan Shaohua, "Chongqing jianli chengshi zuidi shenghuo baozhang zhidu de zuofa" [Chongqing's method of establishing an urban minimum livelihood guarantee system], *ZGMZ*, no. 5 (1997): 23.

25. Ibid. The director of Hubei's Department of Civil Affairs set down a similar set of procedures (Zhang Laosheng, "Quanmian tuijin guifan guanli—Hubeisheng jianli chengshi jumin zuidi shenghuo baozhang zhidu de jingyan" [Fully promote standardized management—Hubei province's experience in establishing urban residents' minimum livelihood guarantee system], *ZGMZ*, no. 9 (1998): 24; Qinghaisheng minzhengting jiuzai jiujichu [Qinghai province Civil affairs Bureau, Disaster and Economic Relief Office], "Wanshan chengshi jumin zuidi shenghuo baozhang zhidu" [Perfect the urban residents' minimum livelihood guarantee system], *ZGMZ*, no. 10 (1999): 24.

26. Meng Jiawu and Tan Zhilin, "Wuhan chengshi zuidi shenghuo baozhang zhidu de sige tedian" [Four characteristics of Wuhan city's minimum livelihood guarantee system], *ZGMZ*, no. 7 (1996): 19.

needs and to attempt to verify the paperwork presented. A thorough physical search of the home follows, along with close inquiry of the household members. Next comes a particularly intrusive, sometimes even insidious, procedure: interviewing neighbors and visiting the candidate's place of work, if any, to make sure that the applicant has spoken truthfully.

Most embarrassing and painful of all, the results of the scrutiny are posted upon a public board (the *gongshilan*, 公示栏), visible to all passersby, in order to solicit the views not just of immediate neighbors but of everyone in the community acquainted with the applicant family's true state of eligibility and of anyone in a position to see the targeted family members' daily comings and goings.[27] This board proclaims the number of members living in every payee household; the sum of money each family is receiving, including any special subsidies; and the amount of "voluntary" work (e.g., neighborhood sanitation, public security, guarding, gardening, etc.) that its relevant members had performed in a given week, such activity usually being a necessary condition of enjoying the allowance, provided at least someone from the household is physically capable of doing it.[28]

Once community officers have made their tentative appraisal of a case, the file goes up one administrative level to the street (*jiedao*, 街道), where another week or so is spent reviewing the materials, with street officials' deliberations then posted on the community's public board. After one more week has passed, the records are delivered to the next echelon, the district (*qu*, 区) level, where managers reexamine them. The judgments about those who seem to have met the necessary conditions must once again be subjected to public view. Only if there are no objections, finally, the city Civil Affair Bureau gives its stamp of approval, and the candidate becomes a full-fledged "*dibaohu*."

At this point, families admitted into the program are extended a "*baozhangjin lingquzheng*" (保障金 领取证, certificate for collecting the funds), which their head is to carry, along with his/her household registration booklet and identification card, to claim the allowance, either monthly or by quarter, depending upon the method adopted in the community. Subsequent regular inspections (sometimes every three months, and in other cases, just every six) are made to certify that the family remains qualified to enjoy the subsidy, by checking whether any of its members have found work or received a pension, or if there has been any change in the numbers of persons living in the household.[29] When its situation or income changes, the household's head is

---

27. Interview with officers at community W, which had about 1,600 residents, with only 1 percent *dibaohu*, August 30, 2007, Wuhan.

28. Interviews at communities Y, containing over 4,000 people, and Z, August 29, 2007, Wuhan.

29. Interview with director of the *dibao* office at the Gansu provincial Civil Affairs Department, September 5, 2007, Lanzhou.

to notify the *dibao* office in the community to arrange for stopping, reducing, or increasing the outlays.[30]

How should we characterize these subjects, people put through such a rigmarole of rules and regulations, welfare targets clearly under some official suspicion despite their worrisome travails? I turn now to examining the individuals granted the *dibao*.

RECIPIENTS: DEMOGRAPHY AND STATE OF HEALTH

Demographic Traits: Age, Employment, Education

The first notable demographic feature of the *dibaohu* is their shared age range. According to a 2002 urban dataset collected by the China Household Income Project, the bulk of the recipients then clustered between the ages of sixteen and twenty and between forty-one and forty-five.[31] Data amassed in an investigation of 500 low-income families in Shanghai seven years later, at the end of 2009, showed a mean age of forty-nine, with over half ranging from forty-six to fifty-five.[32] As late as 2014, 63 percent were still of working age (sixteen to fifty for women, sixteen to sixty for men).[33]

These figures suggest that most of the recipients were retrenched laid-off workers and their offspring. In fact, using data from the then-Minister of Civil Affairs Duoji Cairang, two social policy scholars assert that about 85 percent of the recipients in 2002 were laid-off workers, retirees, unemployed workers, and their dependents.[34] Fulong Wu, citing a 2002 article in the official journal *Liaowang*, likewise estimated that, at the beginning of that year, 90 percent of 12.35 million *dibao* holders were laid-off workers and unemployed staff.[35] In line with this approximation, a 2008 investigation in

---

30. Interview with *dibao* workers, community X, where there were 1,099 households, of which 7.9 percent were *dibaohu*, August 27, 2007, Wuhan; Wang Zhikun, "Chengshi jumin zuidi shenghuo baozhang: buru fazhihua guanli guidao" [Urban residents' minimum livelihood guarantee: Step into the orbit of legalized managment], *ZGMZ* no. 11: 19.

31. Bjorn A. Gustafsson and Quheng Deng, "Social Assistance Receipt and its Importance for Combating Poverty in Urban China," (Bonn: Institute for the Study of Labor, Discussion Paper Series, No. 2758, 2007), quoted in Tony Saich, *Providing Public Goods in Transitional China* (New York: Palgrave Macmillan, 2008), 181.

32. Qin Gao, "Public Assistance and Poverty Reduction: The Case of Shanghai," *Global Social Policy* 13, no. 2 (2013): 193–215.

33. *Idem.*, *Welfare, Work and Poverty: China's Social Assistance 20 Years After* (New York: Oxford University Press, 2017), 40.

34. Xiaoyuan Shang and Xiaoming Wu, "Changing Approaches of Social Protection: Social Assistance Reform in Urban China," *Social Policy and Society* 3, no. 3 (2004): 269.

35. Fulong Wu, "Urban Poverty and Marginalization under Market Transition: The Case of Chinese Cities," *International Journal of Urban and Regional Research* 28, no. 2 (June 2004): 408; Qin Gao, Jiyoung Yoo, Sooko-Mee Yang, and Fuhua Zhai, "Welfare Residualism: a Comparative Study of the Basic Livelihood Security Systems in China and South Korea," *International Journal of Social Welfare (IJSW)* 20 (2011): 119, report that more than half were unemployed (laid off or on the job

six cities found that while 40.8 percent of the *dibaohu* studied had the ability to work and were of working age, just 17.7 percent were laboring. But what they were doing was only "flexible (i.e., intermittent, unstable, without benefits) labor"; those in formal employment accounted for a terribly tiny 2.7 percent. Thirty-seven percent were registered or unregistered unemployed (23.3 and 9.7 percent, respectively).[36] As Athar Hussain pointed out, "Unlike the old urban poor, a large percentage of the new are able and willing to work but have no jobs."[37]

Drawing on information from the Ministry of Civil Affairs, Qin Gao reported that even after another six years, in 2014, 63 percent of the *dibao* targets were still of working age. But, most unfortunately, a mere 2 percent managed to obtain either part- or full-time employment, and another 23 percent were laboring in jobs that were merely temporary. A full 38 percent remained unemployed, whether unregistered (21 percent) or registered (17 percent)—hardly a change from 2011.[38] All this indicates that a decade and a half following their displacement from their original positions, about three-fifths of working-age *dibao* recipients had not managed to attain any form of steady work.

Turning to tabulations of their educational status, a 2002 study of poverty households in Nanjing uncovered that 80 percent of respondents had been educated only through junior high, whereas in the city's total urban population, the comparable figure was about 50 percent.[39] When Han Keqing and his collaborators carried out their stratified, random, six-city survey of *dibao* recipients (in Beijing, Chongqing, Changsha [Hunan], Zhongshan [Guangdong], Tianshui [Gansu], and Hanyang [Liaoning]) in 2008, 74 percent of the 1,209 returned questionnaires showed education only through junior high. The average level of schooling was 8.9 years, just short of the nine years of compulsory education.[40] More than likely, most unskilled laid-off factory workers had missed out on education during the Cultural Revolution, when schools were shut, coinciding with the years when they should have been in school.

roster but not working or being paid). Also, Duoji Cairang et al., *Urban Poverty and Minimum Living Security: Main Report of China Urban Anti-Poverty Forum* (Beijing: Ministry of Civil Affairs, 2002).

36. Han Keqing et al., eds., *Chengshi zuidi shenghuo baozhang zhidu yanjiu* [Study of China's Urban Minimum Livelihood Guarantee System] (Beijing: Zhongguo shehui kexue chubanshe [Beijing: Chinese Social Sciences Publishing Co.], 2015), 105, 128.

37. Hussain, "*Urban Poverty*," 1; see also King-lun Ngok, "Social Assistance Policy and Its Impact on Social Development in China: The Case of the Minimum Living Standard Scheme (MLSS), *China Journal of Social Work* 3, no. 1 (2010): 42.

38. Qin Gao, Fuhua Zhai, Sui Yang, and Shi Li, "Does Welfare Enable Family Expenditures on Human Capital? Evidence from China," *World Development* 64 (2014): 220. See also Qin Gao, Shiyou Wu, and Fuhua Zhai, "Welfare Participation and Time Use in China," *Social Indicators Research* 124 (2015): 863–87.

39. Yuting Liu, Fulong Wu, and Shenjing He, "The Making of the New Urban Poor in Transitional China: Market Versus Institutionally Based Exclusion," *Urban Geography* 2, no. 8 (2008): 821.

40. Han et al., *Chengshi*, 105, 128.

State of Health

One more striking feature of the group's demography has been its members' poor health. A 2003 national survey of 10,000 *dibao* recipients found that 34 percent of the households getting aid had disabled members, and 65 percent had chronically ill ones (possibly some families fit into both categories and so were double-counted).[41] In Han Keqing's 2008 project, about one-third of the subjects had become poverty-stricken because of sickness or disability.[42] With time, problems were aggravated: the Asian Development Bank's 2012 three-city research on 2,810 households found that 74 percent of the families investigated had at least one chronically sick member, and 30 percent had at least one who was disabled.[43]

What was the connection between this state of poor health among the *dibao* recipients and their recent induced poverty? During the socialist era, it is likely that at least some, if not most, of these ill and infirm people would have received gratis medical care from their work units. But with the lifting of medical responsibilities from the shoulders of state enterprises, costs for health care were transferred to cities and families, the poor among them totally unequipped to pay. By 2006, "per capita private spending [on health care], in real terms [had] increased . . . to a level 35 times higher than in 1978."[44] So, for the post-1995 poor, a new, stark choice arose between paying for medical care and medication or for other basic necessities, such as food, clothing, or shelter.

Following the installation of a health insurance scheme for urban residents lacking formal employment in 2009, two researchers found no evidence that the plan had reduced out-of-pocket expenditure.[45] As evidence of the little help such insurance provides, China's National Development and Reform Commission reported that, in 2016, the government subsidy for this insurance had been raised from just 380 yuan to 420 yuan per capita per year (or from about US$54 to a mere US$60 per person).[46] Accordingly, Qin Gao wrote in 2017, "The new resident health insurance schemes have been helpful in pro-

---

41. Gao, "Public Assistance," 199, quoting Joe C. Leung, "The Emergence of Social Assistance in China," *IJSW* 15, no. 3 (2006): 188–98.

42. Han et al., *Chengshi*, 105.

43. Gao, *Welfare, Work,* 82.

44. China Institute for Reform and Development, "China Human Development Report 2007/08: Access for all, Basic public services for 1.3 billion people," (Beijing: China Translation and Publishing Corporation, 2008), 16.

45. Hong Liu and Zhong Zhao, "Impact of China's Urban Resident Basic Medical Insurance on Health Care Utilization and Expenditure," IZA DP No. 6768 (Forschungsinstitut zur Zukunft der Arbeit [Institute for the Study of Labor], Bonn, Germany, July 2012).

46. National Development and Reform Commission, "Report on the Implementation of the 2016 Plan for National Economic and Social Development and on the 2017 Draft Plan for National Economic and Social Development," delivered at the Fifth Session of the Twelfth National People's Congress on March 5, 2017, 23.

viding coverage for the two left-behind groups [rural residents and urbanites without formal jobs], but their premium levels can be high relative to their low income levels, especially among the poor, and their coverage remains narrow and benefit levels remain low."[47] There was improvement by 2018, with the government's share having risen to 28 percent of the total and individuals paying 29 percent.[48] But despite insurance in place by 2019 available to all urbanites, out-of-pocket costs still amounted to about 36 percent of the cost of treatment, a figure prohibitive for the poverty-stricken.[49] In Japan, that average is under 13 percent.[50]

Bringing these statistics to life, I turn to interviews. I observed that where someone was in poor health, s/he stayed at home, lay on a bed nearly all the time, was unable to work, and contrived to subsist, if barely, by swallowing a minimal amount of what might well be questionable medicine, visiting a hospital only in times of dire emergency. Here are several typical examples:

In one home, an old mother was prostrate, paralyzed on her bed, as she had been for half a year. "Now she's very old," explained her daughter-in-law. "Her health situation is very poor, her pension is all used up seeing doctors and buying medicine." In another desperate scenario, a wife, aged forty-seven, was likewise confined to her bed. She had contracted thyroid disease nine years before. "At first, it wasn't serious, and we didn't pay much attention to it," she recalled. Then she continued:

Afterward, it slowly got severe, and I took a lot of hormone-type medicine. Now you can see I got fat, it's a side-effect of the medication. Each month, must take about 100 *yuan* of pills to control the illness. The doctor can examine me every month and check my body signs. But a general check-up costs 300 to 400 *yuan* and we just can't afford it. . . . Ordinarily I'm at home and keep track myself. I do what I can to regulate it, don't lightly go to the hospital.[51]

The following year, in 2008, in Beijing, forty-six-year-old Mr. Wang, asked about medical treatment, had this to offer: "Last month, the kid got a cold twice. The cost was over 300 yuan, but it didn't reach the threshold—one must spend 1,500 yuan to be reimbursed."[52] A citizen of Shanghai, Ms. Li, the mother of a teenaged daughter, told the questioner: "One day, the

47. Gao, *Welfare, Work*, 165.
48. China Power, CSIS, "Is China's Health Care Meeting the Needs of its People," https://chinapower.csis.org/china-health-care-quality, accessed October 2, 2020.
49. Noah Smith, "China Steps Up Health Care Spending Just in Time," *Bloomberg Opinion,* October 27, 2019 (https://www.bloomberg.com/opinion/articles/2019-10-27/china-steps-up-health-care-spending-just-in-time). Besides individuals and the government, public and private insurance contributed about another 44 percent.
50. China Power, "Is China's Health."
51. Interview, August 26, 2007, Wuhan.
52. Han et al., *Chengshi,* 50.

community told me I have a little high blood pressure, *zaogao* (糟糕, awful, what a mess)! I was told to go have a check-up. I said: 'Use what? Pay with what money?'"[53] Some years later, in 2012, speaking of medical insurance, a Shanghai scholar made this remark: "Even though the premium is rather low, [the poor] have no funds to pay it; after getting sick, [they've got] no way to bear long-term treatment and recovery costs."[54]

All told, we have here a conglomeration of middle-aged, poorly educated, scantily employed (if working at all) comrades of the old proletariat, many of whom suffer from disease and disability. Given that the *dibao* was designed and delivered in order to keep them subdued, just how "unstable" were/are they?

STABILITY AND INSTABILITY

After about seven years of threatening and widespread street demonstrations by laid-off workers, such mass protest among the *xiagang* ceased after 2004. But officials' fears and worries about *dibao* recipients acting on their grievances were tenacious. Moreover, granting the *dibao* to the newly destitute did not fully resolve the resentment among the retrenched any more than it quelled the unease among the rulers about the perceived potential for inciting instability among those laid off.[55] Thus, in 2002, outgoing Party General Secretary Jiang Zemin emphasized the critical nature of welfare in his political report to the Sixteenth Party Congress that year. There he decreed that, "Establishing and improving a social security system compatible with the level of economic development constitutes an important guarantee for social stability and long-term peace and order in the country."[56] Years later, this remained the creed. Two social policy scholars remarked, in 2008 and 2010, respectively, "its [the *dibao*'s] main justification is its contribution to social stability."[57] Still one more researcher asserted that the *dibao* fell under the

---

53. Ibid., 88.

54. Xiaoyi Zhang, "Wanshan shehui jiuzhu zhidu, shixian gongping gongzheng" [Perfect the social relief system, realize fairness and impartiality], in 2013 *Shanghai lanpishu: Shanghai shehui fazhan baogao* [2013 Shanghai bluebook: Report on Shanghai's social development], eds. Lu Hanlong and Zhou Haiwang (Beijing: shehui kexue wenxuan chubanshe, 2013), 276.

55. Jennifer Pan, *"Welfare for Autocrats: How Social Assistance in China Cares for its Rulers* (New York: Oxford University Press, 2020) deftly analyzes how the passion, antagonism, and even fury occasioned by not getting (as large a share as one wishes of), or being removed from the rolls of, the *dibao* is paradoxical: what was meant to pacify the unemployed proletariat in practice enraged those disappointed by how it treats—or fails to treat—them.

56. https://www.fmprc.gov.cn/mfa_eng/topics_665678/3698_665962/t18872.shtml, accessed January 2, 2020.

57. Linda Wong, "Mending the Chinese Welfare Net: Tool for Social Harmony or Regime Stability?" presented at a conference on "Authoritarianism in East Asia: Viet Nam, China, North Korea," June 29–30, 2010, City University of Hong Kong, 19.

category of a *ningjuli gongcheng* (cohesion project, 凝聚力工程) or a *wen-ding gongcheng* (stability project, 稳定 工程).[58]

By 2012, whatever fracas was associated with the program—engendered by those not admitted into it, those who believed their share was lower than appropriate, or those prodded to leave the program—was probably magnified in the minds of the political elite. At this point, the State Council even alerted the public security organs to become involved. A document put out that year (see Chapter Nine) directed attention to such behavior (though it seems to have been relatively rare) when it declared that, "The public security organs must criticize, educate, and extend relevant punishment toward those who unreasonably raise hell [or] adopt threatening methods."[59] Perhaps aware of this new thrust, an informant in Shanghai noted, in 2013, that, "The government fears that the hearts of the poor are imbalanced, so it uses the *dibao* to keep them quiet."[60] The same year, the deputy general director of the Department of Social Assistance at the Ministry of Civil Affairs confirmed that, "Naturally *dibao* is related to stability [*weiwen*, 维稳], protection against instability."[61] In 2014, the theme persisted. A group of professors and students at Central China University of Science and Technology in Wuhan agreed that, "The *dibao* is given for social stability, to people who would make trouble, since the government fears them."[62]

Regardless of so much anxiety about *dibaohu*'s disruptions, interviews with them appeared to attest that they, in fact, are not prone to gather in oppositional groups and provided a sense of why not. Principally, though they share a fate, few reported so much as speaking with other beneficiaries, should they—and this was not always the case—even know who they are. One, a bit cryptically, claimed to "talk about the *dibao* with our neighbors, and we basically agree on it," without mentioning what they might be agreeing to.[63] A telling comment from another, however, reveals a great deal: "The *dibao* definitely isn't enough, there's no way to save money, and we have no way [to deal with that]. Some people "curse [ma, 骂] the government for the small amount of the money we're given . . . we don't know other *dibaohu*, so we don't get together with them to complain, and we don't converse about this with the *dibaohu* we do know."[64]

---

58. Zhang, "China's Social Policy," 228.

59. Zhonghua renmin gongheguo Guowuyuan [State Council of the People's Republic of China], Guowuyuan guanyu jinyibu jiaqiang he gaijin zuidi shenghuo baozhang gongcuo de yijian [State Council's Opinions on Progressively Strengthening and Improving the Minimum Livelihood Guarantee Work], Guofa (2012), 45 *hao* [issuance no. 45], www.gov.cn/zwgk/2012-09/26/content_2233209 .htm, accessed September 2012.

60. Interview, June 24, 2013, Shanghai.

61. Interview, September 9, 2013, Beijing.

62. Interview, November 3, 2014, Wuhan. This is the argument in Pan, *Welfare*.

63. Qianjiang, Hubei, July 6, 2010.

64. Lanzhou, July 15, 2010.

Respondents in Guangzhou seemed especially distant from their fellow grantees. As one remarked, "As to our neighbors, our relations are all very good, but with other *dibaohu*, there's basically no interaction, it's just saying hello"; "there's a lot of exchange with our neighbors, but since there's mutual anonymity [ni ming, 匿名], we don't even know who's a *dibaohu*."[65] In another Guangzhou community, there appeared to be outright unfriendliness, as disclosed by this description: "Ordinarily, each person comes back home and then closes the door; it's different from the past; before, each family opened the door and everyone had connections. Now . . . what our neighbors to the right and left are surnamed, what they are called, we don't know at all. At present people talk with you very little."

This feeling was seconded by another resident, who observed that, "We have very little interchange with our neighbors . . . we chat or even say hello rather little and we have no exchange at all with other *dibaohu*." And a third one acknowledged that, busy with assisting her son, "I have no relations with my neighbors, just pass and greet, get no help from them, very rarely chat with them, and this saves me trouble. . . . [As to the other *dibaohu*], I don't know other people," she reflected. At best, one offered these words about others in her community getting the *dibao*: "I see them and know them a little . . . what their name is I don't know in detail, I've just seen them, usually when I [do voluntary] work, I see them and recognize them . . . if appropriate, we'll converse, if not we don't say much . . . we don't want to quarrel or have a dispute."

A man whose mother is "sick from head to toe, if it's not this kind of sickness it's that kind" has no relations at all with his neighbors: "Everyone shuts the doors . . . I only know they live here when I see them, just nod hello, some people [when I nod] pay no attention to me." He does, however, at least admit to some awareness of other *dibao* targets when he states that, "We sometimes congregate to hold a meeting and say hello, and sometimes participate in obligatory labor together." But another man from this community, though also noting that he comes across other recipients while doing mandatory work (*yiwu laodong* 义务 劳动 either voluntary labor or obligatory labor), finds there is "no way to chat, just go together and don't talk, you can talk or not talk, when there's been enough time, you finish the job and that's it . . . whomever I work with doesn't matter to me [*mei suoweide*, 没所谓的]."[66]

Still, there are tales that feed managers' and politicians' fears, though they appear to be egregious, not the work of a crowd and not frequent. Because they are vivid, I relate a number of them here, but most suggest relative rarity or ultimate harmlessness. They do, however, convey a sense that the apprehensions that surround the perpetrators are not without any foundation. Along these

---

65. Interviews, July 12, 2010.
66. Interviews, June 30, 2010.

lines are accounts that mention "throwing and smashing"; "sleeping on the ground and won't get up"; and "everywhere making chaos, staying around in the room, maybe lying down and not moving . . . and wanting to go to cadres' homes to eat."[67] Community officials in Lanzhou in 2010 described the sorts of nuisance that the occasional dissatisfied person stirred up when angry: They would "stand in the doorway obstructing our work and cursing us. We have to send for the community's civil police to get them to shut up. They come one-by-one."[68] In Wuhan, a community *dibao* manager imparted this story: "They threaten community managers that they'll jump off the Yangzi Bridge or go to Beijing to petition" [which could damage an official's career].[69] As researchers in Shanghai explained, citing one distraught, harassed local cadre:

> If they *nao* (闹, stir up trouble) or *shangfang* (上访, petition) local leaders will become afraid and give the *dibao* to the *diaomin* (刁民, wicked person).[70] We're a punching bag, dealing with the lowest stratum of people . . . he thinks they're in the right and should get the *dibao*, if we explain the requirements, they don't pay attention to you, very many people pound the table, glare at you, a common occurrence.[71]

A few other examples, though horrific, seem exceptional. One local officer recounted:

> According to policy, you get the *dibao* where you live; her *hukou* was here but she lived in another district, after divorce last July [2007], she ran over here and said she wanted the *dibao*. Our work personnel knew her situation so told her she can't get the *dibao*, but they'd recommend her for work. The next day there was a recruitment fair, he took her there and found several jobs for her, but she didn't want to: "I don't work, I want the *dibao*!" The worker said, "You can't be choosy, you're in this kind of a situation, and you aren't without labor ability." She listened, then took out a knife and hacked him. . . . This kind of situation happens a few times a year.[72]

Similar rage inspired this situation: In 2011, a Wuhan resident, inflamed by getting a *dibao* 20 yuan lower than others, attacked a student in the area, having mistaken him for a community staff member.[73] A June 2013 incident

---

67. Han et al., *Chengshi,* 134.
68. Interview, July 13, 2010, Lanzhou.
69. Interview, late August 2008, Wuhan.
70. Discussion, Shanghai Academy of Social Sciences, June 28, 2013. This matches the argument in Xi Chen, *Social Protest and Authoritarianism in China* (New York: Cambridge University Press, 2012).
71. Han Keqing, ed. *Zhongguo chengshi dibao fangtanlu* [Interviews with Minimum Livelihood Guarantee Recipients in Urban China] (Jinan: Shandong renmin chubanshe [Shanghai people's publishing], 2012), 303–4.
72. Ibid., 343, 355, 365.
73. Interview with Professor Ding, August 3, 2011, Wuhan.

in Anhui made the national news when a man whose *dibao* had been terminated after he left home to go to (or, perhaps, look for) work. His choice of
revenge was to set a bus on fire, killing forty-seven people.[74] A few Changsha work cadres spoke of threatening behavior, such as one who termed the
aggrieved "very ferocious. . . . We meet up with some who, if they don't
get the *dibao,* want to kill people or take something and run to us cursing,
'You're a stinky whore . . . if you don't let me have it, I'll take a cigarette
stub against someone.' We absolute majority of *dibao* cadres have received
different degrees of personal attacks, verbal injuries, even our family members walking on the street do too." Another described behavior that was
more fearsome: "If you don't let people apply for *dibao*, or not give people
money they want, he takes a knife and stabs people."

And yet, in the face of such assaults and angst, a number of community
work personnel praised the *dibao* for its pacifying influence and for its contribution to a state of general restraint in the neighborhoods. In spite of trepi-
dation on the part of policy makers and the disaffection of and disruptions
by some *dibaohu*, there is evidence that the *dibao* has achieved a measure of
peace. This overall success is apparent in that, to a person, my interlocutors
all reported that after the inauguration of the program, trouble was most often
instigated by individuals acting out singly, not by groups of sizable masses.

Mun Young Cho, who did her fieldwork in the northeast from 2004 to
2008, observed this as well; she "rarely saw organized action to express
grievances." At most, she observed people in small groups accosting and
threatening officials with their grievances and displeasure.[75] The reflections
of Chinese scholars and officials across several cities coincided with Cho's.
Tang Jun, living in Beijing, remarked, in 2009, that, "Individual anger is
common, but not group protests . . . [large-scale] incidents happened in 2002
and 2003; now things are more calm."[76] In Hanyang, Liaoning, one official
advised that, "The *dibao* has had a very great role in community work and
community stability"; in Changsha, the word was that, "In increasing security, maintaining stability, there have been changes, definitely [with the introduction of the *dibao*]," and "The basic livelihood of the masses in difficulty
has gotten a real guarantee, now they're rather stable."[77]

In both Changsha and Chongqing, local program staff contrasted the time
before the scheme had been installed with the situation afterward: "At the time
of the transformation of state enterprises, the *dibao* played an absolute stability
role," said one. Another related how bridges had been blown up and streets

74. Reported to me in an interview, Shanghai Academy of Social Sciences, June 28, 2013.
75. Mun Young Cho, *The Specter of "The People": Urban Poverty in Northeast China* (Ithaca,
NY: Cornell University Press, 2013), 87–88.
76. Interview, July 28, 2009, Beijing.
77. Han et al., *Zhongguo*, 446, 352, 362.

destroyed before the system was implemented, but that thereafter "the anger wasn't so great, and the *dibao* had a very big role in social stability."[78] So, for the authorities, given their aim of mollifying the outrage among the past, now retrenched proletariat, the *dibao* was a kind of victory, the nuisance that *xiagang* wrath had earlier occasioned largely resolved. This judgment surely held for the local cadres who administered the program and who dealt directly and daily with its beneficiaries; it was the case for central leaders as well.

CONCLUSION

Throughout the lifespan of the *dibao* program, the saga of its aims, the nature of its procedures, the amount of investment it received, and the content of the propaganda that accompanied it all add up to a simple story line: The policy elite has employed this project to placate and pacify the workers whom its orders had released from their lifetime positions. Its target was, in particular, the portion of the pre-1995 labor force who were middle-aged, under-educated, and often unhealthy; being deprived of income and occupation, and without the gratis healthcare they had previously enjoyed, many of them saw their well-being decline further. It was the policies of the state itself that produced the new urban poverty. But once that privation became manifest and pervasive among the old workforce, after several years of raucous protest, the potential, largely imagined menace posed by these poor yet continued to unnerve the leadership, at least for some years. Still, on the ground, the *dibao* scheme seems to have had a triumph in calming down the *xiagang*.

Nonetheless, for its targets, the platform's upshot—intended or not—was to render the recipients, quieted but politically repressed, socially marginalized and excluded, silent and discarded, in effect, the detritus of the country's modern, metropolitan development. Thus, a people whose plunge in prestige was manufactured by a state-sponsored market incursion was further manipulated by the powers-that-be. And since the provisions of the *dibao* program confined the payees and their progeny to a long-term life of penury, operatively ensuring that they are denied any opportunity for upward mobility, it seems fair to see it as a ticket to membership in a permanent underclass.

Chapter Four goes on to portray the experiences and sentiments of these laid-off workers who became the new urban poor when they were let go from their posts. It also charts their plummeting shift in status from being "masters," positioned at the top of the masses' hierarchy down to being instead unemployed, "reemployed," or informalized labor subsequent to their retrenchment.

---

78. Ibid., 372, 426. Again, this jibes with Pan, *Welfare.*

Section II

EXPERIENCES OF LAYOFF (XIAGANG) AND LIVELIHOOD GUARANTEE (*DIBAO*)

Chapter Four

Xiagang: **From Master to Mendicant**

This chapter depicts city streets from 1998 to 2002, just after layoffs had been enforced and before the *dibao* was extended widely. That expansion did not get underway until 2001 and occurred mainly during and after 2002. The chapter supplies a picture of what befell China's bygone urban proletariat immediately after its dismissal and how its members tried to cope and survive in their guise as the legions of the new urban poor. In their posture as informal laborers in those years, these people constituted a sizable component of the transition to capitalism in China, a blight on that rosiness of reform with its supposed all-around rising prosperity. Those comprising this mass consisted of that sorry section of the country's manual laborers whose posts were snatched from beneath them in the name of efficiency and profits in the course of the reform of the national economy, mostly in the years after 1994, and in huge numbers after 1997.

Some government officials believed, in 1999, that the real number of workers who should be counted as unemployed—including all those labeled as "waiting for work" but not included in the unemployed statistics—could be as high as one hundred million.[1] Whatever the precise total, even China's own National Bureau of Statistics admitted that nearly 31 percent of those employed in the state sector as of year-end 1997 were cut (from 110.4 million to 76.4 million) within the following four years.[2]

---

1. William H. Overholt, "China in the Balance," Nomura Strategy Paper, Hong Kong, May 12, 1999.
2. Dali L. Yang, "China in 2002: Leadership Transition and the Political Economy of Governance," *Asian Survey* (*AS*) 43, no.1 (2003): 34 (Yang references the State Statistical Bureau but without providing a citation); Hiroshi Imai, Special Report: "China's Growing Unemployment Problem," *Pacific Business and Industries RIM* (Tokyo) II, no. 6 (2002): 25, states that in the 1980s, 99.2 percent of urban workers were employed in the public sector (76.2 percent in state-owned firms, 23 percent in collectives). By 2000, those employed in state firms and collective enterprises had fallen to 38.1 percent and 7.2 percent of all urban workers, respectively, for a combined total of 45.3 percent.

This was a group of mainly unskilled workers who, summarily dismissed from the plants where they had toiled for decades with what they had thought to be life-long job security, had to discover new modes of livelihood from scratch in the midst of middle age. We can picture their efforts to eke out a living in the early days after their severance from their employment, as I observed them in the years 1998 through 2002.

STREET SCENE: THE NEW INFORMALS

Along the streets of Chinese inland cities then, the service sector, starved nearly to death until the early 1980s, seemed full of life, packed with business, its practitioners a literal crowd. You could get your shoes shined for 2 yuan[3] by three different peddlers on just one block, buy what was essentially the same pair of nylons for the same 10 yuan five or six times, or the same style ballpoint pen for 2 or 3 yuan, all the sellers lined up alongside each other in the same lane. Or you could choose any one of ten pedicabs to deliver you as far as a couple of miles away, for as little as a piddling 3 to 5 yuan.[4]

Besides such self-employed city folk, others among the millions of state-abandoned, suddenly informal[5] urban laborers were working for wages. A trade union study done of 553 laid-off and "reemployed" workers in ten large and medium cities and one county in 1999 found that 48.7 percent of the "reemployed" it counted were self-employed, while well over half (59 percent) of the rest, who had been hired, were engaged in work that was only temporary.[6] One of my Wuhan informants was a woman who, first let go by her own firm, had later been sacked from a private enterprise when its business deteriorated and was dishwashing at a restaurant for twelve hours per day for 300 *yuan* a month (equivalent to about USD$1.20 per day) when we spoke. Another, on her third post-enterprise position, was charged with simply standing at the gate of the idle plant where she had once been gainfully employed. A third woman did housework when contacted by the Women's Federation, which could be as rarely as just once a month. She would then be

---

3. A Chinese yuan was equal to about 12 cents USD at that time.
4. The following several paragraphs come from my article, "Labour Market Reform and the Plight of the Laid-off Proletariat," *The China Quarterly* (*CQ*), no. 170 (June 2002): 308–9.
5. The term "informalization" refers to a process whereby employment conditions become "flexible," entailing elimination of entitlements and benefits, reduction of safety and other humane provisions at the workplace, and denial of job security, where all of these guarantees once existed. This is accompanied by a surge in short-term, temporary jobs having these features and an upswing in petty projects of brief self-employment.
6. Xue Zhaoyun, "Dui xiagang zhigong zaijiuye xianzhuang de diaocha, sikao yu jianyi" [Research, reflections, and suggestions about the reemployment situation of laid-off staff and workers], *Gonghui gongzuo tongxun* [Bulletin of trade union work] 7 (2000): 8.

paid by the hour, at the measly rate of 3.2 yuan, thus, in slack times, perhaps just USD$4 for the entire month.[7]

People doing this second type of informal work, those who were hired, were described in sobering vignettes that graced the pages of the local newspaper in the central China city of Wuhan in early summer 1998, as the numbers of those making up the new informal class of retrenched (*xiagang*) workers mounted steadily. One read: "Three hired as transport workers for a store's household appliance department were paid only 200 yuan after a month, while the store's regular workers' monthly income averaged more than 1,000 yuan." And another:

> According to relevant regulations, staff and workers [were to] have a three month-probation period, in which wages are rather low. But after the three months a clothing enterprise fired those it had taken on. Of all those placed out of the [reemployment] service center, 44 percent were soon fired for reasons that had nothing to do with their job performance.[8]

On top of having to cope with the psychological shock of losing their jobs, those able to find work—the new informals—were severely strapped financially. In a 1997 investigation in fifty-five cities across seventeen different provinces, 1,300 returned questionnaires revealed that more than half (58 percent) of the laid off in the study were obtaining an income under 200 yuan per month.[9] With the growing numbers of people who had lost their jobs, it is not surprising that by early 2000, 73 percent of China's urban population had incomes below the national average, according to a study done in eleven major cities by the Macroeconomic Research Institute of the State Planning Commission.[10]

The discharged urban-registered people—individuals whose livelihoods and positions had once been guaranteed and whose spot in society was valued highly for decades—were often at a loss in getting hired. Meanwhile, the better-educated, more youthful confreres of these unfortunates generally could more readily retain their jobs or else find a place in the thriving modern

---

7. Street interviews, September 1999, Wuhan.

8. *Changjiang ribao* [Yangzi daily], June 2, 1998, 2.

9. 'Chengzhen qiye xiagang zhigong zaijiuye zhuangkuang diaocha' ketizu [Task force on 'the investigation of the employment situation of urban enterprise laid-off staff and workers'], "Kunjing yu chulu" [A difficult pass and the way out] from *Shehuixue yanjiu* [Sociology research] 6 (1997) [reprinted in *Xinhua wengao, shehui* [New China manuscript, society] 3 (1998): 21.] In 1999, the National Bureau of Statistics announced that the national average monthly wage of an urban state-employed worker was 695 yuan (N.a., "1998–1999 laodong baozhang tongji baogao" [Report on 1998–1999 labor insurance statistics], *Laodong baozhang tongxun* [Labor insurance bulletin], 3 (2000): 35–36.)

10. Guojia jiwei hongguan jingji yanjiuyuan ketizu [State Planning Commission, Macroeconomic Research Institute Task Force], "Jianli shehui baohu tixi shi wo guo shehui wending de guanjian" [Establishing a social protection system is the key to our country's social stability], *Neibu canyue* (*NBCY*) [Internal consultations], no. 511 (May 5, 2000): 9.

sector. Or their younger, rural-born cousins migrating into town, fresh from the countryside and prized by employers for their brawn and their grit—and for their readiness to reap the most meager of recompense that assembly-line drudgery, construction-site exertion, or menial service and market stall jobs provided—had far less trouble getting work. There were other workers, demographically similar to those let go, who were attached to firms doing marginally better but which were sufficiently strapped financially as to be withholding wages and pensions. (For more, see Chapter Ten.) In the case of those who are the subject of this chapter, however, for all practical purposes, the tie with their former employers was sundered irrevocably.[11] The startling thing is that those who had become demeaned menials making up this crowd were city-born and registered citizens, members of the once-celebrated factory proletariat,[12] turned, in the 1990s and thereafter, into the cohort of the *xiagang*;[13] no longer, thus, were inmigrating peasants, who had made up the principal set of the debased urban residents a few years back, the only marginalized urban dwellers.[14]

In illustration of this crumpling of status hierarchies, the term "*mingong*" (民工, loosely, a label specifying casual labor), which, in the past, had been used just to refer to surplus rural workers from the interior, in 1998 sometimes designated the urban laid-off and unemployed as well.[15] In 2008, one jobless

---

11. Ching Kwan Lee, "Pathways of Labor Insurgency," in *Chinese Society: Change, Conflict and Resistance,* eds. Elizabeth J. Perry and Mark Selden (London: Routledge, 2000), 41–61; *idem.,* "Three Patterns of Working-Class Transitions in China," in *Chinese Politics: Moving Frontiers,* eds. Francoise Mengin and Jean-Louis Rocca (New York: Palgrave, 2002), 62–91; Jean-Louis Rocca, "Three at Once: The Multidimensional Scope of Labor Crisis in China," in Mengin and Rocca, *Chinese Politics,* 3–30; and Feng Chen, "Industrial Restructuring and Workers' Resistance in China," *Modern China (MC)* 29, no. 2 (April 2003): 237–62.

12. On these workers' status and situation in the 1950s, when the myth of their leadership took hold, see Elizabeth J. Perry, "Masters of the Country? Shanghai Workers in the Early People's Republic," in *Dilemmas of Victory: The Early Years of the People's Republic of China,* eds. Jeremy Brown and Paul G. Pickowicz (Cambridge, MA: Harvard University Press, 2007), 59–69. On workers' lasting sense of loss of "social recognition and honor," see Mun Young Cho, *The Specter of "The People": Urban Poverty in Northeast China* (Ithaca, NY: Cornell University Press, 2013), 6–7; on their ongoing "strong sense of their superiority and nobility," Guangxu Ji and Youqin Huang, "Mobile Phone Culture among the Information Have-Less: A Case Study of Laid-Off Workers in Shenyang City, China," in *The Emergence of a New Urban China: Insiders' Perspectives,* eds. Zai Liang, Steven Messner, Cheng Chen, and Youqin Huang (Plymouth, UK: Lexington Books, 2012), 141–61.

13. Officially, a *xiagang* worker had to meet these conditions: 1) began working before the contract system was instituted (1986) and had had a formal, permanent job in the state sector (plus contract laborers whose contract term had not yet concluded); 2) was let go because of his/her firm's problems in business and operations but had not yet cut off relations with the firm; and 3) had not yet found other work (Guo Jun, "Guoyou qiye xiagang yu fenliu you he butong?" [What's the difference between laid-off and diverted workers in state firms?] *Zhongguo gongyun* [Chinese workers' movement] *(ZGGY),* 3 (1999): 32).

14. In 1987 Beijing, three-quarters of the employees in the private sector were from the countryside (Lora Sabin, "New Bosses in the Workers' State: The Growth of Non-State Sector Employment in China," *CQ,* no. 140 [1994]: 969); Shi Xianmin, "Beijing's Privately-Owned Small Businesses: A Decade's Development," *Social Sciences in China* 14, no. 1 (Spring 1993): 161–62.

15. *Ming Pao,* [Bright Daily] (Hong Kong), February 12, 1998.

laborer lamented that, "The original workers became the *ruoshi qunti* (弱势群体, weak masses), definitely their hearts are very unbalanced."[16] Strikingly, a decade on from their time of trauma, former workers could be found who had not yet been able to come to terms with this precipitous drop in status, as a Mr. Han charges: "In the past, workers were 'leaders,' now they're just *dagongzhe* (打工者, colloquial name for workers who do low-paid, low-skill, informal labor), the most disadvantaged. There's no difference between rural migrant labor and urban workers, they all get about the same wages."[17]

A writer in the journal of the official trade union bemoaned the troubles of these workers: "For a long time, they've been drifting outside the enterprise in a socially marginal situation, especially those in small-scale, scattered, mobile informal departments. . . . They meet up with many problems and annoyances, but lack any organization's loving care, are without any opportunity to get education or to participate in society."[18] Another lamented that, "Some households in special difficulty suffer discrimination in trying to become re-employed." Going on, he called attention to their sorry circumstances:

> Their legal rights and interests are harmed arbitrarily by employers, and they are bearing economic and social burdens. They feel lost and in a negative mood. Pessimistic and depressed, they're hopeless, lost their confidence. . . . This is especially so for those who had made a big contribution to their enterprises in the past . . . they feel abandoned by society.[19]

As these abuses ground on, it was just a small step from feeling deserted by society to withdrawing faith in the state. For in the nearly thirty years before the restructuring of the economy began after 1980, urban Chinese workers, especially those on the payroll of state-owned firms, could count implicitly upon a kind of covenant with the state that employed them, an agreement to provide for the bulk of their basic needs.[20] With the coming of the capitalist market order, that connection workers used to draw between their jobs and their government led some to blame the state—which they viewed as having thrown them aside—for their current jobless plight.[21]

---

16. Han Keqing, ed., *Zhongguo chengshi dibao fangtanlu* [Interviews with Minimum Livelihood Guarantee Recipients in Urban China] (Jinan: Shandong renmin chubanshe [Shandong people's publishing], 2012), 372.

17. Interview, July 30, 2011, Wuhan.

18. Xue, "Dui xiagang," 10.

19. Zhang Yuanchao, "Guoyou qiye tekun zhigong shenghuo de zhuangkuang ying yinqi gaodu zhongshi" [The livelihood situation of state-owned firms' especially difficult staff and workers ought to promote taking it seriously], *Zhongguo gongren* [Chinese worker] 7 (2000): 5.

20. Andrew G. Walder, *Communist Neo-Traditionalism: Work and Authority in Chinese Industry* (Berkeley: University of California Press, 1986).

21. Typically, in the late 1990s, dissatisfied workers accused their factory leaders of corruption and mismanagement, believing this was what had led to their firm's bankruptcy or collapse. See Feng Chen, "Subsistence Crises, Managerial Corruption and Labour Protests in China," *The China Journal*, no. 44 (July 2000): 41–63.

Laid-off workers in Wuhan, for instance, told me in the summer of 2002 that:

> The laid-off workers and those in money-losing enterprises are very dissatisfied with the government. It should take responsibility for our situation, but from the center to the localities all the governments are problematic. The Communist Party, as just one party, can't find a solution. Our government's leadership is poor. What we need is a political solution: our leaders should be elected as they are in the United States. The policies of our government can't be of any help to us.[22]

Though separated not just by several centuries but by space and culture as well, this disenchantment resonates with that of English working people of the eighteenth century, as depicted by E. P. Thompson. For those folk, too, the coming of capitalism similarly destroyed a moral economy that had long sustained an allegiance of laborers to their leaders.[23] Thompson delineates the predicament of the "crowd" he describes when its members realized that prices were overriding the take from their efforts at sustenance. In Thompson's words:

> By the notion of legitimation, I mean that the men and women in the crowd were informed by the belief that they were defending traditional rights or customs . . . [their] grievances operated within a popular consensus as to what were legitimate and what were illegitimate practices in marketing, milling, baking, etc. This in its turn was grounded upon a consistent traditional view of social norms and obligations, of the proper economic functions of several parties within the community, which, taken together, can be said to constitute the moral economy of the poor . . . this moral economy . . . supposed definite, and passionately held, notions of the common weal—notions which, indeed, found some support in the paternalist tradition of the authorities.[24]

In China, these newly displaced members of the sometime city-based pro-letariat—with their changed stance with respect to, and their altered treatment by, the state—appear as a powerful symbol of what has shifted and what has not in the posture and behavior of the "people's" government in the PRC after the late 1990s, as compared with its Maoist predecessor. Thompson's image of the legitimacy-challenging "crowd" can serve as well for presenting this transformation of the workers and of their relational bond with their no-longer-trustworthy state; the notion of "crowd," a conglomeration, acts to underline the group-ness of all those undergoing a switch from angry laid-off worker to pacified *dibaohu*.

---

22. Interview, August 19, 2002, Wuhan.

23. E. P. Thompson, "The Moral Economy of the English Crowd in the Eighteenth Century," *Past and Present*, no. 50 (February 1971): 76–136.

24. Thompson, "The Moral Economy," 78–79.

In what follows, I first construe continuities and contrasting visions between today's and yesterday's crowds and their respective connections to the state. I then supply some empirical material about the altered work situations of the constituent members of this urban crowd, as of the year 2001, and about how they were affected by then-current state policies. One can observe the draining away of their loyalty to their leaders and of the legitimacy they once accorded their state.

THE CROWD IN PEOPLE'S CHINA: CONTINUITIES AND CONTRASTS

Just as the crowd—the "masses"—in Mao's time inspired awe—by its huge, unfathomable numbers, its eerie internal conformity, and its ostensibly unstoppable vigor—so in the period of this account, untold millions were, once again, engaging in similar activities, for seemingly endless stretches of time. But if the awe felt by the viewer of the crowd of yore was inspired by that crowd's apparent (sometimes simulated) passion, the spectator's wonder became, in the late 1990s, more a case of pathos. For where the earlier crowd, its members unified in collaboration,[25] was allegedly accomplishing miracles, the crowd of 1998–2002 was composed of people struggling, usually singly, to stay alive.

Another writer, Elias Canetti, also wrote of crowds. He offers images that illustrate the sullying and debilitation of the liaison that once linked the Chinese laborer and the state.[26] Canetti's portraits also provide a picture of the antitheses between the remains of the proletariat from the mid-1990s and the proletariat from the socialist past.[27] According to Canetti, equality is one of the four chief attributes of the generic crowd.[28] And indeed, in both cases, though in disparate ways and for very different reasons (both times having much to do with the posture of the state), the respective crowds' components indeed were, respectively, equals in some fundamental respects. For those in each collectivity were, respectively, more or less homogeneously affected by

25. Joel Andreas, *Disenfranchised: The Rise and Fall of Industrial Citizenship in China* (New York: Oxford University Press, 2019), 168, speaks of workers' past "strong collective identity . . . as part of a working class celebrated as the vanguard of socialist construction and 'masters of the factory.'"

26. Elias Canetti, *Crowds and Power*, trans. Carol Stewart (New York: Viking, 1963).

27. There were great discrepancies between the treatment accorded workers in firms of different sizes and degrees of importance under the socialist regime (1949 to 1978) (Andrew G. Walder, "The Remaking of the Chinese Working Class, 1949–1981," *MC*, 10, no. 1 (1984): 3–48). But then the working class was treated better than were the members of any other social group, barring officials, top leaders, and the military.

28. Canetti, *Crowds*, 29. The other three—the desire to grow, love of density, and need for direction—do not fit the Chinese crowd.

the state in gross terms and thus reacted comparably.[29] And the plight of both crowds' members could be seen as the same in another regard: their situations were largely involuntarily constituted, coerced, if to varying degrees and in quite dissimilar ways.

And yet, the chasm between the two mammoth throngs was deep, reflecting a sea change in the state's choice of social coalition and its vastly altered ambitions. Under Mao's reign, municipal workers—the urban mass's members—were "masters," in name and in privilege, with the rural peasants (though treated as far inferior) their purported partners. Both the workers and the peasants—when officially mobilized—comprised the self-styled socialist regime's most legitimate political actors. In that state, supposedly and discursively based upon the working classes, the formal social status of the crowd's partisans was high; to be a constituent element within this crowd meant one stood as decidedly *included* within the ranks of the renowned. The legitimacy these then-laborers accorded the state was, consequently, unquestioned.

As historical actors, when stirred into motion, these Maoist partisans were (at least in rhetoric) a rapidly moving and mighty force with fearsome power. For Canetti, this would be the "baiting crowd," which "forms with reference to a quickly attainable goal," toward which it heads "with unique determination." It "has speed, elation, conviction." For the Chinese masses in the days of socialism, though, these traits were increasingly merely feigned. Canetti also notes that "the [baiting] crowd have [*sic*] immense superiority on their side."[30] This was, in the Mao-era Chinese case, because of capabilities like these: they were said to produce such marvels as to spark a prairie fire, stage a revolution, reshape the structure of ownership of agricultural land, appropriate for the state the wealth of the bourgeoisie, and forge steel in the fields while surpassing all prior grain growth targets. Too, they surged through the streets in the persons of Red Guards, wantonly deposing and shaming their superiors.

In stark opposition to that vision of potency, the crowdspeople of 2001 in the cities were the *xiagang*, off-post or laid-off workers. In the year 2000 in Wuhan, a man out of work offered his observation, one not wholly without foundation: "*Zaiyede hen shao, gongren chabuduo yiban dou xiagangle*" (在 业 的 很 少, 工人 差不多 一般 都 下岗了, Those still at work are very few, in general, the workers have been laid off).[31] These folk were perceptibly slowed down, as against their customarily portrayed robust style in the past, and pretty impotent, in the face of the regime's switch of alliance away from laborers, along with its stacking the status hierarchy in favor of those

29. For disparities within the working class from the 1950s to the 1970s, see Elizabeth J. Perry and Li Xun, *Proletarian Power* (Boulder, CO: Westview Press, 1997).

30. Canetti, *Crowds*, 49.

31. Interview, night market, September 12, 2000, Wuhan.

with capital, technical know-how, and the means of easily acquiring more of both,[32] as fits nicely with Jiang Zemin's "Three Represents," discussed in Chapter One. To be a component of this new crowd, then, was to be among the *excluded*, the abandoned. This sense of things is illustrated in what Eva Hung and Stephen Chiu heard from the *xiagang* workers they interviewed in this period, such as, "How come I suddenly fell from the superior working class to become someone's slave? I can't make sense of this," and "How could they just throw us away like this and ask us to be on our own?"[33]

Where the old, secure, entitled, full-time proletariat was agent (if without much volition of its own), this new set of part-time or over-time informals was victim; where the former was wound up by the Party, the latter was unwound, undone by it. These people correspond to Canetti's "flight crowd," which is "created by a threat," in this case of perishing from hunger or untreated illness. He explains that "the same danger faces them all." Such a crowd could become a panic, Canetti explains, should mass flight turn into a "struggle of each against all who stand in its way."[34] While the old crowd was the protagonist in earthshaking mass movements, the second one was reject, resulting in a sort of immobile mass stasis (in Canetti's terms, these are, respectively, the "rhythmic crowd," for which "everything depends on movement," and the "stagnating crowd")[35]—or, at best, pawns in the leadership's grand project of global ascent.

Moreover, while the crowd of the past was a united body, an internally relatively uniform aggregation that worked in unison, in the 1990s, that mass was dismantled and disaggregated, atomized first into families by the household responsibility system in the countryside, which cut up the commune after 1980. These family units, in turn, were further carved up, first into individual actors with the state's permission to migrate, which created a population of "floaters," and then by the state's license to launch private businesses just a few years later. As for the urban crowd, many of its constituents were, after the late 1990s, tossed one by one from their posts in their once collective work units (*danwei,* 单位)—or, even if retrenched in batches, still left to scrounge for subsistence as individuals.

So as this brief comparison highlights, the modalities of the crowd in China have both changed and not changed. But by way of summary, "the crowd" provides an image, by myriad means, whether of a mob or a herd churned into agitation by political campaigns, or of people in multitudes chased from their

---

32. Jaeyoun Won, "The Making of the Post-Proletariat in China," *Development and Society* 34, no. 2 (2005): 210, states, "Workers have become the lowest class among ten classes at the bottom of the class hierarchy . . . [and] have been pushed from society."

33. Eva P. W. Hung and Stephen W. K. Chiu, "The Lost Generation: Life Course Dynamics and *Xiagang* in China," *MC* 29, no. 2 (2003): 217, 223.

34. Canetti, *Crowds*, 53.

35. Ibid., 30.

workplaces as accounts ran dry and plants collapsed. Up to that point, the components of these two Chinese crowds greatly resembled each other. At the same time, they revealed in their features, and in their forms and manner and degree of dynamism, the program, the direction, and the aims of the state at each of two respective junctures. Accordingly, as they were switched from beneficiary to butt of the state's designs, their own belief in the legitimacy of that state shifted 180 degrees. I turn now to a closer look at the urban crowd's chances for reemployment in the age of efficiency and flexible labor.

THE URBAN CROWD OF THE YEAR 2000: "REEMPLOYMENT?"

Numbers, some of which are uncertain, still tell a chilling story that confirms redundant workers' feelings of neglect and their consequent lack of trust in the state. Though official statistics on the "reemployment" of these folk are notoriously slippery, their very collection does suggest that the leadership was well aware of the general situation.[36] Unfortunately, the increasing grimness of the data over time indicates that the state's several efforts to help these people were by no means adequate.

One might be suspicious when even those who compiled the figures had to admit, as one of them did in Wuhan in 2000, that, "One can't be clear about these statistics; they're relative, not absolute. The situation is dynamic and there's no way to count them (说不清 . . . 相对的 . . . 没办法 统计, *shuobuqing . . . xiangduide . . . meibanfa tongji*)."[37] According to this official, who cited a figure of about 30 percent "reemployed" in Wuhan as of mid-2000, it was the numbers of positions (人次, *renci*) known to be newly filled, not the number of people with new jobs, that was counted up once each month; each year, this data was added up, eliminating from the total the jobs known to labor administrators to have ended. These figures very likely involved recounting the same person, who may have held several very short-term posts in a given year. Moreover, an official pronouncement asserted that a late 1990s study of 10,000 laid-off workers in ten cities showed that as many as 68 percent of those with new jobs had held the jobs for just six months or less, including 40 percent of the total who had done so for under three months. A mere 17.26 percent managed to hold onto their new positions for longer than a year.[38]

---

36. Dorothy J. Solinger, "Why We Cannot Count the 'Unemployed,'" *CQ*, no. 167 (2001): 671–88.
37. Official, Wuhan General Trade Union's Professional Introduction Service Center, September 13, 2000.
38. N.a., "1998–1999," 35.

In addition to this vagueness about how to tally the reemployed, there were wide variations in official announcements about their proportions among the laid off. An internal publication cited a miserable rate of just 27 percent nationwide who had found new placements as of the end of June 1999.[39] But the All-China Federation of Trade Unions reported, on the basis of local labor departments' statistics, even worse news: there was a trend of annual deterioration. In 1998, the reemployment rate was 50 percent; in 1999, it was 42 percent; and in the first eleven months of 2000, down to a mere 16 percent.[40] According to a 2002 Xinhua release, the rate had dropped to just 9 percent in the first half of 2002.[41]

Another cause for concern about numbers was the amount of time people were spending out of work: In Hubei Province, a September 1997 random sampling of three thousand laid-off workers in 580 firms in ten cities and counties revealed that, although 47 percent were said to be reemployed, as many as another 26 percent had already been without any employment for three years or more, while 29 percent had been jobless for less than a year.[42] Not only were so many languishing laborless, but also the occupations they took up, if they did find work, were most unpromising. According to this same study, 18.6 percent of the "reemployed" had turned into odd-job manual workers, 10 percent did various sorts of hourly work (which usually referred to activities such as picking up others' children from school), 5.2 percent had seasonal jobs, 60 percent were individual retailers operating stalls, and a mere 6.8 percent had obtained formal, contracted employment. Among stallkeepers, a worrisome 45 percent were discovered to be working as vulnerable, mobile peddlers, selling in shifting sites without a license, easy prey to the urban police.[43]

Other research in 1997 among 360 reemployed staff and workers in Wuhan found that over a third of them (34.54 percent) had set up a stall, were operating a pedicab, or driving a taxi; by autumn 2000, a pedicab jockey claimed in private conversation that he had a startling 26,000 competitors in the city![44] If

---

39. Yang Yiyong, "2000 nian wo guo jiuye xingshi fenxi" [An analysis of the employment situation in our country in the year 2000], *NBCY*, 4 (January 28, 2000): 11.

40. Quanguo zongtonghui baozhang gongzuobu [All-China General Trade Union Security Work Department], "Guanyu xiagang zhigong laodong guanxi chuli ji shehui baozhang jiexu wenti de diaocha" [Investigation on handling laid-off staff and workers' labor relations and the issue of the continuation of social security], *ZGGY* 5 (2001): 14.

41. Terence Tan, "China's Jobless Can't Get New Work," *The Straits' Times*, September 27, 2002.

42. Hubei sheng zonggonghui shenghuo baozhangbu [Hubei province general trade union livelihood guarantee department], "Yunyong zhengce he falu shouduan, quanli tuijin zaijiuye gongcheng xiang zongshen fazhan" [Utilize policy and legal methods, fully promote the reemployment project to develop in depth], *Lilun yuekan* [Theory monthly], 2 (1998): 18.

43. Ibid., 8–9. Numbers in the source do not add up to 100 percent.

44. Interview, September 16, 2000, Wuhan. Interviewees at Wuhan branch of the All-China Federation of Trade Unions, October 31, 2001, gave the official figure as 40,000 then.

there was any accuracy at all in such a sum, it is not surprising that after 1997 (until the early 2000s) the streets of the city were crammed with a crowd of men pedaling their empty carts in search of customers and that their daily take was tiny.[45] As these new informals saw no change in their incomes or their placements year after year and as they perceived the worthlessness of the niche they were forced to fill, many increasingly repudiated the state whose policies put them where they were.

THE PRODUCTION OF INFORMALIZATION: A PARTNERSHIP ABANDONED

Despite appearances, the unregulated economic activity adopted by the laid-off did not represent just a straightforward manifestation of the metamorphosis of the Chinese urban economy, some uncomplicated consequence of that system's steadily deepening marketization. Nor did these sellers and service people merely symbolize an instance of the widespread process of privatization[46] attending the advance of capitalism on a global scale.[47] It is also inappropriate to view their labor as only the latest incarnation of the secondary sector of China's longstanding "dual market," as if a market, operating according to principles of supply and demand, had merely become bifurcated along some new fault line.[48]

It is the case that what is usually billed as the "secondary economy" across the world is a sector comprised of marginal and/or denigrated people, usually migrants or minorities, who have been relegated to the least desirable

45. In spring 2003, the city government attempted to clear the streets of these carts by buying the carts from their owners for some eight thousand yuan apiece and offering these drivers low-paying, low-status jobs. Communications from Huang Xiangchun, then editor of a local party journal, Wuhan, June 11 and July 6, 2003. Other sources said this occurred in 2002.

46. At the same time that employment in state units dropped 19.6 percent between 1995 and 1998, jobs in urban privately and individually owned enterprises increased by 44.8 percent, according to Hu Angang (*Jingmao daokan* [Economic and trade guide], December 30, 1999, in *Summary of World Broadcasts* (*SWB*), FE/3750, G/10, January 29, 2000); between 1991 and 1995, self-employed and private business provided 40 percent of the newly created jobs in cities (*SWB* FE/3098, G/5, December 10, 1997, from *Xinhua* [*XH*], December 9, 1997). A 1999 ten-city study of 553 reemployed staff and workers laid off from state firms found that 77 percent had switched from state to non-state firms, half of whom went into the private sector (Xue, "Dui xiagang").

47. P. Connolly, "The Politics of the Informal Sector: A Critique," in *Beyond Employment: Household, Gender and Subsistence*, eds. N. Redclift and E. Mingione (Oxford: Blackwell, 1985), 55–91; Alejandro Portes and John Walton, *Labour, Class and the International System* (New York: Academic Press, 1981) (both cited in Michael Pinches, "'All that we have is our muscle and sweat': The Rise of Wage Labour in a Manila Squatter Community," in *Wage Labour and Social Change: The Proletariat in Asia and the Pacific*, eds. M. Pinches and S. Lakha [Clayton, Australia: Centre of Southeast Asian Studies, Monash University, 1987], 104).

48. Louis Putterman, "Dualism and Reform in China," *Economic Development and Cultural Chang*, no. 40 (1992): 467–93; Flemming Christiansen, "The Legacy of the Mock Dual Economy: Chinese Labour in Transition, 1978–1992," *Economy & Society* 22, no. 4 (1993): 411–36.

and most unstable work available. Their lives, however, no matter how bitter, have generally improved significantly in material terms as a result of having joined such markets, as compared with what their existence was like before.[49] But as distinct from the usual secondary market worker elsewhere, these laid-off Chinese workers were *downwardly*, not upwardly, mobile.

Another difference is that, unlike informals in other places, the urban people on Chinese streets of 2001 were not situated in this niche voluntarily with dreams of bettering their lot by building businesses and amassing capital. Rather, they found themselves in this spot because their former rice bowl had been snatched away, and for them, there were no other means of survival. Since most of these small-time sellers of odd merchandise and manual labor had quite recently been full-time, life-tenured, completely welfare-entitled, and state-employed manufacturing workers, one needs to go beyond the surface signs of their quotidian practices—their superficial appearance as a reborn "private sector" linked to economic "reform" in the urban areas—to get a good grasp of the totality of what was going on.[50]

Official formulations aimed at enticing urban residents into the new tertiary (chiefly service) or private sectors (within the second economy) can lead one astray if attempting to grasp the situation of these individuals. A deceptive ruling was the 1999 National People's Congress amendment to the state constitution proclaiming the private sector a "component part" of the national economy. Cited as a hopeful sign was the expanding portion of the national economy occupied by this branch: in spring 1999, the State Economic and Trade Commission announced that "private enterprises" were accounting for almost one-fifth of the gross value of industrial output nationally and for over one-third of the retail trade in consumer goods,[51] figures that were probably much lower than the reality. Despite these promising bits of information, most private sector practitioners were seriously constrained

---

49. Michael J. Piore, *Birds of Passage: Migrant Labor and Industrial Societies* (Cambridge: Cambridge University Press, 1979); David Stark, "Bending the Bars of the Iron Cage: Bureaucratization and Informalization in Capitalism and Socialism," *Sociological Forum* 4, no. 4 (1989): 637–64 says that the "second economy" is "a broad range of income-gathering activity outside the boundaries of the redistributively coordinated and managed economy."

50. A re-born private sector appeared after the early 1980s. But the informals of the mid-1990s emerged from a very different social process from those that produced the earlier segments of this sector. The earlier marketers were or hoped to become capitalists, if often just petty ones: young people waiting for their first state jobs; rural migrants; ex-convicts; demobilized soldiers; rural cadres; and officials and state enterprise managers (Susan Young, *Private Business and Economic Reform in China* [Armonk, NY: M.E. Sharpe, 1995]; Ole Bruun, *Business and Bureaucracy in a Chinese City: An Ethnography of Private Business Households in Contemporary China* [Research Monograph 43] [Berkeley: Institute for East Asian Studies, University of California, 1993]; Ole Odgaard, "Entrepreneurs and Elite Formation in Rural China" *Australian Journal of Chinese Affairs* 28 (1992): 89–108; and David L. Wank, *Commodifying Communism: Business, Trust and Politics in a Chinese City* [New York: Cambridge University Press, 1999]).

51. *SWB* FE/3520, April 27, 1999, G/11, from *XH*, April 26, 1999.

by a lack of funding channels,[52] which remained the case for years. In the especially stricken northeast, but elsewhere too, people attempting to open their own businesses were often unable to obtain any government support at all, and they were heavily taxed besides.[53]

In short, the predicament of these people was by no means a product of "the market" acting alone. Instead, it derived primarily from state policies as they had evolved over time and in the then-recent past. Under the planned economy, government policy and the incentives it had promoted led local managers to overstaff and set up unnecessary construction projects that eventually demanded more and more investment. Later, massive enterprise losses and bankruptcies broke out when official credit tightening occurred. Indeed, in the second half of the 1990s, the Communist Party adopted a brand-new agenda quite unrestrained by the nature of the social coalition that had formerly buttressed its rule: it abandoned its putative past political partner, the working class, quite callously, in a step it disingenuously justified as being in labor's own "long-term interest."[54] Just as the sacking campaign was getting underway in force, the 1997 May Day editorial in the Party paper, the *People's Daily*, warned its readers that, "It's possible benefits of some workers may be temporarily affected. Seen from [the standpoint of] long-term benefits, the pains are worth enduring."[55]

Ironically enough, even as the Chinese leadership unleashed and encouraged the forces of the market in its march toward modernization and economic reform, at the same time, it arrested the full unfolding of some of the chief social processes that generally issue from marketization elsewhere. Thus, in China, in addition to the advancing affluence, rising levels of education, and embourgeoisement of one section of the working class that took place in many societies along with economic development—and quite markedly so in China's East Asian neighbors, South Korea, Japan, and Taiwan—this informalization of the urban economy represented a regression, not an ascent, for a substantial portion of the urban populace. Though one could label those newly jobless as members of a lower-class-in-formation, their situation was defined more by their status as *xiagang* workers than it was by some new class category. The overwhelming majority of them had been deprived of

---

52. Ibid.

53. *South China Morning Post* (Hong Kong), June 7, 1999.

54. *Jingji ribao* [Economic daily], April 27, 1998; Deng Baoshan, "Zhengfu, qiye, he xiagang zhigong zai zaijiuye gongcuozhong de cuoyong" [The role of government, enterprise, and laid-off staff and workers in reemployment work], *Zhongguo laodong* [Chinese Labor] (*ZGLD*) 3, 1999: 11; Zhu Rongji, "Zaijiuye gongcheng guanxi guoqi gaige chengbai" [The reemployment project relates to the success or failure of the reform of state enterprises], from *Jingji guanli wengao* [Drafts on economic management], in *Gongyun cankao ziliao* [Workers' movement reference materials] 3 (1998): 5; Dorothy J. Solinger, *States' Gains, Labor's Losses: China, France and Mexico Choose Global Liaisons, 1980–2000* (Ithaca, NY: Cornell University Press, 2009).

55. *Renmin ribao* [People's Daily], May 1, 1997, in *SWB* FE/2908, May 2, 1997, G/6.

formal education from having been compelled to quit school and join in the Cultural Revolution (including, for most, a lengthy stint in the countryside) over a decade or so after 1966, and therefore they lacked any skills beyond those elementary ones connected with the simple factory jobs they had lost. This group of people, chiefly of middle age, together and all at once fell onto a downward trajectory in their lifestyles and in their prospects.[56]

With the demise of the planned economy, economic forces played a critical role in changing Chinese society in many ways. For one thing, markets infringed on state institutions' old monopoly on shaping people's fates, so certainly some changes have been positive for many. There also was a diminution in the determining power over urbanites' lives of specific institutions such as the *danwei*.[57] But the move away from the state's planned economy, with its shunting aside of the former urban workforce, did not eventuate in any meaningful autonomy for what was probably most members of this contingent.[58] For their lives became constricted by the urgent need to scrape up a pittance to keep themselves and their families alive. The meager take of those at work around the year 2000 was, to a large extent, the result of the lack of any genuine demand-driven economic activity in the emerging labor market, at least insofar as the work done by—and the goods on offer from the hands of—the dislocated was concerned. This was the case because, given the immense proportions of those hit by the official program of enforced dismissals, plus the unspecialized nature of the labor the affected workers could supply, there could not be demand sufficient to forge a decent livelihood for the tens of millions made redundant, struggling to find buyers for their cheap wares and simple services.

So, the Chinese leadership fostered a novel style of economic growth and development, one entailing sacrificing and discarding the selfsame working class that once laid the foundation for the country's present rise to prosperity. In short, in the state's very rush to reform its municipal economy, most of the marketization's typical social concomitants were suppressed or halted for many, that is, for those as of the late 1990s and after, lamenting the loss of a former day where they had stood supreme—at least relative to other social groups—in the state's rhetoric and in its treatment.[59]

56. Mo Rong, "*Dui guoyou qiye zhigong xiagang yu zaijiuye wenti de renshi*" [Thoughts about state enterprises' staff and workers' layoffs and the question of reemployment] *ZGLD* 2 (1998): 12.

57. Lowell Dittmer and Lü Xiaobo, "Personal Politics in the Chinese Danwei Under Reform," *AS* 36, no. 3 (1996): 247–49; Barry Naughton, "Danwei: The Economic Foundations of a Unique Institution," in *Danwei: The Changing Chinese Workplace in Historical and Comparative Perspective*, eds. Xiaobo Lü and Elizabeth J. Perry (Armonk, NY: M.E. Sharpe, 1997), 169–82.

58. Ming-kwan Lee, "The Decline of Status in China's Transition from Socialism," *Hong Kong Journal of Sociology* 1 (2000): 72.

59. Ching Kwan Lee, "The Labor Politics of Market Socialism: Collective Inaction and Class Experiences Among State Workers in Guangzhou," *MC* 24, 1 (January 1998): 3–33; Ching Kwan Lee and Guobin Yang, eds., *Re-envisioning the Chinese Revolution: Politics and Poetics of Collec-*

What became of the old proletariat represented a fundamental and quite sudden reconstruction of the nature of the tie between the state and its former premier workforce. For more than forty years, the Chinese state and its elite laborers, the workers at the urban state-owned enterprises, enjoyed a relationship that was multifaceted, to be sure. But at its core, this tie embodied a strong dose of paternalistic protection, of succor, albeit one laced with surveillance. As is well-known, workers labored under a reign of "organized dependency,"[60] in which plant leaders could consider themselves caretakers—for the employees—but for the state as well, under whose commission managers controlled their charges. In prosaic terms, factory officials were there to administer the daily business of production and workers' welfare. But in a larger sense, they were joined with the Chinese state in acting as benefactor as well as guardian (if a very intrusive one).

All that changed in the space of just a few short years. Increasingly as the last century came to a close, the nature of this once often-benign connection turned sour. With the sudden surge in the shedding of state workers in the years after the Party's Third Plenum of its Fourteenth Party Congress in December 1993, when its heightened commitment to marketization was publicly enunciated—a move that had already seen a start in the late 1980s—the key component of the linkage between the state and this laboring segment of society became fear, or at least suspicion, on both sides. At the same time, many of the one-time intermediaries standing between these two players, the plant officials—especially those in failing firms—shed their pose of custodian and took on that of embezzler, thereby no longer serving either the central state (except insofar as they obeyed orders from above to push the workers from their plants) or their original worker-wards.

Thus, the more or less clear line of command and superintendence of old—according to which plant management acted toward labor as the agent of the center, which was its principal, directing production and disbursing benefits—was deflected, such that the three parties (state, enterprise administrators, and workers), once supposed allies, in some ways became mutually antagonistic. In the relation between state and this recast-turned lower portion of society, the state's moves became motivated primarily by its fear (though possibly also, at least for some among its staffers, by guilt), as it abandoned its prior roles, along with its prior proteges. At the same time, the workers, in turn, experienced despair mixed with fear and, in some cases, embitterment and daring (at least during the years of large-scale pro-

tive Memories in Reform China (Washington, DC: The Woodrow Wilson Center Press and Stanford: Stanford University Press, 2007); Feng Chen and Mengxiao Tang, "Labor Conflicts in China; Typologies and Their Implications," *AS* 53, no. 3 (2013): 559–83.

60. Walder, *Chinese Neo-Traditionalism.*

tests in 1998 to 2003). For many, their old bestowal of legitimacy upon the state dissolved, along with their prior posts.

That was the mid-term inter-echelon and inter-personal dynamic developing with the informalization of the urban economy around the year 2000, as the process transformed a crowd of once so-styled "masters" into one of paupers. The upshot was that the state and its rulers fell captive to an increasingly pronounced paradox in the trio of their then oft-stated aims— "reform, development, and stability." While the leaders strove to develop the economy through market reforms, they were compelled to balance a treacherous trade-off between their objectives: development, that is, growth and marketization, which meant massive discharges and the creation of a new crowd of the dispossessed, on the one hand, conflicted with a resultant and mounting social instability among those disenfranchised,[61] on the other. In the process, contestation occurred, but that was only one outcome. Often, as well, intimidation was evident among both parties—the state, in its at-once offering favors and funds to compensate the jobless, but also in battling and jailing protesters, on the one side, and many timorous workers, in retreating into a crushed quiescence, or else exhausting themselves with full-time income-seeking, on the other.

CONCLUSION

In the China of 2000—where rampant economic reforming and enterprise dismantling was decimating a great proportion of the old state sector and dispossessing the crowd it had sustained as its partner for decades—unemployment meant much more than being out of work on an individual level. Rather, it served as the symbol of a collective and sudden informalization of the urban economy, a reforging of a crowd once ennobled and proud, into a new crowd, one most commonly cowering and déclassé.

Thus, formal Chinese workers, dignified and advantaged for decades, became idle or informal ones in and after the late 1990s. In place of the miraculous world propagandized as occupied by the crowd of yore, one saw instead a grim and lackluster scene inhabited by undistinguished masses, those let go by their firms. In the altered social status hierarchy that evolved in Chinese cities, to be a laborer became lowly, not lordly, as it had been not so long before. There was, too, quite a transformed tie between the state and its one-time working class (the new crowd), a bond characterized much more by mutual fear and shame than by the original socialists' shared and

---

61. To borrow the term from Andreas, *Disenfranchised.*

cooperative mission of constructing, with and through their honored crowd, a more fair and egalitarian China.[62]

What of those *xiagang* staff and workers who managed to become *dibaohu*—those provided with an allowance by the *dibao* program—how have they fared? That is the subject of the two chapters that come next, one on the failures of management and the other on how these people struggle to survive. We will see that, with receipt of the *dibao*, the stance of at least some among them turned to some extent less directly hostile toward the state and rather more ambivalent.

---

62. Ibid. portrays that lost world.

Chapter Five

Dibao: Management and Missteps

The straits and distress of the laid-off workers denoted in the last chapter clearly called for some relief. In this chapter, I review what sort of aid the *dibao* really provided. This will entail a look at the administrative procedures and funding that comprise the *dibao* scheme in its actual, quotidian practices; the extra subsidies and benefits that are supposed to (at least are said to) accompany it; the exclusions of eligible individuals and households; and its prohibitive restrictions. I begin by recounting the ultimately futile frenzy of the campaign-like style of promoting the reemployment program that preceded it.

I pepper my exposition with quotations from interviews with recipients—from my own conversations in nine cities but mostly from Wuhan—and also from an edited volume of talks with beneficiaries in six cities in 2008 compiled by Chinese social policy researchers.[1] I will convey these people's words in a manner close to how they expressed themselves. I do not claim that the informants are representative of the *dibaohu* as a whole. My aim instead is to illustrate their issues by setting down views, opinions, and feelings one frequently encounters in interchange with these subjects. What comes across is the state's (and its most-local agents') inability to fulfill—or, put yet more starkly, even a near undoing of—most of the intended (or at least publicly announced) promises that the designers of the *dibao* initially put forth. The most effective effort was the one targeted at stability: the aim to shut up the poor.

---

1. Han Keqing, ed., *Zhongguo chengshi dibao fangtanlu* [Interviews with Minimum Livelihood Guarantee Recipients in Urban China] (Jinan: Shandong renmin chubanshe [Shandong people's publishing company], 2012).

CAMPAIGN-STYLE REEMPLOYMENT

When the layoffs first occurred, their victims were handled as if targets of a Chinese "political campaign." Certainly, most of what happened in the early post-layoff days differed in both style and content from full-fledged Maoist era "campaigns" (also called "mass movements").[2] The reemployment program's methods were neither characterized by tension and struggle, confessions and coercion as mass movements under Mao had been, nor did this movement focus on promoting the "progress of socialism," "socialist production," sociopolitical transformation, or "construction," as did many such upheavals of earlier times. But the take-off of the project to pacify retrenched workers beginning in 1998, which the *dibao* followed, did share with the *yundong* (运动, mass movement) some of its basic characteristics.[3]

Common features included most prominently the typical movement's "intensive mass mobilization of active commitment."[4] A prime instance was that still-employed staff members were required temporarily to set aside their regular work to focus on a decreed objective. And, like the mass campaign, this period saw "concentrated attack on a specific issue."[5] Other descriptions of mass campaigns fit as well: they are "'a type of policy implementation involving extraordinary mobilization of resources under political sponsorship' to achieve a specific policy target within a defined period of time.' . . . The Party today adopts campaigns to tackle weak implementation in important policy areas and to address problematic policy outcomes that could potentially undermine regime legitimacy and social stability."[6]

Starting in 1998 and into the early 2000s, conscious attention was demanded from offices of all kinds at the unit level and, on an individual scale, from officials in every manner of agency. An unexpected but telling example involved the chroniclers at a city's local gazetteer's workplace having been assigned four poverty-stricken, laid-off workers' families to visit regularly and to care for. The chroniclers' mission, no doubt like that

---

2. Sebastian Heilmann and Elizabeth J. Perry, eds., *Mao's Invisible Hand: The Political Foundations of Adaptive Governance in China* (Cambridge, MA: Harvard University Asia Center, 2011). See especially Elizabeth J. Perry, "From Mass Campaigns to Managed Campaigns: 'Constructing a New Socialist Countryside,'" in ibid., 32–35; and Gordon Bennett, *Yundong: Mass Campaigns in Chinese Communist Leadership* (China Research Monograph, No. 12) (Berkeley: Institute of East Asian Studies, University of California, Berkeley, 1976).

3. Kenneth Lieberthal, *Governing China: From Revolution Through Reform* (second edition) (New York: W.W. Norton & Co., 2003), 65–68. See also Xin Sun, "Campaign-Style Implementation and Affordable Housing Provision in China," *The China Journal*, no. 84 (July 2020): 76–101.

4. Bennett, *Yundong*, 18.

5. Lieberthal, *Governing China*, 65. See also Kristen E. Looney, *Mobilizing for Development: The Modernization of Rural East Asia* (Ithaca, NY: Cornell University Press, 2020).

6. Sun, "Campaign-Style," 76, 80–81 (the first part of the citation is a quotation from a source in *Public Administrative Review* 75 [2015]).

of state employees in units throughout urban China, was to bring gifts to the impoverished households at holidays and to search for jobs their members might be able to fill. One of the researchers took me with him to meet this unit's families in the summer of 1999. A household we visited consisted of a fifty-four-year-old man and his wife, also over fifty. Both had had jobs of administrative authority in a collectively owned asbestos plant, but let go, they were then being given just 150 yuan per month (about US$20) as basic living cash. The husband, too ill with kidney disease to go out to work, sat at home waiting for his pension, then six years away, while his wife worked twenty-six days a month cooking lunch for various workplaces at the rate of about 7 yuan, or less than US$1, per day. I wondered that day whether he would ever see his pension.[7]

Aside from activating all manner of staff to put aside their own work to administer to those cast off, municipal authorities set in place a vast array of arrangements designed to service the discharged; these activities resembled a crusade more than they did a simple drive to return those dismissed back to work. As Wang Shaoguang commented in early 2004, the central government installed a "total mobilization, launching hundreds of ten thousands of people to participate in a nationwide effort" to provide new situations for the new poor.[8] Wang, and also a news release in 2005,[9] trace the regime's adoption of "active employment policies" to the year 2002, following which, they observe, all financial, monetary, taxation, and industrial and commercial departments were to promote employment.

But in fact, this effort began earlier: already in 1998, local organs had flown into a furor of action to assist the jobless. Beginning in Wuhan in the summer of 1998 and for several years thereafter, my many interviews and site visits, arranged by the city, brought these orders to life. An official at a labor employment management bureau under the city's Bureau of Labor explained that the whole society and every official agency (including residential districts [streets], trade union branches, the Women's Federation, the Bureau of Labor, the chemical and machinery industries, relevant departments within enterprises, industrial and commercial organs, and tax offices) were charged with finding means of supporting the laid-off.[10] The tertiary sector planning

---

7. Interview, August 29, 1999, Wuhan.

8. Wang Shaoguang, "Shunying minxin de bianhua: cong caizheng zijin liuxiang zongguo zhengfu jinqi de zhengce tiaozheng" [A Change that complies with popular sentiments: a recent policy readjustment in the flow of financial funds toward the Chinese government], paper presented to the Center for Strategic and International Studies, Washington, DC, unpublished manuscript, January 16, 2004, 6.

9. "Xinwen zhongxin jiuye fuwu, peixun jianding laodong guanxi yu gongzi shehui baozhang zhengci cixun shuju fenxi dushu pindao" [News center employment service training appraisal, labor relations and wages, social security policy consultation, statistical analysis readers' frequency channel], May 11, 2005.

10. Interview, September 7, 1998.

and coordination office of the city's Planning Commission revealed that cadres' success in arranging laid-off people had become a target governing the assessment of each cadre's work. Concurrently, officials in government departments, pressured to locate jobs for the displaced, could find their careers affected if they failed at this chore.[11] Every enterprise and each department was to receive preferential treatment—such as reduced or waived fees and taxes—if its leaders hired the unemployed. Special "night markets" trading in cheap products, such as those I frequented (see Chapter Four), were set up throughout cities to allow the jobless to earn small bits of cash and were charged fees only for electricity and trash removal but were not made to pay rent for a space on the street. Neither were there any taxes on these petty businesses.[12]

Wuhan was said to have permitted as many as somewhere between 26,000 and 100,000 (both figures were bandied about) three-wheeled pedicabs to roam the avenues, picking up customers who were billed just a mere pittance (3 yuan for a short ride). Organs in the city designed so-called reemployment bases to train and hire dismissed personnel. Base types ranged widely: one was a "university instructing women in household work," established by the Women's Federation, the Labor Bureau, the trade unions, and every city district.[13] Leaders at the city's branch of the official trade union conveyed that they had collaborated with private firms to establish as many as thirty-seven bases, which, by September 2000, had placed 6,300 laid-off workers in work posts. The union also worked with the city's Labor Bureau to convene four large job fairs per year, which entailed communicating with over a thousand enterprises in a search for unfilled slots.[14]

Officials at the Wuhan Industrial and Commercial Federation regularly received lists from the city government and Labor Bureau of people with very low incomes who were to be supplied with positions in private firms.[15] In at least one of the city districts, Jianghan, the Women's Federation arranged for each of its thirteen subordinate streets, respectively, to develop a specialty, such as running a night market, selling flowers, knitting sweaters, making items for daily use, lettering signs, and so forth.[16] In another district, Qiaokou, the Women's Federation, in conjunction with the district labor department, held monthly meetings on the problems of the *xiagang*, as well as regular job fairs.[17]

11. Interview, September 9, 1998.
12. Interview, Wuhan Bureau of Statistics and Labor, September 7, 2000.
13. Interview at Wuhan Modern Household Work University, September 10, 2000, and at the Jianghan District base for household labor, September 12, 2000.
14. Interview, head of social security work in the city's trade union, September 13, 2000.
15. Interview, September 15, 2000, Wuhan.
16. Interview at the district headquarters, September 12, 2000.
17. Interview, September 12, 2000.

The city established a centralized official labor market, and each city district created one as well, where the *xiagang* could register for free. Such markets listed available jobs, maintained intercity computer connections about the state of the market elsewhere, held two job fairs each month, and provided one to three months of training per jobless person. Classes organized by these "markets" included ones in using computers, serving as nursemaids, repairing small appliances, styling hair, performing community service, driving cars, cooking, accounting, and marketing.[18] But the jobs actually on offer—washing dishes in restaurants, household labor, preparing food, sweeping floors—which often paid between 4 and 9 yuan per hour or 400 and 600 yuan per month—"can't support a livelihood," complained a man of age forty in a 2001 interview.[19]

As a piece typical of the times commanded at the close of a national work forum on reemployment, "We must concentrate force to develop reemployment posts, realize policies to support reemployment, increase investment in funds for reemployment, strengthen training, perform services for reemployment, and change people's concept of what employment is." All told, this statist mobilization to promote labor marketization and job placement was extensive, even totalistic. Given that it was this state itself, and its policies of modernization, global involvement, and removal of those workers whom decision makers viewed as obsolete, it is deeply paradoxical that that same state was at once engaging in essaying to resettle the sacked by diktat, even as it was attempting to insert its business into the market-based, capitalist world economy.[20] And it is critical to note that the nature of a campaign is that it is

---

18. Interview at the labor market, September 7, 2000.

19. Interview, October 29, 2001.

20. There was a similar rush of urgency at the start of 2016, when large-scale protests mounted with cutbacks in jobs in coal and steel (1.8 million jobs cut and talk of more than five million more to come. See Qi Yue, "Danyou di'er bo xiagangchao: xian lai suansuan chuqing 'jianghu qiye' yingxiang duoda" [Concern about the second wave of Layoffs, First calculate how great the influence of the "zombie factories" is], December 29, 2015, at http://m.wallstreetcn.com/node/228055 (accessed December 30, 2015)). The government pressured businesses to settle disputes and allocated billions of dollars for welfare and retraining. See Javier C. Hernandez, "More Protests by Labor Vex China's Rulers," *New York Times*, March 14, 2016, A1, A6. And in late 2019, following the Fourth Plenum of the Nineteenth Party Congress, the State Council produced "Guowuyuan guanyu jinyibu zuohao wen jiuye gongzuo de yijian" [Opinion on Progressively Doing Well the Work of Stabilizing Employment], Guofa [2019] 28 [State Council Issuance No. 28], December 13, 2019, http://www.gov.cn/zhengce /content/2019-12/24/content_5463595.htm (accessed December 25, 2019). This document came at a time of nationwide economic slowdown, high pork prices, and an ongoing and inconclusive trade war with the United States, and, consequently, a time when the leadership was notably concerned about the economy (see George Magnus, "Beijing's Delicate Balancing Act Relies on Job Creation," *Financial Times*, January 2, 2020, at https://www.ft.com/content/cfff7a9a-2262-11ea-b8a1-584213ee7b2b (accessed January 3, 2020). At that Plenum, "six stabilizes" were announced, the first of which was employment. That document had the same ring of all-hands-on-deck urgency, as did the period twenty years earlier, calling for strengthening financial support to enterprises, supporting enterprises' stabilizing of work posts, lowering fees for insurance, developing subsidies for on-the-job training, guiding enterprises to open internal markets, adjusting work times, using rotation, giving compensation for

usually short-lived; just as in previous periods, the mobilization that marked the reemployment *yundong* lasted a few years at best. Even as it petered out, fast on its heels, the *dibao* was to take its place.

OPERATING MECHANISMS AND MODALITIES

Administration, Funding of the *Dibao*

The regulations formalizing the *dibao* system called for setting the outlays locally in accord with the costs of the amount of food, clothing, and housing needed for minimal subsistence in a particular area. Designers of the program ordered local authorities to set the poverty line (i.e., the *dibao* norm, *dibao biaozhun*), since prices, the pattern of consumption, and the average income per capita vary by area, and also because it was the city that was to fund a sizable portion of the outlay.[21]

Originally, under a policy entitled "whoever's child it is should pay" [*shei jia haizi shei jia bao*, 谁 家 孩子 谁 家 保], enterprises were to put up the funds for the allowances for employees whose families had become indigent.[22] Yet this practice soon became unfeasible. For it was precisely those enterprises in financial distress whose staff was being dismissed, underpaid, or not paid at all. By the time of the announcement of the final *dibao* regulations in 1999, local financial departments, not firms, were to share responsibility for underwriting the program with the central government, at varying rates.[23]

Then the bureaus of civil affairs, labor, finance, auditing, personnel, statistics, and prices, along with the local branches of the trade union, were jointly to stipulate and, when deemed necessary (as in times of inflation, when a city's financial receipts have a good turn, or when the standard of living among the general population of a city has risen), hike up the local cut-off line.[24] Other departments were directed to perform other, related

layoffs and reimbursement for delayed wages, and creating more jobs. The big difference with the past was an emphasis on "high-quality employment," college graduates, and upgrading the industrial structure's optimization. See the official *China Daily* story laying this out at https://china.chinadaily .com.cn/a/202001/03/WS5e0f09daa31099ab995f5432.html (accessed January 3, 2020).

21. Athar Hussain, "Urban Poverty in China: Measurement, Patterns and Policies," Ms. (Geneva: International Labour Office, January 2003), 64–76; H. Wang, "Chengshi zuidi shenghuo baozhang zhiduzhong de zijin ji guanli" [Funds and Management in the Urban Minimum Livelihood Guarantee System], *Zhongguo minzheng* (*ZGMZ*) (Chinese civil affairs) 8 (1996): 34.

22. Wang, "Chengshi zuidi," 25.

23. Wang, Zhikun, "Chengshi jumin zuidi shenghuo baozhang: buru fazhihua guanli guidao" [Urban residents' minimum livelihood guarantee: Step into the orbit of legalized management], *ZGMZ* no. 11 (1999): 19.

24. Y. Lu, "Shishi zuidi shenghuo baozhang zhidu de sikao" [Reflections on implementing the minimum livelihood guarantee system], *ZGMZ* 4 (1998): 20; Wang, "Chengshi jumin," 18, 19.

functions (e.g., the education bureau had to make sure that the targets' children's miscellaneous school fees were not cut or canceled; medical departments were to do the same for medical fees). Most places also created a special leadership small group, located within the bureau of civil affairs, to take overall control.[25]

Each city's poverty line (*dibao* norm) was to be set below the local minimum wage and also lower than the benefits for unemployment insurance, supposedly to encourage employment. But, ironically, even a recipient's acquisition of a tiny increment in income through occasional labor could result in a drastic reduction in his/her household's *dibao* disbursement. An article in the civil affairs journal stated that, "The scientific determination of the norm mainly depends on four factors: residents' basic livelihood needs; a place's price level; the degree of development in the region; and that locality's financial ability to contribute to the program."

Thus, the financial situation of the city has a determining impact upon where the poverty line is set in that city; poorer urban jurisdictions set the standard low, to minimize the numbers for which they are responsible. Alternatively, cities with more revenue and where, often, the numbers of the poverty-stricken are fewer, peg the line at a higher level. Besides, larger cities tend to have higher living standards and prices as well as bigger budgets. While initially it was projected that the costs would be shared relatively equally between the central government and the localities, in practice, the portion born by localities has varied significantly, from places where the city pays out the bulk or even all of the allowances to other municipalities where essential, sizable assistance from the central government means that a locale bears almost no expenses, the variance a function of a municipality's economic strength.[26]

Within cities, variable ratios between the municipality and its districts are also locally defined.[27] To give one example, as of 1998, Wuhan divided up

25. Mao, Jiansheng, "Liguo limin de ningjuli gongcheng—Fan Baojun fubuzhang jiu chengshi jumin zuidi shenghuo baozhang zhidu jianshe hui benkan jizhe wen" [A cohesive project benefiting the nation and the people—Vice Minister Fan Baojun answers this journal's reporter's questions about the minimum livelihood guarantee system's construction], *ZGMZ*, 4 (1997): 5.

26. Z. Wang and H. Wang, "Luoshi chengshi jumin zuidi shenghuo baozhang zijin ying chuli hao wuge guanxi" [In order to implement urban residents' minimum livelihood guarantee funds we need to handle five relationships well], *ZGMZ*, 3 (1998): 18, 19; Hussain, "Urban Poverty," 70; Tang Jun. "The New Situation of Poverty and Antipoverty," in *2002 nian: Zhongguo shehui xingshi yu yuce (shehui lanpishu)* [2002: Analysis and Forecast of China's Social Situation (social blue book)], edited by Ru Xin, Lu Xueyi, Li Peilin, et al., January 1, 2002. [FBIS Translated Text]. Hussain stated that only twenty-one of the thirty-one provincial-level units were then contributing toward the cost of the *dibao*. But Tang Jun's article, published in the same year, states that, "With the exception of Beijing, Shanghai, Shandong, Jiangsu, Zhejiang, Fujian, and Guangdong, all the other provinces got the central government's financial subsidies."

27. N. a., "Jianli zuidi shenghuo baozhang zhidu de jige wenti" [Several issues in establishing the minimum livelihood guarantee system] *ZGMZ* 9 (1996): 14.

responsibilities such that each district got half its funds from the city government and had to supply the other half itself; in neighboring Hubei municipalities, such as Xiangfan, Shiyan, and Huangshi, the ratios of city-level to
district-level contributions were 6:4, 7:3, and 3:2, respectively.[28]

In practice, the process of underwriting the *dibao* at the municipal level
begins with the City Finance Bureau's annual determination of how much
of the municipal budget to allocate to that city's Bureau of Civil Affairs; in
2008, this amount was in the range of 5 to 10 percent of the city's total expenditure.[29] Civil Affairs then resolves how much of its total allotment to accord
to the *dibao*. In the next step, the district (*qu*, 区) civil affairs bureau, just
below the administrative level of the city, decides which applicants will be
given the allowance and how much each can receive, based on the discretion
of district officials.[30] While district administrators approve the final selection
of recipients, they do so on the basis of recommendations from community
officers who live among and often know the potential recipients and who
have a rough idea of their circumstances. The district also is the authority
that sets the limits on how much each of its subordinate streets (*jiedao*, 街道)
and, below that, each community (*shequ*, 社区), obtains for the individual
"targets" (*duixiang*, 对象) it approves. Indirectly, the district likely sets a ceiling as to how many recipients each street, and perhaps even each community,
will accommodate.[31]

Grassroots cadres control the flow of information to residents about new
policies and modifications of old ones, and so they are well-positioned to
direct funds not necessarily to the poorest but to people with whom they are
close, with whom they sympathize, or whom they find fearsome.[32] Another
deviation from policy is those city governments whose administrative capability and resources are in short supply dole out a quantity of money for
the *dibao* purely as a function of the amount of resources the city's finan-

---

28. Meng, Jiawu, and Tan Zhilin, "Wuhan chengshi zuidi shenghuo baozhang zhidu de sige
tedian" [Four characteristics of Wuhan city's minimum livelihood guarantee system], *ZGMZ* no.
7 (1996), 19; Zhang, L., "Quanmian tuijin guifan guanli—Hubeisheng jianli chengshi jumin zuidi
shenghuo baozhang zhidu de jingyan" [Fully promote standardized management—Hubei province's
experience in establishing urban residents' minimum livelihood guarantee system], *ZGMZ* 9 (1998),
24. The Wuhan ratio was set in 1996 when the program began in that city. Figures for the other cities
are in ibid. Zhang was then director of the Hubei provincial Department of Civil Affairs.

29. Interview, Professor Ding Jianding of Central China University of Science and Technology,
August 30, 2008.

30. Sophie Fenghua Zhou, "Selectivity, Welfare Stigma, and the Take-up of Social Welfare—How
Do Chinese People Manage Welfare Stigma," prepared for "Social Welfare Development and Governance Transformation in East Asia," May 17 and 18, 2012, Central China Normal University in Wuhan, China, sponsored by the Harvard-Yenching Institute and the Central China Normal University.

31. Chen Honglin, Wong Yu-cheung, Zeng Qun, and Juha Hamalainen, "Trapped in Poverty?
A Study of the *Dibao* Programme in Shanghai," *China Journal of Social Work* (*CJSW*) 6, no. 3
(2013): 333.

32. Ibid., 331.

cial officers decide the city can bear. Unfortunately for potential recipients, leaders with the power to determine that sum tend to rank the *dibao* as a low priority expenditure.[33]

Variation marks local implementation, as my 2010 interviews in two similar cities illustrated. Xiantao and Qianjiang, both at the subprefectural level in Hubei Province with roughly the same population (in 2010, Xiantao had a population of 1.175 million; Qianjiang's was 1.03 million), handled the *dibao* differently. Professor Ding Jianding, a specialist on the program, judged that Qianjiang had sufficient revenues for underwriting the policy. But its decision makers preferred to use the funds to construct tall buildings and to grace the city with modern facilities;[34] Xiantao, to the contrary, was more generous to its poor, disbursing the allowance not only in relation to a family's income (as policy dictates) but also with consideration to any physical/health-related difficulties its members were experiencing.

In Xiantao in 2010, the urban *dibao* was apportioned 0.25 percent of GDP and 2.5 percent of the city's expenditure, and recipients were, on average, accorded an amount near 30 percent of the city's average disposable income,[35] all higher than the national average. That year, the urban *dibao* nationally represented just 0.127 percent of China's total GDP and 0.58 percent of all government expenditures. Also, nationwide, the urban *dibao* amounted to just 15.8 percent of average urban disposable income.[36] Professor Ding had an explanation for Xiantao's largesse: the city's revenue had expanded quickly in the previous years while its price level had also increased, forcing residents to spend more on their basic subsistence.[37] So not just poor families' need but also city politicians' policy preferences and the state of local economies play roles in setting assistance expenditures.

Additional Subsidies?

Beyond the *dibao* allowance itself, recipients are alleged to be eligible for a range of attached "preferential policies" (*youhui zhengce*, 优惠 政策), or special benefits.[38] In a 2007 interview, the manager of the *dibao* program in the Wuhan Civil Affairs Bureau proudly listed the twelve preferential

---

33. Joe C. B. Leung and Yuebin Xu, *China's Social Welfare* (Cambridge, UK and Malden, MA: Polity Press, 2015), 88.
34. Interview, Wuhan, July 11, 2010.
35. Interview, Xiantao, July 8, 2010, street *dibao* office.
36. See Tables 2.1 and 2.4.
37. Interview, Wuhan, July 11, 2010.
38. Yao Jianping, "Zhongguo chengshi zuidi shenghuo baozhang biaozhun shuiping fenxi" [An Analysis of the Level of Minimum Livelihood Standard in Urban China], *Keji yu shehui* [Technology and society], no. 11 (2012): 62 claims that "the reason for welfare dependency is the benefits attached to it" and that "more than 30 kinds of fees are reduced or eliminated."

benefits supposedly accruing to *dibaohu* in the city (two more than Beijing offered, he boasted). Perks included an exemption from paying miscellaneous educational fees and grants to help with ordinary school fees; reduction in in-patient costs in hospitals and waiver of registration for outpatients; rental assistance for state-owned housing; funds for food and water; home-heating fuel; and so on.[39]

Alas, interviews with purported beneficiaries revealed that these subsidies were far from always extended. The chief problem was that realizing the promise of these policies required that relevant city departments either relinquish or at least suffer cutbacks in the fees they were accustomed to collecting for providing the services. Besides, bureau managers already resented having to watch as their old control over prices for goods and services fell away with the progress of marketization, diminishing their revenues in a different way.[40]

Still, without citing any evidence, many sources claim that those angling to be accepted onto the *dibao* rolls—with the piddling allowances they would thereby acquire—are really hoping not so much to pocket the funds themselves as to obtain these extra subsidies. For instance, in a 2012 interview at the Shanghai Academy of Social Sciences, an interlocutor told me that, "People want the related benefits that go with the *dibao*, so they lie about their income to make themselves appear qualified."[41] Other sources, however, disclosed that, in fact, there are significant slips in these favors' distribution. One researcher explained that, "Though some local governments have provided program recipients with special social assistance, such as medical aid, educational subsidies, and housing allowance support, these are not incorporated . . . into the *dibao*. . . . None [of the proclaimed benefits] . . . has been established nationwide and the coverage is limited."[42] Adding more specificity to this view, the Asian Development Bank's 2012 three-city survey of some 2,800 *dibaohu* found that only 34 percent got educational aid; 22 percent were helped with housing; and just 9 percent received assistance with medical costs.[43] Another investigation found that only about half of those

---

39. Interview, Wuhan, August 28, 2007; Yang Zongchuan and Zhang Qilin, "Wuhanshi chengshi jumin zuidi shenghuo baozhang zhidu shishi zhuangkuang de diaocha fenxi" [Analysis of an investigation of the implementation of Wuhan's urban residents' minimum livelihood guarantee system], *Jingji pinglun* [Economic review no. 4 (1999): 100.

40. Li Chunyan and Ding Jianding, "Wuhanshi dibao guanlizhong cunzai de wenti yu gaijin duice fenxi-yi Wuchangqu weili" [Existing problems and analysis of measures for improvement in Wuhan's *dibao* management: Wuchang District as an example], *Changjiang luntan* [Yangtze Forum] 1, no. 76 (2006): 27–28.

41. Interview, June 28, 2013.

42. King-lun Ngok, "Social Assistance Policy and Its Impact on Social Development in China: The Case of the Minimum Living Standard Scheme (MLSS), *CJSW* 3, no. 1 (2010): 49.

43. Qin Gao, *Welfare, Work, and Poverty: Social Assistance in China* (New York: Oxford University Press, 2017), 7–8.

eligible were collecting one or more forms of supplementary assistance. And Jennifer Pan, whose fieldwork was undertaken in late 2012 and early 2013, came up with a similar finding, concluding that, "Few ad hoc benefits are provided to all *dibao* households, and most are limited in quantity."[44]

The situation appears not to have improved with time. As late as 2018, two scholars advised that, "China's various supplementary measures and services—such as job training and medical service aid—are *not yet* [emphasis added] perfected or spread; the majority of districts stagnate in the stage of just issuing funds. The other affiliated policies have either not yet been developed fully or their effect is sub-optimal."[45] Given the ongoing difficulties in implementing this effort, the following quotations from deprived *dibaohu*, even if from over a decade ago, can likely still serve to illustrate the situation for many. The first came from a very typical poor thirty-seven-year-old woman living in Chaoyang City in the frigid northeast province of Liaoning (Q stands for Questioner; R for Respondent):

Q: How much are your monthly expenses?

R: Haven't calculated concretely, but we spend almost all that's earned.

Q: Including rice, noodles, grains, oil, salt, soy, and vinegar, plus daily necessities, like for washing-clothes powder, what do you spend?

R: A lot, each month we need a bag of rice and one of noodles, that's 150 yuan! [a yuan is a Chinese dollar, equal at the time to about US$0.12] oil, salt, etc., probably about 20 or 30 yuan, each month use two packs of laundry soap, several yuan.

Q: Do you normally eat meat; how many eggs/month?

R: Very rarely eat meat, just once last month, just over a *jin* [a bit more than a pound], about 15 yuan, eat more eggs than meat, but mostly give the eggs to the kids, we eat them very little.

Q: Your rent?

R: 180 yuan, our *dibao* isn't even enough for that.

Q: When you cook, what do you usually use?

R: We use coal.

Q: And how much do you spend on that per month?

---

44. Jennifer Pan, "Buying Inertia: Preempting Social Disorder with Selective Welfare Provision in Urban China," PhD dissertation, Harvard University, 2015, 32.

45. Feng Jie and Zheng Hong, "'Yinfa langchao' shiyuxia chengshi 'dibao' de kunjing ji fazhan lujing" [On the Dilemma and Development of 'Minimum Livelihood Guarantee System' in Urban Areas in View of the 'Grey-hair Wave'], *Guangxi shifan xueyuan xuebao* [Journal of Guangxi Teachers Education University] 39, no. 5 (September 2018): 131.

R: Don't know exactly; we buy some coal and use it for two to three months, that's 400 or 500 yuan, so about 100 yuan per month.

Q: Do you have a subsidy for warmth?

R: We got it last year, but only 100 yuan; they said our one-story building gets only a small amount of coal; basically, it's not enough, and don't know if we'll get it this year.

Q: Any other subsidies?

R: No.

Q: Water?

R: Seems we do, but I'm not clear.

Q: About how much help with school fees per month?

R: For the girl, because she's in junior high, about 100-plus yuan per month; son is in primary school, each day he comes home for lunch, several 10 yuan is enough; but the school always makes them pay for this and that, it's just arbitrarily collecting fees.

Q: About how much do you spend on medicine per month?

R: Usually he [her ill husband] doesn't take medicine, when it's unbearable he buys some pain medication, his mother continuously takes it; this is the biggest expense, in a month at least 60 or 70 yuan—and it's not even good medicine.[46]

Even in Xuanwu District, Beijing, where the *dibao* allotments are higher than in most other cities, a Ms. Li, aged forty-three, related her situation:

Q: What are your expenses?

R: Mainly it's medicine, how much do I spend on it each month? About 100-plus yuan, 200 yuan. We two get 690 yuan from the *dibao*, so about 490 is left, let's say 500 is left, but then we have to scoop out cash for rent, water fees, electrical fees, fuel, not mentioning other things; as to the phone—we don't dare use it—monthly limit is 20 yuan. So our daily expenses come to more than 100 yuan [per month]. You save a little water, in a home like ours, you have to turn on the light or basically no way to entertain anyone.[47]

All this suggests that extra subsidies are not reaching her, or certainly not in an adequate amount.

In Lanzhou in 2010, when I was fortunate on one occasion to speak with informants without community officials sitting in, I encountered a tense and

---

46. Han, *Zhongguo chengshi*, 202–03.
47. Ibid., 79.

easily exasperated thirty-nine-year-old man who had contracted liver disease the year before, the father of a ten-year-old girl. He had worked in a large state steel firm for ten years but had lost his place when the firm went into bankruptcy because of "the system," in his words. He had been given the *dibao* earlier that year, having first tried to survive on part-time work for eight years. His daughter was studying English once a week at the cost of 550 yuan per semester; he was getting no subsidy for her schooling. Thinking they might be eligible for a benefit, I urged him to look into the possibility. But, he railed, making no effort to conceal his frustration: "Too complicated to ask for school subsidies; I've already spent a month applying for this [referring to the *dibao*]," throwing up his hands in vexation.[48] His sense of aggravation recalls the plight of welfare-takers in the United States, as characterized by Frances Fox Piven and Richard A. Cloward in their classic study, *Regulating the Poor.* There they detail how "applicants . . . had to prove their pauper status repeatedly . . . by completing elaborate forms, providing . . . documentation," while their neighbors and relatives were compelled to undergo all manner of interrogation as to the applicant's situation.[49]

Commenting on such complaints from recipients, an apparently jaded and unsympathetic thirty-five-year-old civil affairs street cadre in Xuanwu pontificated in response to queries:

Q: Are there people who come to see you who say, "ai-ya, this money is too little?"

R: Yes, there are; they're all of working age with labor ability, the majority are the type who stir up trouble. They have labor ability but don't go to work, have money, say this isn't enough, that isn't enough.

Q: What do you think is their mentality?

R: It's clear that their psychology isn't too healthy, possibly hostile toward the government, in a dissatisfied mood, unbalanced; they see that other people are doing well and they're not, they're angry, but they're not trying, they just blame their own mistakes on other people or blame the government, feel it should be the government gives you money and I get money, you aid me, this is how it should be; I'm miserable all because of what you've done.

Q: Isn't the *dibao* the people's right [*quanyi*, 权益]?

---

48. Interview, July 13, 2010, Lanzhou.
49. Frances Fox Piven and Richard A. Cloward, *Regulating the Poor: The Functions of Public Welfare* (updated edition) (New York: Vintage Books, 1993), 154–55. For an almost identical set of procedures in China when soliciting the *dibao,* see Jennifer Pan, "*Welfare for Autocrats: How Social Assistance in China Cares for its Rulers* (New York: Oxford University Press, 2020), 82–83; Dorothy J. Solinger, "The Urban Dibao: Guarantee for Minimum Livelihood or for Minimal Turmoil?" in *Marginalization in Urban China: Comparative Perspectives*, eds. Fulong Wu and Chris Webster, 253–77 (Houndmills, Basingstoke: Palgrave/Macmillan, 2010).

R: Yes, but it's just to protect their basic livelihood. But they say: "I have to pay housing fees, water, and electrical fees, have to pay for this, pay for that, I have to see a doctor, etc. etc. So this money is insufficient."[50]

Here again is evidence of recipients not being accorded the extra benefits meant to accompany the *dibao*.

In a Lanzhou street office, the remarks of a cadre also highlighted the lack of extra subsidies, if putting it much more solicitously:

Q: Do you feel anything should be improved?

R: Give them more preferential policies, like education, water and electricity, supply warmth, reduce or waive fees, give them cheap rental housing.[51]

Consider educational and medical benefits. In 2008, a disabled father of two in Wuhan fretted about the family's inability to finance his nine-month-old child's kindergarten: "Even going to kindergarten is something we can't afford—it's 400 to 500 yuan per month. But if he doesn't go, his contacts with other people and with society will be narrow, this can damage his personality, making him become introverted, not lively, and his ability to study may be influenced."[52]

At the higher end, another parent agonized over his daughter's inability to attend senior high, which, like kindergarten (and unlike the nine years of compulsory education), is not free. In this family, the man, laid off from an electrical factory, had lost his labor ability because of a stroke and had no way to work while the mother had diabetes. Their little bit of savings was all used up, likely on medical treatments. "Now our greatest worry is our little daughter, she's just fifteen, and immediately must go on to high school. Where's the money to pay for her schooling?" he lamented.[53]

As late as 2013, the issue of financial want also plagued even parents of children at middle school, whose education was supposed to be publicly funded. A Shanghai mother of a 10-year-old son spoke of the free schoolbooks and uniforms they had received as *dibao* beneficiaries but went on to complain: "He has no outside-school tutor, even though having one is common for the other students. But it's too expensive. And for lack of funds, he couldn't participate in a summer outing costing 100 yuan."[54] The issue did not disappear. In 2014, Haomiao Zhang found that many of her interview

50. Han, *Zhongguo chengshi*, 323–24.
51. Ibid., 386.
52. Home interview, late August 2008, Wuhan.
53. Interview, July 21, 2009, Wuhan.
54. Interview, June 27, 2013, Shanghai.

subjects in Chengdu had gotten no educational assistance.[55] And even in mid-2018, Yang Lixiong deemed it still appropriate to pronounce the following in a meeting at the United Nations: "The state should [the word "should" implies that this is something the state is not doing] provide educational assistance to students in the compulsory educational attendance stage who are members of families covered by *dibao*."[56]

Turning to medical assistance, in 1998, when the government launched the Urban Employee Basic Medical Insurance plan, 420 million urban residents who were not formally employed were left without insurance.[57] This situation was partially addressed in a new program set up in 2009, the Urban Residents' Basic Medical Insurance, which, as of 2013, serviced 300 million urban residents.[58] Its features included voluntary participation, a minimum local government contribution of 40 yuan per person per year as of 2012, coverage mainly for major illnesses requiring in-patient treatment, and a low level of reimbursement.[59] The National Development and Reform Commission's 2016 annual report proclaimed that the government subsidy for medical insurance (for the premium) had been increased that year from 380 yuan per person per year up to 420 yuan (approximately US$55 to $60 at that time); it also noted that the government subsidy for basic public health services had been increased to 45 yuan per capita per annum, a sum equivalent to merely about US$7 to $8.[60]

Despite this national regulation, individual cities make their own determinations for the rates. For instance, in 2016, Tianjin raised its adult premium per capita rates from 760, 990, and 1,290 yuan for varying levels of treatment

55. Haomiao Zhang, "The Meaning of Social Assistance for Women Recipients in China," *Asian Women* 32, no. 1 (2016): 53–75.

56. Yang Lixiong, "The Social Assistance Reform in China; Towards a Fair and Inclusive Social Safety Net," Prepared for "Addressing Inequalities and Challenges to Social Inclusion through Fiscal, Wage and Social Protection Policies," United Nations Headquarters, New York, June 25–27, 2018 (unpaginated), https://www.un.org/development/desa/dspd/wp-content/uploads/sites/22/2018/06/The-Social-Assistance-Reform-in-China.pdf.

57. Hong Liu and Zhong Zhao, "Impact of China's Urban Resident Basic Medical Insurance on Health Care Utilization and Expenditure," IZA DP No. 6768, Forschungsinstitut zur Zukunft der Arbeit [Research Institute to Study the Future of Labor], Bonn, Germany (July 2012): 3–4.

58. Qin Gao, Sui Yang, Yalu Zhang, and Shi Li, "Three Worlds of the Chinese Welfare State: Do Health and Education Change the Picture?" Paper prepared for the IARIW 33rd General Conference, Rotterdam, the Netherlands, August 24–30, 2014; Leung and Xu, *China's Social Welfare*, 83–84.

59. Gang Chen and Xiao Yan, "Demand for Voluntary Basic Medical Insurance in Urban China: Panel Evidence from the Urban Resident Basic Medical Insurance Scheme," *Health Policy and Planning* 27, no. 8 (December 2012): 658–68, https://doi.org/10.1093/heapol/czs014.

60. National Development and Reform Commission, "Report on the Implementation of the 2016 Plan for National Economic and Social Development and on the 2017 Draft Plan for National Economic and Social Development," delivered at the Fifth Session of the Twelfth National People's Congress, March 5, 2017, 23. The subsidy for basic public health services helps with such activities as immunizations (email from Xian Huang, December 6, 2019).

respectively, per annum to 850, 1,080, and 1,380 yuan per capita. This meant that the individual premium payment in that city rose from 90, 320, and 620 yuan per annum to 120, 350, and 650 yuan, with the city government's subsidy increasing from 670 yuan up to 730 yuan per person per annum, according to the official notice, an amount much above the national rate but still quite low (around US$96).[61] So, for people living hand-to-mouth, these sums—regardless of the subsidies—were prohibitive.

And even after the government had introduced these increments in the subsidies for non-formally employed individuals, and while the reimbursement rate for employees' in-patient treatment averaged 70 to 80 percent of the bill, for residents without formal jobs, reimbursement was just 50 to 60 percent of the cost.[62] Perhaps most critically, patients were required to lay out the total fee for their treatment ahead of the procedure, to be recompensed later. But the full cost was certainly well above the resources of the poor. Being permitted to put down just a copayment initially instead would possibly have been affordable.[63]

In interviews, respondent after respondent bemoaned his or her inability to manage medical costs, either being driven into deeper poverty by trying, taking cheap and inferior medications, or simply not seeing doctors at all. Indeed, homes in which the chronically diseased or disabled lay prone on a bed day and night, bereft of any relief, were frequently encountered. In one home beset by medical problems whose treatment costs were far beyond the family's means, twin nineteen-year-old sons had some media training but, without any connections, "basically can't find work that fits their specialty." To raise the money for their education, their mother explained, "I and their father worked day and night, a year ago. We both got so worn out we had to go to the hospital. But as soon as we got in, we got right out; it was too expensive, there was nowhere we could afford to go."

Children, too, are afflicted and perforce left medically unattended to. In one family, a twenty-two-year-old son was born blind and had never worked, but, according to his father, he had no way to acquire entree into a work unit for the disabled (not stated but, probably, they had no personal connections to achieve this). In a household that a divorced wife had abandoned, a fifty-nine-year-old husband was compelled to stay at home to minister to his twenty-six-year-old son, born with no upper limbs or left leg. Variously, but

61. "Guanyu 2016 niandu jumin jiben yiliao baoxian chouzi biaozhun tiaozheng" [On adjusting the norm for the 2016 residents' basic medical insurance premium], http://www.cpic.com.cn/c/2018 -04-19/1425447.shtml, accessed December 9, 2019.

62. Qin Gao, Sui Yang, Yalu Zhang, and Shi Li, "The Divided Chinese Welfare System: Do Health and Education Change the Picture?" *Social Policy & Society* 17, no. 2 (2018): 231.

63. Qin Zhou, Gordon G. Liu, Yankun Sun, and Sam A. Vortherms, "The Impact of Health Insurance Cost-Sharing Method on Healthcare Utilization in China," *CJSW* 9, nos. 1–3 (2016): 38–61.

similarly pitiful, in a third, the medical needs of a mentally disabled daughter, then nineteen, had devoured the family's entire savings.[64]

These cases illustrate that even households fortunate enough to be given the *dibao* remain mortally in need of extra assistance beyond the mere cash allotment the guarantee provides. Clearly, many people who live on the *dibao* are not, in addition, accorded extra subsidies. But how good is the scheme even at reaching appropriate recipients?

Quotas

The slogan "*ying bao jin bao*" (应保 尽保, as much as possible guarantee the allowance for all who deserve it) was purportedly the operative order about dispensing the *dibao* beginning in 2001. In point of fact, however, multiple sources have confirmed that, rather, a train of quotas beginning in Beijing is passed down the hierarchy, with decisions reached on restrictions and upper limits at every administrative level. This is not openly announced, and so it has been surrounded with some speculation. A 2013 study surmised that, "It is likely that there is a budget for the program, and that officials cannot accommodate more applicants than the budget allows. There's suspicion that there's an undisclosed ceiling on *dibao* payments."[65] When asked, community cadres managing the *dibao* routinely denied that they were working under quotas.

But the process of setting limits was already implicitly revealed in a 2005 policy paper, which read that, "We have to use insufficient funds to set the numbers of people [who will get cash]; there's a manmade control of the *dibao* numbers."[66] The statement implied that, in practice, it is predetermined shares at least as much as it is need that regulates who become recipients. Relatedly, in 2008, Professor Ding affirmed that the city Civil Affairs Bureau first calculates how many recipients it has decided that the city should have. Next, the bureau wrangles with its peer urban bureaus, for instance, arguing that increases in prices influence people's livelihood and thus affect stability and, in this way, presses for a rise in the threshold line or for funds to cover more applicants.[67]

---

64. Interviews, Wuhan, August 2007.
65. Chen, Wong, Zeng, and Hamalainen, "Trapped," 333.
66. Hong Dayong, "Chengshi jumin zuidi shenghuo baozhang zhidu de zuixin jinzhan" [Recent progress in the minimum livelihood system], in Hong Dayong, *Zhongguo de chengshi pinkun yu zuidi shenghuo baozhang* [Poverty and the Minimum Livelihood Standard Assistance Policy in Urban China], Disan zhang [Chapter Three] (Beijing: Zhongguo shehui kexueyuan, shehui zhengce zhongxin [Social Policy Research Center, Chinese Academy of Social Sciences], 2005) http://www.chinasocialpolicy.org/Paper_Show.asp?Paper_ID=38, accessed August 2007.
67. Interview, August 30, 2008, Wuhan.

Another five years on, the same evidence was offered by Liu Xitang, deputy general director of the Department of Social Assistance at the Ministry of Civil Affairs, when he acknowledged that, indeed, quotas do exist in the allocation of the *dibao*. He specified that local governments place caps on the number of citizens who can obtain the grant, as follows: "The local *dibao* norm is set in direct relation to a locality's funds. A lot of [city] departments together decide on how much money to give to the *dibao*. All the bureaus [in the city government] debate about this. Finally, the city leaders decide [on a level of outlay for the city's *dibao*]."[68]

Besides what these two informants revealed, in 2012, the Ministry of Finance issued an order stating that upper-level finance departments were to send a quota for using subsidy funds to the finance department one level down the hierarchy. Following that, each of the thirty-one provincial finance offices nationwide was to set a ceiling for the number of *dibaohu* who could be beneficiaries in its jurisdiction.[69] There is grassroots evidence that the directive held in practice: In 2016, Ben Westmore, an investigator at the Organization for Economic Cooperation and Development (OECD), learned during fieldwork in Inner Mongolia, Guangdong, and Beijing that, "The county [in cities, the city district] government often determines a quota of *dibao* payments that can be made based on available funding. This quota is then allocated across townships in the county [or, in cities, by districts to street offices], before the township [street] government allocates its quota across local villages [in cities, across communities]." Perhaps this quota system is a reason why a full three-quarters of eligible urban households in Gansu province did not receive the *dibao* in 2014.[70]

Taken altogether, these various sources provide a firm foundation for accepting that there are quotas—despite denials from my *dibao*-managing local interlocutors. These limits must surely cut into allocators' ability to observe the directive to "*ying bao jin bao*."

Exclusions and Prohibitions

Not just quotas restrict the delivery of the *dibao* to all the destitute. Jennifer Pan advances an argument that eligible families may fail to be granted the *dibao* because funds are reserved for people whom officials believe are potential troublemakers, such as individuals recently released from prison.[71]

---

68. Interview, September 9, 2013, Beijing.
69. Caizheng bu, minzhengbu tongzhi, "Guanyu yinfa."
70. Ben Westmore, "Do Government Transfers Reduce Poverty in China? Micro Evidence from Five Regions," OECD Economics Department Working Papers no. 1415 (Paris: OECD Publishing, 2017), 7, 15.
71. Pan, *Welfare for Autocrats.*

There are also purposive constraints placed on the disbursements. As two scholars of the *dibao* wrote more than a decade ago:

> The more a place's economic situation isn't good and its financial ability is weak, the more people there will be who fit the qualifications for the *dibao*. Then all the more the present social security system, like pensions, medical insurance, assisting the poor, etc. must be covered by local finance. This makes the local government hard pressed for money . . . and finally must lead to the locality producing some "local policies," making those who deserve to get the *dibao* unable to get it.[72]

Such "local policies" (*difang zhengci*, 地方 政策) include prohibitions commonly found in cities as of 2006 and thereafter. These prevent households, however poor, from getting the *dibao* if their members engage in any one of eighteen sorts of forbidden behavior, including possessing or even using a motorized vehicle; purchasing a refrigerator; having recently obtained air conditioning or a computer; spending more than fifteen yuan per month on electrical fees or over forty yuan on phone fees; owning a color television; having a family member who uses a cell phone or other hand-held communication device (even if having acquired it as a gift or a loan); or having a member at work outside the city whose income is hard to verify.[73] An indigent resident, one forty-two-year-old male recipient in Chongqing, remarked:

> And what if your relative sends you a television, what's it worth? Now they calculate the amount of money [they think it cost], but it was sent to you and you didn't buy it? If you bought it and you're on the *dibao*, what money would you use to buy it? Can't have a drinking water machine! Can't use the air conditioner! The microwave! What if you want to buy a microwave, feeling you can economize [on electricity], it's not permitted, the *dibao*'s limits don't allow you to use it, can't turn on the air conditioner [but then] if you get heatstroke and see a doctor, you'll use up all your money, what can you do![74]

Also forbidden is arranging for one's children to select their own schools, enrolling them in special classes for study or training, or arranging for them

---

72. Zhang Shifei and Tang Jun, "Chengxiang zuidi shenghuo baozhang zhidu jiben xingcheng" [Urban and rural minimum livelihood guarantee system has basically taken form], in *2008 nian: Zhongguo shehui xingshi fenxi yu yuce* [2008: Analysis and forecast of China's social situation], eds. Ru Xin, Lu Xueyi, and Li Peilin (Beijing: Social Sciences Academic Press, 2008), 62.

73. "Zhongguo chengshi jumin zuidi shenghuo baozhang biaozhun de xiangguan fenxi, jingji qita xiangguan lunwen" [Relevant analysis of Chinese urban residents' dibao norm; economic and other related treatises] ("Zhongguo chengshi"), http://www.ynexam.cn/html/jingjixue/jingjixiangguan/2006/1105/zhonggochengshijimin . . ., accessed August 18, 2007.

74. Han, *Zhongguo chengshi*, 411.

to have a foreigner as a tutor.[75] Grantees like this mother of a sixteen-year-old boy took these guidelines seriously:

> This year his grades qualify him to transfer to the Number Three Senior High School, a provincial-level "keypoint" institution. But I don't have the money, and secondly, if it's discovered that there's a child in the family who transferred to a "keypoint" high school, our *dibao* qualification would be eliminated. We can't take this risk. He really wants to study in that school, but he knows the family's conditions, so he doesn't demand it of me; I feel I have really let my son down.

Another way cadres restrict the outlays concerns recipients' going to work. Several Wuhan interviewees found their families' *dibao* funds reduced or even altogether cut off when a member took on some wage-earning work. In one representative case, the wife in a family of three bravely reflected that the following: "The family has one person working, so our subsidy was lowered a lot. We're not thinking of arguing about it, we all are very submissive people, so we don't think of haggling over money. If you give us 200-plus yuan [per month], it still can be of use." Speaking to another woman, aged thirty-four, the questioner pointed out that the woman's husband was out of the city doing odd jobs (*dagong*, 打工) and that she was managing a stall. He then inquired whether the family's monthly *dibao* allowance was, therefore, decreased. "Yes," she replied and continued: "It's a no-way affair [*mei banfa de shiqing*, 没办法的事情]. In my stall in one month, I can earn only so much money, his work also isn't stable, but now our work is calculated into our income, and then they lower our allowance. But this income fluctuates, sometimes we have it and sometimes we don't, only relying on the *dibao*, that little money, means that basically there's no way to live."

From a cadre's perspective, recipients concoct their ways to transgress these rulings: "They find a hole in the policy, in so many ways! Like about their home, a family has several rooms, rents them out, and then [the guy living there] says:

> "This home doesn't belong to me." But turns out the landlord is his father, these rooms are his father's property, it's he who rents out these rooms, and the guy says the rent money goes to his father, you have no way to tell.

> They aren't permitted to have house pets, or a cell phone, or drive a private car. But now people do have cell phones because you only regulated they can't have it but didn't regulate that people can't use it, so people say, "I'm using it, such-and-so person gave it to me." What way do you have? Is it really what they say? We don't know!

---

75. The following three comments were made during home interviews, late August 2007, Wuhan.

And then there's a pet in the household, very many people don't put pets on their household registration. This way, if you ask them, they'll allege, "This pet isn't mine, it's my mother's; this is my brother's." The excuses are many, just won't say it's their own! But all day he walks the dog. You can see it but there's no way to verify it. Also driving a car; you check the car registration, the owner isn't him.

R: Yes, even now there's a family running a restaurant but also taking the *dibao*!

Q: And doesn't use his own name?

R: That person really is a bully, so no one dares to touch him.[76]

Or, from another interviewee:

Q: Do you feel estimating their hidden income is the biggest problem?

R: Yes; we haven't the power to investigate, no way to investigate [no official or legal power]. If they do have work we first have to know where—we can secretly check on it, but we really don't know! We have an example, there's a person who applied for the *dibao*, we suspected he's working in a certain place, we went to look, found out it's really there. Afterward, we withdrew his *dibao*. Often, it's uncovered in fights or conflicts between the neighbors. If no one gives us information, we basically have no way to check.[77]

Besides these disqualifying behaviors—real or assumed—that reduce the numbers of beneficiaries or their take from the welfare, there are in addition two principal modes cadres rely upon to contrive a basis for rejection. The first is what is termed "assumed" (or "notional") income (*xuni shouru*, 虚拟收入), a practice already in play at least as far back as 2002. According to this practice, cadres deem that a person has the income s/he would have if s/he had the job the cadre supposes s/he should have; the other is to keep able-bodied individuals off the rolls, even if the person cannot find any work.[78] Both of these apparent subterfuges (whether at the level of practice or as explicit policy) amount to means of curbing the numbers of takers and, correspondingly, of the amount of funds doled out. Whether these tactics are meant to avoid exceeding quotas, to save money to prioritize allowances for purportedly dangerous citizens, or simply to set aside monies for city beautification

---

76. Han, *Zhongguo chengshi*, 326.

77. Ibid., 306.

78. Hong, "Chengshi jumin," 5, wrote, in 2005, that "those with labor ability but no labor opportunity are [nonetheless] excluded." Also, Liu Wenhai, "Guanyu wanshan chengzhen zhumin 'dibao' zhidu de jianyi" [Suggestions on perfecting the urban residents' 'minimum income' system], *Canyue* [Consultations] no. 37 (September 26, 2003): 20; Xiaoyuan Shang and Xiaoming Wu, "Changing Approaches of Social Protection: Social Assistance Reform in Urban China," *Social Policy and Society* 3, no. 3 (2004): 259–67, and Hussain, "Urban Poverty," 25.

or for cadres' friends and relatives, as early as 2003, in many places, local officials were already refusing both those who appeared to be capable of labor and those counted as having "assumed" incomes they did not really have.[79] Indeed, long before doing so became a matter of policy around 2009—and, it would seem, in contradiction to the original authorizing directive for the *dibao*, which said nothing of the sort (see Chapter Nine)—around 2004, most localities were already denying the *dibao* to those capable of labor.[80]

Much later, Westmore, the OECD researcher, found in a 2014 survey in five provinces (Shanghai, Liaoning, Henan, Gansu, and Guangdong) that a full three-quarters of those eligible were denied the *dibao*;[81] he also learned that a frequently employed stratagem is to "use the average or statutory minimum wage" in the locale in which a family member is working (or looking for work) as the person's actual income (a variant of "assumed income"), thereby rendering the household's income too high to meet the standard for the allowance.

Adding all these bits together, it is clear that the regulations proclaimed in 1999 to guide the granting of the *dibao* have long been undermined in their execution. That is, rulings that were supposed to bring the level of household income among the poverty-stricken up to a threshold line set in each city are countered in the implementation, whether by new pronouncements or by hidden motives. The editors of a 2015 work analyzing the transcripts of six city interviews done in 2008 had to agree that the system was deficient, as their concluding proposals suggested: "The [*dibao*] system isn't all-powerful, we can't expect it to solve every problem. The solution is to establish a separate, related system that includes housing assistance, help with education, medical aid, unemployment services, and so on. We need to form a ramified structure of assistance based on the masses' needs."[82]

CONCLUSION

So, in characteristic fashion, the regime originally pulled out the stops in its energetic crusade to reemploy and revive the retrenched in an effort to compensate them for their abrupt joblessness. Alongside the campaign but gathering heightened force as new jobs were mostly not to be had, the government

79. Shang and Wu, "Changing Approaches," 267–68; Hussain, "Urban Poverty," 25.

80. Joe C. B. Leung and Yuebin Xu, *China's Social Welfare* (Cambridge: Polity Press, 2015), 93; Shang and Wu, "Changing Approaches," 267; Haomiao Zhang, "China's Social Assistance Policy: Experiences and Future Directions," *CJSW* 7, 3 (2014): 223.

81. Westmore, "Do Government Transfers," 15.

82. Han Keqing et al., eds., *Chengshi zuidi shenghuo baozhang zhidu yanjiu* [Study of China's Urban Minimum Livelihood Guarantee System] (Beijing: Zhongguo shehui kexue chubanshe [Beijing: Chinese Social Sciences Publishing Co.], 2015), 266.

unveiled the *dibao* as a relief scheme, which, however well-intentioned and for a range of reasons, was riddled with flaws from its start. Consequently, once enrolled in the program, *dibaohu* have discovered that it often offers much less than promised, with its uncertain or absent additional benefits and subsidies; its secret quotas; its exclusions; and its onerous and seemingly haphazard prohibitions.

A glaringly deprecating aspect of the platform is that it keeps its beneficiaries marginal (though perhaps not consciously calculated to do so) by disallowing the disbursal of the *dibao* to households whose behavior might help them ascend out of poverty—such as by purchasing a computer or using a cell phone.[83] Other such forbidden behaviors are arranging for one's child to attend schools of his/her choice or private schools; enrolling a child in special classes for learning or training; or having a child study with a foreigner. Some places have banned people from becoming recipients if they have a family business, regardless of its profits or losses; even owning a firm losing money and incapable of supporting the family's livelihood could spark quarrels between civil affairs officials and an applicant.[84] All these strictures condemn the poor to persist in poverty while keeping them from mixing into the wider and modernizing society.

Perhaps without actively and specifically meaning to mold their situation in this way, the state has dealt with these *dibaohu* in a manner that maintains them and their children either sickly and, therefore, off the streets (as seen in Chapters Three and Six) or else insufficiently schooled to advance in society, out of work and eating too little to grow strong. And those able to improve their prospects by providing extra education for their children or by using computers, or to brighten their existence by communicating on cell phones, become for these reasons ineligible. This chapter has demonstrated that both the regulations that shape this program and the regimens used in enforcing it—whether by design or by subterfuge—marginalize the most indigent among the officially registered urbanites. As the rulings do so, rather than assisting the poor to throw off poverty, they succeed in forging what for China is a sizable, unaccustomed, if mostly invisible, urban underclass.

Beyond or in addition to depending on the *dibao*, might these citizens support themselves by way of other means of relief? And how do the beneficiaries of this wanting scheme experience and perceive their changed situation? Chapter Six explores these questions.

---

83. "Ji'nan guiding mai diannao jingchang yong shoujizhe buneng xiangshou dibao" [Jinan regulates that those who bought a computer or often use a cell phone can't enjoy the *dibao*], Zhongguowang, October 9, 2006, china.com.cn, accessed August 17, 2007.

84. "Zhongguo chengshi."

Chapter Six

Dibao: Survival and Perspectives

The last chapter demonstrated the range of lapses and bureaucratic hassles that only amplified the shortcomings of the already inadequate *dibao* scheme. It would appear that recipients (and even worse, *xiagang* staff and workers who had not been admitted into the program) must find it more than challenging to survive. In this chapter, I explore the possible solutions, as well as the non-solutions, that should—but usually do not—furnish them with some much-needed additional cash. The routes they travel in search of some relief usually fail them, one way or another: trying to get a job; relying on the state to supply them with a position; or turning to family members for succor. I also provide data on their quality of life and present typical feelings I encountered in my meetings with *dibaohu* and in reading about them: their hopes and despair; their shame and isolation; and the rebelliousness among some. I conclude by presenting conflicting perspectives on the plight of these people.

SURVIVAL STRATEGIES

Working

Apart from official policy on this (see Chapter Nine), there is sentiment in society—and sometimes among the personnel who work on the *dibao* program—that the takers of the money should be at work, not on welfare. A forty-year-old street-level officer in Xuanwu District, Beijing, expressed this view, displaying her resentment over her charges' failure to go to work: "If you give them a job, they'll say they're sick and can't work or say it's too far from home. . . . The most infuriating is two people, we introduced them to a job, but they say, 'Wages are too low, what can you do with so little money?'

Are *dibao* wages high? If you ask them how much they want, they'll say 3,000 or 5,000 yuan!"[1]

Yet many *dibaohu* are not, in fact, shirking work or choosing to rest on alms. One of my interviewees was quite representative: a man of forty-four, reflecting on his possibilities, despairingly offered this defeatist perspective:

> We all grew up in the city, didn't eat any bitterness [*mei chi ku,* 没 吃 苦, didn't suffer] and didn't do any heavy physical labor. Now in the labor market, there's some construction work, and it all demands rather a lot of such labor. They wouldn't want us forty-year-old laid-off workers, and there's some work that, if you give it to us to do, we couldn't manage such intensity, eventually we'd just damage our health and have to take medicine, and trying to work would become even more untenable.[2]

The same sentiment appeared in a conversation in Chongqing with a forty-five-year-old woman, who, along with her husband, had been laid off (Q is the questioner, R the respondent):

Q: Did you want to take the *dibao*?

R: No, I wanted to work, now I'm old, going out to look for work, people ask your age, once you say forty-five or forty-six, they don't want you. I'm embarrassed to take the *dibao*, working definitely is better, why would you want to take the *dibao*! Other people will think if you take the *dibao* you must be very poor, but now there's no way [*mei banfa*] because society already has become this way . . . if you don't take it, go out to look for work*,* how can you do it, because age limits you, women all must be under forty, over forty they don't want you, so at this age, we can only drift along, there's some years before retiring, *mei banfa*.

Q: What measures do you want from the government to help you get employed?

R: Help me find work! Why would I want to take the *dibao*; it's just several 100 yuan, how can it be enough! Mainly it's temporary work, you go to do it, the community and the street committee say, 'Good, good, good,' you go and then they [the employers] make you get out. They say, 'We have too many people, we can't afford to eat' [presumably meaning that their firm can't make a profit if it hires more people than it needs].' If you go out to the shopping mall to work, if you're young, you can work on the computer, how could we do the computer, sometimes can't see; they demand twenty-plus-year-olds![3]

---

1. Han Keqing, ed., *Zhongguo chengshi dibao fangtanlu* [Interviews with Minimum Livelihood Guarantee Recipients in Urban China] (Ji'nan: Shandong renmin chubanshe, 2012), 306.

2. Interview, late August 2007, Wuhan.

3. Han, *Zhongguo chengshi,* 273–74.

As an informant in Wuhan complained, "If it's not young, educated people, employers want, it's peasants for strenuous jobs that the laid-off workers are not fit to do."[4] In yet another dialogue, in Beijing, a forty-eight-year-old male makes the same points:

Q: Have you met anyone who's gone through these [skill training] courses and gotten employed?

R: You finish the training, and he chooses the younger one.[5]

One more case is this nearly fifty-year-old, a Guangzhou recipient, who, half-paralyzed and suffering from high blood pressure and diabetes, was still yearning somehow to be gainfully at work. But he fretted: "Because I'm too old and sick, if you were a boss, you wouldn't look for a forty-plus-year-old sick person, it's this simple." As a one-time state-owned oil depot employee, later laid off, he summed up the general situation of the *xiagang* thusly:

Everything requires a high educational background; I have only primary school education; naturally, they won't hire me; talented people are numerous, so they won't take me. You say go sell things, that needs start-up money [*benqian*, 本钱], private businesspeople wouldn't invite us, private bosses have no reason to ask a both sick and old person to work, right? I've already tried to find work, but it's no use; no one hired me, I'm too old, and I'm sick. The main reason is sickness; when the boss hears you're sick, he wouldn't want you; being young is much better, this is the way it is.[6]

A forty-two-year-old female *dibao* recipient in Tianshui, Gansu, confirmed this with her own self-appraisal: "The computer is impossible, my brain is no good."[7]

Or take this fifty-two-year-old man in Chongqing:

R: I actively demand, I told the community leaders several times, you say you want to place me there, I still can labor, who's going to accept me? I'm fifty-two, what post wants me? The key is a social reality—you say I should act as a business worker, he'll [the boss] say you're old; and no education, now everywhere wants the educated. Give the phone to us, don't know how to use it, what's the use? What unit will want us?

Q: Does the community offer training?

---

4. Interview, August 27, 2007.
5. Han, *Zhongguo chengshi*, 96.
6. Interview, June 30, 2010, Haizhu District, Guangzhou.
7. Han, *Zhongguo chengshi*, 239.

R: It does supply training, I can't learn it; train to be a tailor, I'm going to study that? My eyes can't see. Become a cook? Stir-frying vegetables—even the salt and the MSG I can't see.[8]

And what if a poor person dares to give some thought to doing business independently? This does not seem to be the case often, but there are instances: A thirty-two-year-old man in Changsha pled for the government to help with loans and preferential reemployment funds so he could afford to set up a small stall in the streets. But his request fell on deaf ears.[9] Likewise, a younger man (but, at thirty-five, still considered by employers "too old" for the labor market of the day) in Chaoyangshi, Liaoning (like Tianshui, a city of about three million), had no capital to open a shop and couldn't get a loan.[10] In Chongqing, a man of fifty-six did begin a business, but after it failed, he concluded that he was simply "too old."[11] Another recipient, a Chongqing woman of thirty-seven with a high school education, warned, perhaps from experience: "Hoping to be self-sufficient you might start a little business; yet after a while they'll confiscate it."[12] Moreover, in the poverty-beset locations where these "older" workers are concentrated, their neighbors are themselves too poor to serve as customers.[13]

One more case was a fully discouraged man living in Changsha, Hunan. Aged thirty-two and released from prison, he had this to say about his chances (in addition to no one wanting him because of his past incarceration): "I have no skill, in a company if they ask me to do something I don't understand it, can't keep up with society."

Q: Do you know this from personal experience?

R: Yes, I tried ordering newspapers, but my vision is rather deficient, my speaking is inferior, haven't had much exchange with others, sometimes can't do what I hope to do; now, there's rather a lot of talented people in Changsha; people like me, if you can't do the work, just forget it. Like my soliciting newspaper subscriptions and didn't get any orders, everywhere you go, they deduct some money; it's like kicking me out.

Q: So, did you think of participating in some skill training? Now there's some free training, did you know?

R: I hadn't heard! I hope I can study a skill, but I've only read a little, can't do *pinyin* [the Romanization of Chinese characters based on their pronunciation]

8. Ibid., 402–3.
9. Ibid., 156.
10. Ibid., 215.
11. Ibid., 276.
12. Ibid., 404.
13. Interview, August 27, 2007, Wuhan.

or English; I'm thinking of studying some skill like electrician, in principle I know some, I could practice, but have to study. But even looking at pictures, I don't understand.

Q: If you get the chance to study, what would you study?

R: I'm afraid I couldn't learn.[14]

This perspective is buttressed by a 2012 study undertaken of 8,191 *dibao* beneficiaries in three cities: this man's hometown of Changsha, in Ji'nan, and in Baotou. The researchers discovered that just a mere 12 percent of the subjects had received even some reemployment training. But then half of these considered it to be of little help in a job search.[15]

Family encumbrances frequently interfere. In the Liaoning city, a thirty-seven-year-old woman was caring for four people and couldn't think of going out to work. The interchange with her went like this:

Q: How much *dibao* does your family get?

R: 153 yuan, what do you think that amount of money can do? Not even enough for a child's school, and my husband gets 700 or 800 a month [from what source was not specified]; he's sick.

Q: Why don't you go look for work?

R: I've got two kids, one in junior high, one in primary school, every day have to take care of them going to school. . . . Really, my family should be considered five people, there's also my mother who lives with us; she has cerebral thrombosis, lies on the bed and can't move, I have to stay home all day to care for her, so basically can't go out![16]

Also stressed by her familial obligations, a forty-year-old woman in Tianshui, Gansu, went searching for odd jobs. But, she fretted: "In a month, I found just two days of work, and those two days, I had to take care of my in-laws too. Attending to old people is busy, my health isn't so good, so I have to consider."[17] Many informants were unavoidably stuck indoors, barely able to exit even for short periods. A fifty-six-year-old Guangzhou man, who had lost sight in his right eye and who was burdened with a mentally ill wife, was asked if he had done any part-time work. He replied, "I'm not afraid of doing it, but can't do it, must take care of my wife. If it weren't for this, long ago I'd go on duty . . . when I'm gone for a long time it's no good . . . if she

---

14. Han, *Zhongguo chengshi*, 144.
15. Xu Yuebin and Ludovico Carraro, "Minimum Income Programme and Welfare Dependency in China," *International Journal of Social Welfare* (*IJSW*) 26, no. 2 (2017): 144.
16. Han, *Zhengguo chengshi*, 200.
17. Ibid., 250.

doesn't see me, she worries. Often, I have to supervise her taking medicine. When I'm at home she'll be very stable; when I'm gone, she's unstable."[18]

In another case, a laid-off forty-five-year-old woman, also in Guangzhou, had an intellectually disabled son aged twenty-two. Here is her sorry situation:

> Majority of the time, I'm at home, caring for my son. Every day, I boil eggs for him; he eats very well because he's very large, robust . . . I can't leave my son, he can't do anything. I have to feed him three meals a day; if he were to boil some hot water, I fear he'd get scalded. He's completely without intelligence; if he sees something, he'll want to go play, like with those electrical plugs. I don't dare to get away, something could bring disaster to other people.[19]

Perhaps the most compelling case of home-boundedness caused by relentless family care was an enraged junior-high graduate who had sold food on the street in the past but was put out of business by fierce competition. His wife was out doing "sanitation work" much of the time, with him left to manage his children and his mother. Gradually he revealed that his mother was "not too agile, can't care for herself," and his two daughters were rather young. "So, it's hard to get away. In the morning," he went on,

> I must cook for my mother, at noon also have to cook for her, so there's no way to work. . . . Problem is can't get away, my mother's problem and arranging kids' school. . . . Sometimes, my mother talks a lot; I'm very angry, she sometimes speaks incoherently, and I scold her; this is true. I think the neighbors talk about this. Sometimes I get very angry, she has something to do but doesn't do it. Everything depends on us. She doesn't even cook the family's New Year's dinner. Although she doesn't have a major illness, compared to other people, she's sort of dull-witted . . . I can't abandon my mother. . . . If she could make rice for me and her granddaughters, we could go out to work, life would be peaceful, we'd come home and eat, this is how I think, but that's impossible. My mother has no ability; I must boil water to give her a bath. Sometimes, if not careful, she'll harm herself, and then she has to call me to take her to the doctor.[20]

A Mr. Li, aged forty-two, in Chongqing, offered a different sort of persuasive explanation for why he was reluctant to look for work: "If you go out this month, they'll stop your *dibao*; next month, there might be no odd jobs, and you've lost your *dibao*. Then you have to wait four months to reapply for it. You're better off not working. I tried working for those four months and earned 500 yuan; that's 840 yuan of funds from the *dibao* that I lost."[21]

---

18. Interview, July 8, 2010.
19. Interview, June 30, 2010, Guangzhou.
20. Interview, June 30, 2010, Guangzhou.
21. Han, *Zhongguo chengshi,* 410–11.

Apart from individuals' experiences and feelings, the labor market is far from capable of generating the multitude of positions needed. "Around here, my god, there are nearly 200 *dibao* households; each one has three people, so that's about 600 people. If we count 400 adults, maybe one hundred of them might have labor ability. Where would we have that many positions to let them labor?" vainly asked a street-level cadre in Xuanwu District, Beijing.[22]

Despite suspicions that *dibaohu* prefer handouts to hard labor, and in support of the laments of these informants, appraisals of numerous scholars of poverty challenge the concept of "welfare dependency" (i.e., the notion that social assistance breeds helplessness, irresponsibility, and sloth). Armando Barrientos, a researcher of poverty and social policy in less developed nations, has judged that, "There is little evidence that social protection programs have observable adverse effects on work incentives."[23] Commenting on China's *dibao* specifically, World Bank economists Martin Ravallion and Shaohua Chen determined that, "Even in Beijing [where the allowances are among the highest nationwide], the incentives built into the program as it works in practice are unlikely to create a poverty trap."[24]

Tang Jun reflected in 2004, that, "Our standard [for the *dibao*] is very low . . . it's so little that no one would want it if not pressed,"[25] a viewpoint echoed eight years later by sociologist Han Keqing and colleagues when they concluded that, "The amount of the *dibao* is so low that the possibility of 'welfare dependency' is rather low."[26] Adding to the analysis, Xu Yuebin and Ludovico Carraro used data drawn by the Asian Development Bank in 2012 from over eight thousand informants in three cities to assert that, "The issue of welfare dependency has been overstated." This is the case, they argue, since those who allege the presence of such behavior among beneficiaries ignore the personal and household circumstances—such as caregiving duties for the aged, the ill, and the young—as well as design factors embedded in the scheme itself that act as barriers and disincentives to taking a job.[27]

---

22. Ibid., 332–33.

23. Armando Barrientos, "Introducing Basic Social Protection in Low-Income Countries: Lessons from Existing Programmes," in *Building Decent Societies: Rethinking the Role of Social Security in Development*, ed. Peter Townsend (Houndmills, UK: Palgrave Macmillan 2009), 270.

24. Martin Ravallion and Shaohua Chen, "Benefit Incidence with Incentive Effects, Measurement Errors and Latent Heterogeneity," Policy Working Paper No. 6573 (Washington, DC: The World Bank, Development Research Group, Poverty and Inequality Team, August 2013), 6.

25. Tang Jun, "Jiasu zuidi shenghuo baozhang zhidu de guanfanhua yunzuo" [Speed up the dibao's normalized operation], in *2004 nian: Zhongguo shehui xingshi fenxi yu yuce* [2004: Analysis and forecast of China's social situation], eds. Ru Xin, Lu Xuejin, and Li Peilin (Beijing: shehui kexue wenxian chubanshe [Social science documents publishing company], 2004), 127.

26. Han Keqing et al., eds., *Chengshi zuidi shenghuo baozhang zhidu yanjiu* [Study of China's Urban Minimum Livelihood Guarantee System] (Beijing: Zhongguo shehui kexue chubanshe [Chinese Social Sciences Publishing Co.], 2015), 253.

27. Xu and Carraro, "Minimum income programme."

A 2008 survey of 1,209 recipients of the *dibao* backed up these social scientists, as it yielded the finding that, in fact, more than 90 percent of the subjects offered an affirmative reply to this query: "If you had labor ability, would you want to actively look for work?"[28] In the phrasing of a forty-eight-year-old Beijinger named Mr. Sun:

> Who wants to eat this *dibao*? To stretch out your hands to the government for money, not willing to! *Mei banfa*! I'm not willing to eat it . . . I just want to do some business, set up a stall, be self-sufficient . . . if you try to set it up, the *chengguan* (城管, urban management police) will confiscate. . . . Can we put up a stall? Of course *chengguan* will kick us out, can't argue back.[29]

Written sources consulted make it seem that only the occasional cadre comprehends the troubles of the *dibaohu*. There are no surveys of the providers of which I am aware. But here is an example of a sympathetic female community worker in Hanyang, Liaoning, who had this to say: "Many lack skills but do have labor ability, we connected them with work and thought of training them, but some are really no good [*buxing*, 不行] at it . . . even if they worked well in the factory, they can't do anything, can't go to study."[30] Probably her judgment comes from more than negative bias. For as a group of social policy scholars in Wuhan admitted in 2014, "They do get training but often it's not successful."[31] In Beijing's Xuanwu District, a compassionate *dibao* office chairwoman in the civil affairs bureau pointed out the following in 2008: "Going to work, paying for transportation, the prices for meals outside the home have gone up, leaving home there are costs for necessities while traveling, social interactions costs, all of these have to be calculated."[32]

These reflections add up to a sorry story highlighting a range of reasons why those on the *dibao* might prefer to—or be compelled to—remain on the rolls and to refrain from entering the labor market. These are circumstances that many cadres in charge of these people have not grasped.

State-Supplied Work

If *dibao* recipients encounter such hardship locating or being accepted for jobs or earning a living wage from work in the standard labor market (whether formal or informal), does the government help them out? The answer is that it has assisted some of them. Beginning in 2004, most provinces and cities

---

28. Han et al., *Chengshi zuidi*, 253.
29. Han, *Zhongguo chengshi*, 99.
30. Ibid., 446.
31. Interview, November 3, 2014, Wuhan.
32. Han, *Zhongguo chengshi*, 319.

implemented labor activation measures to prod recipients capable of doing so to take on paid work.[33] Such inducements included gradually reducing their *dibao* benefit (instead of immediately cutting it off), job training and placement, and tax incentives for the employers.[34] Unfortunately, the project was judged to be largely without effect.

But a few years later, in 2008 or 2009, the governments of many cities initiated a new approach. This entailed arranging for able-bodied, laid-off, older impoverished residents to perform menial make-work activities that were more or less the same ones they were obliged to execute gratis in exchange for the *dibao* (*yiwu laodong*, 义务 劳动, translated either as voluntary labor or as obligatory labor[!]). According to one source, people accepting these positions were required to leave the *dibao* roster while the community paid them wages, though trifling ones.[35] Their assignments included sweeping streets; distributing leaflets; cleaning up within the community; helping the police or community officials with security work, sanitation, or gardening; handing out leaflets; assisting people crossing public streets; performing household labor; and even pulling down obsolete advertisements from the walls of the community.[36]

In 2008, an official at a Changsha District civil affairs bureau remarked that the city's Party committee had created several hundred such public-interest (*gongyixing*, 公益性) jobs, entitled *xieguanyuan* (协管员, assistant management personnel) to handle the ongoing issue of unemployment, with the city finance bureau contributing to the wages.[37] Liu Xitang at the Ministry of Civil Affairs variously reported that such positions were allocated by the city districts (at the administrative echelon just below the citywide Bureau of Human Resources and Social Security).[38]

The next year (2009), a Wuhan teenager from a *dibao* family informed me that his mother had become a paid security guard, obliged to stand for long hours at her community's entrance gate, while his father was doing occasional hauling work for the community. Both of these positions had been arranged by the community. His mother was being recompensed at the rate

---

33. Xu and Carraro, "Minimum Income," 143–44. Xinwen zhongxin jiuye fuwu, peixun jianding laodong guanxi yu gongzi shehui baozhang zhengce cixun shuju fenxi dushu pindao [News center employment service training appraisal, labor relations and wages, social security policy consultation, statistical analysis readers' frequency channel], May 11, 2005, dates this back to 2002.

34. Xu and Carraro, "Minimum Income," 143–44.

35. Han, *Zhongguo chengshi,* 342.

36. Interview with a social worker in Shanghai, June 27, 2013, who referred to these jobs as *bao'an* (保安, security protection), *baojie* (保洁, sanitary worker), *jiazheng* (家政, housework), and *fuwuyuan* (服务员, service worker). A Lanzhou interviewee's wife was assigned to pull off ads (interview, July 13, 2010).

37. Han, *Zhongguo chengshi,* 430; Suzanne E. Scoggins, *Policing China: Street Level Cops in the Shadow of Protest* (Ithaca, NY: Cornell University Press, 2021), 54–55, 65.

38. Interview, September 9, 2013, Beijing.

of 500 yuan per month, which amounted to under 20 percent of the average wage of regularly employed workers in the city at the time, of about 2,650 yuan.[39] This is comparable to the wages then being paid for those in similar "public-service jobs" in Shenyang, where the rate was 550 yuan in 2008 and 2009.[40] By 2011, in Wuhan, these jobs were being compensated at 660 yuan per month, when the average wage for employed staff and workers was 3,804 yuan per month, representing a drop to 17.35 percent of Wuhan's average worker's pay.[41]

In Guangzhou, the pay for an official city management worker was over three times that for a public-service assistant doing precisely the same work (6,000 yuan per month for the former, 2,000 for the latter in 2015).[42] A Beijing informant related that an aide to a formal worker could earn about 1,400 yuan per month there in 2014. Finding such jobs, though, required either personal connections with officialdom or having been involved in big trouble-making, as by having participated in a sit-in appeal or sending a petition to a higher level.[43]

These data suggest that, whether in light of roadblocks in the pathway of the poor finding, engaging in, and retaining work on their own, or in terms of the unattractive pay—never mind the likely difficulty of even landing a state-supplied "assistant" position in the first place, it seems fair to conclude that the government was really doing little to help these people escape from poverty.

39. Emails about his mother's wage, September 2 and 11, 2009. Zhongguo tongjiju, chengshi shehui jingji diaochasi, bian [China Statistical Bureau, urban social economic investigation office, ed.], 2010, *Zhongguo chengshi tongji nianjian* [2010 China urban statistical yearbook] (Beijing, Zhongguo tongji chubanshe [China Statistics Press], 2010) does not give Wuhan's average wage for staff and workers in 2009. But I calculated its approximate amount by extrapolating from the percentage rise from 2008 to 2009 (about 12 percent) in six cities (Taiyuan, Wushun, Changchun, Zhengzhou, Shaoxing, and Zhuhai) whose 2008 average wage was close to Wuhan's (in the 2009 edition of this yearbook).

40. Guangxu Ji and Youqin Huang, "Mobile Phone Culture among the Information Have-Less: A Case Study of Laid-Off Workers in Shenyang City, China," in *The Emergence of a New Urban China: Insiders' Perspectives*, eds. Zai Liang, Steven F. Messner, Cheng Chen, and Youqin Huang (Lanham, MD: Lexington Books, 2012), 157.

41. Interview, August 2, 2011, Wuhan, with a woman whose husband was disabled. She was working as a library assistant and helping people cross the street. For the 2011 average wage, Zhongguo tongjiju chengshi shehui jingji diaochasi, bian, [China Statistical Bureau urban social and economic investigation office, ed.], *2012 Zhongguo chengshi tongji nianjian* [2012 China city statistical yearbook] (Beijing: China Statistics Press, 2012), 289.

42. Xu and Jiang, *op. cit*, 76. Unfortunately, despite hours of effort, I am unable to locate the original source nor any further citation information. But "Guangdong shiye danwei, 2015 nian Guangzhou Tianhenanjie chengguan xieguanyuan zhaopinwang [2015 advertisement for Guangzhou Tianhenan street *chengguan* assistant], http://gd.huatu.com/sydw/2015/0922/1327898.html cites 1,900 yuan as the basic pay for this position in Guangzhou in 2015, accessed February 4, 2021.

43. Interview, September 17, 2014, Hong Kong; Xi Chen, *Social Protest and Contentious Authoritarianism* (New York: Cambridge University Press, 2012).

Family Support?

Given the Chinese tradition of strong intrafamilial support, the expectation would be that those impoverished by losing their jobs ought to be able to survive by relying on family members' financial assistance.[44] But interview data undercut that assumption. Informants advanced a number of reasons why they could not count on family to prop up their lives; several explanations cropped up repeatedly:

A Mr. Huang, aged fifty-one and a father of two in Wuhan, forlornly disclosed that "no relatives or friends help because we're too poor so they don't want to get close; everyone would rather get close to people with money."[45] A forty-two-year-old woman in Wuhan acknowledged that her relatives were "all taking care of their own difficulties, so I can't ask them for any help."[46] In slightly better shape was a divorced Ms. Hong, age fifty, living with her two grown children (ages twenty-six and eighteen) in Shashi, Hubei. Her relatives were giving some material help, but usually just in the form of occasional fruits and cakes for the younger family members, or by buying new clothes for them—even that only at New Year's. Otherwise, extended family might supply what she termed "spiritual assistance," such as tutoring when the children were younger.[47] A Jingzhou, Hubei, couple of which both spouses were aged fifty-eight did benefit from a bit of generosity from the husband's younger brother, who provided 300 yuan, again, however, just once a year, at New Year's.[48]

Several families with adult sons fared worse. In Qianjiang, a couple had three sons—aged thirty-four, thirty, and forty-one—all living away, in Guangzhou, Qingdao, and Jinmen, Hubei, respectively, all laid off, and so sent no money home, needing it for themselves. One relation, an uncle, had once lent some money, but they had been obliged to pay it back.[49] A man with a disabled leg and a wife who was deaf and dumb, both in their early sixties, were living in Xiantao, Hubei. But their two sons had gone off to Dalian and Qingdao in search of work. Neither sent any money back home nor did they ever return; the parents confessed they were even "not too clear what [their] sons were doing." No other relatives helped, since "each has

---

44. Myron L. Cohen, "Developmental Process in the Chinese Domestic Group," in *Family and Kinship in Chinese Society*, ed. Maurice Freedman, 21–36 (Stanford: Stanford University Press, 1970). Cohen wrote in an email: "Membership in a family meant participation in a unified family economy" (December 11, 2019).
45. Interview, late August 2008.
46. Interview, August 2, 2011.
47. Interview, August 28, 2008.
48. Interview, August 28, 2008.
49. Interview, July 6, 2010.

his own hardship."[50] Beyond Hubei, in Lanzhou, a woman with two sons, both involved in unstable work for some seven or eight months of the year, whose "wages were too low," could not find a way to give any money to their seventy-three-year-old mother.[51] And in a family mentioned earlier, in which the husband had had a stroke and the wife was afflicted with diabetes, the son had "muddled along without a decent career, then went out to become a security guard and never returned." He, like the others, never sent his parents any money.[52]

There are surely families with members poised to help their unfortunate relations who have come upon hard times. But a common tale matches the larger socioeconomic circumstances in which these subjects find themselves: In the massive layoffs of the turn of the century, many from the same city—often enough the same family—had been employees in the same enterprise and had all lost their jobs at the same time. On top of that, the irregularities and precariousness of the informal labor market—usually the only arena in which anyone of their ilk can find work—leave those fortunate to land a job earning too little to share their wages with others.

QUALITY OF LIFE

So, what is the quality of life that *dibaohu* are left with—if work is hard to come by and low in pay, and if family cannot be depended upon to make up the gaps, how do these people manage to survive? Over the years, maybe some have received their pensions (see Chapter Ten). But before they do, or if they do not, what is their existence like?[53]

Several surveys expose the penury marking the lives of these near cast-asides. One 2008 study of 1,209 people in six cities found that just 3 to 7 percent felt that the benefits they were receiving from the *dibao* covered their basic livelihood;[54] another piece of research done in 2008 by wealthy Shanghai's Bureau of Civil Affairs showed that for as many as 82.5 percent of the 1,182 people living in the 400 households covered by the survey, even

---

50. Interview, July 8, 2010.
51. Interview, July 13, 2010.
52. Interview, July 21, 2009, Wuhan.
53. Harriet Evans, *Beijing From Below: Stories of Marginal Lives in the Capital's Center* (Durham, NC: Duke University Press, 2020) contains sagas of urban poverty; *idem.*, "Patriarchal Investments: Expectations of Male Authority and Support in a Poor Beijing," in *Transforming Patriarchy: Chinese Families in the Twenty-first Century*, eds. Goncalo Santos and Stevan Harrell (Seattle: University of Washington Press, 2017), 182–98.
54. Qin Gao, *Welfare, Work, and Poverty: Social Assistance in China* (New York: Oxford University Press, 2017), 63.

essential necessities were unaffordable.[55] A third investigation, tapping the opinions of 2,550 working-age recipients in three cities in 2012, concluded that the allowance helped half of the subjects to meet about one-third of their total needs, while an additional 30 percent could afford less than half what they had to buy.[56]

Welfare officers concurred with these assessments. Researchers who spoke in a focus group with eight of these people (from both street and community offices) in Guangzhou in 2010—a city which at the time had the third-highest level of *dibao* disbursement among China's thirty-six major cities—heard that, "The threshold is far from sufficient for subsistence." "Beneficiaries . . . must find every means to survive," said one group member, "as they scramble to locate the lowest prices, purchase the very minimal amount of food, and cut down on other consumption." One quoted a recipient who had admitted that, "To save fuel, I cook lunch and supper at the same time," and "I buy a whole chicken and cut it into small pieces—this way can eat it for a month." Still another saved money on meals by biking to a market an hour and a half away.[57] A Xuanwu District, Beijing, street office worker summed up the situation this way: "If you're talking about full, balanced nutrition, this won't do; for most, it's just basically [barely] sustaining your life."[58]

Among recipients, a fair number mentioned compromised nutrition above all. More than a few were subsisting on nothing but green vegetables and rice gruel, such as a seventy-four-year-old Ms. Chen in a family of five in Wuhan; two other women, aged fifty-two and forty-two, members of a focus group in Chongqing, complained about their level of nourishment. The first found it "annoying, can eat only a little gruel, just two meals a day, when other people are getting three"; the second reflected that, in the supermarket, she could buy only what no one else wants. "Anyway," she griped, "Taking the *dibao* is like this, there's no way [once more, the refrain of *mei banfa*], after our rent, water, and electricity, how much is left? Several hundred yuan, how can it be enough; really, it's scarcely surviving."[59] A moving case involved a Lanzhou woman with a ten-year-old son: "Our son saves money by not eating well, he eats only *mantou* (馒头, a steamed bun)," she lamented, in tears.[60]

Also chilling was a Ms. Li, a Wuhan woman, aged fifty-six, who had a daughter, twenty-eight, whose job was collecting money in an Internet cafe

---

55. Zhang, "The Meaning," 227.

56. Gao, *Welfare and Work*, 101.

57. Jie Lei and Chak Kwan Chan, "Does China's Public Assistance Scheme Create Welfare Dependency? An Assessment of the Welfare of the Urban Minimum Living Standard Guarantee," *International Social Work* 12, no. 2 (2019): 495, https://doi.org/10.1177/0020872817731142.

58. Han, *Zongguo chengshi,* 323.

59. Interview, late August 2008; Han, *Zhongguo chengshi*, 400–1.

60. Interview, July 13, 2010.

and who ate just thick gruel for her nourishment. Ms. Li was very much worried about her daughter's future: "You can see society is so chaotic, having the *dibao* means our child needn't go out to steal. . . . She is preparing to get married. After that I'm thinking of suicide because I don't want to burden her," she confessed. A community worker in Changsha described the meals of an especially impoverished resident as consisting of vinegar, vegetables, and pig's blood soup. This miserable man was also living with no electricity, so he bedded down at seven at night.[61]

A Mr. Xu, fifty-six years old and living in Chongqing with occasional help from his daughter, was bravely essaying to stay afloat on his very meager funds. Here is a short conversation with him:

Q: Last month, how much were your income and expenditures?

R: I've got no income other than the *dibao*; that's 210 yuan, not enough to live on, each month spend 400 or 500 yuan. Mainly, I spend on eating, I can't cook at home, have no refrigerator; in this weather, if you buy a lot, it quickly goes bad. And spoiling it is a waste. So I get two or three bowls of noodles outside for 3 yuan; a bowl of fried rice is 4 yuan. This way is simpler, I don't have to cook. If I buy vegetables and don't finish them, it's a waste. Eat two meals a day; every day, that's 10 yuan. It's effortless, but it's not enough. A bowl of vegetable soup is 2 or 3 yuan, so it adds up to 10 to 13 yuan a day.[62]

Mr. Fang, in his fifties, encountered in a tall apartment structure in Wuhan, was able to find shelter only by living under a staircase where he could avoid paying rent. He was divorced and suffered from four different health problems (heart disease, a stomach illness, and kidney stones, plus being severely near-sighted) and, with all of his three younger sisters themselves in straitened cirucmstances, got no help from relatives. "I'd be dead without the *dibao*," he observed.[63]

Others, however, were more exasperated than they were grateful. Ms. Zhang, a forty-five-year-old mother of two in Chongqing, fumed to her fellow focus-group members:

They control you; we're regulated to death: for water, electricity, and gas can't spend over 80 yuan a month, every month have to bring your bill for those things to the community office for checking. If you go beyond this amount, the next month they'll stop your *dibao*. And they don't consider the season—on hot days, don't dare use an electric fan, you just have to go soak in the river

61. Interview, August 30, 2008; Han, *Zhongguo chengshi,* 417.
62. Ibid., 277.
63. Interview, August 25, 2008.

. . . [obeying all their rules] you could die of suffocation in your room from fear they'll remove the *dibao*. . . . If someone reports that you went to buy a watermelon, you worry it seems you don't want to get the *dibao* anymore . . . so I don't risk carrying a big watermelon home; they immediately will stop you, will you really ever be able to eat that watermelon?

she plaintively continued.[64] When asked what he would do if under great financial duress, a Mr. Wang, in the same focus group, responded: "I first think of robbing people; people can't starve to death! The *dibao*, after all, only lets you barely survive, [but] if you rob people, you'll sit in jail . . . so have a little *dibao* to barely survive."[65]

Some were beyond simple bitterness, such as one Lanzhou woman in her early forties with a half-paralyzed husband and a daughter about to enter senior high school, who was at the end of her rope. Her two younger brothers provided no help, so she sold noodles in the evenings, earning 4 to 10 yuan per night. Though the family's *dibao* amounted to 728 yuan per month, senior high was going to cost the family 1,000 yuan a semester. "The *dibao* definitely is not enough, we've got no way [*mei banfa*], the pressure is so heavy I can't breathe. Can't think about it too much or I wouldn't revive," she wailed.[66]

Have these issues been addressed with the passage of years? Apparently not in a major way, or not for all. For well into the 2010s, the problems persisted. In 2014, a scholar reported that laid-off staff and workers were continuing to face hardship, with employment opportunities scarce and unreliable, incomes low and unstable. Besides, he noted, beyond just surviving, these people still bore the burden of raising and supporting children, taking care of their old, and contributing to their pension funds, if they could. Surely, they remained strapped for the wherewithal to carry out their lives.[67]

VARIOUS FEELINGS OF THE *DIBAOHU*

Hopes and Despair

Their own choice of language provides a telling window into the mood of these "social assistance" beneficiaries. Their dreams of the future all fixate on their children; their despair always resides in their seemingly endless coping

64. Han, *Zhongguo chengshi*, 403.

65. Focus group member in ibid., 401–3.

66. Interview, July 15, 2010.

67. Zhou Shoujing, "Xiagang shiwunian: ronghui yi cheng wangshi" [Laid off for 15 years: the glory is already in the past], *Juece tanso* [Policy explorations] No. 4 (2014), 50–53.

with what has befallen them. I take as examples of their aspirations the words of three interviewees encountered in Wuhan in July 2009.[68] The first, Ms. Xiong, aged forty-two, had become blind from illness at a young age; when I met with her, she was living with her eleven-year-old child. She had managed to find work as a masseuse, but soon her husband "began to pass his days in the world of women and wine, wasting money," and mistreating Ms. Xiong, after which they divorced. "I'm now longing for my son to quickly grow up and become independent," she fantasized.

The second, a forty-year-old Ms. Lu, was married to a Mr. Hu, both of whom had a senior high education and were physically in good health. Ms. Lu, however, was mentally ill and could not find work, while her husband had a position in a fruit wholesale market. Their daughter, aged sixteen, was studying at a vocational school (*zhongzhuan xuexiao*, 中专 学校). Mr. Hu acknowledged that he felt helpless about the family's situation: "Mainly, it's our daughter's studying is not good, and she doesn't know how to land any job. Now we can put up with things (日子将就还 能过, *ridz jiang jiu hai neng guo*). But if we think about the long term, once you get sick, it's difficult." So the aspirations of this pair rested on their child as well: "I hope my daughter soon finds a marriage with good conditions," appeared to him as their only refuge.

And the third subject, thirty-two-year-old Mr. Liang, also suffering from mental illness, lived with his wife and their young son. The family depended on the wife's making breakfast for neighbors and on their parents' financial help, in addition to a *dibao* allowance of 100 yuan per month, plus a small salary for the husband from "public-service employment." His wife explained: "Because of my husband's mental problem, up to now, he's had no formal job. If it's not watching the gate, then it's security work, for a monthly income of 500 yuan." Their son was then in kindergarten, for which they were paying very high fees. "Our little money is basically insufficient for this," she lamented. "Our hope is that later after he grows up, our son somehow won't be like us; he definitely must study well and be a person with ability!" she cried.

In other cities, the story was very much the same. In a similar state of mind, another woman, aged forty-five, in Chongqing, was despondent:

Only eating the *dibao* (*chi dibao,* 吃 低保, colloquial for relying on the *dibao*) [we] can't throw off poverty, only can get poorer and poorer . . . the cheapest things all are a *kuai* (块, Chinese dollar, then equaling about US$0.125) a *jin* (斤, just over a pound), only relying on eating the *dibao* simply isn't ok. If an older child goes out to work, if you have no culture how can he find work, will

68. Interviews, July 21, 2009.

be one generation after another being poor. Very many *dibao* households put their desire to throw off poverty on their kids, wish to escape inter-generational inheritance of poverty.[69]

A longitudinal study of forty households in each of three cities (Guangzhou, Beijing, and Shanghai), initiated in mid-2009, encountered respondents who had lost all confidence in gaining further employment, despite being relatively young. As one bemoaned, "I'm already forty-one and will just let it be. . . . Our generation is finished."[70] Equally pitiful was a woman in Shanghai, interviewed in a study of over 1,100 subjects in 2008: "I think I'm already eliminated by society," she grieved.[71]

Shame and Isolation

Sometimes informants opened up their feelings during interviews. What follows are selected comments from subjects in Wuhan in the summer of 2007. For some, shame lurked behind the material discomforts of being a recipient. The young wife of a schizophrenic man, though in absolutely dire straits, was "embarrassed to go to apply, feel[s] too young to take it." She should be supporting herself, she judged, sobbing, but saddled with rearing a one-and-a-half-year-old baby, she could not. A couple in their late forties, both laid-off workers, "feel we as people getting the *dibao* are not too honorable (*guangcai*, 光彩); since our son got out of school for the summer, he has just stayed home, won't play with other kids; during vacation, he rarely goes out, has a sense of inferiority."

Like this boy, a common sense of disgrace prevents the beneficiaries from initiating exchanges with neighbors. One related common feelings: "Ordinarily *dibaohu* talk very little among themselves about how much money they get, generally keep it a secret." A sixty-seven-year-old widow without formal education still had her pride: "We don't communicate with other *dibao* targets; I basically don't know other people's situation . . . I'm also embarrassed to raise the issue with other people, after all, taking the *dibao* isn't a very honorable thing."

Another woman in her sixties pointed out that a lot of her neighbors were also receiving the *dibao* but that they didn't discuss it among themselves. The wife of the schizophrenic man replied in the negative when queried as

---

69. Han Keqing and Guo Yu, "Fuli yilan" shi fu cunzai?—Zhongguo chengshi dibao zhidu de yige shizheng yanjiu" [Does "welfare reliance" exist or not?—concrete evidence on China's urban minimum livelihood system], *Shehuixue yanjiu* [Sociological studies] 2 (2012): 162–63.

70. Wong Yu-Cheung, Honglin Chen, and Qun Zeng, "Social Assistance in Shanghai: Dynamics between Social Protection and Informal Employment," *IJSW* 23 (2014): 339.

71. Haomiao Zhang, "Frustration, Shame, and Gratitude: The Meaning of Social Assistance for Women Recipients in China," *Asian Women* 32, no. 1 (2016): 61.

to whether she talked about her situation with those living in her community. "No," she responded, "the family's affairs are not easy to speak of much with others, now too many people will look at you and laugh at you."

Opposition

Still, among the litany of sufferings—both of the body and of the heart—only a mere handful of informants were challengers, such as one who had had spats with the management personnel, leading to her estrangement from the community. In another case, a father asked whether he had been given extra subsidies to deal with then-recent inflation, refrained from criticizing the system, but claimed, "I've heard that we *dibaohu* are to have a price subsidy of 30 yuan, but actually getting it is not too clear. Each month when they issue us our money, I don't know concretely how it's calculated. They give us a certain amount, and that's just it (*gei duoshao, jiushi duoshao*, 给多少，就是多少), haven't inquired." Here it is possible that what could be anger was masked as mystification.

The wife in a three-person household, a junior high graduate, seemed to have given up in what she presented as a state of ignorance, though perhaps her perplexity belied some dissent: "We understand some, but not too much," she claimed. "We only know there's some price subsidies, and in winter, there's funds for warmth. The specifics really aren't too clear. Anyway, it's such a small amount of money, it's hard to calculate. However much there is, that's it, we don't haggle over the details." Two other informants were more straightforward about the futility of expounding upon their grievances. One father, queried whether he had any suggestions for the system operators, offered this rejoinder: "Suggestions I do have, but it's no use. I wish the government would give more money. Now *laobaixing* (老百姓, ordinary people) don't have the right to speak. Going to the doctor is expensive, studying is hard, how can we solve the problems in a short time? But raising it is useless (提了是白提, *tile shi baiti*)." In the same state of mind, a forty-four-year-old woman had this to say: "Raising it hasn't much use, just hope I can enter a hospital, now seeing a doctor is something I can't afford. . . . Basic-level implementation lacks supervision and guarantees, the *laobaixing* don't know much about the actual policy, how the subsidy they issue us each month is really figured, we're all unclear." From the tone of these complaints, this bewilderment appears to be experienced with at least some modicum of annoyance.

In the midst of these fatalistic and phlegmatic postures, one pugnacious and forthright sixty-seven-year-old widow stood out; she dared to wrangle with the administrators in her community. Convinced that her family was not being treated fairly, she charged that, "In 2003, when we got into the system, the subsidy was very transparent, the public bulletin board told how much income each household had every month, what their subsidy was, how much was deducted. But these past two years, it's not this way. Among us *dibaohu* we don't know how much other people are getting." Questioned whether she was being given a larger subsidy after inflation had set in, "It's not like that," she inveighed. Then she went on to give a fuller explanation:

> Since my daughter-in-law went out to work, and the residents' committee found out, my son's *dibao* was cut back. Getting one-hundred-plus yuan each month is not as good as when it first began. We're a family with an old person [herself], my son can't see and has no labor ability, my daughter-in-law's little money can take care of her son, but [because of this] the *juweihui* (居委会, residents' committee, the old name for what is now called the community) cuts back our family's allowance. Other families have two people going out to work and their allowance wasn't reduced. Since I argued opinionatedly with the *juweihui*, they said I shouldn't compare myself with other people. But our family has no money, no connections, so things can only be this way.[72]

Asked if she had any communication with other *dibaohu*, she ranted on: "Since my son's subsidy was taken away, I very rarely go to the *juweihui* office, don't speak to other *dibaohu*, and when the *juweihui* holds a meeting, they don't call me. So, I basically don't know other people's situations." Did she get a recent increase, the interviewer wanted to know. Her answer was, again, defiant:

> It increased some, but I don't know why, the *laobaixing* (ordinary people, 老百姓) are all very bewildered, sometimes more money comes, and we don't know why, when the total is more, we're very happy. I just hope to understand how this subsidy is granted, we ordinary people don't get to see the civil affairs department's documents. . . . The *juweihui* ought to treat people equally, everyone should be equal before the regulations, it shouldn't happen that because of a certain family's connections they can do whatever.

Of all the informants, only this one older subject had the nerve to give full voice to her vexations. And yet, it must be underlined, hushed up among her neighbors by her feelings of humiliation, and pushed aside by her program managers, she poses no threat to the so-precious stability of the party-state, as Chapter Three has argued.

---

72. Interview, late August 2007, Wuhan. Jennifer Pan, *Welfare for Autocrats: How Social Assistance in China Cares for its Rulers* (New York: Oxford University Press, 2020), 28 and 30 explains this.

APPRAISALS OF THE *DIBAOHU*

Cadres' Views

As noted above, some local management personnel are sympathetic to the *dibao* subjects. But these cadres are caught in a bind, one with several features. First of all, they must try to mediate between their higher-ups with their rules, on one side, and their charges, who, perforce, have no redress but must suffer from those rules, on the other. Annoyances, frustrations, and improprieties abound on both sides, in many ways the product of the structure of their relationship and of the program to which both parties are bound. These issues feature the near impossibility cadres frequently face of investigating potential beneficiaries' undeclared (so-called hidden) assets; uncovering income that is occasional or inconsistent; and/or learning about any assistance their subjects may be receiving from others, especially when, as is usually true, it is unpredictable. That administrators have to rely on the self-reports of the residents renders nearly futile an accurate calculation of the true means of people who either conceal or are unable fully or accurately to supply such data. An article commented on this conundrum already in 2003, soon after the inauguration of the program,[73] but the problem went on to bedevil practitioners for years thereafter.

Another source of irritation appears in these comments from a *dibao* management cadre in a Zhongshan, Guangdong, community: "If you work with humaneness, it just creates lazybones . . . very many people come to find me. I say, 'You look, you have hands and feet, right? Now go do some work in society, just help sell things . . . you're taking advantage.'"[74] At least in part, this impatience can be attributed to these officers' own imperfections. Among the failings, a chief one is that the majority of those filling these positions are themselves laid-off, unemployed people with only limited education, lacking both professional training and its related skills. Though training is sometimes provided, its content is brief and inadequate to the task, being more theoretical than it is related to the practical needs of the job.

Moreover, the targets of their work are members of the cities' new underclass, whose proper handling requires forbearance from the cadres and an inclination to serve the poor, both virtues that are in short supply. Under these conditions, the negativism managers sometimes exhibit can doubtlessly spark conflicts and tension between giver and taker. On top of this, the pay for the work is very low (only 450 yuan in Wuchang District, Wuhan, in 2006, then

---

73. Liu Wenhai, "Guanyu wanshan chengzhen zhumin `dibao' zhidu de jianyi" [Suggestions on perfecting the urban residents' `minimum income' system], *Canyue* [Consultations] no. 37 (September 26, 2003), 20.

74. Han, *Zhongguo chengshi*, 392.

equivalent to about US$56.25 a month, about one-fifth of the city's average wage[75]), the tasks many and complex, both factors that undermine the workers' commitment to the job at hand. Among their chores are examining the finances and family exigencies of all claimants; inspecting their homes; making inquiries at any possible places of work and at their neighbors' homes; and managing multiple accounts, tables, files, and forms. This array of burdens can easily dispose exhausted and grudging personnel to forego painstaking analysis and to resort to relying just on rumors about the suppliants. Their behavior, when they are thus exasperated, can incite anger, cursing, and even violence among rejected or otherwise irritable welfare candidates.[76]

Often this configuration of contradictions between agents and applicants can frame the context for corruption. Examples are cases in which *dibaohu* intentionally falsify their finances or present gifts to officials in order to encourage a raise in their allowances. By the same token, cadres are often charged with favoring undeserving friends and relatives (*qingbao*, 情保) or even pocketing or misappropriating funds intended for beneficiaries.[77] (See Chapter Nine.) Still, some cadres' mindset of opposition to their target subjects clearly has a structural foundation.

Official and Media Justification

Official rationalization of this situation is manifested in the media's downgrading of the *dibaohus'* abilities and worth. Journal articles around the turn of the century describing the newly unemployed—those discarded by the enterprises after 1995 in response to official orders—routinely characterized these individuals as "lack[ing in] understanding of the realities of market competition,"[78] unable to grasp the need for behavior that is "normal in a market economy," such as moving one's residence for a job. This so-called inadequate thinking amounted, it was claimed, to a "regression back to the world of the state-owned enterprises,"[79] a formulation clearly castigating

---

75. In 2007, the average wage in urban units of fully employed staff and workers in Wuhan was 2,094.7 yuan per month. See Wuhanshi tongjiju, bian [Wuhan City Bureau of Statistics, ed.], *2008 Wuhan tongji nianjian* [2008 Wuhan statistics yearbook] (Beijing: Zhongguo tongji chubanshe [China Statistics Press], 2008), 55.

76. Li Chunyan and Ding Jianding, "Wuhanshi dibao guanlizhong cunzai de wenti yu gaijin duice fenxi—yi Wuchangqu weili" [Existing problems and analysis of measures for improvement in Wuhan's *dibao* management—Wuchang district as an example], *Changjiang luntan* [Yangtze Forum] 1, no. 76 (2006): 27.

77. Han, *Zhongguo chengshi,* 187.

78. Chengshi shiye xiagang yu zaijiuye yanjiu ketizu [Research task force on urban unemployment, layoffs and reemployment], "Wo guo chengshizhong de shiye xiagang wenti ji qi duice" [The issue of our country's urban unemployment and layoffs and measures to handle it], *Shehuixue* [Sociology] 3 (2000): 83.

79. Ibid., 84.

these unfortunate workers as laggards. Indeed, a commonly called-upon moniker in the media—and in social media as well—tarred these forsaken people as *dibaozu* (低保族, disparagingly, the *dibao* tribe, a term similar in function to President Ronald Reagan's stigmatizing label "welfare queen" used to denigrate people on welfare in the United States).[80] Their overall "quality and their concept about a market economy is 'inappropriate,'" states another writer, posing "an obstacle to our country's economic opening and speedy transition."[81]

According to the Hong Kong newspaper *Ming Bao* [Bright News, 明 报], in 1997, just as the mandated layoffs were gathering force, the Ministry of Labor announced that, "We should work hard to educate this group of people to wake up to the fact that the market economy needs competition, competition is bound to lead to bankruptcy and unemployment, enterprises no longer have the iron rice bowl, two-way selection exists between employers and employees, and we should rely on indomitable work for survival."[82] Around the same time, a tabloid called *The Shopping Guide* (*Gouwu daobao*, 购务 导报) proclaimed in the late 1990s that, "The process of reform requires some enterprises to go bankrupt, to make others feel the pressure of survival . . . it also needs to lay off some people, who will pose a threat to those remaining on the job and motivate them to work harder . . . unemployment is essential to social progress." The author of this piece went on to scorn what he perceived to be "the character weaknesses of laid-off workers, [as apparent in] their sense of dependence and archaic notions of job security, welfare entitlements and social status."[83]

Several years later, in 2000, the press continued to essay to edify those its publicists tagged "excess workers," as in the following extract:

The superiority of socialism should not be manifested in supporting idle and lazy people. We hope to see such a moving scenario: units can survive on the basis of their efficiency; people get rewards on the grounds of their capabilities. There will be no place of existence for lazy people. And those who are complacent will, naturally, be removed. If so, the phenomenon of extra personnel, which has put unbearable burdens on government finance, will disappear by itself.[84]

80. Mun Young Cho, *The Specter of "The People": Urban Poverty in Northeast China* (Ithaca, NY: Cornell University Press, 2013), 89; email from Cho, October 2, 2020.

81. Mo Rong, "Jiaru WTO yu woguo de jiuye" [Entering the WTO and my country's employment] *Laodong baozhang tongxun* [Labor security bulletin] (*LDBZTX*) 4 (2000): 20.

82. *Ming Bao* [Bright News], December 19, 1997.

83. Yuezhi Zhao, "The Rich, the Laid-off, and the Criminals in Tabloid Tales: Read All About Them!" in *Popular China: Unofficial Culture in a Globalizing Society*, eds. Perry Link, Richard P. Madsen, and Paul G. Pickowicz (Lanham, MD: Rowman & Littlefield, 2002), 111–35.

84. *Fazhi ribao* [Legal Daily], May 28, 2000.

It should be noted here that, as Jaeyoun Won has observed, the appraisal of what were for decades seen as fine socialist principles—employment security and comprehensive welfare—became objects of castigation for their perceived role in nurturing laziness, inefficiency, low productivity, and underperformance.[85]

By the 1990s, the political elite was poised to join forces with the global economy, as its members prepared to ready the country for entering the World Trade Organization. Accordingly, it seemed impossible to these leaders to accommodate people whose "cultural level and business skill isn't high," making it "difficult [for such people] to completely meet the demands of market economic structural readjustment and international competition," according to an internal publication.[86] The commentator even went so far as to urge that, "We should as early as possible . . . establish the view that [only?] 'those who can adapt should exist,' to blend our enterprises into the international competitive environment."[87]

Essayists must have known that what they described as an intractable mindset among the laid-off personnel had to be traced to the long-term influence of the planned economy, with its employment security and gratis infusion of state funds for their firms, as well as the various generous, cheap, or free state social and educational policies that accompanied that economy. Still, they nonetheless tarred former laborers with sustaining a "traditional employment concept," allegedly knowing only to "wait, depend, and demand," victims of "their own backward ways of understanding employment."[88] This analysis explicitly linked the laid-off with what was by the turn of the century seen as China's discredited past under the pre-reform regime. One writer labeled such workers "ensnared in passivity."[89] The only solution for such sad cases, these detractors insisted, was to "modernize their concept of value," to "get rid of their past backward and narrow mentality."[90]

---

85. Jaeyoun Won, "The Making of the Post-Proletariat in China," *Development and Society* 34, no. 2 (2005): 192.

86. Zhongguo qiye lianhehui "qiye yingdui 'rushi' celue" ketizu [Task force for Chinese enterprise unions' "enterprise strategy for handling 'entering the WTO'"], "Jiaru WTO hou wo guo qiye mianlin de xingshi ji duice" [The situation and response measures facing our enterprises after our country enters the WTO], *Neibu canyue* [Internal consultations], 561 (April 27, 2001): 14.

87. Ibid., 15.

88. Shoudu jingji maoyi daxue, laodong jingji xueyuan shequ jiuye ketizu [Capital University of Economics and Trade, Labor Economics Institute, Community Employment Task Force], "Shequ jiuye fuwu tixi jianshe de lilun yu shijian" [Theory and Practice in the construction of the community employment service system], *Renkou yu jingji* [Population & Economics] 5 (2001): 61.

89. Xu Liqi, "Xiagang zhigong xintai diaocha fenxi" [An analysis of research on laid-off staff and worker's psychological state], *LDBZTX* 5 (2001): 29.

90. Hu Xinhua, "Woguo qiye zhigong duiwu de yuce bianhua ji baozhang duice" [Expected changes and security response measures for the ranks of our enterprise staff and workers] (Unpublished ms., 2001).

Xiagang workers internalized this outlook as early as 1999, as I found in interviews that summer. A female worker in her late thirties, having lately lost her job in the electronics system, told me, "For China to progress, we have to go through this process, [even if] people like us will be affected by it," and "We need to sacrifice for the next generation . . . so the country can get stronger [even as their children, quite likely to become members of the new urban underclass, were in fact also being consigned to poverty in future days] . . . eliminating people is a necessary law of social development," clearly quoting the government's pitch.

Parroting the official line was another laid-off woman, aged thirty-eight, whose thread-making unit had gone bankrupt earlier that year: "For middle-aged people [like us], it's hard to learn new things," implicitly admitting her unsuitability for the challenging world of market competition that she found confronting her.[91] Thirty-four-year-old Mr. Kong of Xuanwu District, Beijing, the father of two young children, had concluded by 2008 that, "If a person doesn't work, he's finished."[92] Most humbling of all was a short man, formerly an employee of a small cloth shoe factory, assigned to mopping my hotel's marble entrance pillars, whom I encountered at 1:30 in the morning. He announced to me with tears in his eyes that, "Without reform and opening, China will remain behind (*luohoude*, 落后的) . . . there's no other future for it."[93]

These denigrating comments did not cease with time. In 2011, for instance, an academic journal instructed laid-off staff and workers to "actively transform their thinking, raise their quality (*suzhi*, 素质), and take the initiative to seek opportunities for reemployment."[94] And still, nearly another decade on, an analyst penned an essay pointing to "an overwhelming undeclared campaign from above to shape popular opinions of the poor," which blamed the victims, "demoniz[ing] people situated at the bottom of the social pyramid."[95] Plainly put, those who had been discharged became scapegoats in the transition to a market economy. These disturbing remarks—from both the critics and the criticized—serve to symbolize the interpretative dialogues that have undergirded the administration and impact of the *dibao*.

---

91. Interviews, September 1 and 6, 1999, Wuhan.
92. Han, *Zhongguo chengshi*, 13.
93. Interview, September 11, 1999, Wuhan.
94. Xiong Yang, "Guizhou qiye xiagang zhigong zaijiuye wenti fenxi" [Analysis of the issue of the reemployment of Guizhou's staff and workers laid off from enterprises], *Xueshu tantao* [Academic Inquiry], no. 5 (2011): 389.
95. Jasmine Wang, "Poor Attitudes Towards the Poor: Conceptions of Poverty among the Rich and Powerful in China," *Made in China* (April–June 2019): 63.

CONCLUSION

Anguish and anxiety have resulted from the features of a program meant to keep at bay the people struggling to live the lives delineated above. Those critical features, outlined in Chapter Five, include its rigid, exclusionary procedures and niggardly allowances, plus impediments stacked up against entering the labor market, with its subsistence wages, even if one should somehow contrive to get into it. This chapter points as well to the many sorts of barriers against working and to the issue of kin no better placed to extend a helping hand than are those in distress.

These circumstances, combined and projected on a large scale, have had their damaging effects: nourishment that borders on starvation, and forlorn and forsaken subjects cherishing dreams quite impossible to fulfil. And, most likely, their children—the subjects of these dreams—will have little choice but to carry on in their place and with their plight.

This portrayal of the consequences of the *dibao* program for its recipients, and of the perspectives that the three players in it—its subjects, its administrators, and the policy elite who designed the system—entertain is unsettling. But how prevalent is such a scene in welfare ventures internationally? The next chapter investigates how China's social assistance compares with similar schemes in other nations. The point of that exercise is to query whether the Chinese example truly deserves the label "social assistance."

Section III

COMPARISONS AND VARIATIONS

Chapter Seven

"Social Assistance?"

A Comparative Perspective

This chapter poses a provocative question: Should China's *dibao* be catego-rized as "social assistance," properly understood? Or is it best perceived in other terms? Here I develop a framework to situate this scheme in relation to other programs that, writ large, are positioned as "social assistance"—defined by poverty scholar Armando Barrientos as "anti-poverty transfer programs" that "provide direct transfers of cash and/or goods in kind to individuals or households experiencing poverty or vulnerability, *with the aim of facilitating their permanent exit from poverty.*"[1] Alternatively but similarly, Gao and her co-authors define the related term, "safety net programs," as being schemes "designed to target those most in need and alleviate extreme poverty . . . [which] focus only on a small proportion of the population who are *unable to earn a sufficient living* and would fall below the minimum livelihood level if without the social safety net"[2] [emphases added].

That the *dibao* was initially designed to placate and pacify laid-off work-ers—the great majority of whom were quite *able to earn a sufficient living,* and not to *facilitate permanent exit from poverty*—suggests that this policy may not constitute social assistance, as defined above. Two quotations make this point: One Chinese scholar told me in 2009, "The *dibao* is not a *tuopin* [脱贫, throw off, or escape from, poverty] strategy, it's just to maintain livelihood";[3] and in mid-2011, years after the program was installed, a provincial-level cadre in Shaanxi Province who had been managing the program for ten years—

---

1. Armando Barrientos, *Social Assistance in Developing Countries* (Cambridge, UK: Cambridge University Press, 2013), 3.

2. Qin Gao, Sui Yang, and Shi Li, "Welfare, Targeting, and Anti-poverty Effectiveness: The Case of Urban China, *The Quarterly Review of Economics and Finance* 56 (2015): 30.

3. Interview, July 26, 2009, Wuhan. An official at the Ministry of Civil Affairs agreed, July 28, 2009, Beijing.

almost from its inception—disclosed that the majority of *dibao* recipients in his province remained laid-off workers. "The purpose of the *dibao* is to cover the *xiagang* [下岗, laid-off]," he averred.[4]

The comparative exercise I perform in this chapter is aimed at appraising the nature of China's "social assistance" program by pitting it against other national-scale ventures of this name. I tackle this project in two ways: First, I posit a set of abstract, ideal-typical political goals that drive politicians to allocate welfare. I take these goals—or motives—that either explicitly or implicitly guide rulers to succor the needy as the foundation for three welfare program models, respectively. The models refer to three dominant political incentives that propel leaders to install projects purporting to supply sustenance to the poor and other weak portions of the populace, namely, "productivist," "partisan," and "pacifying/policing," respectively. In devising this tripartite classification, and in determining where individual states belong within it, I rely on the judgments of specialists on these places, whose assessments are based upon the countries' leaders' policies, behaviors, and statements. In Chapter Eight, which looks at variation within China, economic variation drives the comparison.

My second approach in this chapter is to draw on statistics to assess the level of generosity the various programs provide. I employ standard measures of generosity—on spending, on the proportion of the populations served, and on what would seem to be the munificence displayed by the respective programs—to gauge how Chinese authorities manage their program of relief as against how officials in other states do and have. The places I refer to are the following: other East Asian nations, chiefly Japan, South Korea, and Taiwan, plus India in South Asia; several Latin American countries, especially Mexico and Brazil; some African states, along with "developing countries," generally; a few Eastern European nations and the region as a whole; and members of the European Union (EU) and of the Organization for Economic Cooperation and Development (OECD).

I proceed to construct the tri-fold typology of programs, each type with a different intent, and assign explanations for the choice among these that leaders have made. I then lay out features of specific support schemes in different countries and analyze the causes behind any changes these countries have made among types over time, whether expansions or contractions of official aid. Next, I refer to statistics. At the chapter's end, I use this material to gauge how China's *dibao* should be evaluated.

---

4. Interview with civil affairs official, July 27, 2011, Xi'an.

THREE IDEAL-TYPICAL MOTIVATIONS FOR EXTENDING ALLOWANCES TO THE POOR

I begin by proposing that states—that is, the politicians at their helms—aspire to attain and maintain their citizens' views that their governance is legitimate.[5] I suggest that a principal means of doing this is by—at a minimum—*appearing* to protect their citizens. Accordingly, I propose that a basic impetus behind a regime (and its rulers') granting welfare is to convince those under its jurisdiction that its mode of exercising power—its political system or its regime—is appropriate, justifiable, and acceptable. Thus, supplying assistance to the needy is, at the most basic level, meant to engender a belief that the regime rightly commands loyalty and obedience, the bastions of legitimacy, at least among some substantial segment of the populace.[6]

In China's case, Ho-fung Hung has written of "the ruling Communist leaders' emphasis on the merit of securing . . . subsistence rights as the source of their legitimacy."[7] The work of Joanna Handlin Smith on charity in the late Ming dynasty alludes to this commitment dating from imperial times: she notes that local magistrates were expected to care for the people, as well as to rely on provisioning as a hedge against potential riots.[8] On this same point, as trials of the *dibao* program were underway in 1995, Doje Cering,[9] then Minister of Civil Affairs, explained to a *People's Daily* reporter that one of three reasons China needed this policy was to bolster the legitimacy of the government and the party. For, he went on, it would allow the leaders to demonstrate that the state was responsive to its citizens' condition, while also embodying the superiority of China's socialist system.[10]

---

5. Christian Aspalter, "The East Asian Welfare Model," *International Journal of Social Welfare* (*IJSW*)15 (2006): 290. Bruce J. Dickson, Pierre F. Landry, Mingming Shen, and Jie Yan, "Public Goods and Regime Support in Urban China," *The China Quarterly*, no. 228 (2016): 859–80, argues that welfare enhances a state's perceived legitimacy.

6. Chan Kwan Chan, "Re-thinking the Incrementalist Thesis in China: A Reflection on the Development of the Minimum Standard of Living Scheme in Urban and Rural Areas," *Journal of Social Policy* 39, no. 4 (2010): 627–45; Yu-Cheung Wong, Honglin Chen, and Qun Zeng, "Social Assistance in Shanghai: Dynamics between Social Protection and Informal Employment," *IJSW* 23 (2014): 334.

7. Ho-fung Hung, *Protest with Chinese Characteristics: Demonstrations, Riots, and Petitions in the Mid-Qing Dynasty* (New York: Columbia Press, 2011), 197.

8. Joanna Handlin Smith, *The Art of Doing Good: Charity in Late Ming China* (Berkeley: University of California Press, 2009), 8–9. Also, Pierre-Etienne Will and R. Bin Wong, with James Lee, *Nourish the People: The State Civilian Granary System in China, 1650–1850* (Ann Arbor: University of Michigan Press, 1991); and R. Bin Wong, *China Transformed: Historical Change and the Limits of European Experience* (Ithaca, NY: Cornell University Press, 1997).

9. This is a different transliteration of Duoji Cairang, mentioned earlier.

10. *Renmin ribao* [People's Daily], September 14, 1995, cited in Jennifer Pan, *Welfare for Autocrats: How Social Assistance in China Cares for its Rulers* (New York: Oxford University Press, 2020), 34.

Different state leaders hope to attain legitimacy by employing their state's welfare transfers to embody disparate values. I understand these values to be perceived by leaders as ideal-typical goods: the first is a state's ability to foster economic growth, along with the national power, both domestically and externally, that growth bestows. States where the value of economic accomplishment overrides all other state objectives, including welfare for its own sake, have been termed "productivist" in the literature. Although funds may be transmitted in order to build up "human capital" in such states—as through investments in the education and health of the citizenry—that expenditure is extended ultimately to serve the state; it also is often directed toward those already poised to succeed. This was so in East Asian and Latin American nations prior to 1990, where much welfare was targeted at formal-sector employees, those at work in state firms and government offices.[11] Aspalter calls investment of this kind "part of the strategy of nation building."[12]

In these places, historically, much reliance was placed on private-funded, not state-funded, sources of sustenance, such that the bulk of state resources could be reserved to be directly pumped into developmental projects and purposes. Accordingly, in Japan and Korea, in both of which productivist welfare has long been the primary goal behind governmental giving, enterprises, families, and civil society groups were traditionally the suppliers of social services and benefits, from postwar times at least up to the period of democratization, in 1952 in Japan and in the late 1980s in Korea.[13]

A second value driving leaders to fund social welfare is their own political advantage (i.e., using allowances to function as patronage for obtaining electoral support). In these cases, elections provide legitimacy, and welfare is given to secure votes. I refer to this usage of social assistance as "partisan." Scholars have often attributed this motive to politicians in Latin America (especially in Mexico) and in India, among other places. And the third ideal-typical value, and, thus, role for relief, is to disperse funds to the disadvantaged to secure domestic peace, order, and stability, lest those left without sufficient means to survive (at least minimally) should create disturbances and fuel opposition to the regime, thereby diminishing its legitimacy. This type of giving I characterize as "pacifying/policing," which has been the impetus for the Chinese regime's provision of the *dibao*,[14] and also for some

---

11. Stephan Haggard and Robert R. Kaufman, *Development, Democracy, and Welfare States: Latin America, East Asia, and Eastern Europe* (Princeton, NJ: Princeton University Press, 2008), 4.

12. Aspalter, "The East Asian," 291, references the work of Ian Holliday and Ian Gough.

13. Haggard and Kaufman, *Development*, 231.

14. Dorothy J. Solinger, "The Urban Dibao: Guarantee for Minimum Livelihood or for Minimal Turmoil?" in *Marginalization in Urban China: Comparative Perspectives*, eds. Fulong Wu and Chris Webster (Houndmills, Basingstoke, UK: Palgrave/Macmillan, 2010), 253–77; Pan, *Welfare*.

states in Latin America.[15] Some scholars allege that this motive lies behind the US authorities' disbursal of benefits as well.[16]

Accordingly, in ideal-typical terms, politicians have employed public assistance to enhance state productivity; to achieve their own political ambitions; and to ensure or secure social peace. In all these ways, the larger mission is to shore up their personal—or their regime's—legitimacy. I claim, despite the promise (and, to varying degrees, the reality), that a package of relief will protect the individual recipient, researchers have alleged that these modalities of assistance address other objectives, primarily those related to politicians' purposes.

Three caveats: First, there are instances or situations in which there is truly an aim to protect or relieve the needy and where doing so is rooted in an individual politician's or his/her political party's ideology. According to the work of Gosta Esping-Andersen and that of Evelyne Huber and John D. Stephens, left-wing political parties in Western Europe and elsewhere have espoused such ideology;[17] the same claim has been made for former South Korean President Kim Dae Jung (1998 to 2003);[18] this position seemingly played a part too in twentieth-century so-called communist administrations run by socialist parties, whether in the former Soviet Union, Eastern Europe, Cuba, or elsewhere.[19] The second caveat is that there may be more than one of these ideal-typical motives at play in any given instance; and third, a particular government's approach can change with time, as I discuss later in this chapter.

This classification is markedly different from the oft-cited, three-fold one proposed some thirty years ago by Esping-Andersen, in his well-known treatise, *The Three Worlds of Welfare Capitalism*. The study explicated historical reasons why "advanced capitalist democracies" vary considerably with regard to their accent on welfare. The author alleges that, "Even if the lion's

---

15. Alex Segura-Ubiergo, *The Political Economy of the Welfare State in Latin America: Globalization, Democracy, and Development* (New York: Cambridge University Press, 2007), 260.

16. Frances Fox Piven and Richard A. Cloward, *Regulating the Poor: The Functions of Public Welfare* (updated edition) (New York: Vintage Books, 1993); Joe Soss, Richard C. Fording, and Sanford F. Schram, *Disciplining the Poor: Neoliberal Paternalism and the Persistent Power of Race* (Chicago: University of Chicago Press, 2011); Michael B. Katz, *The Undeserving Poor: America's Enduring Confrontation with Poverty* (second ed.) (New York: Oxford University Press, 2013); and Loic Wacquant, *Punishing the Poor: The Neoliberal Government of Social Insecurity* (Durham, NC: Duke University Press, 2009).

17. Gosta Esping-Andersen, *The Three Worlds of Welfare Capitalism* (Princeton, NJ: Princeton University Press, 1990); Evelyne Huber and John D. Stephens, *Development and Crisis of the Welfare State: Parties and Policies in Global Markets* (Chicago: University of Chicago Press, 2001).

18. J. J. Yang, "The Korean Welfare," 60, refers thusly to Korean President Kim Dae Jung.

19. Linda J. Cook, *The Soviet Social Contract and Why it Failed* (Cambridge, MA: Harvard University Press, 1993); Elizabeth Kath, *Social Relations and the Cuban Health Miracle* (Milton Park, Abingdon, UK: Routledge Press, 2017.); Haggard and Kaufman, *Development*, 357.

share of expenditures or personnel serves welfare aims, the kind of welfare provided will be qualitatively different, as will its prioritization relative to competing activities." For him, it was "the history of political class coalitions" that was "the most decisive cause of welfare-state variations." Esping-Andersen's argument was that the degree of decommodification, the nature of social stratification, and the management of employment are "keys to a welfare state's identity." This insight enabled him to formulate three diverse welfare-regime types among democracies, each centered on a distinct logic of economic organization, social stratification, and societal integration. Regimes then "owe their origins to different historical forces, and they follow qualitatively different developmental trajectories," he asserted, as he clustered the states that observe one or another of these patterns into "conservative," "liberal," and "social democratic" welfare.[20] My triple model is aimed at comparing not just democracies but also programs in countries with differing regime types; it also can be useful in assessing the extent to which it is appropriate to judge that a particular scheme meets the objectives of "social assistance" as defined previously.

Under all three of my rubrics or models, funds or goods are, admittedly, allocated to people in distress, regardless of the giving government's deeper political purpose and, therefore, on that basis alone, could all qualify as "social assistance" (but not according to the definitions above). But the level of generosity of the allowance is also relevant, as measured by the total amount bestowed as a percentage of the state's gross domestic product (GDP) and/or of governmental expenditures; and also, by the allocation's percentage of a place's national (or local) average per capita income and/or of its national (or local) average wage. If one or more of these percentages is notably small compared with those provided by other states, one could debate whether the subsidy ought genuinely to be viewed as social assistance, as defined above, by Barrientos.

I go on to elaborate on each of these welfare model types—productivist, partisan, or pacifying/policing—and also illustrate each type by reviewing countries or regions that fit into one or the other of the groupings. As noted, these three styles of, or, more precisely, motives for, protection are ideal types. Thus, in a given instance, there may be a mix of any two or three of these types; in such cases, I will either emphasize the motive that appears most prominent in the views of specialists, or else I will appeal to trans-

---

20. Joseph Hanlon, Armando Barrientos, and David Hulme, *Just Give Money to the Poor: The Development Revolution from the Global South* (Sterling, VA: Kumarian Press, 2010), 28–37, 89–97. See also Yuan Yuan and Fulong Wu, "Multiple Deprivations in Urban China: An Analysis of Individual Survey Data," in Wu and Webster, eds., *Marginalization,* 218; Han Keqing, ed., *Zhongguo chengshi dibao fangtanlu* [Interviews with Minimum Livelihood Guarantee Recipients in Urban China] (Ji'nan: Shandong renmin chubanshe [Shandong people's press], 2012), 262–63.

forming factors that over time shifted a nation's leaders' major, or primary, incentive behind giving.

THREE WELFARE PROGRAM MODELS

Productivist Assistance: Nation Building for the State

Analysts who point to a "productivist" angle in assistance, particularly in East Asia, usually attach it to what Chalmers Johnson branded "the developmental state";[21] this approach is also portrayed as a component of the "bureaucratic authoritarian state."[22] For East Asian states, writes Gregory Kasza, "production" is the "first approach to public policy." These states, he maintains, limit social spending, in the interest of putting finances largely into economic growth.[23]

In another characterization, Ian Holliday and P. Wilding find six dimensions that characterized East Asian welfare states prior to democratization. Their list closely matches Kasza's: political purposes were primary; economic growth and full employment were the main engines of welfare; productivist welfare was the goal; welfar*ism* was shunned; the family took a central role; and the state's involvement was strong but limited.[24] Similarly, Stephan Haggard and Robert R. Kaufman term social insurance in East Asia "minimal" and often turned over to mandated individual savings programs, even if the states did treat education and public health seriously.[25] Mari Miura goes so far as to contend that, in Japan, social protection is officially justified in terms of the state's interest and so amounts to a form of statism. She even sees economic development and growth as "the sole national goal in postwar Japan."[26] According to T. Fleckenstein and S. C. Lee, states of this type took the aim of national productivity to such a degree that they concentrated welfare provision just on what were held to be the most productive segments of

21. Chalmers Johnson, *MITI and the Japanese Miracle* (Stanford, CA: Stanford University Press, 1982).

22. Guillermo O'Donnell, *Modernization and Bureaucratic Authoritarianism* (Berkeley: University of California Press, 1979) coined the term "bureaucratic authoritarianism." Jung-en Woo, *Race to the Swift: State and Finance in Korean Industrialization* (New York: Columbia University Press, 1991) uses it to describe pre-democratic South Korea.

23. Gregory J. Kasza, *One World of Welfare: Japan in Comparative Perspective* (Ithaca, NY: Cornell University Press, 2006), 110, 115–16.

24. I. P. Holliday and P. Wilding, eds., *Welfare Capitalism in East Asia* (London: Palgrave/MacMillan, 2003), 1–17, cited in Yih-Jiunn Lee and Yeun-wen Ku, "East Asian Welfare Regimes: Testing the Hypothesis of the Developmental Welfare State," *Social Policy and Administration* 41, no. 2 (2007): 197–212.

25. Haggard and Kaufman, *Development*, 1, 4.

26. Mari Miura, *Welfare through Work: Conservative Ideas, Partisan Dynamics, and Social Protection in Japan* (Ithaca, NY: Cornell University Press, 2012), 6.

the population, such as skilled workers in large companies, civil servants, and the military, and ensured jobs with lifetime employment in lieu of offering grants of aid. They term this model "welfare through work."[27]

For South Korea (hereafter, Korea), the story is much the same—lifetime employment, emphasis on growth, meager direct spending on social welfare. Jun Sung Hong et al. refer to the nation's "productive welfare,"[28] as do Tae-kyoon Kim and his collaborators, who use the term "occupational welfare" to signify that assistance policy was to operate through enterprises via life-long guaranteed employment, much as in its neighbor country.[29] The family was also to be a strong fallback—again, as in Japan[30]—which some have connected to the Confucian ethos prominent in these societies.[31] True, a Livelihood Protection System for poverty relief was enacted in Korea in 1961. But it assisted just the elderly, the disabled, pregnant women, and children, neglecting the merely indigent.[32] Later, in the words of Mungji Yang, dictator Park Chung-Hee, who ruled from 1961–1979, had as his "ultimate goal" the construction of a "strong and modernized nation-state that would be on equal terms with world powers."[33]

Some believe that even following democratization after 1987, Korea's proclivity to slight welfare officially—by turning most of the responsibility for it over to the firms—persisted. Since, as these scholars argue, economic growth and development still occupied pride of place on the government's agenda, whatever pro-poor policy existed continued to have "little impact on either poverty reduction or income inequality." Rather, it was mainly the country's economic development that could be credited for any lessening of poverty.[34]

Seconding this assessment, Haggard and Kaufman refer to 1990s President Kim Young Sam as another champion of productivist policies. For, despite the welfare reforms he sponsored, the result remained provision by private entities such as firms, non-governmental organizations, and community groups.[35] Though leftist-leaning Presidents Kim Dae Jung and Roh Moo Hyun

---

27. Timo Fleckenstein and Soohyun Christine Lee, "Democratization, Post-Industrialization, and East Asian Welfare Capitalism: The Politics of Welfare State Reform in Japan, South Korea, and Taiwan," *Journal of International and Comparative Social Policy* 33, no. 1 (2017): 36–54. https://doi.org/10.1080/21699763.2017.1288158; Kasza, *One World,* 100.

28. Jun Sung Hong, Young Sook Kim, Na Youn Lee, and Ji Woong Ha, "Understanding Social Welfare in South Korea," in *Social Welfare in East Asia and the Pacific*, ed. Sharlene B. C. L. Furuto (New York: Columbia University Press, 2013), 41–66.

29. Taekyoon Kim, Huck-Ju Kwon, Jooha Lee, and Ilcheong Yi, "'Mixed Governance' and Welfare in South Korea," *Journal of Democracy* 22, no. 3 (July 2011): 125, 127.

30. Ibid., 130.

31. Fleckenstein and Lee, "Democratization."

32. Kim et al., "'Mixed Governance,'" 125.

33. Mungji Yang, *From Miracle to Mirage: The Making and Unmaking of the Korean Middle Class, 1960–2015* (Ithaca, NY: Cornell University Press, 2018), 35.

34. Kim et al., "'Mixed Governance,'" 125.

35. Haggard and Kaufman, *Development*, 231, 250; Hong et al., "Understanding," 45.

(who governed, respectively, from 1998 to 2008) did favor a more welfare-oriented approach, the advent of conservative politicians, beginning with the presidency of Lee Myung-bak (2009–2013), ended their initiatives.[36] In short, states that have accentuated the value of economic growth, primarily but not only the "miracle"-making East Asian states of Korea and Japan,[37] have tended to be ones where the productivist approach has been predominant.

Partisan Welfare Approaches: Assistance for Politicians' Benefit

Researchers writing on Brazil, Argentina, Mexico, Japan, India, Korea, Taiwan, and the United States have all emphasized the impact of upcoming elections on politicians' attention to social spending. Students of Latin American countries, especially of Mexico, have accordingly queried the sincerity of welfare policies and programs there, pointing to their proponents' partisan ambitions. PRONASOL (Programa Nacional de Solidaridad, established by President Carlos Salinas de Gortari in 1988), the first major social welfare program to target poor rural populations in Mexico, has famously been said to have been forged expressly to gain votes for the Institutional Revolutionary Party (the PRI). This judgment is based on the PRI's need for votes in exactly the regions to which funds were directed. As Michelle Dion argues, a series of Mexican administrations over the two decades from 1988 to 2007 instituted noncontributory welfare schemes expressly to strengthen the Party's popularity. Even though some benefit expansions were made in response to economic crisis and accompanying restructuring—and to a concomitant growth in the size of the population in need—the effort also played a critical role in winning votes. And that the hikes in contributions occurred in election years strengthens this interpretation.[38]

Perhaps in the mold of Franklin Delano Roosevelt, leaders in Mexico built and enlarged their political coalitions by spreading allowances. Hanlon and his co-authors note that this phenomenon has existed in Brazil as well.[39] Sergio Simoni Junior maintains that Brazilian President Lula da Silva's Workers Party's 2003 creation of a conditional cash transfer program for poor families with children, the Bolsa Família, was driven partly by partisan aims.

36. Jae-Jin Yang, "Parochial Welfare Politics and the Small Welfare State in South Korea," *Comparative Politics* (CP) 45, no. 4 (2013): 464; idem., "The Korean Welfare State in Economic Hard Times: Democracy, Partisanship, and Social Learning," *Taiwan Journal of Democracy* 8, no. 1 (July 2012): 57, 59–61.

37. Qin Gao, Jiyoung Yoo, Sooko-Mee Yang, and Fuhua Zhai, "Welfare Residualism: A Comparative Study of the Basic Livelihood Security Systems in China and South Korea," *IJSW* 20 (2011): 113–24, especially 122.

38. Michelle L. Dion, *Workers and Welfare: Comparative Institutional Change in Twentieth-Century Mexico* (Pittsburgh: University of Pittsburgh Press, 2010), 192–97.

39. Hanlon et al., *Just Give*, 92.

Moreover, his opponents, and later leaders, behaved analogously. President Jair Bolsonaro, for instance, who took office in 2019, promised during his election campaign to enlarge the plan.[40] Haggard and Kaufman add that in the early 2000s, two successive, expressly populist administrations (that sponsored policies aimed at placating and winning over voters) significantly expanded social assistance to jobless workers.[41]

This practice has also been observed in Asia. In Japan, according to Kasza, welfare policy has aimed not only at national economic development but also at gaining votes for the long-reigning Liberal Democratic Party (LDP).[42] Fleckenstein speaks of "electoral calculation, competition and victory" as leftist parties in both Taiwan and Korea played to voters' demands for improved social policy, once the combination of democratization and fiscal crisis spurred them to do so. And, in turn, after left-wing parties attained power, they did enhance public spending for public works, jobs, and social assistance.[43]

In India, what amounts to outright vote-buying by means of welfare distribution is rampant. By the early 1980s, the Indian state and its politicians had forged an alliance with the business class as economic growth trumped a prior policy of redistribution, Atul Kohli holds. Still, resources have been allocated to the poor, in response to electoral, and also non-electoral, pressures from groups that were excluded.[44] Soundarya Chidambram, writing in 2010, emphasizes that the high degree of competitiveness in Indian elections induced politicians, parties, and voters to build patronage bonds that could smooth the way to electoral victory.[45] In like manner, Anoop Sadanandan attests that both parties and their leaders allocate Below Poverty Line cards to build a political clientele, at both federal and, increasingly with decentralization, at state levels.[46]

When the government announced a new program in 2013 to deposit pension and scholarship payments into people's bank accounts in order to prevent theft by local elites, critics charged that the plan was aimed more at purchasing votes than at fighting poverty; fewer than one-third of the populace even possessed a bank account at the time.[47] Five years later, in early

---

40. Sergio Simoni Junior, "How Bolsa Familia Really Impacts Brazilian Elections," *The Brazilian Report*, October 26, 2018.
41. Haggard and Kaufman, *Development,* 280–81.
42. Kasza, *One World,* 80.
43. Fleckenstein and Lee, *Democratization.*
44. Atul Kohli, *Poverty amid Plenty in the New India* (New York: Cambridge University Press, 2012), 2, 3, 9.
45. Soundarya Chidambram, "The 'Right' Kind of Welfare in South India's Urban Slums: *Seva* vs. Patronage and the Success of Hindu Nationalist Organizations," *Asian Survey* 52, no. 2 (March/April 2012): 298–320.
46. Anoop Sadanandan, "Patronage and Decentralization: The Politics of Poverty in India," *CP* (January 2012): 211–28.
47. Gardiner Harris, "With Deposits, India Aims to Keep Money for the Poor from Others' Pockets," *New York Times (NYT),* January 6, 2013.

2018, with an eye to elections coming up the following year, Prime Minister Narendra Modi announced a measure that was to provide free health care for a half-billion poor Indians. Some speculated that this venture was more likely to succeed than an earlier similar one that was never funded, given the imminence of elections the second time.[48]

The moral here is that elections and party competition have allegedly been the major push behind the promotion of welfare in a number of states. And, even where the primary governmental focus may be on economic results, as in Japan, party competition can significantly shape politicians' behavior too.

Pacifying/Policing as Prod to Welfare

Christian Aspalter considers the hope of instilling political stability and peace in society, along with economic growth, to be two distinct regime goals driving social policy in East Asia.[49] Relatedly, Alex Segura-Ubiergo contends that many Latin American countries introduced social legislation to control mobilized labor movements, citing Chile and Argentina as instances.[50] In this same vein, Barrientos remarks that this impulse to appease opponents and silence troublemakers frequently feeds plans of social protection.[51] In the welfare literature, China and the United States are two outstanding cases in which leaders' concerns over possible loss of state control owing to popular opposition and disorder—especially at times of massive unemployment—have disposed them to design projects that distributed allowances to the needy.

To begin with the United States, Frances Fox Piven and Richard A. Cloward suggest that Franklin Roosevelt's angling for the Democratic Party presidential nomination in the midst of the Great Depression—during which millions of unemployed were clogging the roads in protest—sparked his bond with the unemployed and others in need. Among the raft of new policies his speeches pledged, a major one entailed the federal government taking on responsibility for relief where states had failed to execute their own programs. According to this reasoning, Roosevelt's storied New Deal program was born out of electoral considerations.[52] But "turmoil"—in reference to the laid-off thronging the streets and clamoring for help—was, these authors bluntly judge, the prompt that produced the subsidies and

---

48. Vindu Goel and Hari Kumar, "India Wants to Give a Half-Billion People Free Health Care," *NYT*, February 2, 2018, A6.

49. Aspalter, "The East Asian," 290.

50. Alex Segura-Ubiergo, *The Political Economy,* 260.

51. Armando Barrientos, "Introducing Basic Social Protection in Low-Income Countries: Lessons from Existing Programmes," in *Building Decent Societies: Rethinking the Role of Social Security in Development,* ed. Peter Townsend (Houndmills, UK: Palgrave Macmillan 2009), 263.

52. Piven and Cloward, *Regulating the Poor*, 61–72. By contrast, President Lyndon Johnson's Great Society of 1964–1965 was launched *following* his election in 1964. But perhaps it bolstered his legitimacy as he ruled.

aid dispensed during Roosevelt's administration. Piven and Cloward also point out that, as the upheaval calmed—even in the face of persisting and stubbornly elevated unemployment—relief was cut back. An apt quotation establishes what they term "the moral point": "A placid poor gets nothing but a turbulent poor sometimes gets something."[53]

Appraising procedures in more recent times, Joe Soss and his co-authors attest that programs billed to benefit the poor in the United States have as a major purpose limiting disruptiveness and making the indigent "more manageable."[54] Andrea Campbell agrees, arguing that assistance for the poor can be used as a kind of punishment, as in the case of supplemental social insurance, which condemns its recipients to the most meager level of subsistence imaginable.[55] Sanford Schram, commenting on the aftermath of the 2008–2009 Great Recession in the United States, holds that the working class and the poor, who had already suffered from this setback, were further disciplined by the state for their inability to manage in an economy that offered them no decent place—that is, they were forced to labor in precarious, substandard jobs just to stay barely nourished.[56]

In like vein, both administrators and policymakers in China explicitly instituted, assess the success of, and defend the *dibao* in large part in light of its role in quieting social disorder. They have specifically pointed to its function in appeasing the tens of millions of laid-off workers whose jobs were terminated at one stroke without warning. Patricia Thornton contends that the Communist Party handles those on the "lower rungs" of society with surveillance and "preemptive cum coercive strategies of control."[57] For Korea, Taekyoon Kim et al. note that the Chun Doo Hwan government, which came to power in 1980, similarly used social welfare to ensure social control.[58] Surely these schemes that strive to counter disruption do offer funds to the poor. But the levels of support tend to be exceedingly meager, or, as Gao and her co-authors term it, "residual," referring to China and Korea.[59]

Programs having either a productivist or a pacifying/policing bent tend to be notably stingier than partisan ones, as I document below. This is apparent in the productivist East Asian reliance on private spending. Another unchari-

53. Ibid., 3, 45, 338.

54. Soss et al., *Disciplining the Poor*, 1.

55. Andrea Louise Campbell, *Trapped in America's Safety Net: One Family's Struggle* (Chicago: University of Chicago Press, 2014), 120.

56. Stanford F. Schram, *The Return of Ordinary Capitalism: Neoliberalism, Precarity, Occupy* (Oxford and New York: Oxford University Press, 2015), 4, 25, 26.

57. Patricia M. Thornton, "A New Urban Underclass? Making and Managing 'Vulnerable Groups' in Contemporary China," in *To Govern China: Evolving Practices of Power*, eds. Vivienne Shue and Patricia M. Thornton (New York: Cambridge University Press, 2017), 260–61, 270, 273.

58. Kim et al., "'Mixed governance,'" 122.

59. Gao et al.,"Welfare Residualism," 113–24.

table dimension of such programs is that they frequently are meant merely for those incapable of working to earn a living and exclude the able-bodied poor. One example is the 1999 Korean National Basic Livelihood Security Act, according to which the state would be responsible for guaranteeing just a "social minimum"—and even of that, only for those between the ages of eighteen and sixty-four who were unable to work[60]—even in the aftermath of the devastating Asian financial crisis of 1997–1998. Similarly, in Japan, most welfare recipients have not been able-bodied, even in 1999, when unemployment reached its highest level in years.[61] Instead, public assistance has aimed at bringing poor families over the poverty line only if they have members who are elderly or diseased, injured, or disabled.[62]

Welfare in the United States has often been marked by this same slant. Piven and Cloward uncover a vicious cycle, according to which ambitious aid schemes have dwindled as disorder has subsided, leaving behind "categorical-assistance programs for the impotent poor" (i.e., schemes meant just for those who are older, blind, orphaned, and so forth). And, the authors go on, "Relief systems ordinarily exclude able-bodied men no matter how severe their destitution or prolonged their unemployment."[63] Means-tested Supplemental Security Income, inaugurated in 1972 as a federal program to supplement Social Security for those with scant income or resources and who are disabled, blind, or over the age of sixty-five, has much in common with the Japanese program of the late 1990s noted above: both demand that recipients first deplete their savings and any other possible sources of financial sustenance before they can get assistance. Its niggardly treatment of its clients, as spelled out graphically by Andrea Campbell in her heart-rending saga of her own family, sends a definite message about the frugal stance of the American government in aiding those who are helpless and very needy: as of 2013, a family in possession of more than $3,150 in assets would not qualify.[64]

Clearly, such restrictions set up situations in which members of the subsequent generation receive as their birthright biting poverty with no evident exit from it.[65] Moreover, schemes and approaches that give out meager allowances are degrading, intrusive, stigmatizing, and humiliating. This has been true both in China's *dibao* and in the United States, when relief has

---

60. Kim, "'Mixed Governance,'" 130.

61. Kasza, *One World*, 100.

62. Leonard J. Schoppa, *Race for the Exits: The Unraveling of Japan's System of Social Protection* (Ithaca, NY: Cornell University Press, 2006), 46.

63. Piven and Cloward, *Regulating the Poor*, 117, 126.

64. Campbell, *Trapped*, 17; Edward D. Berkowitz and Larry DeWitt, *The Other Welfare: Supplemental Security Income and U.S. Social Policy* (Ithaca, NY: Cornell University Press, 2013); Julie Turkewitz and Juliet Linderman, "The Disability Trap," *NYT*, October 21, 2012.

65. Campbell, *Trapped*, 68.

been offered chiefly to muzzle the potentially unruly plaints of the poor.[66] As I show later, there is a correlation between pacification/policing as the principal objective behind bestowing benefits, on the one hand, and low percentages of GDP spent on social assistance, on the other.

CHANGES: TRANSFORMING FACTORS, POLITICAL AND ECONOMIC

Governmental expansion and contraction of benefits both occur, as do switches from one dominant political motivation for giving assistance to another. Two broad kinds of factors drive such alterations/transformations: political, as in regime transitions; and economic, as in heightened global involvement, debt, or other crises (whether having domestic or external causes), and fiscal constraints. Both political and economic factors can be present simultaneously, making it difficult to sort out their separate influences; still, I discuss them independently.

Political Factors: Democratization/Regime Change

A country's move from an authoritarian regime to a democratic one invariably has implications for its welfare package. According citizens the right to choose their leaders, permitting them to form civil society groups that can put forward demands pressuring leaders, and signaling to politicians that they may openly establish new parties and compete for office all can produce programs that enhance existing or create uncharted social welfare policies and programs. Regime change of this sort activates my second major prod to providing assistance analyzed above—the partisan one.

In Korea, Taiwan, Thailand, and the Philippines in Asia, as well as in Mexico and Brazil in Latin America, conversion from authoritarian to democratic regimes in and after the late 1980s led to building brand-new programs of assistance and welfare. But while the Taiwanese and Brazilian governments were able to take this step from a position of economic strength, that was not the case for all these countries.[67] Jae-Jin Yang sees a confluence of economic and political circumstances at work in Korea's move: the 1997 economic crisis prodded large sections of the public suddenly to clamor for state aid, given the massive numbers of abruptly jobless citizens, while the relatively

---

66. Piven and Cloward, *Regulating the Poor*, 3, 166; Soss et al., *Disciplining the Poor*, 204; William Julius Wilson, *The Truly Disadvantaged* (Chicago: University of Chicago Press, 1987), 157.

67. Haggard and Kaufman, *Development*, 218, 8, 232, 282; Kim et al., "'Mixed Governance,'" 122; Hong et al., "Understanding," 45–46; and J. J. Yang, "Parochial Welfare," 457, discussing the late 1990s; Aspalter, "The East Asian," 290–91.

recent democratization there heightened their ability to attain a favorable hearing.[68] As the economy floundered, and a "flexible labor market" took the place of what had been secure, lifetime employment, the government did set up compensatory programs, as those affected by the downturn employed democratic tools to goad it to do so, with public expenditure for social assistance doubling as a percentage of the state budget from before (1997) to after (2001) the crisis.[69]

In Mexico, democratization came at the end of the 1980s with the entry of a new, seemingly challenging party, the Partido de la Revolucion Democratica. Thereafter, one program of social aid followed another with a succession of presidents, beginning with President Salinas. Throughout Latin America, in the 1980s in countries where democratization took hold (if sometimes briefly), demands from the lower classes impelled social assistance initiatives.[70] The upshot included benefits for people who had been outside the system, since their votes could now make a difference.[71]

Regime transition in Eastern Europe also brought concern over welfare to the fore for both the populace and the politicians. But the situation was quite different from that in either Latin America or East Asia, where social policies in authoritarian times had been either scant or else targeted just at formal sector workers and state officials. In the former Soviet region, it was not so much regime transition with its political competition and elections that disposed the post-Soviet leadership throughout Eastern Europe to be as generous as possible, according to Haggard and Kaufman. The issue was that economies fell apart and mass impoverishment surfaced under the assaults of "shock therapy." Indeed, across Eastern Europe, new rulers felt obliged to cater to the multitude of victims of the failed economies, as state-owned firms with all their privileges and prerequisites fell prey to the sudden appearance of an untried market economy.

Rather than simply democratization prompting the authorities to provide assistance, a particular background presaged the largesse in these nations: this was the legacy of expectations from communist days, when the state accorded numerous benefits and provided public goods and subsidies to the population at large. New leaders were at pains to honor these assumptions in

---

68. J. J. Yang, "The Korean Welfare," 54.

69. Kim et al., "'Mixed Governance,'" 123, 130.

70. Yuriko Takahashi, "The Political Economy of Conditional Cash Transfers in Latin America," Prepared for delivery at the 2013 Annual Meeting of the American Political Science Association, August 29–September 1, 2013, Chicago.

71. Wayne A. Cornelius, Ann L. Craig, and Jonathan Fox, "Mexico's National Solidarity Program: An Overview," in *Transforming State-Society Relations in Mexico: The National Solidarity Strategy*, eds. Wayne Cornelius, Ann L. Craig, and Jonathan Fox (San Diego, CA: Center for US-Mexico Studies, 1994), 3–26; Denise Dresser, "Bringing the Poor Back In: National Solidarity as a Strategy of Regime Legitimation," in ibid., 143–65. Nora Lustig, "Solidarity as a Strategy of Poverty Alleviation," in ibid., 78–96 questions this interpretation.

order to cement the legitimacy of their new regime.[72] Besides the power of these memories, new electoral institutions and freedoms permitting popular agitation also did play some part in inducing the increased welfare spending.[73]

The point here is that political regime change, specifically the advent of democracy, transformed not just the political institutions that made up the regimes in question. It also fundamentally revamped the incentives shaping the behavior of politicians in ways that had definite implications for social policy. Where striving for ever-more economic growth and national wealth had been the ultimate objectives in the past for leaders in East Asia and Latin America (as in the countries of the former Soviet Union), with the onset of democratization, the judgments, gratitude, and potential censure of the ordinary masses came to matter much more than they had in the past. For these reactions could determine whether or not current or aspiring officeholders would be able to retain or attain public office. This political metamorphosis, thus, had the capacity to redirect officials in countries where aid had been handed out mainly to strengthen the economic base of the state—for productivity—to begin to adopt a partisan stance on this issue.

Economic Factors: Globalization and Economic Hardship

A state's economic circumstances may undergo change for a wealth of reasons. Examples are a decision to transform the state's economic development model from import substitution to outward orientation, leading to unaccustomed international competition that in turn eliminates jobs; multilateral financial institutions' imposition of restructuring as a condition for providing loans; or shifts in the prices of a country's critical exports. The point is that the motive behind and/or the level of welfare assistance a government supplies may be altered at times of major economic change. The field of international political economy has long debated if states facing pressures from international economic involvement are more likely to cut back on welfare in order to better compete for foreign investment or, alternatively, to increase the level of assistance for the needy, to help poorer citizens adjust to work and income losses caused by involvement.[74] Much of this analysis attributes the direction of change to the class base of the party in power at the time.

---

72. Haggard and Kaufman, *Development,* 1, 4, notes that "comprehensive protections and services," including employment, education, training, health care, pensions, and family allowances, were accorded "to almost all their populations."

73. Ibid., 3, 13, 17, 217, 287, 343; p. 317 states that, in Hungary, though state revenue dropped and fiscal deficits loomed large, there was high social spending; Czechia and Slovakia were also generous (325, 342).

74. Geoffrey Garrett, "Globalization and Government Spending Around the World," *Studies in Comparative International Development* 35, no. 4 (2001): 3–29; Geoffrey Garrett and Peter Lange, "Political Responses to Interdependence: What's 'Left' for the Left?" *IO* 45, no. 4 (1991): 539–64;

The literature takes one of two tacks: The first focuses on *needs among the populace generated by the losses* from structural change, emphasizing policy makers' willingness to submit to new pressures and address them. In these cases, perhaps owing to concurrent democratization that positions politicians to play to aggrieved publics, or perhaps because of leaders' political ideology, international involvement can foster an *expansion* in benefits and programs. The second stance stresses *the economic hardships facing leaders*, whether from externally induced or internally arranged "structural adjustment," buttressed by the neoliberal philosophy that swept across much of the globe in and after the 1980s.[75] That philosophy called for the privatization of state-owned assets, deregulation of industry, cuts in benefits, and freer trade, including reductions in tariffs and subsidies. All these measures spur job losses and/or wage cuts. Whatever the effort and the intention, a bottom-line commentary that fits states adopting this second approach is this one by Lutz Leisering, written in the midst of the 2008–2009 global fiscal crisis: "Dominated by fiscal considerations, in most countries benefits are below the national poverty line, and fail to alleviate poverty substantially."[76]

In Mexico, as firms and assets were privatized and markets opened, companies fell into bankruptcy, and workers lost their jobs in droves in the early 1990s. Such was the backdrop to the new labor "flexibility" that shot up there at the time. And yet, since that jar took place in tandem with the effort of the PRI to sustain its hold on power at any cost once democratization got underway, programs for the poor did expand.[77] But elsewhere in Latin America, following the 1998 debt crisis, social spending contracted in the face of threatening deficits that led to shaving back budgets.[78] There, with the short-term exception of Brazil, the politics of democratization were

Nita Rudra, "Globalization and the Decline of the Welfare State in Less-Developed Countries," *International Organization* 56, no. 2 (2002): 411–45; Markus M. L. Crepaz, "Global, Constitutional and Partisan Determinants of Redistribution in Fifteen OECD Countries," *CP* 34, no. 2 (2002): 169–88; Robert R. Kaufman and Alex Segura-Ubiergo, "Globalization, Domestic Politics, and Social Spending in Latin America: A Time-Series Cross-Section Analysis, 1973–1997," *World Politics* 53 (2001): 553–87; Alexander Hicks, *Social Democracy and Welfare Capitalism: A Century of Income Security Politics* (Ithaca, NY: Cornell University Press, 1999); and Dorothy J. Solinger, *State's Gains, Labor's Losses: China, France and Mexico Choose Global Liaisons, 1980–2000* (Ithaca, NY: Cornell University Press, 2009).

75. Mark Blyth, *Great Transformations: Economic Ideas and Institutional Change in the Twentieth Century* (Cambridge: Cambridge University Press, 2002); Peter A. Hall, "Policy Paradigms, Social Learning and the State: The Case of Economic Policy-Making in Britain," *CP* 25, no. 3 (1993): 275–96.

76. Lutz Leisering, "Extending Social Security to the Excluded," *Global Social Policy* (GSP) 9 (2009): 253.

77. Dion, *Workers and Welfare*, 13; Judith A. Teichman, *Social Forces and States: Poverty and Distributional Outcomes in South Korea, Chile, and Mexico* (Stanford, CA: Stanford University Press, 2012), 166.

78. Segura-Ubiergo, *The Political Economy*, 167, 264, 265; Alan Gilbert, "Neoliberalism and the Urban Poor: A View from Latin America," in *Marginalization*, eds. Wu and Webster, 40; Haggard and Kaufman, *Development*, 2–4, 12, 17, 287.

overridden, even though, as in Eastern Europe, Latin American states had also long boasted an historical consensus holding that the state must furnish public goods, education, and health care, at least for formal-sector workers.[79] Indeed, as Segura-Ubiergo explains, several prior decades of high levels of social spending in the region were actually one of the contributory factors to the fiscal deficits already long-standing by the turn of the century.[80]

In Asia, when debt crisis occurred in tandem with democratization, the power of the vote did dispose leaders to upgrade social commitments where they could. President Kim Young Sam was the first to accelerate the country's turn outward in the early 1990s, with his enthusiasm for globalization and economic growth.[81] But circumstances turned nasty once the Asian financial crisis reared its head in the late 1990s. Korea's plight was dire enough that it was forced to call in the International Monetary Fund at the end of 1997.[82] The Fund, in turn, mandated a major restructuring of the economic system, in finance and in corporate affairs, shutting down many large chaebols and banks and privatizing public firms.[83] Nonetheless, the election of a leftist politician, Kim Dae Jung, in 1998, meant there was an attempt—if brief—to redress suffering, with an expansion of social insurance.[84] But during the next round of upset, in 2008, both regular and irregular workers lost jobs in large numbers, with social policy unable to keep up with the need.[85] So democracy did not trump financial emergency every time.

Taiwan, too, felt the financial crisis of the late 1990s, with cuts in growth undermining guaranteed jobs. And there, as in Korea in 1998, the government did essay to come to the rescue with public works and job promotion incentives, as well as social assistance. In the Philippines, on the other hand, funding was more limited in the wake of, and on account of, the crisis.[86] Japan's saga began decades earlier, with the LDP's submission to the wave of neoliberalism, soon discovering that the electorate responded favorably. Thus, by the 1990s, previous labor market restructuring meant that the ability of firms to dispense welfare started to retract even before the financial crisis had begun.[87] This was on top of competition from inflows of cheaper goods

---

79. Hanlon et al., *Just Give*, 92.
80. Segura-Ubiergo, *The Political Economy*, 264.
81. Hong et al., "Understanding," 40.
82. There was an economic contraction of nearly 6 percentage points and a burst in the unemployment rate from the norm of 2 to 3 percent to over 8 percent (J. J. Yang, "The Korean Welfare," 55; Kim et al., "'Mixed Governance,'" 130; J. J. Yang, "Parochial," 469).
83. Yang, *From Miracle*, 100.
84. Yang, "Parochial," 457.
85. Teichman, *Social Forces*, 148–49.
86. Haggard and Kaufman, *Development*, 218, 252, 258; Fleckenstein and Lee, "Democratization."
87. Miura, *Welfare through Work*, 3, 7, 8.

from newly industrializing countries and,[88] according to Miura, a deceleration in economic growth in the 1990s disposed the government to reduce benefits and limit eligibility.[89] In India, too, a financial crisis in 1991 only pushed the government further on its pro-business, anti-labor course.[90] So having a democratic political system did not necessarily shield workers from cutbacks when economic exigencies demanded.

Finally, Western and Eastern Europe met the structural crises and economic challenges posed by globalization in the 1990s and early 2000s differentially. European Union members became more deeply entrenched in the global market, which drew their labor markets into powerful competition, even as they were bound by the stringent financial criteria of the European Monetary Union. The outcome was that they were compelled to pare down earlier, generous domestic welfare policies.[91] As Anton Hemerijck wrote of the first decade of the twenty-first century, "A 'double bind' of rising social benefit expenditures [paid out to compensate for the adversity caused by international competition], combined with declining government revenues, is forcing policymakers to make significant cuts in welfare services and social transfers to the poor, the unemployed and pensioners, in order to shore up public finance solvency."[92] But in Eastern Europe, the state-socialist belief that it was the government's responsibility to provide sustenance, added to the ambitions of politicians newly appealing to voters, meant that, even under the constraints of fiscal strain, unemployment insurance and social assistance funds were forthcoming for the newly impoverished.[93]

Thus, the impact of political and economic forces upon welfare models is not a straightforward story. In some cases, an original bias toward productivist welfare can be upset when the chief private source of succor, the firms, can no longer play their wonted role under the strain of economic crises in a country undergoing deeper global insertion. Similarly, partisan motives are clearly strengthened and may even trump productivism when elections come to set the terms of governing and leadership. Finally, places where pacification had ruled in the past, as in Mexico, may become more open to partisanship with democratization. But at the same time, nations in Western Europe that had

———————

88. Schoppa, *Race for the Exits*, 68ff.
89. Miura, *Welfare through Work*, 62.
90. Kohli, *Poverty amid Plenty*, 10.
91. Anton Hemerijck, *Changing Welfare States* (Oxford, UK: Oxford University Press, 2012), 83, 104; Anton Hemerijck and Martin Schludi, "Sequences of Policy Failures and Effective Policy Responses," in *Welfare and Work in the Open Economy: From Vulnerability to Competitiveness*, vol. 1, ed. Fritz W. Scharpf and Vivien A. Schmidt (Oxford, UK: Oxford University Press, 2000), 127, 224.
92. Hemerijck, *Changing Welfare*, 1.
93. Haggard and Kaufman, *Development*, 12, 17, 343.

long been democratic thus, generally speaking, partisan, were spurred—in part as a function of the pull of neoliberal economic thinking—to discard much of the left's pro-labor, vote-garnering posture when globalization and supranational rules overcame past modes of conducting social policy.

TWO SUBTYPE PROGRAMS:
CONDITIONAL CASH TRANSFERS AND WORKFARE

Conditional Cash Transfers

President Ernesto Zedillo inaugurated conditional cash transfers (CCTs) in Mexico in 1997 with PROGRESA, the Programa de Educacion, Salud y Alimentacion (Program for Education, Health and Nutrition), which was expressly aimed at building human capital among the poor. The project soon proliferated throughout Latin America, Africa, Asia, and Central Europe, and even in the United States.[94] In Brazil, the Bolsa Familia is the largest program of this kind.[95] Hanlon et al. name South Africa, Namibia, Indonesia, and India as locations where cash is provided to the poor on a long-term basis.[96]

The distinguishing feature of these grants is that funds are allocated provisionally (i.e., only if recipients send their children to school, take them to health clinics for check-ups, and attend seminars). Their purpose jibes with the productivist model of state-giving, as their grants are meant to enhance the productive capacity of the beneficiaries by building human capital, even as they further development at the national level.[97] Ideally, a critical indirect result is to stave off intergenerational transmission of poverty, a serious and likely consequence of parental impoverishment in places, such as China, that lack such programs.[98]

By 2015, less than two decades from the inception of these schemes, as many as seventeen countries across Latin America—where on average 0.5 to 1.0 percent of GDP was then going to CCT programs—had adopted the plan as a core feature of their anti-poverty efforts, benefiting some twenty-seven million households.[99] Interestingly, the World Bank encouraged

---

94. Dion, *Workers and Welfare*, 199.

95. Haggard and Kaufman, *Development*, 282. From its inception, in 2003, to 2015, the program produced an 82 percent reduction in the country's undernourished population (Rick Gladstone, "Brazil to Keep Allowances for the Poor," *NYT*, September 19, 2015).

96. Hanlon et al., *Just Give*, 2.

97. Juliana Martinez Franzoni and Koen Voorend, "Actors and Ideas Behind CCTs in Chile, Costa Rica and El Salvador," *GSP* no. 2 (2011): 1–20; see 3.

98. Ibid.; Hanlon et al., *Just Give*, ix, 2, 4, 6, 20.

99. Haggard and Kaufman, *Development*, 217, 287; Wendy Hunter, review of Ana Lorena De La O, *Crafting Policies to End Poverty in Latin America: The Quiet Transformation* (New York: Cambridge University Press, 2015), *Perspectives on Politics* 13, no. 4 (2015): 1178–79.

China to set up a plan of this type but was ignored.[100] This was unfortunate, as a principal focus of CCT programs is to cut off continuing penury, a goal in which the Chinese leadership apparently showed no interest.[101] Had it complied with the World Bank's recommendation, many criticisms of the *dibao* could have been addressed.

Workfare

Workfare, "welfare-through-work," or "activation"—cutting back aid to those not employed and pushing those who can do so to take on work—was tried out in the United States in the 1960s and 1970s. But it did not become firm, national policy until the elimination of Aid to Families with Dependent Children (AFDC), which had dated back to 1935, and its replacement with Temporary Assistance for Needy Families (TANF) in 1996. Michael B. Katz criticizes workfare, arguing that it "rejects compassion, empowerment and entitlement," all hallmarks of the 1960s-era Great Society.[102] On the other hand, at least TANF does permit people with jobs to receive assistance; in China, to the contrary, since around 2009, those with even the *capability to work* (even if not employed) have often been thrown off the *dibao* rolls or not admitted into the program. (See Chapter Nine)

Unlike AFDC, TANF incorporates restrictions and requirements that were altogether new in the United States: a minimum of thirty hours of work per week for single mothers with young children and thirty-five hours if two parents live with the children, as well as having a five-year lifetime limit.[103] In 2016, the Obama administration even placed a work requirement

---

100. Nara Dillon, "China's Welfare State in Comparative Perspective: A Preliminary Assessment after Twenty Years of Reform," Paper presented at the annual meeting of the American Political Science Convention, Seattle, September 3, 2011, 29.

101. Wu Fulong, Chris Webster, Shenjing He, and Yuting Liu, *Urban Poverty in China* (Cheltenham, UK: Edward Elgar, 2010), 29; Chen Honglin, Wong Yu-cheung, Zeng Qun, and Juha Hamalainen, "Trapped in Poverty? A Study of the *Dibao* Programme in Shanghai," *China Journal of Social Work* (*CJSW*) 6, no. 3 (2013): 327–43. But Qin Gao, Fuhua Zhai, Sui Yang, and Shi Li, "Does Welfare Enable Family Expenditures on Human Capital? Evidence from China," *World Development* 64 (2014): 225, using the 2007 China Household Income Project, found that *dibao* recipient families "invested significantly more in human capital [education and health care] than their non-recipient peers." Also, see Han, *Zhengguo chengshi*, 260.

102. Katz, *Undeserving Poor*, 196.

103. TANF is discussed in Soss et al., *Disciplining the Poor*, 15, 39; R. Kent Weaver, *Ending Welfare as We Know It* (Washington, DC: The Brookings Institution, 2000), 13, 19, 343, 346; John Karl Scholz, Robert Moffitt, and Benjamin Cowan, "Trends in Income Support," in *Changing Poverty, Changing Policies*, eds. Maria Cancian and Sheldon Danziger (New York: Russell Sage Foundation, 2009), 211–12; Harry J. Holzer, "Workforce Development as an Antipoverty Strategy: What Do We Know? What Should We Do?" in ibid., 301–29; Mary Jo Bane, "Poverty Politics and Policy," in ibid., 367–86; Susan Lambert and Julia Henly, "Double Jeopardy: The Misfit between Welfare-to-Work Requirements and Job Realities," in *Work and the Welfare State: Street-Level Organizations and Workfare Politics*, eds. Evelyn Z. Brodkin and Gregory Marston (Washington, DC: Georgetown University Press, 2013), 69–84; and Giuliano Bonoli and David Natali, "Multidimensional Transformations in

on beneficiaries of the Supplemental Nutrition Assistance Program (the food stamp program of the 1960s).[104]

Not only in the United States but also in a number of OECD countries, around the mid-1990s, a shift occurred in welfare policy, according to which people who would have been recipients in the past were made to enter the labor market rather than having the state continue to protect their incomes.[105] While one form of workfare, like CCTs, does strive to upgrade skills to render the unemployed fit for the job market, another, perhaps more prevalent, form entails sanctions and cutbacks in benefits if people do not comply.[106] David Rueda assessed the new situation thusly: "Budgetary concerns and fiscal discipline have replaced unemployment as the main goals of [better put, matters worrying] governments of all ideologies."[107] Unlike in the West, China did not have budgetary problems at the time of its adoption of the *dibao*; rather, its economy was surging. Nonetheless, the low level of benefit the allowance supplies was deeply influenced by the idea of workfare.[108]

To refer to just one case, in the last decade of the twentieth century and at the beginning of the twentieth-first in the United Kingdom, under the moniker "New Labour," the Labour Party instituted harsh tests of disability, enjoining those at all capable of working to become part of the labor force, with penalties if they did not—a move credited to Margaret Thatcher's view of welfare recipients as "scroungers."[109] Despite the similarity to the related impulse in the United States, Jane Waldfogel contrasted the British approach favorably with the American one, for its support for families with children.[110] Evelyn Z. Brodkin and Flemming Larsen also praise European initiatives, noting that,

---

the Early 21st Century Welfare States," in *The Politics of the New Welfare State*, eds. Giuliano Bonoli and David Natali (Oxford, UK: Oxford University Press, 2012), 302.

104. Robert Pear, "Thousands Could Lose Food Stamps as States Restore Requirements," *NYT*, April 2, 2016.

105. Giuliano Bonoli and David Natali, "The Politics of the 'New' Welfare States: Analysing Reforms in Western Europe," in Bonoli and Natali, *The Politics*, 3–5; Peter A. Hall, "Social Policy-Making for the Long Term," *PS* (April 2015): 289–91.

106. Bonoli and Natali, "Multidimensional Transformations," 302.

107. David Rueda, "The State of the Welfare State: Unemployment, Labor Market Policy, and Inequality in the Age of Workfare," *CP* (April 2015): 296–314.

108. Tao Liu, "Urban Social Assistance in China: Transnational Diffusion and National Interpretation," *Journal of Current Chinese Affairs* 45, no. 2 (2016): 29–51; *idem.*, "Epistemological globalization and the shaping of social policy in China," *Journal of Chinese Governance* 3, no. 4 (2018): 461–76, 5, 7, 10, 11.

109. Michael Adler, "Conditionality, Sanctions, and the Weakness of Redress Mechanisms in the British 'New Deal,'" in Brodkin and Marston, *Work and the Welfare State*, 229–48; Michael Hill and Alan Walker, "What Were the Lasting Effects of Thatcher's Legacy for Social Security? The Burial of Beveridge?" in *The Legacy of Thatcherism: Assessing and Exploring Thatcherite Social and Economic Policies*, eds. Stephen Farrall and Colin Hay (Oxford, UK: Oxford University Press for The British Academy, 2014), 77–107; Carol Walker, "'Don't cut down the tall poppies': Thatcherism and the Strategy of Inequality," in ibid., 282–305.

110. Jane Waldfogel, *Britain's War on Poverty* (New York: Russell Sage Foundation, 2010), 3–7.

"In general, European policies have tended to emphasize programmatic features aimed at building human capital and supporting worker flexibility."[111]

Still, while workfare can be sold as a means of heightening a country's productivity, the jobs to which welfare recipients are referred are often precarious, low-paid, informal, and temporary.[112] This mode of "welfare" is best viewed as part of a larger effort to shave off governmental responsibilities instead of as a means of actualizing human capability. Thus, the foundational spirit behind workfare is miserly as compared with the more generous-minded drive behind conditional cash transfers—regardless of the amounts of funds delivered; the proportions of the population covered; or the percentages of governmental expenditures laid out. I turn now to these quantitative issues. My objective will be to consider correlations between welfare model type and generosity level.

QUANTITATIVE COMPARISONS

Here I adopt two approaches: First, I contrast what is termed "social assistance" in various countries using standard measures: the percent of the populace who are recipients; the percent of per capita disposable income the assistance represents in different countries; the percent of the average and minimum wage the outlays amount to; and the percent of GDP for which the investment accounts. Next, I contrast examples of each of the three welfare models outlined above, using statistics to see how they each stack up. These two exercises will help to judge the extent to which China's *dibao* should be deemed social assistance as strictly understood. Both my statistics and my reasoning are meant to be suggestive, not conclusive.

China's *Dibao* Ranked Comparatively

According to research by Martin Ravallion, as of 2004, when the *dibao* existed only in the cities and about twenty-two million people were receiving it, 7.7 percent of the Chinese urban-registered population was technically eligible for it (i.e., lived in households where the per capita income was below a locally-set threshold). But only just over one-quarter (28.6 percent) of these people were getting the *dibao*, such that just 2.2 percent of the city-officially-registered population was appropriately receiving the funds. Also, while 3.9 percent of the urban population were recipients of the *dibao* nationwide that

---

111. Evelyn Z. Brodkin and Flemming Larsen, "The Policies of Workfare: At the Boundaries between Work and the Welfare State," in Brodkin and Marston, *Work and the Welfare State*, 61.
112. Rueda, "The State," 28.

year, as many as 43 percent of these beneficiaries were not eligible for it.[113] The situation had improved by 2007, when 39 percent of the *dibao*-eligible poor were benefiting from the program.[114] But by 2018, just 46.19 million people (both urban and rural) were being granted the funds, or 3.3 percent of the nation's population that year.[115]

In Mexico, by contrast, where partisan motives were in play, 40 percent of the rural population and about 11 percent of the total population were targets of the PROGRESA in 1999.[116] By 2004, under a new name, Oportunidades, this policy had reached twenty-four million people, accounting for 22 percent of the entire Mexican people.[117] Of course, it is possible that in Mexico, a higher percentage of the populace was poor compared to in China; but China was also less generous. In the OECD member countries, there was quite a range: in 1992, just 0.7 percent of the people in Greece were bestowed benefits, but in partisan New Zealand, 25 percent of the population was getting aid.[118]

Looking at another measure, Gao and her collaborators write that in the first quarter of 2008, the national average *dibao* threshold (or poverty line) amounted to just 17 percent of average per capita disposable income in urban China,[119] a substantial decline from 2002, when the average was 22 percent in cities nationwide and as high as 28 percent among twenty-one major cities.[120] (See Table 2.3) The figure dropped to 16 percent in cities in 2010,[121] and then fell to just 15 percent as of 2017.[122] Between 2007 and 2011, the norm's

---

113. In 2014, just 2.5 percent of the urban population was getting the allowance (Qin Gao and Fuhua Zhai, "Public Assistance, Economic Prospect, and Happiness in Urban China," *Social Indicators Research* 132, no. 1 [2017]; 451–73).

114. Martin Ravallion, "A Guaranteed Minimum Income? China's Di Bao Program," ppt. N.p., n.d. (PowerPoint obtained from the author); Zhang Shifei and Tang Jun, "Chengxiang zuidi shenghuo baozhang zhidu jiben xingcheng" [Urban and rural minimum livelihood guarantee system has basically taken form], in *2008 nian: Zhongguo shehui xingshi fenxi yu yuce* [2008: Analysis and forecast of China's social situation], eds. Ru Xin, Lu Xueyi, and Li Peilin (Beijing: Social Sciences Academic Press, 2008), 60–61, write that reports from the World Bank and China's National Statistics Bureau found that recipients accounted for about one-third of the deserving poor, though in a sample from seven extra-large cities, just 12 percent of those who should have been given allowances were not.

115. http://mca.gov.cn.

116. Dion, *Workers and Welfare*, 201.

117. Hanlon et al., *Just Give*, 40.

118. Gao et al., "Welfare Residualism," 114.

119. Ibid., 116. But Chan, "Rethinking," 641, quotes Tang Jun and Zhang Shifei as finding that in 2004–2005, in thirty-six cities, the actual benefit distributed to recipients (the subsidy) was just 9.2 percent of the average per capita monthly income.

120. Dorothy J. Solinger, "Dibaohu in Distress: The Meager Minimum Livelihood Guarantee System in Wuhan," in *China's Changing Welfare Mix: Local Perspectives*, eds. Jane Duckett and Beatriz Carillo (London: Routledge, 2011), 45.

121. Bjorn Gustafsson and Gang Shuge, "A Comparison of Social Assistance in China and Sweden," *CJSW* 6, no. 3 (2013): 304; Tang Jun and Xiu Hongfang, "2010–2011: Chengxiang shehui jiuzhu zhidu de wenti ji duice" [Urban and rural social assistance system's problems and their management], in *2011 nian: Zhongguo shehui xingshi fenxi yu yuce* [2011: analysis of China's social situation and forecast], eds. Ru Xin, Lu Xueyi, and Li Peilin (Beijing: shehui kexue wenxian chubanshe [Social Sciences Academic Press], 2011), 212–13.

122. Table 2.4, based on the Civil Affairs Statistical Yearbook, has just under 18 percent for 2017.

average increase rate per annum was over 7.5 percent lower than the average rate of the increase in the consumer price index.[123] And, as of 2010, the average growth rate of the norm was "obviously lower than the rate of increase of per capita GDP, that of the average wage, and that of per capita financial income and expenditure across various provinces and cities," two Chinese scholars report.[124] Similar to this minimalist, pacifying approach was what TANF offered in most states in the United States, "Less than 10 percent of what a family need[ed] to live," as of around 2013, according to Campbell.[125]

In Sweden, where partisanship (plus ideology) governs assistance, recipients were granted allowances that equaled 35 percent of mean disposable income in 2010.[126] Even more generous, according to Tang and Xiu, nations in the European Union, governed by the partisan model, "generally" had a social assistance norm of 50 to 60 percent of per capita income.[127] Among the more developed countries in the European Union, only Estonia, at 11 percent, had a very low rate.[128] Also well above China's after 2005 (see Tables 2.4 and 7.2) or those distributed in the United States, Mexico's cash grants amounted to 27 percent of the average household income of the rural poor and 20 percent of the urban poor's,[129] where, again, partisanship influenced the outlays.

In partisan Brazil in 2003, cash transfers allotted by the Bolsa Familia were worth 30 percent of the minimum wage. This figure is higher than China's *dibao* as a percent of its average wage even at the *dibao*'s most generous, in 1998, when the average rate was 20.5 percent in nineteen major cities.[130] (See Table 2.2) By 2004, the average rate had already fallen significantly, down to 14.2 percent among eighteen major municipalities.[131] (See Table 7.1) In another five years, in 2009, Tianjin, which had the highest rate nationally, was offering just 11.7 percent of the average wage. By

---

123. Tang Jun, "2012: Zhongguo xinxing shehui jiuzhu tixi jiben jiancheng" [China's new-style social assistance system is basically constructed], in *2013 nian: Zhongguo shehui xingshi fenxi yu yuce*, eds. Lu Xueyi, Li Peilin, and Chen Guangjin [2013: analysis of China's social situation and forecast] (Beijing: shehui kexue wenxuan chubanshe [Social Science Academic Press], 2013), 215.

124. Xiang and Zhao, "Jiyu kuozhan," 43.

125. Campbell, *Trapped*, 77.

126. Gustafsson and Gang, "A Comparison," 304.

127. Tang and Xiu, "2010–2011," 213.

128. Jinxian Wang and Yanfeng Bai, "Development of Minimum Livelihood Guarantee Programmes in Urban China: An Empirical Analysis Based on 31 Regions over 2003–2013," *CJSW* 9, nos. 1–3 (2016): 157.

129. Hanlon et al., *Just Give*, 41. No date is given for these figures.

130. Solinger, "Dibaohu in Distress," 43; for the *dibao* norm, "Xiao ziliao: Quanguo ge chengshi jumin zuidi shenghuo baozhang biaozhun" [Small material: Nationwide various cities' residents' minimum livelihood guarantee norms], *Shehui* [Society], 6 (1999): 26; for the average wage, Wuxi Statistical Yearbook 1999, from China Data Online, accessed May 29, 2008.

131. Solinger, "Dibaohu in Distress," 46. For the *dibao* norm, "Quanguo 36ge chengshi zuidi baozhang biaozhun yilan" [General survey of 36 cities' minimum livelihood guarantee norm], http://china.com.cn/city/txt/2006-11/25/content_740675\hich\af0\dbch\af13\loch\f0 8_2.htm, accessed August 17, 2007 (no longer available); for wages, Wuxi Statistical Yearbook 2005, China data online, accessed May 29. 2008.

Table 7.1.   *Dibao* Norms, Average Wage, *Dibao* Norms as Percentage of Average Wage, Eighteen Large Cities, 2004 (Unit: Yuan/Month)

City Name	Dibao *Line (A)*	Avg.Stf./Wkr. Mon.Wage (B)	A/B (%)
Beijing	290	2,472.83	11.7
Tianjin	241	1,812.83	13.3
Shenyang	205	1,444.33	14.2
Dalian	276*	1,643.25	16.8
Changchun	169	1,159.42	14.6
Harbin	200	1,160.67	17.2
Qingdao	230	1,120.42	20.5
Shanghai	280	2,489.58	11.3
Hangzhou	285*	2,407.58	11.8
Nanjing	220	2,171.92	10.3
Wuhan	220	1,330.92	16.5
Chongqing	185	1,196.42	15.5
Chengdu	178	1,463.00	12.2
Xi'an	180	1,274.67	14.1
Shenzhen	317*	2,660.67	11.9
Xiamen	290*	1,711.58	16.9
Guangzhou	300	2,632.75	11.4
Fuzhou	210*	1,382.17	15.2

*Indicates that figure is average of upper and lower figures for dibao line for city for that year.

Sources: For the *dibao* line, "*Quanguo 36ge chengshi zuidi baozhang biaozhun yilan*" [General survey of 36 cities' minimum livelihood guarantee line], http://china.com .cn/city/txt/2006-11/25/content_740675\hich\af0\dbch\af13\loch\f08_2.htm, accessed August 17, 2007 (Link no longer available); for wages, Wuxi Statistical Yearbook 2005, China data online, accessed May 29. 2008.

2013, nationwide, the average *dibao* norm (poverty line) had dropped to a mere 9.4 percent of the average wage and represented only 30.2 percent of the national average *minimum* wage.[132]

Gao uses Asian Development Bank data to note that China's spending on social assistance for the urban and rural *dibao* combined amounted to a mere 0.25 percent of GDP as of 2009 (see Table 3.1), whereas the average among other developing countries was much higher, at 1.6 percent.[133] Japan spent 0.21 percent of its GDP on family cash benefits in 1995[134] when China had not yet fully abandoned the very parsimonious *sanwu* program. As Japan's economy stagnated, however, the economic downturn led the government to tighten eligibility and to decrease its allowance level; the number of recipients saw a decline as well.[135] For Korea, one observer noted that, in 2018,

132. Wang and Bai, "Development," 168. Table 2.3 shows 8.55 percent of average wage, using figures from the Civil Affairs Statistical Yearbook.
133. Qin Gao, *Welfare, Work and Poverty: Social Assistance in China* (New York: Oxford University Press, 2017), 39.
134. Schoppa, *Race for the Exits*, 46.
135. Miura, *Welfare through Work*, 32, 51.

Table 7.2. *Dibao* **Norms, Average Disposable Income,** *Dibao* **Norm as Percentage of Average Disposable Income, Twenty-One Large Cities, September 2005 (Unit: Yuan/Month)**

City	Dibao *Line (A)*	Avg. *Disp. Inc. (B)*	A/B (%)
Beijing	300	1,471.08	20.39
Tianjin	265	1,053.25	25.16
Shenyang	220	841.50	26.14
Dalian	240	999.50	24.01
Changchun	169	838.75	20.15
Harbin	200	838.75	23.85
Taiyuan	183	873.00	20.96
Jinan	230	1,131.50	20.33
Qingdao	260	1,076.67	24.15
Shanghai	300	1,553.75	19.31
Hangzhou	300*	1,383.42	21.69
Nanjing	230*	1,249.75	18.40
Wuhan	220	904.17	24.33
Changsha	200	1,036.17	19.30
Chongqing	210	853.67	24.60
Chengdu	195	946.58	20.60
Xi'an	200	802.33	24.93
Lanzhou	190	710.75	26.73
Shenzhen	344	1,791.17 [*sic*]	19.21
Xiamen	290*	1,366.92	21.22
Guangzhou	330	1,523.92	21.65

*Indicates that figure is average of upper and lower figures for city for that year.

Sources: For the *dibao* line, *"Quanguo 36ge chengshi zuidi baozhang biaozhun yilan"* [General survey of 36 cities' minimum livelihood guarantee line], http://china.com.cn /city/txt/2006-11/25/content_740675\hich\af0\dbch\af13\loch\f08_2.htm, accessed August 17, 2007; for urban residents' average disposable income, Chengdu Statistical Yearbook 2005, China data online, accessed May 29, 2008; for Lanzhou, *Lanzhoushi tongjiju, bian* [Lanzhou statistical bureau, ed.], *Lanzhou tongji nianjian-2007* [Lanzhou statistical yearbook-2007] (Lanzhou: *Lanzhou dehui yinshua youxian ziren gongsi* [Lanzhou Dehui Printing Limited Responsibility Company], 2007, 297.

the ratio of social welfare spending to GDP was just half the average among OECD countries;[136] another reported that, in 2012, Korea's total social expenditure was only about 39 percent of the average among OECD nations.[137] One could surmise that a productivist heritage, married to economic troubles, accounted for Japan's and Korea's lower levels of generosity then.

Some Latin American nations performed much better. For one example, the Mexican government raised the state's investment in its CCT, Oportunidades, from 0.17 percent of GDP up to 0.36 percent under President Fox over the course of his term (2000 to 2006).[138] In India, the National Rural Employment Guarantee Scheme's total spending amounted to 0.3 percent of GDP in

---

136. Jong-sung You, "State Intervention Can Cut Inequality, But the Current Approach is Wrong," *Global Asia* 14, no. 1 (March 2019): 57.

137. Yang, "Parochial," 458.

138. Dion, *Workers and Welfare*, 205.

2006.[139] Both of these rural programs served the portions of the country where the majority of the population resided, and consequently, where vigorous bidding for votes occurred in these two partisan nations.

In the OECD countries generally, where partisan proclivities mark welfare allocations, as in Mexico and Brazil, the funds committed to social assistance have mostly been significantly above those in China: total spending on social assistance (designated as "the range of benefits and services available to guarantee a minimum [however defined] level of subsistence to people in need, based on a test of resources") in 1992 was 13 percent of GDP in New Zealand.[140] In 1995, when France was allocating 2.23 percent of GDP to family cash benefits, Sweden spent 2.13 percent, and Britain 1 percent, respectively,[141] all well above the level of GDP committed to China's *dibao*. Years later, in 2009, though some members of the European Union (namely, Italy, Estonia, and Hungary) spent a mere 0.1 percent of their GDP on social assistance, in the Netherlands, the figure went up to 2 percent. The mean for this measure of social assistance stood at 0.4 percent for the then-twenty-five members of the Union, all far beyond what China's program of the same name amounted to.[142]

Probably it is appropriate to compare expenditure on CCTs with that on the *dibao*, as their target populations are likely to be similar. Haggard and Kaufman report that as of the late 1990s, CCT programs' outlays in a number of Latin American countries were higher than China's *dibao*, as spending ran from 0.5 to 1 percent of GDP.[143] Similarly, the amount allocated to what Hanlon and co-authors term "family cash transfers" amounted to 1.2 percent of GDP among OECD countries in 2005, also much higher than the *dibao*.[144] Again, partisan-inclined politicians outspent those in the United States and China on a proportional basis.

Matching Generosity with Welfare Model Types

Among the countries for which I have data, I assigned two countries to the productivist category (Japan and South Korea); eight to the partisan heading (Argentina, Brazil, India, Japan, Korea, Mexico, Taiwan, and the United States); and five to pacifying/policing (Chile, Argentina, China, the United States, and South Korea). Several countries sort into more than one category, namely Japan has been in both the productivist and the partisan list; Argentina and the United States are both partisan and pacifying/policing;[145] and Ko-

139. Hanlon et al., *Just Give*, 41.
140. Gao et al., "Welfare Residualism," 114.
141. Schoppa, *Race for the Exits*, 46.
142. Gustafsson and Gang, "A Comparison," 294.
143. Haggard and Kaufman, *Development*, 216–17.
144. Hanlon et al., *Just Give*, 23.
145. Paul Pierson, *Dismantling the Welfare State? Reagan, Thatcher and the Politics of Retrenchment* (Cambridge, UK: Cambridge University Press, 1994); Soss et al., *Disciplining the Poor*.

rea appears under all three headings. The issue is to decide which category (or tendency) fits best at a particular juncture. In Japan and Korea, as in Taiwan, partisan impulses began to predominate with regime change. Japan, democratic since 1952 (at least in institutional structure), demonstrated partisan inclinations in its administration of public benefits, especially at times when the dominant party, the LDP, faced electoral challenges, as in the early 1970s. Argentina has had democratic phases but also authoritarian ones.

Above, I suggested that countries slotted as productivist, specifically Japan and Korea, tend to be less beneficent with their public funds as compared with those chiefly following the partisan model. Indeed, the literature review here does bear this out: In both, recipients of social assistance constituted far lower percentages of their populace than did those in other states, such as Mexico and New Zealand, that have more purely partisan approaches. As noted, Japan spent just 0.2 percent of its GDP on family cash benefits in 1995, while Korea's social welfare expenditures represented a percentage of its GDP that was just half the average of that of its fellow OECD members. So, in places where the timing of bestowing allowances syncs with electoral contests, there is routinely a higher contribution by partisanship-type governments or, one might say, by the party in power at the time of the allotment, than in the two more productivist nations.

As for partisan-style welfare approaches, one case is India, where a national scheme installed in 2006 (at least on paper) guaranteed each rural household one hundred days of paid work per year, ensuring (where it was successfully implemented) a right to work and to an income. If fully enforced, the plan would have cost 0.3 percent of GDP,[146] more than what China was investing in the *dibao* at any time. Jonathan Daniel London shows convincingly that immediately following Taiwan's democratization (as in Korea), the government carried out "steady expansions in insurance coverage and the benefits package."[147] A number of studies demonstrate a superior level of generosity in most EU/OECD developed countries, where elections (i.e., partisanship) have long determined the cast of policy.[148]

Lastly, as for policing/pacifying, polities such as China and in many ways the United States, both of whose welfare efforts have been characterized by surveillance and even coercion, are notably niggardly in their outlays for the poor: China effected a drastic reduction in the numbers of its program's beneficiaries in the decade 2009 to 2019 (see Chapter Ten), as well as financing its *dibao* program with a tiny percentage of GDP. In the United States, similarly, particularly after AFDC—already not a bountiful policy—was downgraded to TANF in 1996, regulations on level of assistance and conditions for eligibility

---

146. Hanlon et al., *Just Give*, 41–42.

147. Jonathan Daniel London, *Welfare and Inequality in Marketizing East Asia* (London: Palgrave/Macmillan, 2018), 227.

148. Huber and Stephens, *Development.*

became especially harsh: the number of recipients fell by 68 percent between 1994 and 2006, and constant dollar spending declined by 48 percent.[149] This pairing suggests that regime type—democratic versus authoritarian—does not always determine the most dominant motive driving assistance allocation.

CONCLUSION

This comparative exercise is by no means rigorous; if anything, it is impressionistic. The goal was simply to grapple with the nature of China's *dibao* by examining it in comparative perspective. This I did in two ways: First, by positing three ideal-typical welfare program models, based on three sorts of intentions that variously inspire governmental assistance. I then assigned the *dibao* to one of these: pacifying/policing. Second, I looked at statistics on measures such as the percentage of various states' total GDP that their leaders allocate to social assistance.

In the process, my appraisal addressed the query that motivated the chapter: Should China's *dibao* be considered true social assistance? This called for determining whether the scheme meets the definitions of social assistance that initiated the chapter. Thus, the question became: Is the *dibao* an antipoverty program that has "the aim of facilitating the permanent exit from poverty" of the indigent population it purports to aid?[150]

In the scheme's early years (up through 2004), it trained its beneficence (such as it was) not necessarily on the poorest but instead mainly on rowdy proletarians recently released from their jobs. Its chief purpose, ensuring stability, was not related to the generic issue—pure poverty—that social assistance as public policy is typically meant to address. In later years (as Chapters Nine and Ten document), as a program that uses welfare to police and pacify its recipients, the *dibao* belongs among countries employing the ideal type least likely to achieve the goal that social assistance is instituted to attain, that is, helping recipients escape from poverty. So neither in terms of its target nor in relation to its objective should the *dibao* properly be cast as "social assistance," as usually understood.

Chapter Eight takes up variation of a different sort. It considers economic contrasts within China, between wealthier and poorer cities, holding this nation-state constant. It will perform this exercise by demonstrating statistically how urban administrations in these two categories of municipalities disparately distribute their *dibao* allowances to specific groups of recipients.

---

149. Bane, "Poverty Politics," 41.
150. Barrientos, *Social Assistance*, 3.

Chapter Eight

Dibao: Differential Disbursement

As noted earlier, the *dibao* was set up to be administered at the municipal level. Given this local discretion, its enforcement has, understandingly, varied among cities. This chapter, focusing on economic differentiation among locales, seeks to find regularity in this disparity.[1] It shifts the analysis from the last chapter, which presented three politically based models for understanding politicians' provision of welfare among different nation-states. Here, I propose instead an economic rationale for governmental welfare programs in this (and perhaps other) authoritarian state(s), in an effort to elucidate unlike motives behind the implementation of the *dibao* in cities with differing economic profiles.

While social welfare has been much studied in the field of comparative politics, with only a few exceptions, it has been analyzed as discharged in *democratic* states.[2] Scholars who treat welfare in democratic contexts posit that politicians dispense it to serve their all-embracing concern with the *electoral imperative* (i.e., in line with the "partisan" approach laid out in Chapter Seven). But in non-democracies, where elections are either empty charades or are nonexistent, this *political* purpose for providing assistance is, obviously, absent.

---

1. The statistical work in this chapter was done by Hu Yiyang, thus the use of "we" throughout.

2. Paul Pierson, *Dismantling the Welfare State: Reagan, Thatcher, and the Politics of Retrenchment* (New York: Cambridge University Press, 1994); Alexander Hicks, *Social Democracy and Welfare Capitalism: A Century of Income Security Politics* (Ithaca, NY: Cornell University Press, 1999); Evelyne Huber and John D. Stephens, *Development and Crisis of the Welfare State: Parties and Policies in Global Markets* (Chicago: University of Chicago Press, 2001); Linda J. Cook, *Postcommunist Welfare States* (Ithaca, NY: Cornell University Press, 2007); Mitchell Orenstein, *Out of the Red: Building Capitalism and Democracy in Postcommunist Europe* (Ann Arbor: University of Michigan Press, 2001); and Stepan Haggard and Robert Kaufman, *Development, Democracy, and Welfare States* (Princeton, NJ: Princeton University Press, 2008).

Against this democratic welfare state paradigm, two older pieces of work on welfare and poor relief—Frances Fox Piven and Richard Cloward's book, *Regulating the Poor*, and Claus Offe's paper, "Advanced Capitalism and the Welfare State"[3]—consider assistance in the context of changes in the *economy*. That is, they pinpoint not just the incentive that voting provides but also *capitalism* (and the vicissitudes of the market that accompany it) as a main causal factor underlying the welfare relation between rulers and the needy portion of the populace. Piven and Cloward see the two pivotal roles of poor relief in capitalist states (of whatever regime type) as *maintaining civic order* and *regulating labor*. This harks back to my "pacifying/policing" motive in Chapter Seven.

Though they do not specify the exact modalities, these authors note two common governmental goals in officialdom's regulation of labor that apply specifically under capitalism: The first is to "absorb and control enough of the unemployed to restore order . . . when mass unemployment leads to outbreaks of turmoil" (or, in the case of China's *dibao* program, to *prevent*, as well as to quell, any outbreaks of disorder at such a juncture). The second objective concerns the time when the labor market expands again; at that point, relief is used, they claim—with the denigration and punitiveness that assistance directs toward those "of no use as workers" (such as the aged, the disabled, and the insane)—as a disincentive to discourage people readmitted into the labor market from "relax[ing] into beggary and pauperism."[4]

Both these studies understand the recipients of welfare as people who had become obsolete, even worthless, when alterations in the nature of the demand for labor made their skills inadequate for a new phase of economic growth. The Piven and Cloward book links the rise in need for aid to times of foundational, historic dislocations in the economy, speaking of the "cata-strophic changes" that appear in eras of rapid modernization, precisely like what China began experiencing in the 1980s.[5]

Several features of the operation of poor relief that Piven and Cloward detail—demands for "good," "moral" behavior on the part of beneficiaries, along with surprise visits to their homes to confirm this; decisions to allocate only so much funding to families as to supplement their incomes up to a bare minimum livelihood; and a principle of "less eligibility," decreeing that

---

3. Frances Fox Piven and Richard A. Cloward, *Regulating the Poor: The Functions of Public Welfare* (updated edition) (New York: Vintage Books, 1993); and Claus Offe, "Advanced Capitalism and the Welfare State," *Politics & Society* 2 (Summer 1972): 479–88.

4. Piven and Cloward, *Regulating the Poor*, 3, 408.

5. Ibid., 5–7, 15–17. Here Piven and Cloward are outlining what causes a need for aid; in Chapter Seven I focused on what they wrote about what motivates politicians to provide that aid.

a welfare subject's portion must be lower than that of the most poorly paid laborer[6]—also are hallmarks of China's *dibao*,[7] as they often are in social assistance elsewhere.

But as we will see, it is just in some, not all, Chinese cities that this scheme operates with an aim of limiting the actions of the poor, frequently sidetracking indigent people away from the mainstream of urban citizenry and its economic activity (i.e., effectively working to *regulate the labor market* by keeping it free of undesirables). This is a variable outcome, we find: such results seem strongest where capitalism and cosmopolitan pretensions are most prominent (i.e., in the richer cities). This distinction suggests a bifurcation of behaviors among Chinese urban officialdom that we explore in this chapter.

Another factor in the paradigm casting social assistance as a concomitant of capitalism is Offe's designation of welfare as a "safety valve," for guarding against "potential social problems." He points to a "benign neglect" informing welfare spending, which spending, he argues, is minimal, since such outlays target population segments whose appeals do not seem particularly worrisome to policy makers.[8] Thus, these writers suggest that not only electoral behavior but also *capitalism* (an economic, but regime-type-neutral, factor)—with its unpredictable and potentially merciless markets in labor—can be a core mechanism driving both need and state beneficence, and the level thereof. This analysis makes sense for China (as does that of Piven and Cloward), where votes mean little to nothing but where using handouts to induce popular passivity, and where removing the unskilled from the labor market—and thereby, ideally, enhancing productivity—can mean a lot.

Following this line of reasoning, four features characterize official giving under capitalism, according to these authors, and are pertinent to our analysis. First, there is the use of relief subsidies to *regulate the labor market* (removing less-able workers from it); second, a concern with *maintaining order*, or, to employ Chinese catchwords, guaranteeing "social stability" and "harmony"; third, targeting *anachronistic* (or useless) *workers*—mostly the old, the undereducated, and the disabled or otherwise infirm[9]—as the ap-

---

6. Ibid., 11, 22, 30, 35.
7. Dorothy J. Solinger, "The Urban *Dibao*: Guarantee for Minimum Livelihood or for Minimal Turmoil?" in *Marginalization in Urban China: Comparative Perspectives*, eds. Fulong Wu and Chris Webster (Basingbroke, Hampshire: Palgrave Macmillan, 2011), 253–77.
8. Offe, "Advanced Capitalism," 479, 485.
9. Here "useless" fits with Zwia Lipkin's usage in *Useless to the State: "Social Problems" and Social Engineering in Nationalist Nanjing* (Stanford, CA: Stanford University Press, 2006).

propriate recipients; and fourth, *token expenditures*[10]-cum-*"benign neglect."* But, we find, some of these features are more strongly exemplified in the wealthier Chinese cities most influenced by the dynamics of capitalism, others in poorer places. This chapter offers an explanation for these distinctions.

Accordingly, we will show that subnational disparity in policy implementation is at least in part a function of cities' fiscal health. For market opening has gone hand-in-glove with a policy of decentralization of finances, while localities have grossly disparate resource bases and revenue streams.[11] Our data indeed show systematic variation in the ways in which local leaders in well and in poorly endowed cities, respectively, dole out state charity among three types of poverty recipients. We do not claim a relationship of cause and effect between the economic health of a city and its *dibao* allocational decisions. But we do uncover a provocative correlation. Our results are consistent with a deduction that prosperous metropolises' welfare choices act to hide away these places' indigent, while less well-financed municipalities are prone to encourage their poor to contribute to their own sustenance.[12] Our data comes from the years 2007–2010, though there is no reason to believe that our conclusions fit only those years.

Besides fieldwork observations and some eighty interviews with *dibaohu,* urban *dibao* administrators, and community officials in six cities (Wuhan, Guangzhou, Lanzhou; and Jingzhou, Qianjiang, and Xiantao, Hubei) over four summers (2007–2010), we also used two datasets. Since the urban registered population living in the city district (*shiqu,* 市区) are the only people eligible for this relief in the cities, we used data only on this population.

Dibao recipient data came from an unusual dataset compiled by the Ministry of Civil Affairs that was available online in 2009. This source disclosed

---

10. Fulong Wu, "Debates and Developments: The State and Marginality: Reflections on Urban Outcasts from China's Urban Transition," *International Journal of Urban and Regional Research 33,* no. 2 (2009), 4, speaks of "deliberate under-investment [in dilapidated neighborhoods] in order for the state to divert capital for new industrial development"; Joe Leung, "The Development of Social Assistance in Urban China," paper presented at Provincial China Workshop 2008, Nankai University, Tianjin (PRC), October 27–30, 2008, 11.

11. Michel Oksenberg and James Tong, "The Evolution of Central-Provincial Fiscal Relations in China, 1971–1984," *China Quarterly (CQ)* no. 25 (1991): 1–32; and Christine P. Wong, "Rebuilding Government for the 21st Century," *CQ* no. 200 (2009): 929–52.

12. Jane Duckett and Guohui Wang, "Poverty and Inequality," in *China's Challenges,* eds. Jacques deLisle and Avery Goldstein (Philadelphia: University of Pennsylvania Press, 2015), 24–41; You-tien Hsing, *The Great Urban Transformation: Politics of Land and Property in China* (Oxford, UK: Oxford University Press, 2010); Yu-wai Li, Bo Miao, and Graeme Lang, "The Local Environmental State in China: A Study of County-level Cities in Suzhou," *CQ* no. 205 (2011): 115–32; Fulong Wu and Chris Webster, "What Has Been Marginalized? Marginalization as the Constrained 'Right to the City' in Urban China," in Wu and Webster, *Marginalization,* 301–6; Youqin Huang, "Low-income Housing in Chinese Cities: Policies and Practices," *CQ no.*212 (2012): 941–64; Ryane Flock, "Panhandling and the Contestation of Public Space in Guangzhou," *China Perspectives* 2 (2014): 37–44; and Christian Sorace and William Hurst, "China's Phantom Urbanization and the Pathology of Ghost Cities," *Journal of Contemporary Asia* 46, no. 2 (2016): 304–22, http://dx.doi.org/10.1080/00472336.2015.1115532.

how over 600 individual cities, respectively, divided up their *dibao* funds among ten categories of welfare recipients (categories included the aged, women, the registered unemployed, those performing "flexible labor" [*linghuo jiuye*, 灵活 就业[13]], the working poor, students, the disabled). The table showed the numbers of recipients in each category in each city in 2009 and the total number of recipients of the *dibao* per city, making it possible to calculate the percentages each category represented of the total recipients per city.[14] We considered three of these categories, each of which conveys information about a city's stance toward people outside the mainstream economy: flexible workers, the disabled, and the registered unemployed. When our research began, these data for the end of June 2009 were the latest available, and there was not any earlier such data.

The other dataset came from another online source, the China Infobank, which supplied basic economic indicators for a large number of Chinese cities. At the time of this research, data for year-end 2007 was the most recent and reliable such data available. Having two datasets with information from time points eighteen months apart (year-end 2007 and June 2009) was, in a way, fortuitous: the disparity in time afforded a lag that could support the analysis. That is, the variable "city wealth," as measured by average wage in 2007, may well have had an impact on a city's handling of poverty-stricken people a year or two later. Thus, officials' policy choices in 2009 about how to allocate *dibao* funds could have been in part a result of decisions that budget writers made after having had time to observe the recent status (as in 2007) of their city's revenue and their constituents' spending patterns.[15]

We first briefly sketch the program in question, highlighting *in italics* the four elements drawn from the Piven-Cloward/Offe interpretation noted above, which, we argue, fit the management of the *dibao* scheme quite well. We then draw upon fieldwork that led to a set of three hypotheses and lay out these hypotheses. The methodology and results come next, followed by a discussion of our own and of alternative explanations and our conclusions. This work developed from my receipt of the Ministry of Civil Affair's dataset in August 2009, followed by my invitation to my then-student, Yiyang Hu, to work with me to develop my ideas using my hypotheses and statistical tests. Given that this is a joint effort, "we" is used throughout, unlike in all the other chapters in this book.

---

13. Baidu.com defines *linghuo jiuye* as part-time, temporary, elastic (*tanxing*, 弹性) work done by unemployed, let-go, or self-employed workers and differs in compensation, work site, welfare, and labor relations from mainstream employment.

14. Hard-copy Civil Affairs yearbooks had this data for later years, but just for provincial-level units, and it was not online. The China Infobank data comes from the National Bureau of Statistics, *Chinese City Statistical Yearbook 2008*.

15. Thanks to Yumin Sheng for this insight.

THE MINIMUM LIVELIHOOD GUARANTEE PROGRAM

Objectives and Character of the Scheme Using Piven-Cloward/ Offe Framework

As industrial restructuring progressed, it was the *anachronistic* workers, as Piven and Cloward articulated would be the case, who became the brunt of the process.[16] For the coming of capitalism—and the comprehensive, if gradual, entry into the world market—induced a state-led streamlining of the industrial economy in favor of the professionally and personally fit.[17] As protests by dismissed workers mounted after 1997,[18] the Chinese leadership agonized over the implications that current and potential *disorder* could have for the state's hallowed objectives of "social stability" and intergroup "harmony" and, especially for our purposes here, for a successful project of state enterprise reform-cum-economic modernization.

So, the political elite's purpose in instituting this program was officially and explicitly stated as being to handle the people most severely affected by economic restructuring, in the hope of rendering them quiescent, that is, to *maintain the order* the leadership deemed essential for seeing the enterprise reform process safely through. Getting rid of obsolescent and money-losing factories and firing all or most of their generally unskilled and physically weak employees thus amounted to *regulating the labor market*, as Piven and Cloward understand the term. Indeed, the target population of the *dibao* (in plural, the *dibaohu* 低保户) is comprised of members of what the government calls the *ruoshi qunti* (弱势 群体, vulnerable groups), whose rejection has been a negative product of China's effective adoption of capitalism. Its members are, for the most part, low- or un-skilled, chronically ill, or disabled.[19]

Once the program was underway, the Ministry of Civil Affairs enjoined the localities to "spend a little money [which could be interpreted—and, as turned out to be the case—as an injunction to *use token expenditures*] to buy stability."[20] In short, the paired objectives of facilitating the firms'

---

16. This material is in earlier chapters, so here I offer only what is needed as background for this chapter.

17. For demographic traits of laid-off workers and *dibaohu*, see Chapter Three; Y. P. Wang, *Urban Poverty,* 72, 79; and Meiyan Wang, "Emerging Urban Poverty and Effects of the *Dibao* Program on Alleviating Poverty in China," *China & World Economy* 15, no. 2 (2007): 79, 80. Statistics in "Zhongguo chengshi jumin zuidi shenghuo baozhang biaozhun de xiangguan fenxi, jingji qita xiangguan lunwen" [Relevant analysis of Chinese urban residents' *dibao* norm; economic and other related treatises], http://www.ynexam.cn/html/jingjixue/jingjixiangguan/2006/1105/zhonggochengshijimin . . ., accessed August 18, 2007, show that those with only primary or junior-high education or below together represented 71 percent of adult recipients. Only 27.6 percent claimed any professional or handicraft skill.

18. William J. Hurst, *The Chinese Worker After Socialism* (New York: Cambridge University Press, 2009).

19. Y. P. Wang, *Urban Poverty*, 72, 79; M. Wang, "Emerging Urban Poverty," 79, 80.

20. Jianli zuidi shenghuo baozhang zhidu de jige wenti" [Several issues in establishing the minimum livelihood guarantee system], *Zhongguo minzheng (ZGMZ)* [China Civil Affairs] 9 (1996): 14.

reform and, to guarantee this, minimal welfare security for the new, very poor to shut them up, lay at the core of the program's publicly enunciated, official justification, precisely as Piven and Cloward and Offe presumed such programs would.

As for outlays, despite steady increases in the funding granted to the program, its overall *expenditures*, as Offe would argue, were kept at a *token* level relative to other official outlays, ranging from 0.113 percent of total government expenditures for the urban *dibao* in 1999 (before the rural component was established in 2006) and rising just up to 1.2 percent for urban and rural recipients combined in 2011, at the peak, but falling thereafter (see Tables 2.1 and 3.1). Furthermore, as government expenditures overall grew at an annual rate of 25.7 percent from 2007 to 2008, the proportion of them that went to the *dibao* rose by just 9.6 percent.[21]

Following the same trend, the money used for the *dibao* as a percent of GDP climbed from 0.016 percent for cities in 1999 up to 0.27 percent for cities and rural areas combined in 2013 at its height and then dropping steadily in later years. (See Table 3.2) By way of comparison, a set of emerging economies in Latin America spent from 0.5 to 1 percent of GDP on targeted anti-poverty programs. In postsocialist countries in Eastern Europe, there was also relative generosity for the victims of reform in the early twenty-first century, as, for instance, in Romania, where a minimum-income scheme cost nearly 0.5 percent of GDP.[22] (Chapter Seven contains more such comparisons.)

There is other evidence of frugal funding, as noted in earlier chapters. While the local *dibao* norm or standard (the local poverty line) on average represented 20.5 percent of the average local annual wage for staff and workers across a set of provincial capitals and other super-large cities in 1998 (see Table 2.2), nine years later, in 2007, the norm had dropped down to just 8.78 percent of the mean wage (see Table 2.4). In these same cities, the *dibao* norm accounted for 28.2 percent of average disposable income in mid-2002 (see Table 2.3). But by the end of 2007, the norm had diminished to only 15.88 percent of average disposable income (see Table 2.4).[23] These data demonstrate that the miserly portion allotted to the poor across the nation coincided with the notion of "benign neglect" articulated by Claus Offe.

Design of the Program: Setting the Urban Poverty Line

Though there are often reports of China's national poverty line, that line applies only to the rural areas. There is no national *urban* poverty line in China. For cities, there is only the *dibao* norm or standard (*biaozhun*, 标准), a municipally

---

21. Calculated from the 2009 Chinese National Statistical Yearbook, online.

22. Haggard and Kaufman, *Development*, 216–17, 340. Chapter Seven has more comparisons.

23. Tables on the period 1998 through 2005 are available from the author.

designated version of this line, which, as noted, varies across cities. Localities were permitted to peg their own lines expressly because average per capita income and prices vary regionally; another consideration, initially, was that each city was to supply a large portion of the outlay.[24] Later, the central government subsidized some of these places, to varying degrees.[25] So variation set in. By 2003, the proportion of subsidies from the center varied from as low as 16 percent in Fujian on the wealthy east coast to more than 70 percent in the destitute western provinces of Gansu and Guizhou. While some cities were contributing next to nothing, the seven wealthiest metropolises and provinces were charged with financing the program entirely by themselves.[26] Interviews in three Hubei prefectural cities in 2008 and 2010 revealed central plus provincial subsidies to them for the *dibao* of close to 100 percent,[27] meaning that these cities made almost no contribution.

The local *dibao* line was to be fixed below the minimum wage in each city, as it normally is wherever social assistance is provided (just as was dictated by the old principle of "less eligibility" mentioned above) and also lower than the amount dispensed in unemployment insurance benefits, supposedly— again, as elsewhere in the world—in order to *encourage* employment. In truth, however, in many, but not all, cities, local policy stated that acquisition of even a tiny increment in income through occasional labor could result in a drastic reduction in the household's *dibao* disbursement, effectively *discouraging* recipients from engaging in informal labor.[28]

Fieldwork Observations: Basis for the Hypotheses

Visits to two very different cities in 2007 initially alerted one of the authors to the variability with which different urban financial endowments correlated

---

24. Wang Hui, "Chengshi zuidi shenghuo baozhang gongzuo zhi wo jian" [My opinion on the urban minimum livelihood guarantee work], *ZGMZ*, 10 (1996): 34, explains the "vegetable basket method," figured by considering the minimum requisite consumption amount of daily necessities and the price index in a given area.

25. Christine Wong, "Central-local Relations In an Era of Fiscal Decline," *CQ*, no. 128 (1991): 691–715; Joe C. B. Leung, "The Emergence of Social Assistance in China," *International Journal of Social Welfare* 15 (2006): 193; Philip O'Keefe, "Social Assistance in China: An Evolving System" (draft), paper for ANU conference, August 27, 2004, 7, 8; Zhaohui Hong, "Lun shehui quanli de 'pinkun'—Zhongguo chengshi pinkun wenti de genyuan yu zhili lujing" [On the 'poverty' of social rights: the roots and path of managing the problem of urban poverty in China], *Xiandai Zhongguo yanjiu* (*Modern China Studies*) 79, no. 4 (2002): 9–10.

26. Leung, "The Emergence," 193; *idem.*, "The Development," 7; Tang Jun, "The New Situation of Poverty and Antipoverty," in *2002 nian: Zhongguo shehui xingshi yu yuce (shehui lanpishu)* [2002: Analysis and forecast of China's social situation (Blue Book on Chinese Society)] [trans. U.S. Foreign Broadcast Information System Translated Text, January 1, 2002], eds. Ru Xin, Lu Xueyi, Li Peilin, et al. states that, "With the exception of Beijing, Shanghai, Shandong, Jiangsu, Zhejiang, Fujian, and Guangdong, all the other provinces got central government's financial subsidies [for the *dibao*]."

27. Qianjiang got 99 percent of its *dibao* funds from higher-level governments; Xiantao got 98 percent of theirs (interviews, July 6 and July 8, respectively).

28. Several of Solinger's informants revealed this.

with local officials' disparate approaches to the very poor. One of these cities, Wuhan, the vibrant capital of Hubei Province in central China and relatively well-off, was then aspiring to cosmopolitanism; the other, Lanzhou, the capital city of northwestern Gansu Province, situated in a barren and rocky part of the country in one of China's most poverty-stricken provinces, was far less geared to appearing modern. Inspection of these two cities suggested the possibility that systematic variation in welfare governance might mark wealthier and more indigent cities, respectively.

Respective statistics for these two locales convey the story crisply: As of 2007, Wuhan registered an urban population of 5.29 million a GDP of 270.9 billion yuan, and a per capita income of 5,121 yuan per year. *Dibao* recipients constituted 4.6 percent of the city population, and expenditures on the scheme amounted to 338.1 million yuan, 1.25 percent of government expenditures (27.15 billion yuan), and an average of 114 yuan per person per month. In Lanzhou that year, the city population was 2,080,344, just under 40 percent of Wuhan's. The *dibao* population, of 111,758, however, accounted for a slightly higher portion, 5.37 percent of total residents, while the city's GDP, 63.43 billion yuan, was less than a quarter of Wuhan's, while its per capita income, at 3,049 yuan per year, was only 60 percent of Wuhan's.

In Lanzhou, though, where the central government subsidized *dibao* expenditures, these expenses totaled 147.7 million yuan of the city's total government spending (6.82 billion yuan), nearly twice as high a percentage as Wuhan's, amounting to 2.16 percent of its expenditures. Allowances of 105 yuan per person per month were the average in the former city, outlays made possible by the subsidization. In 2007, while the average monthly wage among all the sixty-three cities in our sample was 2,113 yuan per month, in Wuhan, the figure was above that, at 2,239 yuan. But in Lanzhou, it was below, at 1,768 yuan, 79 percent of that in Wuhan and far below average for the sample.

Fieldwork in 2007, revealed that the two were adopting very different tactics in managing their poor. This became clear immediately in observing residents' commercial activities (or lack thereof) on city streets. Earlier research had revealed that the cities had had dissimilar approaches from the programs' inception: a 1998–1999 survey disclosed that Lanzhou's leaders were executing a "mobilizational" strategy toward the indigent, with officials there "emphasiz[ing] arousing the *dibao* targets' activism for production, encouraging and organizing them to develop self-reliance."[29]

Nine years later, in 2007, Lanzhou remained lenient toward its poverty-stricken, allowing them to engage in sidewalk (or "flexible") business—the handling of which each city determines itself, and which, in turn, is policed

---

29. Tang Jun, "The Report of Poverty and Anti-Poverty in Urban China—The Poverty Problems in Urban China and the Program of Minimum Living Standard," (ms.) n.p., n.d.

in each by its urban-order-and-appearance managers (*chengguan,* 城管), an official post created in the 1990s. One could say that the *chengguan* governs the effective contraction of urban space, in a manner much akin to what Don Mitchell has referred to as "the annihilation of space by law."[30] In Chinese cities, these functionaries are charged with keeping sidewalks sterile by ensuring the roadways are washed bare of any stalls, as well as of any wheeled vehicle that is not an automobile.

All kinds of curbside business went on in Lanzhou unobstructed at that time, including stalls for fixing footwear and small bunches of young men hawking political-picture posters.[31] That this was a matter of city policy was confirmed in an interview with the section chief of the Gansu provincial *dibao* office in the province's civil affairs bureau, who admitted that, "If the *chengguan,* is too strict, the *dibaohu* cannot earn money. And letting them earn money is a way of cutting down their numbers. If their skill level is low, their only means of livelihood can be the street-side stalls they set up themselves."[32]

These words disclosed not just a relaxed position toward the indigents' street behavior but also the budgetary shortages that disposed urban authorities in Lanzhou to seek out ways of saving funds. Another seven years on, in late 2014, it seemed things had not changed much: A resident of Lanzhou encountered on the street observed that, "Even to now there are many stalls at all times of day, despite regulations, and they seem to be allowed to stay, for the most part."[33] Yet by way of stark contrast, in 2020, the official media of wealthy Beijing City proclaimed that, "The stall economy is not appropriate for first-tier cities . . . allowing the stall economy to make a comeback in those cities is equivalent to going backward in decades overnight . . . it's a departure from high-quality growth."[34]

Although Wuhan is a second-tier, not a first-tier, city, its leaders' aspirations have inclined them to copy practices in the capital. Thus, in Wuhan in 2007, informal business on the streets was simply made illegal. Beautiful, unencumbered thoroughfares were valued to match the towering, modernistic skyscrapers continuously under construction on both sides of the streets. In 2001, when the city was newly stretching toward the future, comments of a laid-off party cadre from a local factory in a private conversation indicated the thrust of policy there:

30. Don Mitchell, "The Annihilation of Space by Law: The Roots and Implications of Anti-Homeless Laws in the United States," *Antipode* 29, no. 3 (1997): 303–35.

31. Street observations, September 3, 2007.

32. Interview, September 5, 2007, Lanzhou.

33. Street interview, November 21, 2014, Lanzhou.

34. Li Yuan, "China's Street Vendor Push Ignites a Debate: How Rich is It?" *New York Times,* June 11, 2020.

Society has to go forward, we need money to create a civilized environment, sanitation to develop a good environment, a clean shopping area, basic construction facilities necessary to build a better livelihood for people in the future. All cities have pedestrian malls or are building them. They can give Wuhan more competitive ability, for business and tourism. People will come here. We've also built a beach along Yanjiang Road, and it did attract tourists here during the National Day holiday.[35]

The actions of the politician Yu Zhengsheng provide further evidence of this proclivity for pristine roadways and for attracting foreigners. Yu was appointed party secretary of Hubei Province at the end of 2001, where he stayed until 2007.[36] While in Hubei, Yu advocated developing Wuhan by encouraging building much infrastructure. "I guess he wanted to make the city look better, so doing small business on the streets was not something he wanted to see," related a Chinese scholar to one of the authors.[37]

Another distinction between the two cities in 2007 was the relative severity with which the needy were excluded from the program. In Lanzhou, a directive from the end of 2001 barred only three kinds of people from receiving *dibao* funds: the labor-able who without good reason refused to take a job; those with working ability who declined to participate in the public service work assigned to them by the community; and those whose household's actual livelihood level was obviously higher than the local minimum livelihood norm.[38] Wuhan's regulations, by contrast, disqualified people engaged in eighteen different kinds of behavior, as did some other cities, as noted in Chapter Five.

Another discrepancy involved municipal generosity. In 2007, when Lanzhou was providing 7.75 percent of its urban population with the *dibao*, Wuhan was underwriting a mere 4.8 percent of its residents.[39] This contrast deserves several caveats: In addition to central government subsidies earmarked for the *dibao*, Lanzhou probably also received substantial funds from the central government as a part of the Party's post-2000 program to develop the western portion of the country and so perhaps had more wherewithal to offer to the needy. Or, possibly, Lanzhou simply had a higher proportion of poor people among its residents. In only a few sections of Wuhan, the pro-

35. Interview, October 27, 2001, Wuhan.
36. After promotion to Shanghai party secretary in 2007, Yu was elevated to serve on the Communist Party's most powerful body, its Politburo Standing Committee, where he spent five years (2007–2012).
37. Email, November 23, 2008.
38. "Gansusheng renmin zhengfu bangongting guanyu zhuanfa 'Gansusheng chengshi jumin zuidi shenghuo baozhang banfa' de tongzhi" [Gansu Province people's government office notice on transmitting 'Gansu Province urban residents' minimum livelihood guarantee method'], *Caikuai yanjiu* [Finance and accounting research] 5 (2002): 59.
39. Interviews, August 28, 2007, Wuhan, and September 5. 2007, Lanzhou.

portion served matched Lanzhou's average: in Community X, in Hanyang District, about 7.9 percent got it, and in Community V, in Qiaokou District, 7.84 percent did, for instance.[40]

Bits of evidence illustrate the atmosphere in Wuhan in the early 2000s. The first was a talented but hard-up woman who complained that the fees for exhibiting her artwork on the streets had escalated substantially over time, eventually forcing her to abandon any effort to try to make sales.[41] The second was this 2009 comment from a foreign investigator: "Wuhan is working hard to catch up with the infrastructure and living standards of wealthier coastal cities. In 2000, there were 350,000 [motor] vehicles on Wuhan's roads; this year, that number will approach one million."[42]

The viewpoint in Wuhan, it would appear, jibes with what has been labeled the "spatial imaginary of modernity."[43] This vision has informed the aspirations of Chinese officials in richer and up-and-coming cities for an *au courant* urban landscape and for governing a class of people they judge appropriate to such locales. Combined with a fixation on the "quality" (*suzhi*, 素质) of the populace, such administrators appear to take the modernization of their towns to be dependent upon fostering in them "superior" individuals, with economic development seen as contingent upon there being a "higher" caliber workforce.[44]

Hypotheses

The contrasts between Wuhan and Lanzhou resonate with Piven-Cloward/Offe's description of social welfare as being about the *management of anachronistic workers*; *regulation of the labor market*; and *maintenance of order*. In Wuhan, these aims were to be met in part by fostering *clear streets*. Street observations and interview data stretching from 1998 to 2014 suggested that handling these objectives varied in two cities having quite differing levels of resources. We hoped to uncover the extent to which this variation held across a larger number of cities. Given that cities are charged with setting their

40. Benkan jizhe/xinwen, benkan tongxunyuan/Liu Jing, "Guanzhu chengshi dishouru qunti: Wuhanshi qiaokouqu chengshi jumin zuidi shenghuo baozhang gongzuo toushi" [This paper's news, this paper's correspondent,/Liu Jing, Pay close attention to urban low-income masses: Perspective on Wuhan's Qiaokou District's urban residents' minimum livelihood guarantee work], *Hubei caishui* [Hubei finance and taxes], 2 (2002): 4.

41. In-home interview, August 26, 2007, Wuhan.

42. Tom Miller, "Case Studies: I. Wuhan" *China Economic Quarterly, March 2009,* 35. In 2003, the city banned pedicabs—for some years, a source of livelihood for the laid-off—from the city's streets, to eliminate disorder to traffic and to the city's appearance (Interview, September 26, 2003). Another source said this was in 2004.

43. Frank N. Pieke, "Marketization, Centralization and Globalization of Cadre Training in Contemporary China," *CQ* no. 200 (December 2009): 960.

44. Borge Bakken, *The Exemplary Society: Human Improvement, Social Control and the Dangers of Modernity in China* (Oxford: Oxford University Press, 2000), 59–74.

own poverty lines, that their level of resources varies substantially, and that wealthier and upwardly mobile cities—having the capacity to do so—are, we reasoned, more apt to be oriented toward presenting their cities to outsiders as modern spectacles, we hypothesized that:

H1: The wealthier the city, the more inclined its officials will be to use their *dibao* funds for *disabled people* (i.e., to have such persons as a relatively high percentage of their total *dibao* recipients). This they do in their desire to maintain an unsullied urban scene by giving these people stipends and, in doing so, keeping them off the streets.

Using the terminology of Piven-Cloward/Offe, disabled people are what city officials in wealthier cities would consider *anachronistic workers,* publicly unsightly, and also unable to be put to work within a modernizing economy. Accordingly, our reasoning went, such officials would have the funds to, and prefer to, get such people out of the way. Indeed, while wealthier places shut down money-losing, special factories for the disabled in the late 1990s, officials in smaller, less prosperous towns related that the *chengguan* there was lenient and that its officials refrained from chasing such people from the avenues.[45] Poorer cities, not so conscious of their appearance and possibly planning to save their *dibao* allocation for other uses, allowed the disabled to create their own means of livelihood, if possible.

Thus, we hypothesized, administrators in poor cities would have comparatively lower percentages of the disabled among their *dibao* recipients. That there are variations in this respect was obvious when we found, for example, that while the disabled accounted for 10 percent of the *dibao* recipients in sixty-three cities across China on average in 2009, the range was about 1.3 percent in Yunnan's Baoshan and Shaanxi's Shangluo (both poor prefectural cities) but as high as 32 percent in the modernized tourist town of super-city Hangzhou.

H2: The richer the city, the more prone its decision makers will be to extend the *dibao* to registered unemployed workers.

This relationship could occur because wealthier cities have more sophisticated, technologically oriented economies.[46] Thus, registered unemployed

---

45. Interviews with local officials, Qianjiang, Hubei, July 6, 2010, and Xiantao, Hubei, July 8, 2010, back this up. At the time, Qianjiang's population was less than one-fifth of Wuhan's, and its gross regional product amounted to far, far below 1 percent of Wuhan's (estimated from Guojia tongjiju chengshi shehui jingji diaochasi [State Statistical Bureau, Urban Society and Economic Investigation Office], ed., *2012 Zhongguo chengshi jingji nianjian* [2012 China City Statistical Yearbook] (Beijing, Zhongguo tongji chubanshe [China Statistics Press], 2013), 16 and 361, for Wuhan and Qianjiang population, respectively; and 100 and 380 for Wuhan and Qianjiang gross regional product, respectively.

46. Fulong Wu and Ningying Huang, "New Urban Poverty in China," *Asia Pacific Viewpoint*, 48, no. 2 (2007): 168, 175–76, notes that firms in industrial sectors that were not competitive internationally were compelled to downsize.

workers are very likely to lack the skills and educational background necessary for participating in the new capital- and knowledge-intensive industries
of twenty-first-century China. Receipt of the *dibao* could encourage them not
to look for work in the formal economy, where, indeed, they are not apt to
find employment in any case. Thus, a wealthier city could be enticing laid-off
laborers to leave—and not attempt to re-enter—the labor market by offering
them the *dibao* funds they need to maintain their minimum livelihood.

Poorer cities' economies, on the other hand, being less advanced, are also
more able to absorb the unskilled registered unemployed. Consequently, we
expected to find a correlation between the poverty of a city and a lower percentage of registered unemployed obtaining the *dibao* among the program's
total *dibao* beneficiaries in that city. Again, the range for the percent of registered unemployed recipients among our sample cities was wide, averaging
19 percent of all recipients across cities but going as high as 40 percent in
Wuhan and Qingdao, both well-off, modernized cities, but in the single digits
in smaller, poorer cities.[47]

H3: In wealthier cities, people engaged in flexible labor will account for only
a small percent of the city's *dibao* recipients.

We suggested this relationship because people doing flexible labor often
do so out on the open roadways, damaging the appearance of the city in the
eyes of their urban governors in wealthy cities; thus, the *chengguan* sweeps
them away, resulting in fewer flexible laborers and, therefore, fewer *dibaohu*
doing flexible labor in rich cities. In poorer cities, on the other hand, where
the *chengguan* is more charitable, flexible labor is much more tolerated. In
richer municipalities, then, those engaged in such work will not be given
dibao funds (or their funds tend to be reduced by the amount of wages they
earn—or are claimed by the *dibao* administrators to be earning—in informal
work), reducing the chance that they will seek a livelihood on the streets.
Based on the Lanzhou official's words, and also the remarks of administrators
in two smaller Hubei cities in July 2010, contrariwise, poorer urban areas are
more likely to let the poor earn money on the sidewalks.

By permitting this activity, the city can save *dibao* funds for the municipal
budget. Officials in poor places are, additionally, less able to appeal to outsiders (whether to attract their visits or their capital), and so are less anxious
about their municipal visage. Thus, both to conserve funds and also because

---

47. Qin Gao, *Welfare, Work and Poverty: China's Social Assistance 20 Years After* (New York: Oxford University Press, 2017), 80, reports on a 2012 study the Asian Development Bank conducted in three cities—Ji'nan, Changsha, and Baotou (in Inner Mongolia). Consonant with our findings here, Baotou, the least developed of the three, had the lowest formal employment rate (3.5 percent) and the highest informal employment rate (67 percent). Ji'nan, the most developed, had the highest formal rate (11 percent) and the lowest informal one (53 percent).

such leaders may well channel less investment into bolstering their cities' images (given their lesser ability to simulate modernity), poor cities should be likely to let flexible workers make money outside, and to give them some, if not much, *dibao* money, as well as not to discourage them from out-of-doors petty labor by reducing their handouts.[48]

Interviews in Wuhan and Guangzhou, both relatively prosperous places, seemed to indicate that wealthy cities, on the other hand, actively discourage informal, or "flexible," employment (灵活 就业).[49] They do this by deducting from the *dibao* allowance any income derived from "flexible" employment that a recipient would otherwise receive.[50] This practice of decreasing the assistance subsidy of people with casual jobs can amount to a disincentive against accepting paid work. Such work is typically onerous, and unpleasant to boot, and promises a less reliable payment than does the *dibao*.[51] Flexible laborers, on average across the sample cities, constitute 16 percent of total recipients, but the percentage goes as low as 1.7 percent in Shanghai and as high as 33 percent in the far smaller and much poorer western city of Guyuan, in the impoverished Ningxia Hui Autonomous Region.

These hypotheses amount to correlations and are grounded in the notion that treatment of the poor is fundamentally different and follows distinctly dissimilar logics, in cities at varying levels of wealth. At base, the hypotheses pit the urge to present a cosmopolitan perspective in more affluent municipalities against a focus upon saving revenue in poorer cities.

STATISTICAL ANALYSIS

Data

We used the China Infobank data for the average wage in the cities in our sample, which we took as a proxy for the wealth of a given city. Even though average wage is not a perfect measure of a city's wealth or resources, we believe it is a reasonable indicator. Our reasoning goes like this: clearly, a city housing firms that can afford to pay higher wages must also be a place with higher tax income and thus more revenue.

---

48. Social policy scholar Tang Jun noted that stalls were much more common in small cities (interview, October 10, 2014, Beijing).

49. Zhang Shifei and Tang Jun, "Chengxiang zuidi shenghuo baozhang zhidu jiben xingcheng" [Urban and rural minimum livelihood guarantee system has basically taken form], in *2008 nian: Zhongguo shehui xingshi fenxi yu yuce* [2008: analysis and forecast of China's social situation], eds. Ru Xin, Lu Xueyi, and Li Peilin (Beijing: Social Sciences Academic Press, 2008), 62.

50. Leung, "The Development," 11.

51. Thomas Heberer, "Relegitimation through New Patterns of Social Security" *The China Review* (CR) 9, no. 2 (Fall 2009): 113.

We chose this proxy rather than GDP per capita, a figure often resorted to in economic research comparing Chinese cities but one that, unfortunately, is not comparable among cities. For many Chinese "cities" contain large stretches of rural areas and rural-registered population. Given wide rural-urban disparities in income, plus a vast variety in types of industry and occupation among and within cities, this renders many city *per capita* indicators not reflective of the true situation in the actual urban portion of what is called the "city." The value of such indicators, instead, is a function of the proportion of the "ruralness" in any given city's so-called urban districts.[52] Besides, most cities report their total GDP (that of the "whole city" [*quanshi*, 全市]), which definitely includes the work output of many rural residents who, however, are not registered in the city and so are not counted as part of the "city's" population. But then these cities go on to count only the urban-registered as members of their populations. This method of calculating neglects rural migrants who resided and produced in the city over long periods of time but who lack urban registration, and whose numbers, in some cases, amount to as much as a third of the city's formal, official urban population. These variable counting practices skew the results differentially in different municipalities.

Our statistical data covers sixty-three cities. Of these, thirty-six are "super-large" cities and include all thirty-one provincial capitals and five other cities having populations above two million. These thirty-six cities are those typically used in research on the urban *dibao*.[53] We added another twenty-four municipalities, all prefectural-level cities belonging to a set called "large" cities.[54] We chose these twenty-four cities by randomly selecting from each province one such city for which the requisite data were available and which also had populations between half a million and a million people as of 2007.[55] We added these "large" cities to investigate the variation that size

---

52. Kam Wing Chan, "Urbanization in China: What is the True Urban Population of China? Which is the Largest City in China?" unpublished ms., (January 2009).

53. Chen Shaohua, Martin Ravallion, and Youjuan Wang, "*Di bao:* A Guaranteed Minimum Income in China's Cities?" World Bank Policy Research Working Paper 3805, January 2006, surveyed these thirty-six cities; Du Yang and Albert Park, "The Effects of Social Assistance on Poverty Reduction," The International Conference on Policy Perspectives on Growth, Economic Structures and Poverty Reduction, Beijing, China, June 2007, use data from five super-large cities; and Shenjing He, Fulong Wu, Chris Webster, and Yuting Liu, "Poverty Concentration and Determinants in China's Urban Low-income Neighbourhoods and Social Groups," *International Journal of Urban and Regional Research* 34, no. 2 (2010): 328–49, studies six super-large cities. One exception is Qin Gao and Carl Riskin, "Generosity and Participation: Variations in Urban China's Minimum Livelihood Guarantee Policy," in *Law and Economics with Chinese Characteristics*, eds. David Kennedy and Joseph E. Stiglitz (New York: Oxford University Press, 2013), which analyzes data from seventy-seven cities of varying sizes.

54. The prefecture is the administrative unit just below the province; provinces typically contain six to eight of these.

55. Kam Wing Chan, "Fundamentals of China's Urbanization and Policy," *CR* 10, no.1 (2010); and Chen Xiangming, "China's City Hierarachy, Urban Policy and Spatial Development in the 1980s," *Urban Studies* 28, no. 3 (1991): 341–67.

might introduce, especially given that nearly all prior *dibao* research had as of 2009 been carried out only on super-large cities, to the best of our knowledge. "Large" cities are especially important to study in work on the *dibao* program, since roughly 85 percent of the scheme's targets were living either in them or in even smaller cities in the mid-2000s.[56]

Variables

Table 8.1 lists all variables and their descriptions. Besides average wage, three other variables match the three hypotheses above: disabled workers as a percent of total *dibao* recipients; registered unemployed workers as a percent of total *dibao* workers; and flexible laborers as a percent of total *dibao* recipients. *Dibao* expenditure as a percentage of city GDP is included to control for a city government's generosity; it strongly and significantly correlates negatively with average wage. This finding suggests either that poorer cities have more poor people and, therefore, are compelled to spend more on the *dibao* or that poor cities get a large injection of funds from the central government for their *dibao* payments. Most likely, both are true.

Methodology

Ordinary least squares (OLS) regression is used to show the variable correlations between average wage and the three other variables. One model is used for each of the variables in our three hypotheses: Model 1 is for the variable number of flexible workers who are *dibao* recipients as a percentage of total *dibao* recipients in a city; Model 2 is for the variable number of registered unemployed *dibao* recipients as a percentage of total *dibao* recipients in a city; and Model 3 is for the variable number of disabled *dibao* recipients in a city as a percent of total recipients.

In Models 4 and 5, the percentage of flexible labor *dibao* recipients is regressed on government revenue in two groups: Model 4 uses as its group cities with lower than median government revenue. Model 5 analyses the group of cities with higher than median government revenue. We split cities into two groups because poorer cities receive much of their *dibao* funding as an earmarked allocation (subsidy) from the central government, while

---

56. John G. Taylor, "Poverty and Vulnerability," in *China Urbanizes*, eds. Shahid Yusuf and Tony Saich (Washington, DC: The World Bank, 2008), 95. Poverty Reduction and Economic Management Department, East Asia And Pacific Region, World Bank, *From Poor Areas to Poor People: China's Evolving Poverty Reduction Agenda: An Assessment of Poverty and Inequality in China* (Washington, DC: The World Bank, 2009), 73, states: "Provincial mega-cities have the lowest incidence [of urban disadvantage], while prefecture-level cities have several times higher incidence"; also "Urban disadvantage is primarily a small-city phenomenon: *more than 80 percent of the urban disadvantaged population lives in prefecture- and lower-level cities* [emphasis added]."

Table 8.1. Index of Variables and Cities

Variables	N	Mean	Standard Deviation	Min	Max	Description
Dbpop	59	54,924.75	76,067.74	1,784	43,7592	Total dibao recipient population in a city
flexwork_dbpop	59	0.164	0.119	0	0.631	% among dibao recipients who do flexible work
Regunemp_dbbpop	59	0.195	0.122	0	0.588	% among dibao recipients who are registered unemployed
disabled_dbpop	59	0.101	0.077	0.013	0.379	% among dibao recipients who are disabled
Dbexpdr	60	91.02	141.11	3.02	798.83	Dibao expenditure (million yuan)
Govrev	59	16,111.19	33,637.16	40.78	2.06E+05	Government revenue (million Yuan)
db_GDP	60	0.001	0.002	0.00006	0.009	Dibao expenditure as the percentage of GDP
Avrgwage	59	26,198	7,411.647	11,644.3	49,439.06	average wage in a city (Yuan)
RegionC	60	0.222	0.419	0	1	1 for central region
RegionE	60	0.365	0.485	0	1	1 for east region
RegionNE	60	0.111	0.317	0	1	1 for northeast region
RegionW	60	0.302	0.463	0	1	1 for west region

richer cities pay for the *dibao* either entirely or mostly from their own municipal revenues. The different sources of funding may cause cities to have different giving patterns. It should be noted here that, despite poorer cities receiving most or all of their funding from upper levels of government, all urban officials interviewed uniformly claimed that there were no quotas or targets dictating limits to the numbers of needy people that could be subsidized,[57] and neither were there specific reporting obligations to their superiors. It did appear in interviews that each city made its own decisions about whom to fund.[58]

Results

We regressed flexible laborers as a percentage of total *dibao* recipients on average wage, after putting data into two groups according to the median amount of government revenue in a city. The regression showed that in low-average wage cities, there was no relationship between the percentage of flexible worker *dibao* recipients and average wage. But there was a strong negative relationship between high average wage and the percentage of flexible worker *dibao* recipients in richer cities. In other words, flexible workers represented a comparatively smaller percentage of all *dibao* recipients in cities with a higher average wage (i.e., in the richer cities); this percentage, however, had no relationship with average wage in poorer cities. Models 4 and 5 supported the correlation proposed in Hypothesis 3. (See Table 8.2)

Hypothesis 1 was buttressed by Model 3 in Table 8.3: the wealthier the city, the more likely that a larger percentage of the city's *dibao* recipients were disabled people—in our reasoning, to keep them off the streets. Hypothesis 2 was consistent with Model 2 in this table: the richer the city, the more prone its decision makers were to extend the *dibao* to registered unemployed workers, since, in our interpretation, these workers could not easily be placed in the city's formal economy.

Governments whose *dibao* spending was a higher percentage of GDP (that is, poorer cities) were more likely to give *dibao* funding to flexible laborers (Model 1) and to the registered unemployed (Model 2). We believed this may indicate that these cities did not want to inhibit informal labor, and so they did not provide a disincentive against working on the streets by withdrawing the *dibao* (or a large proportion of it) when a person was engaged in irregular labor. There is no confirmation of the hypothesis that these governments were less likely to give money to the disabled. Model 3, however, does show that

---

57. See Chapter Five, which refutes this claim.
58. Allocations made by city districts vary also, but we refrained from testing that. That each city makes its decisions about whom to fund does not negate the presence of quotas.

Table 8.2. Regression Models: Explaining Different Percentages of *Dibao* given to Flexible Workers, Registered Unemployed, and the Disabled

Variables	(1) flexwork_dbpop	(2) regunemp_dbpop	(3) disabled_dbpop
Avrgwage	−1.38e-06	6.40e-06**	3.23e-06**
	(2.27e-06)	(2.66e-06)	(1.60e-06)
db_GDP	20.00*	24.66*	−6.703
	(11.84)	(13.84)	(8.329)
Region	0.0234	0.0224	0.0521*
	(0.0405)	(0.0473)	(0.0285)
regionE	−0.00138	−0.0350	0.0166
	(0.0427)	(0.0499)	(0.0301)
regionNE	0.0284	−0.00380	0.0847**
	(0.0478)	(0.0559)	(0.0336)
Constant	0.161**	0.00974	−0.00340
	(0.0756)	(0.0883)	(0.0532)
Observations	58	58	58
R-squared	0.152	0.130	0.262

Standard errors in parentheses: *** p<0.01, ** p<0.05, * p<0.1

Table 8.3. Regression of Flexible Worker Recipients' Percentage on Average Wage, in Two Different Groups

Variables	(4) flexwork_dbpop	(5) flexwork_dbpop
Avrgwage	3.43e-06	−4.53e-06**
	(5.26e-06)	(1.88e-06)
+db_GDP	25.59*	−4.106
	(14.50)	(25.56)
Constant	0.0555	0.278***
	(0.136)	(0.0669)
Observations	28	30
R-squared	0.113	0.200

Standard errors in parentheses: *** p<0.01, ** p<0.05, * p<0.1
Notes: The twenty-eight cities in Model 4 are those with average wage below the median of government revenue (4,836.8 million yuan). The thirty cities in Model 5 are those with average wage above the median.

the western region, the poorest in the country,[59] was generally less likely to give the *dibao* to the disabled than were other regions (especially the northeast and the central regions).

---

59. According to World Bank, "From Poor Areas," 73, 6.8 percent of the urban people living in the northwest region of the country are poor to the extent of twice the World Bank's poverty level; in the southwest, the rate is 6.6 percent. The rates are 4.4 percent in the coastal provinces, 6.3 percent in the northeast, and 6.2 percent in central China. We consider the "west" as: Sichuan, Guizhou, Yunnan, Inner Mongolia, Gansu, Tibet, Qinghai, Shaanxi, Ningxia, Xinjiang, and Chongqing, nearly matching the World Bank's southwest and northwest regions.

DISCUSSION AND ALTERNATIVE EXPLANATIONS

Discussion

These findings provide suggestive correlations between the level of wealth/ poverty in a city, on the one side, and cities' variable treatment of three categories of welfare recipients, on the other. Returning to Piven and Cloward and Offe, we found that several of the features of social assistance they identify (in italics just below) can be seen as characterizing the operation of the *dibao* program in both the richer and the poorer cities. Thus, one can read the data as showing that—as central-level politicians promised in the late 1990s—the *dibao* has been used in a way consistent with *preserving order* (by compensating losers in the state's modernization project), and that decision makers at the urban level do allocate only *token expenditures* to the project; the program also appears to embody a subtext of *benign neglect*.

The findings also enabled us to offer some conjectures about the *differential* implementation of the *dibao* in our sixty-three sample cities, some of which are prosperous and others relatively penurious. For the ways in which local administrators disburse their *dibao* funds seemed to differ in a patterned way among the cities of China. Most crucially, as interviews and street observations in two cities signified, officials in richer cities appeared to set urban management priorities that dictated distributing social assistance funds diametrically differently from how the authorities in poorer locales did: that is, officers in wealthier municipalities were more prone to finance *anachronistic workers* (represented in our data by the *disabled*), care more about *regulating the* (formal) *labor market* (by paying the *registered unemployed*—if minimally—to stay out of it), and insist more on the *order* signaled to outsiders by boasting *cleared, clean streets* (i.e., discouraging *flexible labor* from doing business on them) than did those in the less well-off places.

Alternative Explanations

It is possible that the total number of people who actually constitute each *dibao* recipient category in each city might have affected the percentage each category represented among total *dibao* recipients in that city. Unfortunately, we were unable to locate data indicating the numbers that these categories of poor people represented in the general population of each city. For instance, for the number of disabled in the cities, it could be that poorer cities, presumably having more problems of untreated environmental pollution, have more disabled people. But it could also be that wealthier cities, where manufacturing was rapid and extensive, had more industrial accidents and/or more industrial pollution. Without any way to collect the necessary data, we were forced to posit the presence of a random distribution of these population categories within individual cities, even though the truth may be otherwise.

It is also possible that there is simply more "flexible labor" in poorer cities, for whatever reason. But if that is the case, that would be consistent with our explanation because it would mean that such municipalities permit and encourage this type of work. If true, that datum would still distinguish between cities with more and less wealth, and it would help to explain why flexible workers constituted a larger proportion of the *dibao* recipients in poor than in rich cities.

Finally, it could be that there were simply more registered unemployed people in rich than in poor cities. That is, these peoples' numbers could be higher in wealthier places simply because there were more still-extant firms in these richer cities that had been able to pay into the unemployment insurance fund for their dismissed workers while they were still employed (such payments are a necessary condition for anyone to receive unemployment insurance, and so dispose people to register as unemployed; the result would be more registered unemployed people in the city). Nonetheless, giving the *dibao* to these people would just the same have represented a choice by city governments to placate/pacify these people (i.e., to *preserve order*). That provision would also have served as an acknowledgment that there were no spots for them in the regular economy.

CONCLUSION

Our findings supported a conjecture that in China, where profits, modernization, and foreign investment have become significant to leaders at all levels, there may be a logic undergirding welfare allocation that grows out of an economic, not a political, calculus. Our work suggests that, where lower echelons of administration have authority to make rules about welfare rationing, urban finances appear to correlate with such allocational decisions. This seems to be the case in poor places, where officials attempt to save on funds; it also appears so in wealthier municipalities, where it is well-known and easily observable that authorities design their urban areas as showcases, in the hope of attracting outside tourism and foreign investment. For in well-off cities, a relatively lower percentage of all *dibao* recipients were (at the time of our study) people known to be engaged in "flexible labor" as compared within poorer cities. Preferring clearer sidewalks, welfare distributors in prosperous cities were reducing the *dibao* allowances they gave to impoverished people who tried to make their own money, we argue, in the interest of keeping such people out of the public eye and safely at home.[60]

---

60. This observation is reminiscent of an editorialist's quotation written in 1902, in Janet Y. Chen, *Guilty of Indigence: The Urban Poor in China, 1900–1953* (Princeton, NJ: Princeton, 2012), 22:

At the same time, a relatively higher proportion of people with disabilities, and also comparatively more people who were registered as unemployed, received assistance in wealthier than in poorer municipalities. The explanation we advanced is that officials in the richer cities were more inclined to want those they probably viewed as unsightly or as incompetent workers to stay out of view and away from the regular labor market. Consequently, our story goes, authorities were offering these people official sustenance by means of the *dibao*. We cannot prove these connections definitively. But at the very least, our findings do, in fact, fit remarks made by welfare officials in two cities, one more flourishing and one poorer.

We propose that these findings—whether or not they represent causal connections, and regardless of whether they result from conscious intentionality on the part of city officialdom—are in accord with the known preferences of urban administrators in wealthier locales for achieving a modern appearance in their cities and for fostering technological sophistication in their economies. And it could certainly be that, in the view of the administrators of such cities, to become effectively modern and sufficiently attractive to foreign investors and tourists, the city must keep disciplined, out of the work force, and even out of sight both the new underdogs to which marketization has given birth, and also people with a visible infirmity. These people, thus, were (and still are) encouraged to stay at home by being supplied with the *dibao*, according to our reasoning.

In poorer places, on the other hand, where funds are scarcer and where pretensions to grandeur weaker, our three categories of recipients were being treated in the opposite way from how they were handled in well-off sites. Both the disabled and flexible workers were allowed on the streets without their *dibao* allocation being diminished, as their fending for themselves was probably viewed as saving funds for the city budget. And administrators, presumably, did not worry about an embarrassing urban appearance. For outside visitors were relatively rare and foreign investment unlikely there in any event. Thus, a smaller percentage of all recipients were disabled people in 2009 in these environments.[61] And a relatively higher percentage of beneficiaries were informal workers, as compared with in the wealthier cities, because, we contended, officials in poor places preferred to conserve their city's *dibao* funds for other uses and did not object to the sight of people earning money informally on the city's roads.

"Today the number of poor people in our nation can be said to have reached an extreme," alluding to unemployed vagrants, widows, orphans, and cripples, whom, he alleged, were "found everywhere." He went on to surmise that, "When foreigners see this, how they must collapse in laughter." This is the same linkage of poverty with national shame suggested in this chapter.

61. One more observational datum: in a destitute section of Guilin, Guangxi, I saw disabled people, uninterrupted, performing calisthenics on city streets in fall 2008.

The registered unemployed, on the other hand, represented a lower proportion of the *dibao* beneficiaries in less well-off municipalities than they did in the wealthier locales. This could be the case because the economies in such places—less advanced and less technologically driven, as well as less foreign-invested—were more likely to have spots for these people, even as local officials were less disposed than were the ones in rich cities to keep them at home and out of work. There were also apt to be fewer successful firms that could manage to fund their unemployed people's insurance, thereby rendering the *registered* unemployed scarcer. The upshot is that laid-off workers were considered suitable for regular employment and so were less liable to constitute a large proportion of the *dibao* recipients in cities that were more strapped for funds.

In sum, our research suggests that an influential formulation stating that welfare giving is geared toward catering to voters is purely regime-specific. In an authoritarian regime undergoing capitalist-style development, modernization, and globalization, we submit, the logics of governance and of social policy are plausibly driven by quite a different line of reasoning, one in line with writings from fifty years ago that instead emphasize an economic rationale for poor relief.

The next chapter moves from analyzing differences in implementation of the *dibao* scheme among cities to reviewing modulation in its execution according to changes in broader national policies over time. What constituted the program by the late 2010s, Chapter Nine will report, diverged considerably from what it was announced to achieve at its instigation.

Section IV

HARSH CHANGES

Chapter Nine

Policy Manipulations

As Chapter Two recounted, the *dibao* came on board in 1999 ostensibly as a program of social assistance—but, pointedly, in the midst of rising numbers of factory worker retrenchments, resultant new poverty, and, what was most potent for policy makers, accompanying protests. But as demonstrations subsided, the program shifted, as a range of modifications were made to the scheme, with some subtle and others obvious.

This chapter spells out five formal changes, largely in and after the rise to leadership of Xi Jinping in 2012, some of which had become practice informally earlier, or at least been advocated. It contrasts these Xi-era initiatives with what the Minimum Livelihood Guarantee had initially put forth as its aims and mechanics.[1] It also presents adjustments in the amounts of funding invested in the program over the years. I interpret the new rules, rhetoric, and statistics related to the program's outlays to demonstrate transformations in the *political* goals that were attached to the program. In conclusion, I highlight how the revisions and political shifts were altered in line with new objectives of the regime, such that its original form was nearly twisted out of shape by the mid-2010s.[2] One conclusion is that the program as a whole,

---

1. State Council Order No. 271, "Chengshi jumin zuidi shenghuo boazhang tiaoli" [Urban residents minimum livelihood guarantee regulations], dbs.mca.gov.cn/article/csdb/cvfg/200711/200711 00003522.shtml, accessed August 13, 2013; also in *Zhongguo minzheng* (*ZGMZ*) [Chinese civil affairs] 11 (1999): 16–17.

2. My analysis is related to, but different from, Jennifer Pan's concept of "seepage," as articulated in *Welfare for Autocrats: How Social Assistance in China Cares for its Rulers* (New York: Oxford University Press, 2020). My argument is in line with that of Yao Jianping, "Zhongguo chengshi dibao miaozhun kunjing: zige zhang'ai, jishu nanti, hai shi zhengzhi yingxiang?" [Chinese urban *dibao* targeting predicament: qualifications obstacles, technical difficulty, or political influence?] *Shehui kexue* [Social science] no. 3 (2018): 72. He writes that, "There's a certain freedom of judgment, discretionary power. The policy environment to a great degree decides whether a borderline person can get it"—which I found after writing this chapter.

including its mission, has been downplayed over the years, as it has been made to serve different goals and as the out-of-work quieted down. Thus, I argue that the original aim of the scheme—to keep the laid-off proletariat passive in order to avoid wrecking enterprise restructuring—was no longer a concern for central-level decision makers. But even as the program's import likely decreased, the scheme did not escape central-level attention. Apparently, the *dibao* continued to be deemed worthy of enough deliberation that it was altered to match Xi's larger ends, and it did so in five different ways.

BACKGROUND: PROTESTS ATTENUATE

I first situate the shift in policy within the context of growing silence among the retrenched workforce after 2004. This quietude had been preceded by dramatic and large-scale *xiagang* and retiree protests—which sparked both the creation of the program and also its extension—as mentioned in Chapters Two and Three.[3] Leaders' response to the decline in organizing and outbursts accords with a view advanced by Frances Fox Piven and Richard A. Cloward. They found a pattern they termed a "cycle" in the mid-twentieth-century United States: worker turbulence, once pacified, tended to be followed by a relief program that was later converted to work relief and then cut back, with the "able-bodied unemployed" disqualified.[4]

That demonstrations slid with time is in line with Lynette Ong's work that showed that, whereas disturbances related to state-owned enterprise labor disputes accounted for over 37 percent of eighteen different grievance types in 2003, in the years 2010 to 2012, they ranged between a mere 6 to 8 percent.[5] Eli Friedman also uncovered a drop-off in labor disputes, though he placed that change earlier, from 2008–2011.[6]

In the view of other observers, too, it was the dying away of the great mass of protests after 2004 that led to the twist in the government's spotlight in giving—away from donating to once-noisy dislocated persons and toward nurturing the abject poor. Jaeyoun Won, who spent much time on the ground during the critical period, reported on numerous protests in 2004 in many

3. Jane Duckett, "Debate: Neoliberalism, Authoritarian Politics and Social Policy in China," *Development and Change* 52, no. 2 (2020): 526. On the protests, see William Hurst and Kevin J. O'Brien, "China's Contentious Pensioners," *The China Quarterly* No. 170 (June 2002): 345–60.

4. Frances Fox Piven and Richard A. Cloward, *Regulating the Poor: The Functions of Public Welfare* (updated edition) (New York: Vintage Books, 1993), 117, 124.

5. Lynette H. Ong, "Reports of Social Unrest: Basic Characteristics, Trends and Patterns, 2003–12," in *Handbook of the Politics of China*, ed. David S. G. Goodman (Cheltenham, UK: Edward Elgar Publishing, 2015), 352.

6. Eli Friedman, *Insurgency Trap: Labor Politics in Postsocialist China* (Ithaca, NY: Cornell University Press, 2014), 4.

cities. But he observed that these tended to mitigate after that, for a variety of reasons: people affected became concerned with finding ways to improve their subsistence level, so they busied themselves looking for and doing work instead of resisting policy; they had lost their prior trust in the fairness of the political processes, a faith that previously had disposed them to believe that defiance was a safe bet; and they had come to understand that challenging the state would probably bring on severe repression.[7]

A second analyst, Kevin Lin, recorded that, "The decline of state-sector workers' protests follow[ed] the end of the most intense period of restructuring." He illustrated this point by stating that state-sector-worker protests fell from constituting 80 percent of all workers' actions down to only 20 percent in the decade from 2000 to 2010. The drop, he held, was due to the failure of previous efforts at complaining and rallying. With the irreversible dismantling of the welfare regime that had for decades obtained in state firms, he wrote, "There's not a great deal left to defend."[8] Reflecting on this point several years after putting it into print, Lin explained that, "Many had no way to reclaim their lost pensions and unpaid wages [nor to make good their inadequate] early retirement buyout, and protests dissipated over the years."[9]

One angle on the vanishing of *xiagang* outbursts was provided by a Beijing social researcher, who, after agreeing that this waning had contributed to enhanced frugality with regard to the *dibao*, offered a different insight. His view was that, unfortunately, the people attempting to make do on its provision had simply gotten accustomed over the years to the enforced meager level of living it prescribed and, consequently, had given up.[10]

FIVE CHANGES IN POLICY

What is clear, in any event, is that beginning near the end of 2012, a raft of new restrictions and regulations, already brewing for several years, became formal policy. The initial sign was a State Council Opinion published in late September 2012, containing several mandates that were either novel to the program or that had been unofficially present but much less accentuated earlier.[11] The first of these was a change of emphasis in providing social assis-

7. Jaeyoun Won, "The Making of the Post-Proletariat in China," *Development and Society* 34, no. 2 (2005): 201–5.

8. Kevin Lin, "Recomposing Chinese Migrant and State-Sector Workers," in *Chinese Workers in Comparative Perspective*, ed. Anita Chan (Ithaca, NY: Cornell University Press, 2015), 81–82. Protests by migrant, non-state-sector workers rose appreciably in that period, affecting this result.

9. Kevin Lin, email, April 5, 2019.

10. Interview, October 10, 2014, Beijing.

11. Zhongguo renmin gongheguo [People's Republic of China], Guowuyuan [State Council] (2012), "*Guowuyuan guanyu jinyibu jiaqiang he gaijin zuidi shenghuo baozhang gongzuo de yijian*"

tance. Instead of offering allowances, community *dibao* distributors were to arrange employment for the able-bodied impecunious.[12] Secondly, the document urged localities to take the seriously/chronically diseased and disabled, the totally destitute and the deserted—in short, those who amounted to the recipients of the former "three-withouts" (*sanwu*) welfare—as the significant beneficiaries (see Chapter Two). The third alteration was that, moving away from the former focus on stability, the document beamed a spotlight on local cadre corruption and misappropriation of funds. Along with that were calls for stepped-up auditing of and supervision over what were thought to be potential and actual recipients' intentional misrepresentations of their financial status. According to the official press, these sorts of misallocations and flaws were rampant in the conduct of the scheme.

Fourth, and prominently, the September 2012 State Council Opinion for the first time formally ordered that household assets, including bank savings, securities, and other forms of property, such as vehicles and housing, be taken into account in assessing a family's eligibility for the *dibao*. The upshot was that now an applicant's local residence registration, family income, and in addition, the amount of his/her household assets became the three criteria in determining who was to obtain the allowance. There was, in addition, a fifth new priority, though not a part of the 2012 injunction: funding for poor people resident in the rural areas began to rise relative to that earmarked for the indigent in the cities, perhaps a forerunner of Xi Jinping's campaign to eliminate rural poverty that began soon after.

First Change: Those Able to Work Must Work

The first alteration amounted to a call to cut off from—and not admit to—the rolls people capable of work but unemployed. That modification can be distinguished from the formal, inaugurating 1999 regulations on the *dibao*, which gave three fundamental conditions for qualifying for the aid: 1) being one of the "three withouts"; 2) being unemployed, with one's term for drawing unemployment relief having ended but being unable to get reemployed and having a family average income below the local poverty standard; and/or

---

[State Council's Opinion on Progressively Strengthening and Improving the Minimum Livelihood Guarantee Work], *Guofa* [2012] [State Council Document no. 45], www.gov.cn/zwgk/2012-09/26 /content_2233209.htm, accessed September 15, 2012; Caizhengbu, minzhengbu tongzhi [Ministry of Finance, Ministry of Civil Affairs Circular], "Guanyu yinfa 'Chengxiang zuidi shenghuo baozhang zijin guanli banfa' de tongzhi'" [On the issuance of the circular on the management of urban and rural minimum livelihood funds], *Caishe* [Finance and society] 171 *hao* [no. 171] 2012, baike.baidu.com/ view/9452029.htm, accessed October 2012.

12. This move was influenced by models in use in the United States and Europe (Tao Liu and Li Sun, "Urban Social Assistance in China: Transnational Diffusion and National Interpretation," *Journal of Current Chinese Affairs* [August 2016] https://doi.org.10.1177/186810261604500202, accessed November 11, 2020).

3) being at work, laid-off, or retired but, with all of one's sources of income combined, still having insufficient funds to bring one's household's average income up to the local poverty line. No mention was made then as to whether or not a person was capable of working. Practically speaking, there were just two requirements that really mattered in the beginning: having an income below the local poverty line and possessing household registration in the city where one applied for the subsidy.[13]

Besides, that earlier document had made only passing reference to whether recipients should work: it just prescribed "encourage[ing] labor self-support." The 2008 Civil Affairs Statistical yearbook shows that, in 2002, as many as nearly half (48.7 percent) of all *dibao* recipients were either laid-off, retired, or unemployed workers; 44.3 percent were laid-off or unemployed.[14] (See Table 9.1) In the same year, Athar Hussain (2002) recorded that "a large percentage" of the *dibaohu* "are able and willing to work but have no jobs," though without giving a figure.[15] No mention was made of their labor capacity.

Table 9.1. Numbers of Laid-off (LO), Unemployed (UE), and Retired Workers as Percentages of Total *Dibao* Recipients, 2002–2007 (Unit: 10,000 People)

Year	Total Dibao Recipients	# of Laid Off (LO)	LO as % of Total Recipients	# of Unemployed (UE)	UE as % of Total Recipients	# of Retired	Retired as % of Total Recipients
2002	2,064.7	554.5	26.9	358.3	17.4	90.8	4.4
2003	2,246.8	518.4	23.1	409.0	18.2	90.7	4.0
2004	2,205.0	468.9	21.3	423.1	19.2	73.1	3.3
2005	2,234.2	430.7	19.3	410.1	18.4	61.3	2.7
2006	2,240.1	350.0	15.6	420.8	18.8	53.2	2.4
2007	2,272.1	627.2	27.6	364.3	16.0	n.a.	n.a.

Source: *Zhongguo minzheng tongji nianjian 2008* [China Civil Affairs' Statistical Yearbook 2008] (Beijing: Zhongguo tongji chubanshe [China Statistics Press], 2008), 76.

---

13. Joe C. B. Leung and Yuebin Xu, *China's Social Welfare* (Cambridge, UK: Polity, 2015), 90–91.

14. Calculated from the 2008 *Minzheng nianjian* [Civil Affairs Yearbook], 76. These figures do not include dependents of the unemployed workers. Shang Xiaoyuan and Xiaoming Wu, "Changing Approaches of Social Protection: Social Assistance Reform in Urban China," *Social Policy and Society* 3, no. 3 (2004): 259–71, differs by a large margin, as it claims that laid-off workers, together with retired people, the unemployed, *and their families* [emphasis added] accounted for a much larger percentage, even as many as 85 percent of those covered by the *dibao* in 2002. "Retired people" in Table 9.1 likely included those forced into early retirement as firms downsized or disappeared, and for this reason, they were included with the laid-off and unemployed, all of whom were eligible for the *dibao* if their income was below the local poverty line, as noted above. Or, possibly, this retired category referred to those whose pensions were insufficient to live on. In any event, "retired" as a category disappeared from tables after 2006. A person was considered "unemployed" if s/he had no further connection to his/her former firm; a "laid-off" worker at least nominally maintained "labor relations" with the firm (i.e., the firm theoretically remained responsible for contributing to the worker's welfare funds). In truth, neither had a job any longer.

15. Athar Hussain, "Urban Poverty in China: Measurement, Patterns and Policies," Ms. (Geneva: International Labour Office, January 2003), 1.

Not long thereafter, a decline gradually ensued in the provision of relief for people considered able to work, although without there being a formal order to that effect. In the middle of 2004, an official from the civil affairs bureau of Shijiazhuang, Hebei, suggested in a letter published in *Chinese Civil Affairs* (*Zhongguo minzheng,* 中国民政, the journal of the Ministry of Civil Affairs, the unit responsible for the *dibao*) that whether a person had labor ability, whether s/he had the will to work, and the nature of the cause for the loss of his/her labor ability should all be considered in deciding whether to offer him/her the *dibao.* In fact, the writer argued that an applicant's possession or lack of labor ability should be the "decisive factor" in according the assistance.[16] At the same time, most cities began implementing activation ("workfare") measures to encourage healthy recipients to take jobs.[17]

In 2008, social welfare researcher Joe Leung still recorded that, "the majority of recipient families are unemployed, and the need for employment assistance is paramount."[18] But by 2009, the registered and unregistered unemployed (essentially, the *xiagang*) together accounted for only 39.5 percent of all *dibao* subjects nationwide—though the numbers of retired among the *dibaohu* was no longer tabulated after 2006, making it difficult to compare earlier and later years—possibly a drop of almost ten percentage points in just seven years, from 2002 to 2009. A 2009 World Bank publication commented, "In practice only those unable to work are likely to be provided with long-term assistance."[19] At that point, however, this state reluctance to underwrite the able-bodied was not yet promulgated as an order.

After 2009, the central government began formalizing this modification, demanding that localities arrange for impoverished individuals capable of doing so to move to the labor market to sustain themselves—irrespective of whether that market had a place for them, which, approximately one hundred interviews revealed, often enough it did not. Informants at the grassroots level in several cities perceived this alteration, even though there was yet to be an authoritative pronouncement. For instance, in 2008, forty-seven-year-old Mr. Zhang, living in Beijing with a wife and one child, insisted that, "If you're not paralyzed and lying on the *kang* (炕, a brick Chinese bed common in north

---

16. Xing Zhaohui, "Fenlei shibao ruhe fenlei" [How to make distinctions in executing the *dibao*], *ZGMZ* 4 (2004): 41.

17. Haomiao Zhang, "China's Social Assistance Policy: Experiences and Future Directions," *China Journal of Social Work (CJSW)* 7, no. 3 (2014): 229–30; Leung and Yuebin Xu, *China's Social Welfare,* 93.

18. Joe Leung, "The Development of Social Assistance in Urban China: The Residualisation of Social Welfare," paper presented at Provincial China Workshop 2008, Nankai University, Tianjin (PRC), October 27–30, 2008, 9.

19. The World Bank, Poverty Reduction and Economic Management Department, East Asia, and Pacific Region, "From poor areas to poor people: China's evolving poverty reduction agenda: an assessment of poverty and inequality in China" (Washington, DC: The World Bank, 2009), 145.

China), you don't meet the conditions . . . if a normal person has a chronic illness, like high blood pressure, might get it and might not."[20]

My first encounter with the changed approach was in 2011, when a *dibao* researcher informed me that, "It seems the program got stricter in recent years, with *xiagang* being pushed out and only the *sanwu* being admitted."[21] In Wuhan interviews in summer 2012, just before State Council Opinion of 2012 was announced, community officials mentioned a new stringency greeting applications. As one local leader explained, "A person who is under fifty years of age and has work ability can't get the *dibao* now; the policy has become very strict. If s/he can't find work, that's not a condition for getting the *dibao*. We encourage them to go work."[22] In a different Wuhan community the same summer, the *dibao* manager asserted that,

Now it's almost impossible for a healthy laid-off person to get the *dibao*. Only the seriously ill and disabled can get it. Getting the allowance depends on age and ability to work; it's only for the old, weak, those with ill health, and the disabled. If one has working ability, he's unlikely to get it. In the past, the policy was more relaxed and there were lots of laid-off people [receiving it].[23]

The year after the order came out, in Shanghai in 2013, a seventy-two-year-old female recipient with two grown daughters explained definitively, "If you have work ability you have to work, unless you're a veteran, a child, or disabled."[24]

The issue was clearly nationwide. Statements in 2014 by a range of academic informants all concurred with this information. In Beijing, Tang Jun noted that, "Around 2010 the policy got tighter with regard to the able-bodied."[25] Faculty members at the Central China University of Science and Technology in Wuhan related that, "Recently we especially care about work ability,"[26] and a Lanzhou street committee cadre held that, "Policy has gotten stricter . . . if you have work ability you should work." He went on to remark that, "In the past a lot of laid-off workers got the funds, but things are stricter now." Consonant with this assessment, an interviewee from Heilongjiang observed that, "At first, the qualifications for the *dibao* were easier [to meet],

---

20. Han Keqing, ed., *Zhongguo chengshi dibao fangtanlu* [Interviews with Minimum Livelihood Guarantee Recipients in Urban China] (Ji'nan: Shandong renmin chubanshe, 2012), 40.

21. Interview, Wuhan, August 18, 2011.

22. Interview, Huazhong shifan daxue [Central China Normal University] community, Wuhan, June 26, 2012.

23. Interview, June 30, 2012, Hongshan District, Wuhan.

24. Interview, June 25, 2013, Shanghai.

25. Interview with social policy researcher, October 10, 2014, Beijing.

26. Interview with a group of social policy faculty, Huazhong keji daxue [Central China University of Science and Technology], November 3, 2014, Wuhan.

but it's gotten harder now."[27] Furthermore, data collected from the years 2003 through 2013 showed that, "In practice only people who are disabled are provided with regular or long-term benefits . . . to maintain a work ethic, it is usually difficult for the able-bodied to get minimum livelihood guarantee benefits."[28] The following complaint from a community leader in Lanzhou went along the same line: "If they have labor ability, then we introduce them to work and train them. But it's a nuisance (*mafan*, 麻烦). Their qualifications don't fit the jobs, but they want it anyway and then they get angry."[29]

Nailing this trend down even more securely, State Council Document No. 649 "Interim Measures for Social Assistance" of February 27, 2014, supplemented the 2012 State Council Opinion. This new mandate decreed that the responsible locality must ensure that at least one person in a family becomes employed if all family members have the capacity to work, even in cases where every adult member was without employment and unable to find any. Otherwise, the family was not to be given an allowance.[30] A last corroboration comes from a 2018 article, which attested that, "At first, government policy was to expand recipients' numbers, so it was lenient, admitted all who could qualify . . . later *dibao* workers got stricter and left out border-line cases."[31] So, from the program's earliest days in 2004 up through the late 2010s, there was a definite switch in its targets, one away from laid-off workers and the able-bodied.

Second Change: Care for (Only) the Very Most Needy

Moving on to the second closely related modification of early policy, near the start of the program in 2002, *sanwu* people constituted just 4.5 percent of the total beneficiaries of the *dibao*. There was no separate category for the "disabled" listed then; perhaps they were sorted together with the *sanwu*. By 2009, the disabled and the *sanwu*, added together, had jumped to 11.8 percent of the national total of recipients (over two and a half times as large a percentage as seven years before). (See Tables 9.2 and 9.3) That datum could bolster a claim that the totally pauperized and bereft, plus those physically incompetent to work, had begun to get a boost, likely at the expense of the able-bodied non-working. Possibly the trouble that some of these unfortu-

---

27. Interviews, Lanzhou, November 21, 2014, and with a student from Heilongjiang, November 14, 2014, Hong Kong.

28. Jinxian Wang and Yanfeng Bai, "Development of Minimum Livelihood Guarantee Programmes in Urban China: An Empirical Analysis Based on 31 Regions Over 2003–2013," *CJSW* 9, nos. 1–3 (2016): 159.

29. Interview, Lanzhou community, July 9, 2010.

30. www.sourcejuice.com/.../People-Republic-China-State-Council-Order-64 . . ., accessed August 2015. (No longer available.)

31. Yao, "Zhongguo chengshi," 71.

Table 9.2. Classifications of Urban *Dibao* Recipients; as Percentages of All *Dibaohu*, 2001–2018 I: Disabled; Three Withouts (*sanwu*); Laid-Off (*xiagang*)
(Unit: 10,000 People)

Year	Urban Dibao Recipients	Disabled	Disabled Percentages	Three Withouts ("sanwu")	Three Withouts Percentages	Laid-off ("xiagang")	Laid-off Percentages
2001	1,170.7	n.a.	n.a.	n.a.	n.a.	n.a.	n.a.
2002	2,064.7	n.a.	n.a.	91.9	4.45	554.5	26.86
2003	2,246.8	n.a.	n.a.	99.9	4.45	518.4	23.07
2004	2,205.0	n.a.	n.a.	95.4	4.33	468.9	21.27
2005	2,234.2	n.a.	n.a.	95.8	4.29	430.7	19.28
2006	2,240.1	n.a.	n.a.	93.1	4.16	350.0	15.62
2007	2,272.1	161.0	7.09	125.8	5.54	n.a.	n.a.
2008	2,334.8	169.1	7.24	106.9	4.58	n.a.	n.a.
2009	2,345.6	181.0	7.72	94.1	4.01	n.a.	n.a.
2010	2,310.5	180.7	7.82	89.3	3.86	n.a.	n.a.
2011	2,276.8	184.1	8.09	80.3	3.53	n.a.	n.a.
2012	2,143.5	174.5	8.14	64.9	3.03	n.a.	n.a.
2013	2,064.2	169.2	8.20	58.0	2.81	n.a.	n.a.
2014	1,877.0	161.1	8.58	50.0	2.66	n.a.	n.a.
2015	1,701.1	165.7	9.74	43.8	2.57	n.a.	n.a.
2016	1,480.2	156.5	10.57	n.a.	n.a.	n.a.	n.a.
2017	1,261.0	159.9	12.68	n.a.	n.a.	n.a.	n.a.
2018	1,007.0	145.5	14.45	n.a.	n.a.	n.a.	n.a.

Table 9.3. **Classifications of Urban *Dibao* Recipients; as Percentages of All *Dibaohu*, 2001–2018 II: Informally Employed; Registered Unemployed; Unregistered Unemployed (Unit: 10,000 People)**

Year	Informally Employed	Informally Employed Percentages	Registered Unemployed	Registered Unemployed Percentages	Unregistered Unemployed	Unregistered Unemployed Percentages
2001	n.a.	n.a.	n.a.	n.a.	n.a.	n.a.
2002	n.a.	n.a.	n.a.	n.a.	n.a.	n.a.
2003	n.a.	n.a.	n.a.	n.a.	n.a.	n.a.
2004	n.a.	n.a.	n.a.	n.a.	n.a.	n.a.
2005	n.a.	n.a.	n.a.	n.a.	n.a.	n.a.
2006	n.a.	n.a.	n.a.	n.a.	n.a.	n.a.
2007	343.8	15.13	627.20	27.60	364.30	16.03
2008	381.7	16.35	564.30	24.17	402.20	17.23
2009	432.2	18.43	510.20	21.75	410.90	17.52
2010	432.4	18.71	492.80	21.33	420.00	18.18
2011	429.7	18.87	472.50	20.75	426.70	18.74
2012	459.3	21.43	400.40	18.68	422.10	19.69
2013	462.1	22.39	365.50	17.71	416.80	20.19
2014	425.8	22.69	312.50	16.65	398.70	21.24
2015	377.3	22.18	264.10	15.53	394.00	23.16
2016	304.4	20.56	252.90	17.09	370.90	25.06
2017	265.0	21.02	153.50	12.17	399.60	31.69
2018	219.2	21.77	109.20	10.84	320.60	31.84

Sources: Zhongguo minzheng tongji nianjian, 2002–2019 [China Civil Affairs' Statistical Yearbook, 2002–2019]. For Laid-off and Three Withouts from 2002–2006: http://www.mca.gov.cn/article/sj/tjgb/.

nates might have been causing led a Shanghai social work scholar to link servicing the desperate (instead of the laid-off) to stability: "The government fears that the *sanwus'* hearts are unbalanced, so it uses the *dibao* to keep them quiet."[32] It seems that concerns about disorder may have shifted from the *xiagang* to the *sanwu.*

Supporting this supposition, State Council Document No. 649 gave more consideration than in the past to the "especially difficult" (*tekun,* 特困) poor. This regulation was termed the "first legal document aimed at coordinating and regulating a fragmentary social assistance system." It sustained the priorities of the September 2012 State Council Opinion, which, as noted above, had ranked the most impoverished as the "keypoint" of relief work. In introducing it, the premier ordered "open, fair, and timely aid for the needy," using a definition of this cohort strikingly close to that of the old *sanwu* population: "The disabled, the elderly and minors unable to work who lack a legal guardian or income."[33]

The addresses at the National People's Congress in March 2015 displayed similar concerns: In his "Report on the Work of the Government," Premier Li Keqiang laid out a list of five major accomplishments achieved in the previous year, of which the fourth was having "worked on developing a tightly woven and sturdy safety net to secure and improve living standards." When referring to that task, Li explicitly underlined the importance of "ensur[ing] a cushion is in place for those most in need." He went on to disclose a newly installed urgent-aid system, promising in the year ahead to "implement a temporary-assistance scheme nationwide, so that people with critical, immediate, or special needs will have somewhere to go for support, and will be able to get that support straight away."[34]

Pursuing the same policy trajectory, a plan presented in July 2015 further targeted the especially poor, dividing them into categories: the seriously ill or disabled (the "traditional relief targets"—a reference to the pre-1995 *sanwu* beneficiaries) and those who had completely lost the ability to work. These two groups were to receive subsidies from 15 to 40 percent higher, respectively, than those for the other *dibaohu.*[35] This constituted a rewriting of the 2000s practice of separating the beneficiaries into "complete amount"

32. Interview, June 24, 2013, Shanghai.
33. Xinhua, "China Regulates Social Assistance," February 28, 2014.
34. Li Keqiang, "Report on the Work of the Government," delivered at the Third Session of the Twelfth National People's Congress on March 5, 2015, 2–6, http://blogs.wsj.com/chinareal time/2015/03/05/china-npc-2015-the-reports, accessed March 6, 2015. The announcement does not reveal whether a separate pot of funds was made available for this initiative.
35. N.a., "Duodi shixian chengxiang dibao biaozhun binggui, Nanjing biaozhun chao 700 yuan." [Many places are implementing a merger of their urban and rural *dibao* norms, Nanjing's norm has surpassed 700 yuan], http://www.chinanews.com/gn/2015/07-08/7390743.shtml, accessed July 10, 2015.

and "make-up-the-deficiency" subsidy groupings that had distinguished the treatment accorded the desperate from that given to the rest. Overall, the notification amounted to one more indication that the extremely desperate were attracting the central government's special attention, as of 2015, while the less forlorn were not.

Third and Fourth Changes: Charges of Financial Impropriety

Official circulars on the *dibao* did not focus on financial improprieties in earlier years. Already in May 2004, however, the journal *Chinese Civil Affairs* carried a piece by a Jiangxi county civil affairs official testifying that there was "much cheating in *dibao* work: some people issue false documents when they apply or present fake medical records."[36] As was typically the case before 2012, official and scholarly mention of misbehavior in the *dibao* realm pinpointed wrongdoing claimed to have been committed by allegedly dishonest applicants. These supposed indigents were thought to be in possession of secret earnings from off-the-books employment or in covert receipt of cash from family. It was charged that they were wantonly hiding their incomes in the interest of collecting the scant sums the allowance accords. Meanwhile, they were feasting in restaurants, driving BMWs, and hiring tutors for their children, went the suspicion.[37] Making the rounds was also a rumor that some *dibaohu* were furtively owning two apartments and renting out one of them (and thus becoming wealthy while pretending to be poor), a tale that did have some basis but, given the evident poverty in the homes I visited, was not likely to be widespread.[38]

Third Change: Fight Cadre Corruption

In the 2012 State Council Opinion, there was another novel element: Infractions were officially recognized, with both sides of the interchanges being named and blamed. This new feature "emphasized the importance of monitoring, auditing, and public reporting of . . . embezzlement and mis-targeting"[39]

36. Chen Xiaohong, "Dibao gongzuozhong de 'zuobi' xianxiang ji duice" [The phenomenon of 'fraud' in *dibao* work and measures to deal with it], *ZGMZ* 5 (2004): 48.

37. N. a. "Minzhengbu jiang jianli dibao jiating caichan hedui jizhi" [The Ministry of civil affairs will establish a mechanism for checking the figures on *dibao* households' assets], www.21.cbh.com /HTML/2012-9-27/ONNjUxXZuZmduona.html, accessed October 16, 2012, professed that, "The situation of driving a BMW on the one hand and taking the *dibao* on the other would become history" [i.e., would cease to exist].

38. Interview with social policy researcher, October 10, 2014, Beijing. Of course, there is no way to know how pervasive this practice was/is.

39. Qin Gao, *Welfare, Work and Poverty: China's Social Assistance 20 Years After* (New York: Oxford University Press, 2017), 30.

(i.e., corruption by cadres, as well as the asset hiding and misconduct said to be perpetrated by applicants and recipients). So, beginning in 2012, many lurid accounts started appearing in the news telling of the misdeeds not only of *dibaohu* but of grassroots-level leaders, now charged with crookedness as well.

One encounters an ongoing concern with the cadre malfeasance attacked in the September 2012 State Council Opinion, as Xi Jinping's comprehensive battle against bribery unfolded, seemingly unstoppably, at higher levels. Accordingly, following 2012, the media (both official and social) suddenly became rife with reports of venality by those holding office at lower levels. In one case from 2012, local officials had reportedly refrained from conveying to upper levels numerous changes in recipients' financial situations, leading higher officials to issue 300 million yuan that likely lined the pockets of those in charge at the base. Another story told of more than three million people involved (*renci*, literally person-times, 人次) when *dibaohu* who were to be awarded funds never saw them delivered.[40]

Then again, 80 percent of households approved for the *dibao* who were surveyed in five provinces went entirely without their subsidies, while 60 percent of those funded were, in fact, not at the poverty level, according to a 2014 investigation.[41] In Henan, nearly 20,000 people in authority were found to have flouted regulations, using more than 100,000 yuan worth of *dibao* funds for their own purposes.[42] In Wuhan, the former deputy chief of a street-level welfare office had allegedly used his position to falsely claim *dibao* cash amounting to over 500,000 yuan, which he used as wage supplements for his workers and for building renovation and office expenses.

Meanwhile, nationwide, over 1.5 million people's names were said to have been wrongly omitted from the *dibao* rolls between June 2013 and September 2014. Most egregiously, in a township under Luoyang City in Henan, a former civil affairs department chief reportedly had 267 bank deposit books in his possession, allegedly collected from the especially poor masses (people who normally did not have accounts in a bank). Using these books, he had gone on to misappropriate over 500,000 yuan of these indigents' money. In other places, records of democratic assessment meetings of residents (charged with evaluating eligibility for the *dibao*) were falsified, as villagers' representatives were discouraged from attending the meetings. In yet additional instances, it was asserted that cash was given

---

40. Tang Jun, "2012: '*Zhongguo xinxing shehui jiuzhu tixi jiben jiancheng*,' [China's new-style social assistance system is basically constructed], in *2013 nian: Zhongguo shehui xingshi fenxi yu yuce* [2013: analysis and forecast of China's social situation], eds. Xueyi Lu, Peilin Li, and Chen Guangjin, (Beijing: shehui kexue wenxuan chubanshe [Social Science Academic Press], 2013), 218.

41. "Low-income Subsidy Fraud in China," *Jiancha Daily*, June 23, 2014; Tang, "2012," 213–25.

42. www.hi.chinanews.com/hnnew/2015-07.../391673.html, accessed August 5, 2015. (No longer available.)

to people who had already died,[43] just as forging recipients' names was not uncommon, so it was said.[44]

Suggesting that these perceived ills of sloppiness and subterfuge had not disappeared, Document No. 649 of 2014 persisted in attacking corruption and misappropriation of *dibao* monies by local cadres, as well as falsification by recipients. In his February 2014 address presenting this order, Premier Li pointedly referred to graft by welfare officials, banning "any group or individual from misappropriating social assistance funds." "Swindlers are to be fined up to three times the worth of the materials and funds" they had wrongly seized, he charged.[45] A researcher in the field whose work stretched from 2010 to 2015 did, in fact, notice an "introduction of fines for local government officials or *dibao* recipients who were [thought to be] acting improperly."[46] This was likely a part of the larger movement to wipe out graft and corruption that General Secretary Xi had been waging (and continues to wage) on a national scale.

Fourth Change: Count All Assets

The fourth, related, thrust embedded in the State Council Opinion of 2012 was an insistence that not just a potential recipient's (and household's) income be carefully assessed but also that his/her/their assets of every conceivable type be investigated and added into applicants' and recipients' holdings as well. This new effort was evidently grounded in a foundational distrust of these poverty-stricken people—and what in the overwhelming majority of cases could well have been a misperception—a suspicion that they were concealing property that pushed their worth above what would qualify them for the allowance.[47]

In mid-2010, a precursor of what was to come appeared when the Ministry of Civil Affairs decreed that "as much as possible withdraw those who don't fit the conditions [for the *dibao*]" (*ying tui jin tui*, 应退尽退), a blatant refutation, even an explicit reversal, of the early 2000s appeal to protect all who should be protected (*ying bao jin bao*, 应保尽保) (See Chapters Two and

43. http://home.freedommerchants.com/833k36 . . ., accessed August 5, 2015. (No longer available.)

44. http://shigu.mca.gov.cn/article/gzdt/20158/20150800859146.shtml, accessed August 5, 2015; http://www.cq.xinhuanet.com/2015-08/01/c_1116109627.htm (accessed August 5, 2015). (Both are no longer available.)

45. Xinhua, "China Regulates."

46. Ben Westmore, "Do Government Transfers Reduce Poverty in China? Micro Evidence from Five Regions," OECD Economics Department Working Papers no. 1415 (Paris: OECD Publishing, 2017), 14 (also in *China Economic Review* 51 [2018]: 59–69).

47. Dorothy J. Solinger, "A Question of Confidence: State Legitimacy and the New Urban Poor," in *Chinese Politics: State, Society, and the Market*, eds. Peter H. Gries and Stanley Rosen, (London and NY: Routledge/Curzon, 2010), 243–57.

Four). Then the 2012 State Council Opinion arrived, stressing that assets of all kinds had to be calculated into a household's income in assessing its eligibility.[48] Cadres' check-up of the household was to examine all bank savings, securities, insurance, business profits, mortgages and other forms of financial assets, and any vehicles or housing property in the applicant's possession, in the interest of assuring that the basis for the disbursements was accurate.[49]

To accomplish this task, local civil affairs departments were for the first time instructed to cooperate with the public security, personnel, housing, and construction departments and offices as well as with the banks. The aim was to establish cross-checking centers charged with ensuring the authenticity of the information that potential claimants supplied.[50] Simultaneously, ministries in Beijing worked in tandem to build databases geared to verify eligibility and cut out fraud.[51] The directive was accompanied by a commentary charging that, "Very many people store their bank savings in other places (*waidi*, 外地) or under the name of a relative."[52] These kinds of nefarious practices, two researchers explained, rendered validating the true incomes of the recipients onerous and prone to error.[53]

Yet another innovation appeared after the issuance of that 2012 mandate: a center was created within the Ministry of Civil Affairs for the "Identification and Guidance of Low-Income Families" to improve the means-testing and targeting of recipients.[54] A central objective of the new thrust was to stamp out what was thought to be serious fraud in the dispensation of the *dibao*. As the premier underlined in his 2014 speech, "People applying for or receiving assistance should declare their income and property status truthfully for verification by local governments."[55] The 2014 edict he was presenting then, like the 2012 State Council Opinion, continued to call for calculating a family's assets in

---

48. Minzhengbu [Ministry of Civil Affairs], "Minzhengbu guanyu jinyibu jiaqiang chengshi dibao duixiang rending gongzuo de tongzhi" [Ministry of Civil Affairs Circular on progressively strengthening the work of identifying urban minimum livelihood guarantee targets], Minzhengbu tongzhi 140 hao [Ministry of Civil Affairs Missive no. 140], 2010. http://www.mca.gov.cn/article/zwgk/fvfg/zdshbz/201008/20100800096408.shtml.

49. Leung and Xu, *China's Social Welfare,* 91; Chen Honglin, Wong Yu-cheung, Zeng Qun, and Juha Hamalainen, "Trapped in Poverty? A Study of the *Dibao* Programme in Shanghai," *CJSW* 6, no. 3 (2013): 339.

50. Yuebin Xu and Ludovico Carraro, "Minimum Income Programme and Welfare Dependency in China," *International Journal of Social Welfare* 26, no. 2 (2017): 141–50.

51. Ben Westmore, "Sharing the Benefits of China's Growth by Providing Opportunities to All," *Journal of International Commerce, Economics and Policy* 8, no. 3 (2017): 9; Yang Lixiong, "The Social Assistance Reform in China; Towards a Fair and Inclusive Social Safety Net," Prepared for "Addressing Inequalities and Challenges to Social Inclusion through Fiscal, Wage and Social Protection Policies," United National Headquarters, New York, June 25–27, 2018, unpaginated, http://www.un.org/development/.../The-Social-Assistance-Reform-in-China.pdf and N. a., "Minzhengbu jiang jianli."

52. N. a., "Minzhengbu jiang jianli."

53. Leung and Xu, *China's Social Welfare,* 149.

54. Email from Xiong Yuegen, Peking University sociology professor, August 2, 2019.

55. Xinhua, "China Regulates."

testing its eligibility for the *dibao*, along with the applicant's household registration and income. The repetition probably indicated noncompliance with the
earlier order, as such recurrence of commands often does in China.

One more attempted remedy against the misdemeanors being unearthed
was making public the names of recipients, along with their incomes, and
the amount of their allowances, plus creating a mechanism that "the masses"
could employ to inquire about *dibao* affairs, all in the interest of satisfying
citizens' rights to know and supervise.[56] In summer 2015, the *People's Daily*
ran a piece demanding that beneficiaries' names routinely be posted publicly.[57] Following this dictate, a number of localities went so far as to place the
namelists of their *dibaohu* on the Internet.[58]

Liuzhou, Guangxi, created special centers to vet the figures on disbursements in the jurisdictions under its control.[59] Separately, in 2015 and 2016,
Guizhou and Yunnan Provinces officially raised their benefit [*dibao*] standards (poverty lines) with the explicit intent of reducing their *dibao* case-
loads, using the slogan, "raise standards, cut amounts" (*biao ti liang jiang*,
标 提 量 减). The result was that the numbers of those meeting the [no doubt
more rigorous] qualifications declined.[60] A fieldworker observed that, "They
are much stricter about tracking informal income, to try to knock people over
the threshold for *dibao* coverage."[61]

At the Ministry of Civil Affairs, an official managing the program seconded the government's line about corruption, and its correction, as the cause
behind the cutbacks in the *dibao* rolls: he insisted that recipients had been removed from the *dibao* because "our ability to investigate households' income
has improved and so we could take people off the scheme who shouldn't be
on it."[62] Even some scholars bought this story, or at least felt compelled to en-
dorse it; one was a poverty researcher who contended that the rules got tighter

---

56. *Chutian jinbao* [Golden News of *Chutian*, which, referring to Wuhan, literally means heaven
of the lower reaches of the Yangzi; Chu was a vassal state of the Zhou dynasty, located there,
founded around the eighth century BC], August 3, 2015, from *Dongfangwang* [Eastern network],
August 4, 2015; http://hulunbeier.mca.gov.cn/article/jcxx/201507/20150700857842.shtml, accessed August 5, 2015.

57. *Renmin ribao* [People's Daily], August 4, 2015, http://zhashui.mca.gov.cn/article/
gzdt/201508/20150800859123.shtml, accessed August 5, 2015. (No longer available.)

58. Two such are http://shigu.mca.gov.cn/article/gzdt/20158/20150800859146.shtml; and http://
qianxian.mca.gov.cn/article/tzgg/201508/20150800859095.shtml, accessed August 5, 2015. (Both
are no longer available.)

59. http://binxian.mca.gov.cn./article/tzgg/20150800859250.shtml; http://liuzhou.mca.gov.cn
/article/jcxx/201508/20150800859281.shtml, both accessed August 5, 2015. (Both are no longer
available.)

60. Wen Zhuoyi and Ngok Kinglun, "Governing the Poor in Guangzhou: Marginalization and the
Neo-Liberal Paternalist Construction of Deservedness," *China Information* 33, no. 2 (2019): 211.

61. Email from William Hurst, February 18, 2019.

62. Two interviews with the same official, September 9, 2013, and October 9, 2014.

after 2010 "because of corruption."[63] This was also the appraisal of two other scholars who surveyed Wuhan in 2016, concluding that, "Over time targets have become more accurate . . . those who got their grants owing to personal relations (*renqingbao, guanxibao*, 人情保, 关系保) but whose situations did not fit the regulations, have been cleared out."[64]

How serious have cheating by recipients and mistargeting by cadres actually been? At the end of 2014, when the total number of *dibaohu*, both urban and rural, was nearly seventy-one million (70.84 million), not so much below the earlier high point of 75.86 million recipients three years before—in other words, less than 7 percent below the all-time national peak—a countrywide recheck of 89 percent of the *dibaohu* was undertaken. Of the 64.3 million beneficiaries in both cities and rural areas examined, just 4.6 million were withdrawn from the allowance, or 6.5 percent of the total number of recipients as of that time, presumably because they were found to be ineligible. It was announced that they were removed because of "normal withdrawal," indicating that their incomes had risen. A tiny 0.4 percent of those reexamined, or 257,000 people, were made to leave for allegedly having obtained the allowance wrongly, through personal ties or other errors.[65] So it would appear that genuine, hidden illicit behavior was terribly negligible (or else very tough to uncover).

Ravallion, Chen, and Wang found that, in the early 2000s, "about 40 percent of the households" who were covered were not qualified, a rate they considered good for such programs worldwide.[66] Yang and Park came up with a similar figure (i.e., that 42 percent of recipient households were unqualified).[67] Luo Wenjian and Wang Wen argued that "over 40 percent" were receiving the *dibao* who should not have been as of 2014, a figure they judged to be "comparatively low."[68]

63. Interview, Beijing shifan daxue [Beijing Normal University], October 13, 2014.

64. Xiang Yunhua and Zhao Lingya, "Jiyu kuozhan xianxing zhichu moshi de chengshi dibao biaozhun yanjiu: yi Wuhanshi wei li" [Research on urban dibao norm on the basis of the extension line expenditure model: taking Wuhan city as example], *Diaoyan shijie* [Investigation world], no. 10 (2018): 44.

65. Pan Fu, "Minzheng xitong fucha jin jiu cheng dibao duixiang; 25.7 wan ren tuichu 'renqingbao' 'cuobao,'" (The civil affairs system rechecked *dibao* recipients; 257,000 people withdraw from the *dibao* because of having received it based on human relations or mistakes), *Renmin ribao* [People's Daily], December 9, 2014.

66. Martin Ravallion, Shaohua Chen, and Youjuan Wang, "Does the Di Bao Program Guarantee a Minimum Income in China's Cities?" in *Public Finance in China: Reform and Growth for a Harmonious Society*, eds. Jiwei Lou and Shuililn Wang (Washington, DC: World Bank, 2006), 317–34.

67. Du Yang and Albert Park, "Social Assistance Programs and their Effects on Poverty Reduction in Urban China," *Economic Research* 12 (2007): 24–33.

68. Luo Wenjian and Wang Wen, "Chengshi dibao de jianpin xiaoying fenxi—ji yu zhongguo jiating zhuicong diaocha (CFPS) de shizheng yanjiu" [Analysis of the urban dibao's effect in reducing poverty—an empirical study based on China Family Panel Survey], *Jiangsu caijing daxue xuebao* [Journal of Jiangsu University of Finance and Economics] no. 5 (2018): 67.

But variously, Yao Jianping uncovered more mistaken allocation, at 56 percent in 2012 and 62 percent in 2014.[69] Another research report had it that mistargeting rates were higher yet in both 2002 and 2007.[70] And a Chinese Academy of Social Sciences survey in five provinces in 2012 found that the rate of misallocation (giving to those who did not deserve the allowance) was also high, at 60 percent. The author, however, advised that though this may seem to be a low degree of accuracy, the *dibao*'s efficiency in targeting was superior to comparable programs internationally.[71] Meanwhile, yet other scholars have averred that "the *dibao*'s performance in this regard is deemed to be better than most other UCT [unconditional cash transfer] programs around the world."[72] Gao attributes such discrepancies among research findings to differences in the design, sampling, and measures used in creating various datasets.[73] But whether China's *dibao* targeting rates are comparatively high or low, the fact is that, taken as a whole, these studies suggest scant improvement in tackling mistargeting during the years in question, when so much effort was allegedly being put into clearing out from the rolls those deemed unqualified to be on them.

As one Chinese scholar perceived, in a view consistent with my own: the numbers fell because the policy emphasis changed. "The new program content has to do with fighting corruption, protecting [only] low-level people and ensuring social stability, not painstakingly guaranteeing everyone we should serve."[74] So, it could well be that those running the *dibao* program at the grassroots got stricter in assigning allowances simply to be in accord with central policy.

Two further observations also challenge the notion that flagrant fraud and corruption were truly besetting the *dibao* scheme. The first comes from Jennifer Pan, who did intensive fieldwork in the years 2012 and 2013, interview-

---

69. Yao Jianping, "Zhongguo chengshi dibao miaozhun kunjing: zige zhang'ai, jishu nanti, hai shi zhengzhi yingxiang?" [Chinese urban dibao targeting predicament: qualifications obstacles, technical difficulty, or political influence?] *Shehui kexue* [Social science] no. 3 (2018): 62.

70. Qin Gao, Sui Yang, and Shi Li, "Welfare, Targeting and Anti-poverty Effectiveness: The Case of Urban China," *Quarterly Review of Economics and Finance* 56 (2015): 30–42. Pan, *Welfare for Autocrats,* 79, determined that 70 to 80 percent of deserving households failed to be granted the allowance, which she termed "a high exclusion rate"; on 129, she reports on a 2014 nationally representative sample in urban China showing that 84 percent of informants whose self-reported income fell below the *dibao* line were not getting the allowance.

71. Cao Yan-chun, "Woguo chengshi 'dibao' zhidu de ba xiang jingzhundu shizheng yanjiu" [An empirical study on the targeting accuracy of minimum living security system for urban residents in China], *Zhongyang caijing daxue xuebao* [Journal of the Central University of Finance and Economics] no. 7 (2016): 4.

72. Gao, *Welfare*, 52. Gao states that this is the view in Ravallion, Chen, and Wang, "Does the Di Bao" and D. Coady, M. E. Grosh, and J. Hoddinott, "Targeting of Transfers in Developing Countries: Review of Lessons and Experience" (Volume I) (Washington, DC: World Bank and International Food Policy Research Institute, 2004).

73. Gao, *Welfare*, 46.

74. Yao, "Zhongguo chengshi," 71.

ing informants in a range of positions connected with the allowance, both distributors and receivers, in one hundred neighborhoods in four provinces. She concluded that, "Corruption practices are relatively rare in China's urban *dibao* program."[75] The other comment jibes with my interpretation of this accusation of dishonest *dibao* delivery: the management of the program "is instrumental; it can serve various kinds of political purposes of the state."[76]

Another caution in deciphering this movement and the seriousness of its mission is this: such suspicion of welfare recipients, paired with a cutback in handouts, is by no means particular to the Chinese *dibao*. This quotation about the Supplemental Security Insurance program of the American welfare system in the last quarter of the twentieth century supports this point: "The reaction against welfare recipients who seemed to be exploiting the vulnerabilities of the system led to measures designed to cut benefits . . . it became a typical welfare program, complete with groups accused of ripping off the government."[77]

Fifth Change: A Shift to the Countryside

The fifth and final switch entailed buttressing the benefits of residents in the agricultural regions. This initiative may well have been a move to shore up the government's (and Party's) legitimacy in these localities, as clashes between farmers and authorities were widespread in the preceding years. Given that land seizures were then the outstanding source of the bitterness felt by farmers, the March 2015 report that the National Reform and Development Research Commission delivered at the annual session of the National People's Conference may have been hinting as to why the outlay of funds began to favor farmers. For this communiqué paired welfare with land confiscation, as it read that, among the plans for the coming year, "We will improve the subsistence allowance system for both urban and rural residents and we will improve the social security policy for farmers whose land has been appropriated."[78] There was also Xi's ambition to wipe out poverty by the year 2020, and he and his government focused this project on the countryside, as noted in Chapter Two.

In any case, when this new drive began, an attempt to placate the restive rural areas had been official policy for some time, one associated mainly with the tenure of leaders Hu Jintao and Wen Jiabao in the first decade of the cen-

---

75. Pan, *Welfare for Autocrats,* 83.

76. Yao, "Zhongguo chengshi," 71–72.

77. Edward D. Berkowitz and Larry DeWitt, *The Other Welfare: Supplemental Security Income and U.S. Social Policy* (Ithaca, NY: Cornell University Press, 2013), 242.

78. National Development and Reform Commission, "Report on the Implementation of the 2014 Plan for National Economic and Social Development and on the 2015 Draft Plan for National Economic and Social Development," delivered at the Third Session of the Twelfth National People's Congress, March 5, 2015, 16.

tury.[79] In 2006–2007, what had been just an urban minimal livelihood scheme for some seven years was extended to the villages after a brief trial period. There were also, concurrently, moves to terminate rural taxes and fees, to institute new cheap and free health and schooling services, and to create a rural pension scheme.[80]

An unequivocal bent to the countryside with respect to the *dibao*, however, began only in the period chronicled here (i.e., after 2011).[81] Back in 2008, when the rural *dibao* was first extended nationally, the urban pot of outlays far, far surpassed that for the countryside (23.34 million urbanites got 39.34 billion yuan, an average of 1,685 yuan per person per year, while in the countryside, 42.84 million people shared 22.87 billion yuan, an average of just 539 yuan per person per year, or a mere 32 percent of what an urban recipient was given). This imbalance obtained through 2010. (See Table 9.4)

But in 2011, the sums for the rural and urban areas were nearly equal, with 66 billion yuan going to the rural areas and 66.76 million yuan to the urban poor, a notable improvement for the countryside, even despite the numbers of recipients in the two regions being vastly different (22.8 million in the cities, and 53.06 in the countryside). See Tables 2.1, 9.4, and 9.5; note the changing balance in 2011 and after.

In 2012, however, 67.43 billion yuan was split up among 21.43 million urban dwellers, an average of 3,146 yuan per person per year, while the 53.45 million rural residents got a total of 71.8 billion yuan, or 1,343 yuan per person per year.[82] This meant that, for the first time, the ratio changed substantially: a rural beneficiary received almost 43 percent of what an urban one did. In both 2013 and 2014, the rural areas as a block got larger amounts of funding than did the urban: 86.69 billion yuan for 53.82 million rural people in 2013, and 87 billion yuan for 52.07 million farmer recipients in 2014.

Simultaneously, for the cities, a lesser amount—just 75.7 billion yuan—was allocated in 2013, a figure that went on to drop to 72.2 billion yuan in the next year, which was meant for distribution among 20.6 million people and 18.77 million beneficiaries, respectively, in the two years. This meant that, in 2014, an average urban recipient (presuming s/he remained on the allowance

79. Jane Duckett and Guohui Wang, "Why Do Authoritarian Regimes Provide Public Goods? Policy Communities, External Shocks and Ideas in China's Rural Social Policy Making," *Europe-Asia Studies* 69, no. 1 (2017): 92–109, argue that policy advisers, shocks from abroad, and new ideas were the most important influences on the creation of new social policies for the countryside.

80. Jeremy Wallace, *Cities and Stability: Urbanization, Redistribution, & Regime Survival in China* (New York: Oxford University Press, 2014), Chapter Five.

81. The past two decades have seen a significant fall in the size of what is counted as the rural population. So, the rapid increase in the numbers of rural *dibao* recipients is especially significant.

82. Zhonghua renmin gongheguo minzhengbu [Ministry of Civil Affairs of the People's Republic of China], "Minzhengbu fabu 2012 nian shehui fuwu fazhan tongji gongbao" [Ministry of Civil Affairs announces 2012's social services development statistical bulletin], June 19, 2013, Renminwang, http://jnjd.mca.gov.cn/article/zyjd/bzjzx/201306/20130600476925.shtml, accessed February18, 2021.

Table 9.4. Number of Urban and Rural *Dibao* Beneficiaries, 1999–2019 (Unit: Million People)

Year	Urban	Rural	Total
1999	2.80	n.a.	2.80
2000	3.24	n.a.	3.24
2001	11.70	n.a.	11.70
7/02	19.30	n.a.	19.30
12/02	20.60	4.08	24.68
2003	22.50	3.70	26.20
2004	22.10	4.90	27.00
2005	22.30	8.25	30.55
2006	22.40	15.93	38.33
2007	22.70	35.66	58.36
2008	23.30	42.84	66.14
2009	23.50[a]	47.6	70.60
2010	22.90	52.28	75.18
2011	22.80	53.06	75.86[a]
2012	21.40	53.45	74.85
2013	20.60	53.82[a]	73.88
2014	18.77	52.07	70.84
2015	17.22	49.33	66.50
2016	14.80	45.86	60.67
2017	12.61	40.45	53.06
2018	10.68	35.51	46.19 (end of 3rd quarter)
2019	8.61	34.56	43.17 (end of 4th quarter)

For 2011, 2012: cws.mca.gov.cn/article/tjbg/2011210/20121000362598.shtml (accessed January 2013).
  2015: http://www.askci.com/news/finance/2015/12/30/163331xfkf.shtml.
  2016: http://www.mca.gov.cn/article/sj/tjgb/201708/20170815005382.shtml.
  2017: www.mca.gov.cn/article/sj/tjgb/2017/201708021607.pdf (accessed January 15, 2019).
  2018: www.mca.gov.cn/article/sj/tjjb/qgsj/2018/20180910291103.html (accessed January 15, 2019).
  2019: www.mca.gov.cn/article/sj/tjjb/qgsj/2019/202002191755.html (accessed February 20, 2020).

Note: [a]Numbers that are the peaks.

Sources: Zhongguo minzheng tongji nianjian [China Civil Affairs' Statistical Yearbook] (Beijing: Zhongguo tongji chubanshe [China Statistics Press]), various years.

for the entire year, which may not always have been the case) got 3,846 yuan per year, while an average rural *dibaohu* got 1,670 yuan per year, again, as in 2012, about 43 percent of the urban indigent's take. (See Table 9.5) That was by no means an equalizing allocation, but it was still a significant relative improvement for rural recipients. At the March 2015 National People's Congress meeting, Premier Li's speech indicated the rise in importance of the rural *dibao* program in his pledge to "continue to raise subsistence allowances for rural and urban residents," notably naming those in the countryside first.[83] He went on to announce projected increases in subsistence allowances (referring to the

83. Li, "Report," 2–6, http://blogs.wsj.com/chinarealtime/2015/03/05/china-npc-2015-the-reports, accessed March 6, 2015.

**Table 9.5.   National *Dibao* Expenditures, Urban and Rural, 2001–2018
(Unit: Million CNY)**

Year	National Dibao Expenditures	National Urban Dibao Expenditures	National Rural Dibao Expenditures
2001	5,086.83	4,617.58	469.25
2002	11,575.26	10,865.17	710.09
2003	15,312.6	15,054.84	257.76
2004	18,897.10	17,273.92	1,623.18
2005	21,724.68	19,192.79	2,531.89
2006	26,768.60	22,420.00	4,348.60
2007	38,644.03	27,736.39	10,907.64
2008	62,213.44	39,341.11	22,872.33
2009	84,506.71	48,211.42	36,295.29
2010	96,975.2	52,472.98	44,502.23
2011	132,763.87	65,994.23	66,769.64
2012	139,227.96	67,432.54	71,795.43
2013	162,361.26	75,670.87	86,690.39
2014	159,200.00	72,174.72	87,026.00
2015	165,080.00	71,930.00	93,150.00
2016	170,240.00	68,790.00	10,1450.00
2017	169,230.00	64,050.00	10,5180.00
2018	163,210.00	57,520.00	10,5690.00

Sources: *Zhongguo minzheng tongji nianjian*, 2002–2019 [China Civil Affairs' Statistical Yearbook, 2002–2019]. For national rural *dibao* expenditures from 2001 to 2002: *Zhongguo nongye tongji nianjian*, 2002–2003 [China Agriculture Statistical Yearbook, 2002–2003]. The national urban *dibao* expenditures in 2001 is calculated from http://www.mca.gov.cn/article/sj/tjgb/200801/200801150093829.shtml.

dibao) per person by 9.97 percent for the urban impoverished but as much as 14.1 percent for the rural needy.[84] This emphasis was echoed by the Beijing city government, which pledged that year that, "We will put emphasis on the rural areas, pay attention to strengthening the readjustment of the rural *dibao* norm, to reduce the gap between the cities and the countryside."[85]

In mid-2015, another striking sign emerged that (at least some of) the rural areas were to be served in a new way: the Chinese News Network broadcast that many places had equalized the amount of the *dibao* norm that was to be delivered to people in the urban and rural areas. That is, these localities had raised both their city and countryside poverty lines to the same level. Though only a handful of major cities, including Beijing, Shanghai, Nanjing, Hangzhou, Changsha, Chengdu, and Hefei, had fulfilled that plan as of mid-year, other cities were said to be considering the move as they carried out their own trials and set up experimental districts.[86]

84. Ibid., 29.

85. "Beijing chengxiang dibao biaozhun tongyi zhi meiyue 710 yuan" [Beijing's urban and rural dibao norm unified to 710 yuan per month], *Xin jing bao* [New capital paper], June 27, 2015.

86. N.a. "Duodi shixian chengxiang dibao biaozhun binggui, Jing Hu norm surpasses 700 yuan" [Many places implement the merger of urban and rural dibao norm, Beijing and Shanghai's norms surpass 700 yuan]. http://www.chinanews.com/gn/2015/07-08/7390743.shmtl, accessed July 10, 2015.

As one case, Beijing raised its urban assistance level from 480 yuan per person per month in 2011 to 710 yuan in 2015, an impressive increase of about 50 percent, while its rural standard over the same years shot up from 300 to 710 yuan, a rise of over 233 percent.[87] It seems likely that those in the "rural" areas who received this hefty increment were residents of suburban places on the outskirts of large cities (but still holding a rural household registration, and so counted as "rural"). But the reform was still substantial, even if for what was probably a limited clientele. This new measure was specifically touted as a means of cutting back the much-criticized income chasm between urban and rural areas. Perhaps the subtext was that the step amounted to a way of addressing the larger issue of gross inequality in the country that has attracted such censure at home and abroad—as well as of trying to tackle the anger that has been so powerful among farmers over the large-scale dispossession of their land.

That choice to favor the farmers in the allocation of *dibao* allowances—in a relative sense, as compared with the past, and also as compared with increases for the cities—continued after 2015. In the subsequent year, Premier Li disclosed that per capita subsidies for subsistence allowances in rural and urban areas were to be increased by 8 and 5 percent, respectively, while average per capita disposable income had risen the previous year by 7.4 percent (thus, the rural rate surpassing the rate of growth in average disposable incomes but the urban one falling short).[88] Another three years on, in 2018, the Ministry of Finance communicated that the average percentage increases in the two types of regions would continue to go up at the same two rates, respectively, as they had in 2016.[89] Again, the regime chose to maintain the urban rise below the rural one and also below the rate of growth in urban per capita disposable income, which had been 6.5 percent in 2017.[90]

Moving forward to 2018, the allotment for the urban *dibao* was 57.52 billion yuan, to be distributed among 10.07 million people; in the rural areas, 35.19 million people were allocated 105.69 billion yuan, a total sum nearly twice as large as the one to be divvied up among the city poor. On a per-capita basis, urbanites on average got 5,712 yuan per year, while countryside recipients on average got 3,003 yuan per annum, a full 52.6 percent of an urban person's allowance. Remarkably, in 2019, the average annual urban *dibao* norm (poverty line) was 7,488 yuan. The rural one, at 5,335 yuan, was over 71 percent of the urban rate. See Tables 9.4, 9.5, and 9.6.

87. "Beijing chengxiang."

88. Li Keqiang, "Report on the Work of the Government," Delivered at the Fourth Session of the Twelfth National People's Congress of the People's Republic of China, March 5, 2016, 33, 2.

89. Ministry of Finance, "Report on the Execution of the Central and Local Budgets for 2018 and on the Draft Central and Local Budgets for 2019," March 5, 2019, 34 (https://www.wsj.com/public/resourses/documents/2019NPC_Financial_Report_EN.pdf?mod=article_inline), accessed November 5, 2021.

90. N. a., "China's Resident Disposable Income rises 6.5% in 2018, *China Daily*, January 21, 2019 (https://www.chinadaily.com.cn/a/201901/21/WS5c4569f1a3106c65c34e5a1f.html), accessed November 5, 2021.

Table 9.6. Comparison of Average Urban and Rural *Dibao* Payouts, Selected Years (Unit: CNY/Year)

Year	Avg. Urban Payouts	Avg. Rural Payouts	Avg. Rural Payouts as Percentages of Urban Payouts
2008	1,685.52	533.85	31.67
2011	2,928.07	1,243.87	42.48
2012	3,146.52	1,343.31	42.69
2013	3,674.76	1,610.74	43.83
2014	3,846.56	1,670.83	43.44
2018	5,712.02	3,003.41	52.58
2019	7,488.00	5,335.00	71.25

Source: Calculated from Tables 9.4 and 9.5.

It is questionable that distributing such small sums as the *dibao* delivers could serve as much in the way of satisfying fractious farmers for their loss of land. And yet, this could well have been viewed by policy makers as a cheap means to at least seem to hear the voices of displaced and shortchanged villagers. If this reasoning is correct, raising the *dibao* was a far simpler palliative than would have been some attempt at restoring confiscated property. So here again was a new decision that, though it was not part of the 2012 State Council Opinion, was like those discussed in this chapter, as it could be read as addressing concerns beyond just poverty. The move was also one more adjustment downgrading the urban segment of the scheme and its participants.

CONCLUSION

This review of modifications in the management of the urban poor—some of the adaptations beginning informally and, in some places, as early as 2004 (incidentally just as the tumult occasioned by factory terminations was subsiding)—exemplifies the nature of policy adjustment in the People's Republic more generally. We have here a welfare scheme, the *dibao*, originally meant to pacify enraged furloughed factory workers (including those capable of working), which later became a plan to favor the most indigent, the type of people characterized as the *sanwu*, the "three withouts," long before the *dibao* was conceived (see Chapter Two). Addressing corruption by aiming at supposed inaccuracy in grassroots' cadres' assessments about eligibility, and at their bribery, followed. Along with that went a doubtful stance that assumed that recipients were hiding their true wealth. And fifth, policy makers shifted the relative focus of the scheme from indigent city folk to impoverished rural dwellers.

As happens not infrequently in China, what amounts to two or even more different Party objectives and resultant policies can, with time, come to be subsumed under one and the same label. This tends to occur as the first initiative evolves into a second one and so forth, in the larger interest of tweaking a given program to fall into sync with critical switches in governmental priorities. It is as if the original project and its title are in a sense turned into available shells, into which new Party purposes can be poured.

What transpired in this instance, then, was that there was a program originally installed to appease protesting proletarians in the cities—and which, it was hoped at its 1999 installation—could somehow substitute for benefits formerly proffered by those defunct industrial *danwei* (单位, work unit) that the reform program had discarded. That program later eventually morphed back into a project aimed primarily at the old *sanwu* as worker-protesters quieted down. This it achieved as it began to bar people who, in the regime's theory anyway, ought to have been able to do some labor (despite the market often not having much on offer). And finally, the program swerved in its thrust away from the cities, where it was born, into the countryside, quite possibly while remaining a plan aimed at pacifying instability.

Put another way, this chapter illustrates how the regime reshaped one initiative to serve the changing political agenda of the Party. Thus, in line with the obsession with wiping out corrupt behavior that characterizes the rule of Xi Jinping, the years since his accession to power have seen the Minimum Livelihood Guarantee training much of its mark on malfeasance, in this case generally in the form of "flies" at the grassroots who must be swatted, not at the big-time "tigers" who are its targets at or near the top of the polity. The demand that the firm of physique go to work, and the subsequent turn to the countryside were also aims of more powerful national priorities. The bottom line is that social assistance and welfare, arguably waning in centrality for policy writers with time, was fashioned to do much more than just to target the poor.

Along with the recasting of the program documented in this chapter went a drastic decline in the numbers of the *dibaohu*. The programmatic alterations recounted in this chapter surely helped in enforcing those cutbacks. But officialdom has neglected to note that policy has been sharply modified, while its spokespersons tend to claim that so many recipients were removed from the roster as they were awarded their pensions. Chapter Ten examines that assertion from a range of angles.

Chapter Ten

Denouement: Drastic Cut in the *Dibao* Rolls

Did Pensions Replace the Dibao*?*

Chapter Nine surveyed a number of reasons why urban *dibaohu* were eliminated from the social assistance program as time went by, with policy being
tightened and rewritten. The cutbacks amounted to a drastic reduction in the
numbers of recipients, as well as heightened stinginess in admitting new applicants: Nearly two-thirds (i.e., 14.9 million) of the number of beneficiaries
being supported when these figures peaked in 2009 (there were 23.5 million
then) were dropped within a decade, resulting in a mere 8.6 million recipients in the cities by 2019.[1] This drop must have been the product of political decisions, I will show. So, did pensions largely substitute for the *dibao*,
thereby sustaining the regime's commitment to the workers it had called for
abandoning in the late 1990s?

   After 2014, when numbers began to slide severely, a number of officials
and academic informants consulted insisted that once-laid-off workers were
able to survive without the *dibao* because of having received their pensions.[2]
The allegation was that, upon arriving at the legal age for retirement (sixty
for men, and fifty for female workers), these individuals would be provided
for with pensions so long as they had paid their annual premium fees into
their enterprises' funds for the requisite fifteen years.[3] Therefore, according

---

1. Rural figures also fell, starting in 2014, from a maximum of 53.8 million in 2013 to 34.6 million
in 2019. See Table 9.5.
   2. Li Zhengang, "2018 nian chengxiang shehui jiuzhu fazhan zhuangkuang fenxi baogao" [2018
report on analysis of the development of urban and rural social assistance], in *2019 nian Zhongguo
shehui xingshi fenxi yu yuce* [2019 Analysis and prediction of Chinese society], eds. Li Peilin, Chen
Guangjin, and Zhang Yi (Beijing: shehui kexue wenxuan chubanshe [Social Science Documents
Publishing Company]), 80, 90.
   3. Interviews with the head of a community *dibao* program, June 26, 2013, Wuhan; an official at
the Ministry of Civil Affairs, October 9, 2014, Beijing; and Liu Yuanwen, deputy director of the Department of Trade Union Study at the China Institute of Labor Relations with Professor Lin Yanting,
Department of Labor Relations, Chinese Institute of Industrial Relations, October 10, 2014, Beijing.

to these accounts, getting a pension sometime between 2009 and 2019—the decade that saw the purge of *dibaohu*—supposedly boosted laid-off workers' incomes sufficiently to render them ineligible for the *dibao*. The other answer sometimes advanced was that someone in the recipient's household had managed to find employment. This chapter asserts that, in fact, it is likely that hordes of workers dismissed from their units never saw a pension coming from that unit when they left it and provides circumstantial evidence to support that argument. Moreover, I will reason, two more recent developments, that is, the creation of a new pension (though a grossly inadequate one) in 2011 for urban residents without a work unit, and a deficit in the national pension funds after the mid-1990s, strengthen the claim that these *xiagang* have not been granted a pension.

I used three kinds of data to challenge the notion that *xiagang* and *dibaohu* got pensions upon being let go and that these could have replaced the *dibao* for any significant number of the laid-off. First, I examined research on the ages of recipients at particular times in the past, to determine whether it was possible that a sufficient number could possibly have indeed reached retirement age (and, therefore, received a pension) in the period during which the number of beneficiaries was declining. Second, I considered information about the types and fate of different kinds of firms that dismissed workers in the critical period, to determine if these enterprises could truly have supplied *xiagang zhigong* (laid-off workers and staff, 下岗 职工, for short, *xiagang*) with pensions. I gleaned much of this material from conversations with laid-off workers and their families from 1998 through 2014. Especially valuable were talks in Wuhan about what had transpired in regard to their own former work units from 1998 through 2003, the years when the vast majority of forced layoffs occurred. I found that nearly all of those I met who were attempting entrepreneurial activities on the streets were discards from "restructured," loss-making, bankrupted, or collective enterprises. My third avenue of inquiry involved stories told to me by *dibao* recipients after 1998, mostly in their homes, about whether they possessed pensions and the reasons why so many did not.

I conclude by explaining why the two new developments—a new pension and a pension fund deficit—may have led officials to believe that those *dibaohu* who bought into this new "residents'" pension could thenceforth leave the *dibao*; unfortunately, this pension's payout is much too low to supplant a family's *dibao* allowance. The second development, the pension deficit, calls into question the capability of pensions to substitute for social

Also, emails from Han Keqing, November 23, 2017; Randong Yuan, January 25 and 31, 2019; William Hurst, February 18, 2019; Tang Jun, February 21, 2019; and Feng Chen, March 26, 2019, all scholars who have worked on pension systems or laid-off workers.

assistance. I deduce from all these pieces of evidence that pensions could not have made good a withdrawal from the *dibao* for recipients nor explained a denial of it to new applicants.

The chapter has a subtext, or, one might say, a subterranean plotline. The main thrust is to demonstrate that many, many *xiagang* workers never got a pension—and the reasons for that—and, thus, that they and other *dibaohu* could not turn to one when they were deemed no longer qualified for the *dibao* after 2009. But the exposition doubles in presenting another story: often using their own words, the material here illuminates the immediately desperate plight of the members of the retrenched proletariat once they lost their work positions, and the regime's failure to succor them.

BACKGROUND: COMMITMENT
TO THE URBAN *DIBAO* SLACKENS

After providing for 22.5 million urban beneficiaries in 2003, the total of *dibao* grantees remained relatively stable for some years. Increases occurred in 2008 and 2009, at the time of the international financial crisis, when many informal-sector jobs—the type that laid-off workers and other *dibao* program participants might have held, if they held any—were terminated, as orders fell from abroad.[4] But following that economic slump, once the economy got back on track, the count of *dibaohu* steadily diminished, to below twenty million in 2014, and then down to only 8.61 million in 2019.[5] (See Table 10.1)

In Guangzhou, the same decline occurred: 2007 was the high point in recipient numbers serviced, and the figures steadily decreased thereafter.[6] For Wuhan, the numbers covered by the allowance also fell precipitously, from 310,900 in 2003 to 82,100 in 2016, a drop of 74 percent in thirteen years.[7] (See Table 10.2) There the coverage rate declined from 6.55 percent of the

---

4. Jinxian Wang and Yanfeng Bai, "Development of Minimum Livelihood Guarantee Programmes in Urban China: An Empirical Analysis Based on 31 Regions over 2003–2013," *China Journal of Social Work* 9, no. 1–3 (2016): 155–75, especially 157; Mo Rong, Zhao Liwei, and Chen Lan, "Guoji jinrong weijixia de jiuye xingshi he zhengce" [The employment situation and relevant policies under international financial crisis], in *2010 nian: Zhongguo shehui xingshi fenxi yu yuce* [2010: Analysis and forecast of Chinese society], eds. Ru Xin, Lu Xueyi, and Li Peilin (Beijing: shehui kexue wenxian chubanshe [Social Sciences Academic Press], 2010), 37–38.

5. See www.mca.gov.cn/article/sj/tjjb/qgsj/2019/202002191755.html for the number of urban recipients as of the last quarter of 2019. Urban plus rural recipients then were 43.17 million, down by 57 percent from 75.86 million in 2011.

6. Wen Zhuoyi and Kinglun Ngok, "Governing the Poor in Guangzhou: Marginalization and the Neoliberal Paternalist Construction of Deservedness," *China Information* 33, no. 2 (2019): 210–33, DOI:10.1177/0920203X18786876.

7. Xiang Yunhua and Zhao Lingya, "Jiyu kuozhan xianxing zhichu moshi de chengshi dibao biaozhun yanjiu: yi Wuhanshi wei li" [Research on urban dibao norm based on the extension line expenditure model: Wuhan as example], *Diaoyan shijie* [Investigation world] no. 10 (2018): 43.

Table 10.1. Number of Urban *Dibao* Beneficiaries, 1999–2019 (Unit: Million People)

Year	Urban	Total
1999	2.80	2.80
2000	3.24	3.24
2001	11.70	11.70
7/02	19.30	19.30
12/02	20.60	24.68
2003	22.50	26.20
2004	22.10	27.00
2005	22.30	30.55
2006	22.40	38.33
2007	22.70	58.36
2008	23.30	66.14
2009	**23.50***	70.60
2010	22.90	75.18
2011	22.80	**75.86***
2012	21.40	74.85
2013	20.60	73.88
2014	18.77	70.84
2015	17.22	66.50
2016	14.80	60.67
2017	12.61	53.06
2018	10.68	46.19 (end of 3rd quarter)
2019	8.61	43.17 (end of 4th quarter)

*Numberss in bold are the peaks.

For 2011, 2012: Minzhengbu wangzhan, retrieved from cws.mca.gov.cn/article/tjbg/2011210/201210003
62598.shtml, accessed January 2013.
 2015: http://www.askci.com/news/finance/2015/12/30/163331xfkf.shtml
 2016: http://www.mca.gov.cn/article/sj/tjgb/201708/20170815005382.shtml
 2017: www.mca.gov.cn/article/sj/tjgb/2017/201708021607.pdf, accessed January 15, 2019
 2018: www.mca.gov.cn/article/sj/tjjb/qgsj/2018/20180910291103.html, accessed January 15, 2019
 2019: www.mca.gov.cn/article/sj/tjjb/qgsj/2019/202002191755.html, accessed February 20, 2020

Sources: Zhongguo minzheng tongji nianjian [China Civil Affairs Statistical Yearbook] (Beijing: Zhongguo
tongji chubanshe), various years.

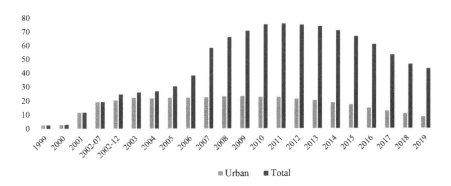

Figure 10.1. Number of Urban *Dibao* Beneficiaries and Total Beneficiaries, 1999–2019

Table 10.2.   Number of Urban *Dibao* Beneficiaries, Wuhan, 2002–2016

Year	# cov'd. (unit=persons)	cov'ge.rate (as % of urb. pop.)
2002	218,500	4.76
2003	310,900	6.55
2004	303,200	6.26
2005	276,400	5.49
2006	259,300	5.00
2007	246,200	4.66
2008	239,100	4.45
2009	232,800	4.30
2010	204,200	3.77
2011	191,500	3.50
2012	169,700	3.06
2013	163,200	2.94
2014	134,000	2.40
2015	114,100	1.95
2016	82,100	1.30

Source: Wuhan Civil Affairs Bureau; coverage rate based on *Wuhanshi tongji nianjian*.

city's population in 2003 down to 1.37 percent 13 years later.[8] Besides these two cities' experiences, an investigation of 16,000 *dibao* households in five provinces (Shanghai, Henan, Liaoning, Gansu, and Guangdong), each situated in a different region of the country, saw significant dips in the share of urban households receiving the *dibao* between the years 2012 and 2014, except for in Henan, as in Table 10.3.

Another disturbing trend is the *relative* decline in the allowance itself over the years. With time, the average urban *dibao* norm (or poverty line) came to

Table 10.3.   Share of *Dibao* Recipient Households Below Local Poverty Line (Norm) (pre-gov't. transfers), 2012, 2014, Five Provinces

Province	Urban		Rural	
Year	2012	2014	2012	2014
Liaoning	25.0	16.0	10.1	16.1
Shanghai	21.8	17.4	6.3	33.3
Henan	19.0	19.5	19.0	24.1
Guangdong	11.9	5.7	14.4	24.7
Gansu	38.3	32.1	25.6	22.4

Source: Ben Westmore, "Do Government Transfers Reduce Poverty in China? Micro Evidence from Five Regions," OECD Economics Department Working Papers No. 1415. (Paris: OECD Publishing, 2017), 15.

---

8. Xiang and Zhao, "Jiyu kuozhan," forty-six states that as the city's revenue increased at an annual average rate of 3.7 percent, its expenditure on the *dibao* dropped from 0.48 percent of revenue in 2013 to 0.23 percent in 2016.

represent a steadily dwindling percentage of the average disposable income of ordinary (non-*dibaohu*) city folk nationwide; the same was so with regard to the norm's percent of the average urban state-factory worker's wage. Thus, just after the scheme's expansion, in 2002 and 2005, the mean *dibao* norm across urban China represented 28 and 23 percent of the average urban monthly per capita disposable income, respectively, a drop over three years but still more than a fifth. (See Tables 2.3, 2.4, 9.2, and 9.5) By November 2011, however, that proportion stood at a mere 15.8 percent. (See Table 2.4)

Similarly, in 1998, the average *dibao* norm nationally equaled 20.5 percent of the mean wage in the largest cities. (See Table 2.2) But by 2007, that proportion had sunk by a full 50 percentage points, down to 10.3 percent. Even in 2011, the year in which the total number of *dibao* recipients (urban and rural combined) reached its all-time high, at 75.86 million, the norm amounted to a tiny 7.8 percent of the mean wage in urban state firms.[9] (See Tables 2.3 and 10.1)

One more calculation reveals that the *dibao* must have attenuated in significance for budget writers: in 2007, urban *dibao* expenditures accounted for 0.10 percent of GDP, a proportion that rose some in 2008, but up to just 0.12 percent (during the financial crisis). One could argue that GDP was rising, along with average incomes—which they both indeed were—such that the face value of the allowances did rise. But the point is that, despite that growth (and thus the state's expanding financial capacity to assist the poor), the government's expenditure on the urban *dibao* as a percentage of GDP remained tiny. And by 2018, the figure had fallen to 0.06 percent. (See Table 2.1) This exercise draws attention not to absolute figures but rather to how *relative* allocations were selected by budget writers. It would seem that provisioning the urban poor progressively dropped in significance for central decision makers.

For a local example, in Wuhan, while the expenditure on the *dibaohu* rose at an average annual rate of 7.3 percent between 2008 and 2016, the city's revenue experienced an annual growth rate of 15 percent, over twice the rate of the *dibaohu* outlay's uptick. Besides, while the annual growth rate of the level of the *dibao* norm (the local poverty line) rose at 11.89 percent in Wuhan over these years, its percentage of urban average disposable income dropped from 21.7 percent in 2012 down to 18.12 percent in 2016.[10] And this decline occurred not just in Wuhan. Wang and Bai state, "All regions have seen decreases" in the percentage that the livelihood guarantee represented of both the minimum and average wage. At the national level, in these researchers' calculations, the average guarantee was 9.4 percent of the average wage

9. Calculated from various editions of the *Zhongguo tongji nianjian* [China Statistical Yearbook].
10. Xiang and Zhao, "Jiyu kuozhan," 44.

and a still-low 30.2 percent of the minimum wage in 2013.[11] (See Table 2.4) All of this material points in the same direction: the urban *dibao* was declining in import for the leadership over time.

QUESTIONING PENSION PROVISION AND JOB ACQUISITION

Doubts about Pensions

And yet, despite clear evidence that the *dibao* no longer mattered very much to policy makers, some researchers claim—or their work could be read to suggest—that pension provisions nonetheless could have supported those dropped from the welfare scheme. Bolstering allegations that pensions were pervasively available to those of retirement age, Barry Naughton has calculated that the number of retirees enjoying a full pension doubled in the decade after 2005, rising to 101 million in 2016.[12] Notably, however, we have no way of knowing how many (if not all) of these people were workers who had been on the job full time during those years, as opposed to those who had been retrenched and become *dibao* recipients before ever reaching retirement age.

Jane Duckett's data and reasoning suggest that the priority in allocating pensions would have gone to those who had been full-time workers. Duckett argues that government public policies and provisions typically favor public servants and those with formal labor contracts, as opposed to informal workers and those without work, or, in other words, that China's social policies are regressive.[13] Another issue is that, according to the terms of the pension system set up in 1951, "Payments to retirees . . . are only as reliable as a given firm's finances and are not backed by the state."[14] And a source from 2014 notes, "Since 2000, more than 74,000 enterprises have defaulted on their pension contribution."[15] True, Clause 13 of the Social Insurance Law of 2010 (whose implementation began in 2011) does mandate that "the government" (but not which level of government) should be "responsible" for this

11. Wang and Bai, "Development," 168, 169. Table 2.4, using official data, puts the percentage of average wage lower, at 8.55 percent.

12. Barry Naughton, *The Chinese Economy: Adaptation and Growth* (Second Edition) (Cambridge, MA: The MIT Press, 2018), 216.

13. Jane Duckett, "Neoliberalism, Authoritarian Politics and Social Policy," *Development and Change*, 51, no. 2 (March 2020): 523–39, DOI.1111/dech.12568.

14. William Hurst and Kevin O'Brien, "China's Contentious Pensioners," *The China Quarterly* (*CQ*) no. 170 (2002): 348.

15. Li Bingqin, "Social Pension Unification in an Urbanising China: Paths and Constraints," *Public Administration and Development* 34 (2014): 289.

insurance.[16] But would state funding have been directed to the long laid-off? There is no mention that it should be.

Several research exercises cast doubt on whether either pension receipt or new jobs might have pushed many *dibao* beneficiaries over the eligibility threshold for the allowance. In one, researchers undertook a two-year study (2009–2011—just when *dibao* numbers began to fall) of forty randomly selected *dibaohu* in three cities (Shanghai, Guangzhou, and Beijing), twenty-seven of whom were long-term unemployed. Their findings show that the allowances of only fourteen of them (35 percent) were terminated or cut back because of getting a pension or a new job.[17]

Another study, this one of informants nationwide, found that those who "should have" gotten pensions were sometimes granted less than they ought to have been, or else that their pensions remained in arrears.[18] Most persuasively, a 2013–2015 survey of 16,000 households depending on the *dibao* in five provinces reached this important conclusion: "The increase in the number of new urban pension recipients has not been sufficient to fully explain the decline in *dibao* coverage."[19] These pieces of research constitute serious challenges to assertions that pension acquisition occurred on a significant scale among the *dibaohu*.[20]

Two ambiguous statements help little: One listed "income increased and withdrew" as only one of several possible causes for the decline in the number of *dibao* recipients in Wuhan but without offering further details.[21] Equally unhelpful was a Ms. Zhang, an employee of a street-level civil affairs bureau in Xuanwu District, Beijing, who noted a fall in the number of *dibao*-recipient households in her community from over 130 originally down to just sixty-six by the year 2008, a cut of about half in under ten years. But she was also vague, attributing the decline simply to "the state's policy."[22]

---

16. *Zhonghua renmin gongheguo shehui baoxianfa* [The Social Insurance Law of the People's Republic of China], October 28, 2010, accessed March 2020 at http://www.gov.cn/zxft/ft209/con tent_1748773.htm. Thanks to Randong Yuan's March 27, 2020, email for pointing this out.

17. Yu-Cheung Wong, Honglin Chen, and Qun Zeng, "Social Assistance in Shanghai: Dynamics Between Social Protection and Informal Employment," *International Journal of Social Welfare* 23 (2014): 334, 337; Wen and Ngok, "Governing the Poor," 11, also found that one-third of their informants had obtained an income disqualifying them for the *dibao*, but none had gotten a pension or found a job.

18. Richard A. Easterlin, Fei Wang, and Shun Wang, "Growth and Happiness in China, 1990–2015," Chapter Three, in *World Happiness Report 2017*, ed. John Helliwell, Richard Layard and Jeffrey Sachs, 48–83. http://worldhappiness.report/ed/2017, accessed September 1, 2017, 63.

19. Ben Westmore, "Sharing the Benefits of China's Growth by Providing Opportunities to All," *Journal of International Commerce, Economics and Policy* 8, 3 (2017): 8.

20. Easterlin, Wang, and Wang, "Growth and Happiness," 63.

21. Xiang and Zhao, "Jiyu kuozhan xianxing," 44.

22. Han Keqing, ed., *Zhongguo chengshi dibao fangtanlu* [Interviews with Minimum Livelihood Guarantee Recipients in Urban China] (Jinan: Shandong renmin chubanshe, 2012), 301.

New Employment?

Adults

So, if, as I argue, pensions did not supplant the *dibao* for the multitudes of potential recipients and removed-from-the-rolls beneficiaries, might income from new employment have boosted household income such that it exceeded the threshold for *dibao* eligibility? This is another common explanation of the drop in *dibaohu* numbers. Could it be that family members or the recipient himself or herself acquired employment between 2009 and 2019? Direct relevant data is missing. But there is demographic research that is helpful: some about adults, some about their children.

As for the adults: as noted in Chapter Three, the Ministry of Civil Affairs compiled statistics showing that, as of 2014, of the 63 percent of the *dibaohu* then still of working age, a mere *2 percent* had either part- or full-time employment (a situation barely changed from 2011[23]). At the same time, another 23 percent were in unstable, irregular, temporary jobs, which would have provided low wages and no benefits. Another 38 percent were unemployed, whether unregistered (21 percent) or registered (17 percent).[24] Such evidence undermines a claim that dismissed *dibaohu* had managed to sustain their livelihood by acquiring new employment after 2009.

New Jobs for Children?

Of course, these data say nothing about recipients' children's possible acquisition of new jobs, but there is no quantitative information pertinent to this that is publicly available, to my knowledge. Consequently, I look at what education has been like for the children of the laid-off, which should have some bearing on these young people's ability to land a labor market position. First of all, even when the basic school fees for the first nine mandatory years were cut back or eliminated with the 2006 amendment to the Compulsory Education Law,[25] superior—or, often enough, even adequate—schooling was

---

23. Qin Gao, Fuhua Zhai, Sui Yang and Shi Li, "Does Welfare Enable Family Expenditures on Human Capital? Evidence from China," *World Development* 64 (2014): 220; Qin Gao, Shiyou Wu, and Fuhua Zhai, "Welfare Participation and Time Use in China," *Social Indicators Research* 124 (2015): 868.

24. Han, *Zhongguo chengshi,* 40.

25. This amendment rendered nine years of compulsory education free. By 2014, the state was contributing 80 percent of the funds for education (see OECD, "Education in China: A Snapshot" [Paris: OECD, 2016], 15–16, https://www.oecd.org/china/Education-in-China-a-snapshot.pdf).

For the 2006 amendment, see State Council of the People's Republic of China, "Compulsory Education Law of the People's Republic of China," June 26, 2006, http://english.www.gov.cn/archive/laws_regulations/2014/08/23/content_281474983042154.htm#:~:text=The%20Compulsory%20 Education%20Law%20of%20the%20People%E2%80%99s%20Republic,go%20into%20effect%20 as%20of%20September%201%2C%202006.

out of reach for the poor. So was switching from one's inferior neighborhood school to a better one at any level, for which a hefty fee was needed. Moreover, beyond basic costs, fees mounted as the student progressed to higher grades, with senior high no longer cost-free as it had been in the past. So, the offspring of the poor have languished in substandard local schools, later unable to advance in the face of new and fierce educational competition.[26]

Interviews in Wuhan in 2007 bear out the plight of the poor in education. One mother, her husband off serving a sentence in labor reform, had become resigned to her son's having dropped out of school: "He's sixteen, after finishing junior high he discontinued his studies, staying home. There's no money for him to go on." Apprehensions exist even about younger children: one mother of ten-year-old twins, considered a precious blessing at their birth—when people like her were all employed—bemoaned her fate after being laid off:

Now while they're at primary school it's okay, don't have to spend too much money . . . later, if they both go on to middle school, expenditures will be too much. Their father and I are very worried, can't not let kids go to school or in the future there will be even less of a way out. And both are boys; if they were girls and found a good marriage, we could be done with it, but with boys, there are more considerations. These are things we ordinarily don't want to give too much thought to; as soon as we think about them, we just worry, so we pass our days like this and then we'll think about it.

Or take the words of fifty-year-old Mr. Wang, also in Beijing, mulling over his thirteen-year-old daughter's schooling:

[Besides the subsidy of 200 yuan per month that we get], still have to buy books, tutoring materials, uniform . . . usually there's unscheduled expenses. Sometimes they say, "Tomorrow there's an activity, must participate, pay 40, 50, 60 yuan," so we have to take it out of our livelihood expenses.[27]

So the poor neighborhood schools these students are compelled to attend and the lack of money in the household for tutors, trips, computers, or other accouterments of a normal education—while competition is intense and their peers with employed parents can easily far outshine them, plus the high, prohibitive costs of secondary and tertiary schooling—surely raise questions about the probability of these *xiagang* youth having landed lucrative jobs. This information injects real doubt into a notion that any newly earned sala-

26. Personal observations and Dang Chunyan and Ci Qinying, "Chengshi xin pinkun jiating zinu jiaoyu de shehui paichi" [Social Discrimination in Education against the Children of the New Urban Poor], *Qing nian yanjiu* [Youth Research] no. 12 (2008): 15–19.
27. Han, *Zhongguo chengshi*, 122.

ries could have appeared that positioned those pushed off the *dibao* to cease qualifying for it. Given the paucity of exact, direct quantitative evidence about these issues, one must rely on circuitous routes to gauge the possibility that pensions or jobs might have replaced the *dibao* after 2009.

THREE ROUTES TO CHALLENGING RECEIPT OF A PENSION

Recipients' Ages

In challenging the idea that by 2019 laid-off workers could have gotten pensions that supplanted the *dibao*, my first avenue of attack draws on the recorded ages of laid-off workers given in four different studies, plus some official data (male workers become eligible for a pension at sixty, women at fifty). My goal was to assess what proportion of these *xiagang* would have reached retirement age between 2009 and 2019, during which the numbers of *dibao* recipients were cut by two-thirds. The first study used a table from the 1999 Chinese Labor Yearbook to show that, in 1998, 75 percent of all officially counted redundant workers (if not yet *dibao* recipients then demographically comparable to those who did become so) were under the age of forty-six.[28] None of the males among them could have turned sixty before 2012. On the basis of this survey, one must wonder how as many as 63.4 percent of the urban *dibao* beneficiaries could have been dropped from the program between 2009 and 2019 purely on account of having become eligible for a pension in those years, never mind whether they were actually given one. (See Table 10.4)

A second piece of research investigated redundant workers from a bankrupted textile plant in Shenyang in the northeast, in the years 2008–2009.[29] By 2018–2019, roughly 70 percent of the sample would have been between the ages of fifty and sixty. But only the females (35 percent of the total) would

Table 10.4. Ages, Gender of Laid-Off Workers, 1998 (Unit = Person)

National Total	Age <35	% <35	Ages 35–46	% 35–46	>Age 46	% >46	Male, %	Female, %
8,769,314	2,917,179	33	3,718,909	42	2,333,226	3%	5,042,754 57.50%	3,926,560 42.50%

Source: 1999 China Labour Statistical Yearbook, 446.

28. Eva P. W. Hung and Stephen W. K. Chiu, "The Lost Generation: Life Course Dyanmics and *Xiagang* in China," *Modern China* 29, no. 2 (2003), 207, refers to this table, which Eva Hung sent to me.

29. Guangxu Ji and Youqin Huang, "Mobile Phone Culture among the Information Have-Less: A Case Study of Laid-Off Workers in Shenyang City, China," in *The Emergence of a New Urban China: Insiders' Perspectives*, eds. Zai Liang, Steven Messner, Cheng Chen, and Youqin Huang (Plymouth, UK: Lexington Books, 2012), 147.

Chapter Ten

have become eligible for a pension—age fifty—(assuming that none had died, and that newly included recipients fell roughly into the same age group), a far cry from two-thirds. None of the males would have become pension-qualified (age sixty or older) during the relevant decade.

In a third survey of 1,209 dibao recipients in six cities done in 2008, just 17.5 percent of the sample was in the age group fifty-one to sixty, that is, those who would have become qualified for a pension during the decade 2008 to 2018. If, as in the total sample, 50.5 percent were male, just 8.84 percent of the sample (17.5 percent x 50.5 percent) would have reached age sixty between 2008 and 2018. And 49.5 percent of the sample was female, while 38.7 percent of the total was aged forty-one to fifty in 2008, and so became pension-eligible in the decade 2008–2018, or 19.16 of the total sample (49.5 x 38.7). Adding 8.84 percent to 19.16 percent of the sample, a mere 28 percent of the total sample—had the sample remained demographically the same over the decade 2008–2019—could have become qualified to receive a pension in that decade. (See Table 10.5.)

A 2012 Asian Development Bank study investigated 2,810 *dibao* recipients in three large cities—Baotou in Inner Mongolia; Changsha in Hunan; and Ji'nan in Shandong—all places where heavy industry and thus layoffs were more pronounced than elsewhere.[30] My calculations using the age data given in the study reveal that just 31.3 percent of the sample could have

Table 10.5. Gender, Ages of *Dibao* Recipients, 2008, Six-City Research, 2008

Gender	Persons	%
Male	608	50.5
Female	586	49.5

Age Groups	Persons	%
< 30	60	5
31–40	234	19.4
41–50	468	38.7
51–60	212	17.5
61–70	111	9.2
71–80	80	6.6
> 81	44	3.6

Source: Han Keqing et al., eds., *Chengshi zuidi shenghuo baozhang zhidu yanjiu* [Study of China's Urban Minimum Livelihood Guarantee System] (Beijing: Zhongguo shehui kexue chubanshe [Chinese Social Sciences Publishing Co.], 2015), 128. The cities are geographically representative of the country: Beijing (North); Chongqing (Southwest); Changsha (Central-south); Zhongshan (Southeast); Tianshui (Gansu, Northwest); and Hanyang (Liaoning, Northeast).

---

30. Qin Gao, *Welfare, Work, and Poverty: Social Assistance in China* (New York: Oxford University Press, 2017), 80.

obtained the annuity between 2009 and 2019, again quite below the percentage of dropped *dibaohu*.

One last note, from year-end 2002: at the time, 17 percent of all laid-off workers were between the ages of forty and fifty, most of whom would have deserved a pension seventeen years later (all the women would have reached age fifty, but not all the men would have reached sixty by 2019). Fifty-five percent of these dismissed workers were male, amounting to 9.35 percent (17 x 0.55) of all laid-off workers known to the authorities,[31] and 45 percent were female, or 7.65 percent of the total (45 x 0.17). Added together, this means that around 17 percent of all laid-off workers would have become eligible for pensions by the end of the decade 2009–2019.[32] Whether any of these eligible people actually obtained a pension is, however, unknowable.

All told, these figures and computations demonstrate that the numbers of *dibao* recipients who were eliminated from the program could not have been reduced by nearly two-thirds between 2009 and 2019 simply because of reaching the age of retirement and, therefore, having been accorded pensions. I move now to draw on data about failing firms and pensionless individuals to understand the pit into which the old proletariat fell after its members' dismissal.

Failed Work Units

If recipients' ages cast a shadow over the claim that most people on the *dibao* got their pensions between 2009 and 2019, thus no longer needed the *dibao*, and if their families' employment situations probably did not change significantly, I adopt a second approach, namely, drawing on my 1998–2003 interviews in Wuhan with laid-off workers soon after they lost their jobs. I did my research in that city because of long-term ties to scholars and officials there; moreover, it was a large city where layoffs were uncommonly high.[33]

---

31. Dorothy J. Solinger, "Why We Cannot Count the Unemployed," *CQ* no.167 (2001): 671–88.

32. Zhongguo tongjiju renkou he shehui keji tongjisi, Laodong he shehui baozhangbu guihua caiwusi, bian [China Statistical Bureau Population and Social, Science and Technology Statistics Department and Ministry of Labour and Social Security, Planning and Finance Department], ed., *2003 Zhongguo laodong tongji nianjian* [*2003* China Labour Statistical Yearbook 2003] (Beijing: China Statistics Press, 2003), 138–40.

33. As of year-end 2002, Hubei officially had 9.4 percent of all laid-off workers in the country, being fourth nationally after Liaoning, Heilongjiang, and Hunan (Zhongguo tongjiju renkou he shehui keji tongjisi, Laodong he shehui baozhangbu guihua caiwusi, bian [China Statistical Bureau Population and Social, Science and Technology Statistics Department and Ministry of Labour and Social Security, Planning and Finance Department, ed.], [2003 *Zhongguo laodong tongji nianjian* [2003 China Labour Statistical Yearbook] (Beijing: China Statistics Press, 2003), 137. In the five years from 1998 through 2002, 2.082 million workers had officially been laid off in Hubei, a figure representing 7.6 percent of laid-off workers in all thirty-one provinces then, making it the province with the third highest number for those years (ibid., 134). In 2003, in Shenyang, one of the most affected cities, people known to have been laid off or who were otherwise unregistered unemployed persons came

Indeed, this was a rich field for finding the recently retrenched: as one seller hawking rubber shoes at a Wuhan night market memorably, if impressionistically, decried, "*Xiagang* is *pubian xingde* (普遍 行的, prevailing everywhere), *zaiyede hen shao* (在业的很少, those working are very few)."[34] Indeed, my street interviews in the late 1990s and early 2000s were with multitudes of former employees subsisting in severe chaos and misery. And, as a seasoned observer reported privately: "Pension protests . . . were mostly staged by retirees from state-owned enterprise and collective firms against nonpayment or arrears of pensions, a serious problem in many inland provinces between the mid-1990s and early 2000s."[35]

Those I spoke with were then newly *xiagang* workers, not necessarily *dibao* participants. But their extremely low incomes—or even their total lack of income—should have qualified them for *dibao* funds had the *dibao* policy been executed according to regulations (i.e., given to those whose household's average per person income fell below the *dibao* line in the household's city). My sample is by no means a representative, formally "random" one. Rather, my informants were people I encountered at street stalls in night markets or in their own homes, having been introduced to the latter by mutual acquaintances or by community (*shequ*, 社区) officials. It could be that the features of such people did not match those of average laid-off workers, whether in Wuhan or elsewhere. Nonetheless, their disclosures were always telling and often chilling.

The story of individuals lacking a pension because of the financial problems of their companies went back at least to the early 1990s, when eligible retirees from state-owned firms were granted reduced pensions or even denied them altogether when their enterprises fell into serious debt.[36] By 1998, a study of out-of-work household heads from firms of all ownership types in eleven central cities found that a tiny 14.4 percent were even participating in pension funds. Nationwide, the urban "coverage rate" was 40 percent, though for those in state firms, it was somewhat higher, at 51.8 percent.[37] "Coverage," though, "is not the same as 'actual beneficiary,'" wrote Linda Wong.

to nearly 29 percent of all enterprise staff and workers. In Shanghai, that figure was 24 percent, and in Tianjin, Chongqing, Wuhan, Xi'an, and Nanjing, it was around 20 percent (Liu Jing and Deng Jingyuan, "Gaishan woguo shiye xianzhuang de shixian fangshi" [A real method to improve our country's unemployment situation], *Juece cankao* [Policy research], 11 [2005], 61).

34. Interview, night market, September 12, 2000, Wuhan.

35. Xi Chen, "The Logic of Fragmented Activism among Chinese State-Owned Enterprise Workers," *The China Journal* no. 81 (January 2019): 76.

36. Daniel R. Hammond, *Politics and Policy in China's Social Assistance Reform: Providing for the Poor?* (Edinburgh: Edinburgh University Press, 2019), 25.

37. Guojia jiwei hongguan jingji yanjiuyuan ketizu [State Planning Commission, Macroeconomic Research Institute Task Force], "Jianli shehui baohu tixi shi wo guo shehui wending de guanjian" [Establishing a social protection system is the key to our country's social stability], *Neibu canyue* [Internal consultations] 511 (May 5, 2000): 9–10.

"The case of unemployment insurance is instructive. In 1994, ninety-five million SOE [state-owned enterprises] employees (95 percent of the eligible) were said to be protected. *Benefit recipients* [emphasis added] were, however, far fewer. . . . In 1995, only two million persons out of a total of seven million [29 percent] unemployed were served," she explained.[38]

"Restructured" State-Owned Factories

The term "restructuring" (改制) stood for a process captured in the slogan "*guanting bingzhuan*" (shut down, stopped production, sold off/merged with a healthier firm, or converted to another line of business, 关停并转), referring to firms operating at a loss and unable to be saved, and, at best, somehow to be resurrected in a form more manageable than the one that was losing money. Such factories were already in evidence in 1994. At that time, documents decreed that if a bankrupt enterprise had not participated in a social pooling insurance fund for pensions—because of being in debt—it would be compelled to make good its debt later by drawing on funds it acquired from transferring the right to use its land.

Large numbers—if not all—of the original employees in enterprises in trouble were typically let go summarily in the late 1990s and early 2000s. By 2001, an official from the textiles division of the City Economic Commission in Wuhan stated that all of the city's one hundred local, state-owned textile firms from the 1980s had been entirely eliminated.[39] At the same session, an administrator from the machinery industry had similarly grievous news: a mere 30 percent of the firms under his supervision were doing well, and 30 to 40 percent were operating in a middling fashion. But the remaining 30 percent had "no way" to go on, as, he related, the sector had "too many people, the equipment was too old, the products could not be sold, all those with talent had already departed of their own accord, and funds were tense. . . . Any way we can solve their problems is okay, sell them off, let them go bankrupt, whatever," he concluded.[40] Even in wealthy Shanghai, a startling 86 percent of the labor force in textiles had been cut back, from 500,000 to 70,000 by the year 2000.[41]

Tang Jun, then directing a research center at the Chinese Academy of Social Sciences, averred that, in addition to loss-making firms, untold numbers of already bankrupted enterprises in heavily industrialized regions were unable to provide pensions for their retirees in those years.[42] As a pension

38. Linda Wong, *Marginalization and Social Welfare in China* (London: Routledge, 1998), 199.

39. Interview, October 29, 2001, Wuhan.

40. Interview, Jingwei [Economic Commission] officials with the Head of the Wuhan Machinery Association, October 29, 2001, Wuhan.

41. Interview, August 9, 2002, Shanghai.

42. Email, February 21, 2019.

researcher pointed out: "If the work unit went bankrupt with outstanding pension contributions, the local social security bureau would negotiate with the unit and the unit might consign some assets to the bureau, such as its building or its land. But in other cases, the outstanding pension contributions remained unresolved, and workers who reach retirement age may not get pensions because of this."[43]

Labor protest scholar Feng Chen explained that if an enterprise was bought out, privatized, or merged, the new owner was to "protect the interests of its former employees. It is the responsibility of local governments to enforce this rule. But there were . . . a lot of violations."[44] John Giles and his research team concurred: "Many cities and enterprises lacked sufficient funds, so that [assistance] programs failed to reach a large share of the dislocated workers."[45] An official source even admitted that, "Some cities refused to help those eligible [for welfare], even when their former work unit and the unemployment fund were giving the laid-off workers nothing."[46]

A researcher in Wuhan in 2000 found that, "Many *xiagang* workers have received neither medical benefits nor salary in recent years because the state has been unable to enforce the law after it stopped giving loans to money-losing enterprises." Yet regulations stipulated that firms pay their laid-off workers' medical costs, as well as some 30 to 40 percent of their salaries.[47] By the year 2002, Ross Garnaut and his team, who sampled 683 firms in eleven cities, found that "many enterprises," apparently left in the lurch by state inattention, were "handicapped by bank debts, unpaid taxes, overdue wages, and pension and social insurance debts." Though it should have been feasible for the earnings from such firms' asset sales to be used to redeploy their workers, this would not have been possible when a factory's net assets were negative, which seems to have often been the case.[48]

Enforcement problems, never resolved, persisted for years. It appears, for instance, that as late as 2008, problems of unpaid or seriously underpaid benefits had yet to be solved. For Premier Wen Jiabao announced in his Government Work Report at the annual National People's Congress meeting that

---

43. Email from Randong Yuan, January 25, 2019.

44. Email, March 26, 2019.

45. John Giles, Albert Park, and Feng Cai, "Reemployment of Dislocated Workers in Urban China: The Roles of Information and Incentives," *Journal of Comparative Economics* 34 (2006): 588–89.

46. "Bian yingde shouru wei shiji shouru; dibao shouru keshi zhengce zuochu tiaozheng" [Change the income owed into real income; readjust the verification policy of the minimum livelihood guarantee], Xinhuanet, October 24, 2002 (http://news.xinhinnet.com/newscenter/2002-10/24/content_607113.htm).

47. Ming Tsui, "Managing Transition: Unemployment and Job Hunting in Urban China," *Pacific Affairs* 75, 4 (Winter 2002–2003): 523.

48. Ross Garnaut, Ligang Song, and Yang Yao, "The Impact and Significance of State-owned Enterprise Restructuring in China," *The China Journal (CJ)* 55, no. 50 (January 2006): 48; Feng Chen, "Industrial Restructuring and Workers' Resistance in China," *Modern China* 29, no. 2 (2003): 241.

over the previous five years (i.e., 2008–2013) the government had "extended social security coverage to retirees of closed or bankrupt enterprises, employees of enterprises with operating difficulties . . . and uninsured employees of collectively-owned enterprises."[49]

While the 2011 Social Insurance Law officially promised to ensure that the government would supply pensions to the entire populace, and did codify the rules on contributions to be made to various insurance funds for both employers and their employees, that pronouncement by no means addressed the fundamental issues.[50] Five years on, in 2016, the *China Labour Bulletin,* asserted that, "In general, as with nearly all labor legislation in China, enforcement [of this Law] . . . has been very lax. . . . A majority of workers are still denied the social security benefits they are legally entitled to."[51] Two years later, that publication declared that, "In many cases, it will still be up to the workers themselves to force their employer to pay not only the contributions they are owed now but the arrears that have accumulated over many years, even decades . . . especially during relocation and bankruptcy disputes."[52] In fact, often enough local officials short of funds ignored their responsibility, as a functionary in the training center of a district-run labor market admitted: "If an enterprise no longer exists," he acknowledged, "its staff will be listed as unemployed" (which could mean no recompense and, of course, no pension, would be coming to them), even if the firm was a state-owned enterprise in the past.[53]

Besides official delinquency in executing the law, there was also deliberate official choice involved. A local cadre in Wuhan explained another cause for lack of state relief: if a firm's output did not influence national security (unlike steel and petroleum, which do have such influence), and if their economic results were poor, the government usually let them go without any support; the same applied to most medium- and small-scale enterprises.[54]

Many of my informants came from plants that had been "restructured" as a result of decisions made by local government officials. A common expression among my subjects was that his/her factory had collapsed or failed totally (*kuale,* 垮了). In a typical case, two men who had held jobs at Wuhan's state-owned Number One Shoe Factory, both laid off in 1990, reported in

---

49. Wen Jiabao, "Report on the Work of the Government," delivered at the First Session of the Twelfth National People's Congress, March 5, 2013, 9.

50. Nara Dillon, "China's Welfare State in Comparative Perspective: A Preliminary Assessment after Twenty Years of Reform," paper presented at the annual meeting of the American Political Science Convention, Seattle, September 3, 2011, 5.

51. *China Labour Bulletin,* June 2016, https://clb.org.hk/content/china's-social-security-system, accessed January 31, 2019.

52. *China Labour Bulletin,* "Workers Fight for Social Security as Government Cracks Down on Malpractice," October 8, 2018.

53. Interview, September 7, 1999.

54. Interview, Jiang'an District, Wuhan labor market training office, September 7, 1999.

2000 that 80 percent of the 200 to 300 people who had been their co-workers had received no money at all in ten years of unemployment.[55] Speaking of his past employer, another retrenched worker charged, "*Ta buguan ni; ni yao zhao ren, zhaobudao*" (他 不管 你；你 要 找 人，找不到, they don't take care of you, if you look for anyone [for help] they can't be found). Still one more, equally unforgettable, street salesman told of his wife, once employed at an electrical appliances firm. The firm had disappeared but somehow was dispensing funds to his wife—though only a piddling 100 yuan per month—which, he related sarcastically, "she can use to buy some toilet paper."[56]

Indeed, the failure of many, many state enterprises to contribute to workers' pension funds led to a situation in which the streets of cities were clogged with middle-aged and older workers, whether protesting over this issue,[57] driving pedicabs for a pittance, or peddling petty goods on the sidewalks. The bottom line seemed to be, as one Wuhan subject told me, "If the enterprise is gone, [no one takes over and] its workers will 'be pushed out to society.'"[58] This harsh appraisal meant that such individuals were simply abandoned and left entirely to their own devices, both when they were first laid off and into the future as well, in an incipient market environment for which they had neither experience nor qualifications.

Severance Payments from Failed Firms

If there were no pensions on offer, retrenched staff might, at best, be handed a lump-sum severance payment (*maiduan gongling*, 买断工龄) upon dismissal, a procedure frequently put into effect. This meant that a firm delivered to its former employees an amount of cash calculated at a given rate times the number of years that person had served in the firm. But there was a definite downside: the ex-worker would be expelled from the plant and told to expect nothing more from it (i.e., that the unit would no longer provide any funds for that person's pension).

The sum a given employee might receive as severance pay varied widely among locales and even within locales among companies.[59] In my interviews, I never encountered anyone who had been accorded an adequate sum. Comments about having expended the entire severance package on a family member's health or having used it to pay for the ex-worker's pension contri-

55. Interview, September 16, 2000.
56. Interviews, Wuhan night market, September 12, 2000.
57. Hurst and O'Brien, "China's Contentious," 345–60. And see chapter four.
58. Street interview, September 4, 1999.
59. Interview, September 9, 2000, Wuhan; Mary E. Gallagher, "China's Older Workers: Between Law and Policy, Between Laid-Off and Unemployed," in *Laid-off Workers in a Workers' State: Unemployment with Chinese Characteristics,* eds. Thomas B. Gold, William J. Hurst, Jaeyoun Won, and Li Qiang (New York: Palgrave, 2009), 145.

butions were common. As the *China Labour Bulletin* charged in 2014, "The increasing cost of living and higher social insurance contributions [that had to be paid by the laid-off worker him/herself after having severed all of his/her ties with the prior company] meant that the one-off payment these workers had received when laid off rapidly evaporated."[60] Others were never even accorded a severance package: "Laid-off workers were entitled to a one-off payment if the firm went bankrupt or was bought out. But they often didn't get it because of firm insolvency and debt," in the assessment of labor studies expert Ching Kwan Lee.[61]

Among my interviewees, settlements could be as little as 8,000 yuan or 12,000 yuan, far from enough to substitute for a pension.[62] Sometimes much more was supplied, but the amount was never enough. One man, formerly a factory statistical worker, had been granted a substantial severance sum of 30,000 yuan (about $3,750 at the time). Still, that money must have been insufficient to meet his needs, since when I met him, he was working as a janitor in a hotel.[63] In Zigong, Sichuan, I met an ex-petrochemical worker who had been employed for his entire working life in a large state-owned company. Because of his lengthy service and the firm's apparent possession of assets, he was fortunate to receive 40,000 yuan at the time of his layoff. He and his wife were nonetheless short of the money needed just for their ordinary daily lives.[64] So some insolvent firms could be said to have made a token contribution to their ex-employees' future livelihood. But the truth is that once again here is a situation where laid-off workers were left without a genuine retirement account or any sort of annuity.

Collective Firms

According to the Chinese authorities, a full quarter of those officially recorded as having been laid off came from collective firms (nearly 2.4 million) as against 6.57 million from state firms, out of a total of 9.11 million officially said to have been dismissed by the end of 2001.[65] Individuals who had worked in collectively owned businesses fared especially miserably. Simon Appleton and co-authors calculated that while workers employed by the cen-

---

60. N. a., "Searching for the Union: The Workers' Movement in China 2011-13," *China Labour Bulletin,* February 2014, 15–16.

61. Email, January 25, 2019.

62. Inteviews, Wuhan, September 4, 1999, late August 2007.

63. Interview, September 15, 2000, Wuhan.

64. Interview, November 4, 2001.

65. Guojia tongjiju renkou he shehui keji tongjiju [National Bureau of Statistics, Department of Population and Society and Science and Technology Statistics, National Bureau of Statistics, *2002 Zhongguo laodong tongji nianjian* [2002 China Labor Statistics Yearbook] (Beijing; Zhongguo tonogji chubanshe [China Statistics Press], 2002), 109.

tral government had just a 16 percent risk of being laid off, for those in urban collectives (at lower levels), the rate was more than twice that, at 34 percent.[66]

Such enterprises, especially those owned by the district level (the administrative level just below the municipality), were considered by officialdom to be justifiably written off altogether, regardless of their financial footing. In addition, in this time of bankruptcies and dismantling, collectives were usually incapable of paying wages on time or in full, much less of contributing to workers' pensions. As late as 2011, the Social Insurance Law made no mention at all of providing pensions to staff discharged from collective firms.[67] A staffer at the Wuhan General Trade Union's Professional Introduction Service Center offered a most telling summation of the rationale for this abandonment: "State-owned enterprises' capital is the state's capital. The state takes care only of its own; the owners of collective enterprises are the laboring masses. Only workers retrenched from state firms are considered to be *xiagang zhigong*."[68]

Another major cause of the desperate straits of collectives' former employees was that—unlike those from state-owned firms—even if they had been on the payroll, they were not usually entitled to any basic living stipends (*jiben shenghuofei*, 基本 生活费).[69] These stipends were a component of the reemployment project, discussed in Chapter Two, instituted before the *dibao* was promoted nationwide. Nor were collective entities permitted to benefit from the right to go bankrupt in accord with official procedures.[70] Local governments regularly had the authority to decide on their own whether or not to deal with the livelihood issues of workers dismissed from collectively-owned firms.[71]

A typical case was a couple attempting to make do by selling trinkets at an outdoor Wuhan night market. The two of them had worked in a collective firm that had collapsed. They denounced their unscrupulous former boss for having absconded with whatever funds remained in the firm, and for providing no means of sustenance to his former charges whatever, for either the present or the future.[72] Jaeyoun Won's reference to "numerous

---

66. Simon Appleton, John Knight, Lina Song, and Qingjie Xia, "Labor Retrenchment in China: Determinants and Consequences," *China Economic Review* no. 13 (2002): 252–75.

67. www.gov.cn/flfg/2010-10/28/content_1732964.htm 1/13, accessed January 27, 2020.

68. Interview, September 13, 2000.

69. Dorothy J. Solinger, "Labor Market Reform and the Plight of the Laid-Off Proletariat," *CQ* no. 170 (June 2002): 304–26.

70. Interview with workers dismissed from failed collectives, August 28 and September 1, 1999, respectively, Wuhan. If firms were allowed to go bankrupt, they were to use whatever assets they had to provide for their dismissed workers.

71. Email from Randong Yuan, January 25, 2019; in an email, social policy scholar Li Bingqin, August 1, 2019, wrote, "Whether it's necessary to pay for the laid-off workers depends on the local policies," August 1, 2019.

72. Interview, September 13, 2000, Wuhan.

cases of inappropriate behaviors of local state officials and managers, such as unfair dismissals, delaying payments, insufficient severance pay, [lack of aid for] injuries on the job, stealing money, and running away with workers' pensions"[73] illustrates that this situation was prevalent.

Then there were those who, like a fifty-four-year-old man questioned in late 2014 in Lanzhou, had worked in a bankrupted, collectively owned firm. This man claimed that his factory had never paid into his pension insurance fund while he was at work. He, therefore, considered himself owed thousands of yuan in insurance money, though he had received a severance allowance of 20,000 yuan.[74] Often, clearly, ex-workers from collective enterprises were in especially dire straits when it came to survival after retrenchment or to a pension later on.

Still Existing Loss-making Enterprises

One more category of enterprises in trouble comprised yet extant, but nonetheless loss-making, firms, which had not disappeared but that still had retrenched much of their workforce. That the issue of falling into deficit and therefore not paying pensions was nationwide by the late 1990s is evident in an injunction that appeared in the newspaper *Jingji ribao* (*Economic Daily*, 经济日报) following a major conference on laid-off workers in May 1998. The article ordered that loss-making firms that were in arrears on pensions contributions must [somehow! But how?] raise the rate of their collection of funds, and that they must also "strengthen their mode of managing funds."[75] Such an injunction indicates the presence of serious mismanagement, a prevalent situation.

At least as early as 1996, as factories teetered on the brink of going under in the face of market conditions for which they had no experience, concerns surfaced among the leadership about "instability"—that is, street demonstrations, attacks on managers, destruction of factory equipment—perpetrated by employees losing their wages, welfare, and pension benefits.[76] In 1997, Wuhan issued City Government Document No. 45, proclaiming that the "reem-

---

73. Jaeyoun Won, "The Making of the Post-Proletariat in China," *Development and Society* 34, no. 2 (2005): 201.

74. Interview, November 22, 2014.

75. Daniel Robert Hammond, "Explaining Policy Making in the People's Republic of China: The Case of the Urban Resident Minimum Livelihood Guarantee System, 1992–2003," PhD thesis, Department of Politics, University of Glasgow, 2010, 85.

76. Reemployment service centers, to be set up by firms retrenching workers, were created in the late 1990s as part of the reemployment project to tend to those who had lost their jobs. Their charge was to provide these *xiagang* with basic living allowances, offer training and job search help, and pay into their insurance funds. (See Chapter Two) But in Wuhan (and likely elsewhere), individuals with connections of any sort with their former firms were not to be admitted into the centers (*Wuhan wanbao* [Wuhan evening news, 武汉 晚报], September 9, 1998, 4).

ployment service centers,"[77] to which retrenched workers from state factories were supposed to be consigned, "must hand over their staff's pension contributions," an exhortation that suggests that this was, in fact, not occurring.[78]

In 1998, I interviewed officials from the Wuhan Economic Commission (Jingwei, 经 委) who acknowledged that "structural change led to job loss, since from 1990 we stopped extending subsidies to enterprises suffering losses." These officials revealed that 367 of the 601 industrial firms in the city (61 percent) were operating at a loss, all the rest having been "released" to the charge of district governments. The officials mentioned a three-year goal to merge or have bought up forty of the one hundred large- and medium-sized enterprises that were losing money. As to the remaining sixty, the local government would have to decide which to merge and which to put through bankruptcy procedures, all of which involved cutting staff to raise efficiency (减员增效, *jianyuan, zengxiao*), in line with the central government's orders.[79] There was no mention of tending to the workers' pensions.

By the year 2001, a full two-thirds of the firms still operating in Wuhan were so strapped financially that they were unable to extend even the tiny basic livelihood stipends that the reemployment project ordered them to extend for three years to their laid-off workers (to say nothing of salaries, medical care, or pensions).[80] This failure exemplifies the gravity of the situation, as that stipend was a sum ranging between only 150 and 200 yuan per laid-off worker per month, the equivalent at the time of around US$20 to $25. And the average disposable income for a household in Wuhan then, at 609 yuan per month, was three to four times the worth of the stipend.[81]

These problems were nationwide. In summer 1999, Eva Hung and Stephen Chui learned that a full quarter of their eighty redundant-worker interviewees in Beijing had not been paid any wages at all, much less given any pensions as their former firms went under. A 2001 survey of a representative sample of all workers and unemployed workers in five cities adds more data: under one-quarter (23 percent) of the dismissed were given what

---

77. Reemployment service centers, to be set up by firms retrenching workers, were created in the late 1990s as part of the reemployment project to tend to those who had lost their jobs. Their charge was to provide these *xiagang* with basic living allowances, offer training and job search help, and pay into their insurance funds. (See Chapter Two) But in Wuhan (and likely elsewhere), individuals with connections of any sort with their former firms were not to be admitted into the centers (*Wuhan wanbao* [Wuhan evening news, 武汉 晚报], September 9, 1998, 4).

78. "Wuhan Shi Fangzhi zaijiuye fuwu zhongxin yuncuo qingkuang huibao" [A Summary report on the operations situation of the Wuhan City Textile Reemployment Service Center], prepared by the center, March 18, 1998, 8; Solinger, "Labor Market Reform."

79. Interview, September 8, 1998. The term was used, perhaps for the first time publicly, in then-Premier Li Peng's address to the Ninth National People's Congress in 1998 (Summary of World Broadcasts, FE/3168 [March 6, 1998], S1/9, from Xinhua, March 5, 1998).

80. Tsui, "Managing Transition," 518.

81. Wuhan shi tongjiju bian [Wuhan statistical bureau, ed.], *2003 Wuhan tongji nianjian* [2003 Wuhan Statistical Yearbook] (Wuhan: Wuhan chubanshe [Wuhan publishing company], 2003), 283.

were supposed to be living stipends; another 6 percent were managing on unemployment or other social welfare grants; 6 percent were being paid an income; 44 percent were relying on help from other household members; and 18 percent were drawing down their savings. But it seems that none of them had pensions.[82] In the next year, Lu Hanlong, at the Sociology Institute of the Shanghai Social Sciences Academy, related that a shocking 76 percent of firms in Shanghai, including firms of all sizes, were suffering losses in the years 1995 to 1998.[83] One must assume that such enterprises could not dispense pensions. Troubles were especially rife in the northeast. Barry Naughton quoted the Chinese labor scholar Mo Rong as having declared that the entire province of Heilongjiang was unable to fulfill its pension obligations in 1997, such that a half-million retirees from state-owned enterprises received no pensions that year.[84]

The roots of this failure were complex. According to a 1998 Wuhan document, some firms "in difficulty" were in arrears on meeting their commitment to the regional-pooled (usually city-pooled) pension endowment fund to which the firms were meant to send their contributions. Consequently, their region refused to honor these firms' reemployment centers' payments for the workers put under their charge.[85] Province-based collection was even more challenging as cities doing well were loath to help out cities with large numbers of firms going under. When a city did not give its share, the punishments were harsh, demonstrating the interdependence of insolvent firms and local administrations: a given city would not be eligible to join its provincial pension pool if the city's collection rate did not reach 90 percent of the enterprises in that city. As of the year 2000, journalists surveying the scene revealed the dismal consequence: "The absolute majority of localities were not able to reach that rate."[86]

---

82. John Knight and Shi Li, "Unemployment Duration and Earnings of Re-employed Workers in Urban China," *China Economic Review* 17 (2006): 105–6, citing J. Giles, F. Cai, and A. Park, "How Has Economic Restructuring Affected China's Urban Workers?" unpublished paper at that time, 2003, http://www.msu.edu/~gilesj/gilesparkcai.pdf. Inexplicably, however, research in Shenyang and Chongqing in 2000 found that 29 percent of laid-off workers had pensions, but half the sample of 802 household heads had no insurance whatever (Zhiming Cheng, "Poverty in China's Urban Communities: Profile and Correlates," *China Report* 46, no. 2 [2010]: 155). Zhu Qingfan, "Jiexu chengzhen pinkun qunti" [The ongoing urban poor mass], *Gaige neican* [Reform internal reference] no.8 (2002), 27 reported on a survey that the Shenyang branch of the official trade union conducted in 2000 showing that 40 percent of the workforce was being shortchanged on its pensions.
83. Interview, August 9, 2002, Shanghai.
84. Naughton, *The Chinese Economy,* 216.
85. "Wuhan Shi fangzhi zaijiuye fuwu zhongxin yuncuo qingkuang huibao" [A Summary report on the operations situation of the Wuhan City Textile Reemployment Service Center], prepared by the center, March 18, 1998, 8.
86. Zhao Zhongheng and Wei Zhikui, "Yanglao baoxian zhidu chuangxin yunxingzhong de san da nanti" [Three big difficulties in blazing a trail in running a pension insurance system], *Zhongguo laodong* [Chinese worker] 1 (2000): 12–15.

It was not only that firms and urban bureaucracies had conflicting interests. Labor departments, personnel bureaus, public health care offices,
and civil affairs and finance departments all wrangled over procedures,
finances, and responsibilities, as each was in charge of a different segment
of what amounted to scattered social security funds, a situation that only
added to the disarray.[87]Also contributing to low compliance was a failure
(presumably of both firms and workers) to pay their required contributions
into their pension funds, which continued, seemingly into the present, seriously to "influence the fund's collective income and the social insurance
system's sustainable development."[88]

Related information comes from a contemporaneous book on the reform
of China's social security system, which records that any enterprise unable to
issue wages should realistically "go bankrupt." The problem, however, was
that many such firms found it "difficult" to do so, since bankruptcy would
have created tumult, both procedural and financial. For these enterprises
lacked the wherewithal to pay off their fired workers, a requirement when a
firm was formally declared to have failed.[89] Consequently, officially bankrupting troubled firms would have entailed consigning factories' surplus employees to open (as opposed to "hidden"—meaning that employees remained
on the firm's roster but had nothing to do) unemployment. The result was
that many, many once-lifetime workers simply had to subsist in utter poverty
without wages even while their names remained on the books of their nonfunctional but legally extant firms and, relatedly, even as they could not be
counted as being among the registered unemployed or the *xiagang.* Nor could
they obtain a pension.[90]

The general problem of near insolvency, and its impact on pensions, remained at least into 2003: the communiqué of the 2003 National Reemployment Work Forum called for firms whose contributions to their pension funds
were greatly in arrears to be "held responsible."[91] Apparently this dictate

87. Gong Li, *Kuashiji nanti: jiuye yu shehui baozhang* [A difficult issue straddling the century:
employment and social security] (Kunming: Yunnan renmin chubanshe [Yunnan people's publishing], 2000), 197; Mark W. Frazier, *Socialist Insecurity: Pensions and the Politics of Uneven Development in China* (Ithaca, NY: Cornell University Press, 2010).

88. Liu Yunying, "Zhongguo yanglao baoxian tizhi de xianzhuang he nanti" [China's pension
insurance system's present condition and difficult issues], *Caixinwang* [Financial news network],
May 16, 2016, http://opinion.caixin.com/2016-05-16/100943804.html, accessed December 6, 2017.

89. Ibid.

90. Song Xiaowu, *Zhongguo shehui baozhang zhidu gaige* [The reform of China's social security
system] (Beijing: Qinghua daxue chubanshe [Tsinghua University publishing, 2001], 147.

91. N. a., Laodong baozhangbu buzhang Zeng Silin zai quanguo laodong baozhang tingjuzhang
zuotanhuishang de jianghua [Minister of Labor and Social Security Zeng Silin's speech in the national
labor and social security department and bureau heads' forum], "Jiakuai tuijin zaijiuye gongzuo,
quanmian wancheng jinnian gexiang laodong baozhang gongzuo renwu" [Speed up the work of
promoting reemployment work, fully complete this year's various tasks in labor and social security
work], *Laodong baozhang tongxun* [Labor and social security bulletin] no. 9 (2003): 12.

often could not be enforced. According to political scientist Xi Chen, in Hunan Province in the first decade of the twenty-first century, a great number of enterprises that had been "restructured" could not afford to pay into their pension funds.[92] Moreover, as late as 2014, the *China Labour Bulletin* noted that, "The aftereffects of state-owned enterprise restructuring in the early 2000s continued to reverberate a decade later in the 2010s . . . workers were often kept in the dark . . . and cheated out of their due severance pay, pension, and welfare payments. . . . A large number of workers were laid off, with no health care or pensions, and no source of income."[93]

The pervasiveness of firms suffering losses, existing but moribund—in addition to those bought out, merged, or gone bankrupt—once more challenges official assertions that laid-off workers who had previously been beneficiaries of the *dibao* no longer needed it because they had come of retirement age and could depend on a pension instead.

Individuals: No pensions

So far, the investigation has reviewed two categories of explanation for the failure of pensions to replace the *dibao*: first, a large majority of *xiagang* workers were still too young for a pension during the decade when two-thirds of 2009's total of *dibaohu* were cut off; and second, so many enterprises became insolvent and/or disappeared and so did not grant pensions in and after the mid-1990s. There is yet a third reason: some people simply did not belong to a pension scheme.

Could Not Afford to Contribute

Some of these were individuals financially incapable of making contributions to the funds after their dismissals. Consequently, they failed to observe a bizarre rule in China—that is, even after separation from their firms, former, unemployed workers were still obliged to go on contributing to a pension scheme. In interviews, people locked out of the system regularly mentioned their sheer lack of cash to hand over for this purpose. And if a person had not subscribed to the fund for a full fifteen years, s/he would not be entitled to a pension, regardless of having reached retirement age—unless that person later on somehow managed to scrounge up the lump sum owed. I learned that a couple in Wuhan finally received a pension in 2015 after struggling since the early 1990s when they were both dismissed from their jobs. To obtain the pension they had to pay the local social security bureau their back contribu-

92. Email, January 21, 2019.
93. N. a., "Searching for the Union," 14.

tions, which they did only once the wife's elder brother provided the necessary 60,000 yuan. The husband got 3,000 yuan and the wife about 2,000 monthly.[94]

Those without the wherewithal to pay in often tried to borrow money from relatives and friends, as "the expected benefits far exceed the costs."[95] Clearly, it would seem that logic would have dictated that people turn in the necessary fees year by year. But, wrote social policy scholar Li Zhu, "When they meet economic hardships they feel they can't find anyone to help, relatives and friends are also poor to the point of having nothing to eat."[96] Or, as put by another commentator, "Raising and supporting children, taking care of ordinary problems makes things even worse, if you add on that they each year must still pay increasing pensions costs, when they have no land or any source of capital, the difficulties can be imagined."[97]

Dozens of conversations with the retrenched bear out these realities. In interviews in late August 2007 in Wuhan, I encountered a husband who lamented: "I feel that at present the monthly pension contribution demanded is too high, this year suddenly went from 160 yuan per month to 220 yuan, still must pay it for fifteen years, we just can't shoulder the burden." Another could afford to pay for only his wife's pension premium, as he simply had no money to defray his own portion. In one family of three, no one was paying for pensions after one of the adults had been bought out with a severance check of 20,800 yuan upon his dismissal. One more husband and wife, aged sixty and sixty-three and living without formal jobs, had no means whatever to manage their payments.[98] I don't recall meeting anyone who could afford this expense.

The following year (2008), interview subjects in a large project in Changsha, Liaoning, and Chongqing were similarly pressed. Mr. Wen, aged forty-five, in Changsha, had worked in an unusually rich collective firm that had graced him with what would seem to have been a fairly generous severance allowance of 40,000 yuan. But he nonetheless bemoaned that, "I don't pay for my pension because I can't afford it; it's 4,000 yuan per year, each year they raise the amount, until I'm sixty, there's another fifteen years, I'd have to pay 60,00 or 70,000 yuan. Where would I get that much money?"[99]

---

94. Emails, February 10, 2020, and phone conversation, March 20, 2021.

95. Randong Yuan, email, January 25, 2019.

96. Li Zhu, Chen Li, and Wu Wei, "Chengshi dibao qunti shengcun zhuangtai diaocha baogao—ji yu Jiangsusheng de wenjuan diaocha" [Report on an investigation of the livelihood situation of urban *dibao* group—based on a questionnaire investigation in Jiangsu province], 4th International Conference on Chinese Society and China Studies, Nanjing University, Nanjing, October 27–28, 2012, 11. Thanks to Beatriz Carrillo for sending me this paper.

97. An Jin, "Ruoshi qunti jiuye cujin yanjiu" [Research on acceleration of the employment of vulnerable groups], *Caijing lilun yanjiu* [Finance and economics theoretical research] no. 1 (2014): 53.

98. In-home interviews.

99. Han, *Zhongguo chengshi*, 15.

Ms. Xuan, a forty-four-year-old divorced woman running a small shoe repair and cleaning business in a crude shop in Chaoyang, Liaoning, was let go from a bankrupted factory. Still, she was required to pay her own pension contribution, at just under 3,000 yuan per year. But, she lamented, "Where's this money going to come from? . . . Have to borrow some more and after that return it, it's all just too difficult."[100] Fifty-four-year-old Mr. Tang, in Chongqing, baldly stated: "The masses living on the *dibao* can't pay for the pension. So what are we going to do later?"[101] Several years on, in 2011, a forty-year-old Wuhan woman with a disabled son confided that, "We don't have enough money for food, how could I afford to pay for social security at 300 to 400 yuan a month?"[102]

Yet another case comes from a focus group of seven middle-aged, junior- and senior-high-school-educated *dibao* recipients in Chongqing interviewed in 2008. The interviewer inquired of the gathering: "Do you pay for your pension insurance?" The reply was unanimous: "Don't have the money, where would it come from? If you pay for it, there wouldn't be money for eating."[103] A local *dibao* manager in Hanyang City, Liaoning, in the same year summed it up: "The pension calls for 5,680 yuan per year (236 per person per month). Let's take a couple with a child in which both adults have been laid off. Do they pay for their pension? They don't, they can't. If they don't, later they'll go directly to poverty."[104]

No Work Contract So No Pension

As compared with these once-workers—who, at least, being on an official register, were eligible for a pension, even if they were not able to contribute to it—there were large numbers formally counted as "reemployed" and so no longer of any official concern. But the truth was that after being retrenched, most such people—cut off from their former firms—at best found only short-term, irregular work offering no benefits whatsoever. One instance from 1998 concerned the 10,000 laid-off textile workers entrusted to Wuhan's first reemployment service center. While part of the center's assignment was to situate these people in new work posts, a mere 400 of them (4 percent) were hired by some one hundred firms. Not a one of these units signed a contract with the workers or paid in pension contributions for them.[105]

A few years later, a 2000 survey conducted in Wuhan and Shenyang discovered that the majority of those finding work (becoming "reemployed") had

---

100. Ibid., 182–83.
101. Ibid., 264.
102. Interview, July 30, 2011.
103. Han, *Zhongguo chengshi,* 407.
104. Ibid., 442.
105. *Changjiang ribao* [Yangzi daily], June 2, 1998, 2.

landed just temporary stints, where they discovered that social insurance relationships they had once possessed with their old employers could not be transferred to their new placements. Though 22 percent of them had been offered
a chance to sign a contract, over half of the rest were working in the private
sector, and of those, just 10 percent had received a promise of a pension.[106]

As Ms. Wang, a thirty-five-year-old Changsha community *dibao* cadre,
described the circumstances she often observed, "In general employing firms
won't sign a labor contract. This is because of labor inspection. If the employer
signs, he'll have to buy insurance for the worker, including pension, work in-
jury, medical, etc. So there are a lot of issues."[107] A worker in a local Beijing
civil affairs office reported in 2008 that, "Some units don't want to give you
this insurance money; instead, they're thinking of ways to fire people."[108] The
trick was to engage a person for a limited period during which it was not necessary to enroll the individual in insurance programs. When the time for enroll-
ment was reached the employer would simply dismiss the new recruit.

The problems did not cease with time. In 2011, a scholar asserted that, "User
firms hiring and then not signing a contract is very pervasive; there's no legal
protection in hiring relations."[109] The situation was still not rectified over the
following decade, the period during which many laid-off workers came of retirement age and allegedly got a pension. A labor researcher wrote in early 2019
that, "Many get no pension [especially] those who didn't have an employment
contract during their careers, including self-employed workers."[110]

Other Causes

Additional reasons for not having a pension were having been employed in a
firm that did not offer one or never having worked at all. Those toiling outside the formal labor market (such as the self-employed or those working for
private owners) "were not required to participate" in insurance schemes.[111]
Naturally, those without the means to do so would have chosen not to join.
As for people who had never worked, a 2011 investigation of 200 persons in
three Jiangsu cities determined that a third of the lowest 10 percent among
them had never had a job and thus had no pension.[112]

106. Mo Rong, "Jiuye: xin shiji mianlin de tiaozhan yu juece" [Employment: the challenge and
decision that the new century is facing], in *2001 nian: Zhongguo shehui xingshi fenxi yu yuce* [2001:
Analysis and forecast of China's social situation], eds. Li Peilin, Huang Ping, and Lu Jianhua (Beijing: shehui kexue wenxuan chubanshe [social science documents publisher], 2001), 224.
107. Han, *Zhongguo chengshi,* 337.
108. Ibid., 321.
109. Xiong Yang, "Guizhou qiye xiagang zhigong zai jiuye wenti fenxi" [Analysis of the issue
of the reemployment of Guizhou's staff and workers laid off from enterprises], *Xueshu tantao* [Aca-
demic Inquiry] no. 5 (2011): 389.
110. Email from Greg Crothall, February 3, 2019.
111. Westmore, "Sharing," 5.
112. Zhu et al., "Chengshi dibao," 5.

These multiple situations combined to create a sizable mass of urban residents who found themselves without security in their old age. Even if a person in this category were capable of labor, their efforts to find work, especially work offering any benefits, were usually rebuffed. Though the *dibao*'s offerings were plainly inadequate, the allowance did provide a vitally necessary cushion for those who had no claim to a pension and probably never received one. So removing such persons from the rolls of the allowance left them dangling in the lurch.

RECENT DEVELOPMENTS

Two developments in the decade in which *dibao* recipients' numbers shrank so dramatically were a new "residents' pension" and a growing deficit in the state's pension fund. The first of these may explain why officials considered it reasonable to expunge such a quantity of former recipients from the allowance and not accommodate new applicants; the second may account, at least in part, for what may simply be the regime's reluctance to go on extending social assistance to people it seems to view as more or less expendable. These changes strengthen my assumption that those removed from the *dibao* were left on their own as they aged.

Urban-Rural Residents' Basic Pension Insurance

A new pension program was created during the 2009 to 2019 decade. Those who had never been employed—or who, after "restructuring," had no attachment to any enterprise or work unit—did get a bit of relief with the emergence of this pension. This insurance was created for rural residents in 2009; then, in 2011, another plan appeared for urbanites without work or a previous employer. Finally, in 2014, a scheme, entitled the Basic Residents' Pension Insurance, merged the two programs. It was directed at all non-working persons of retirement age and those with insecure jobs; anyone ineligible for the employment-based program could also join. The authorizing document for the 2011 urban experiment was "State Council guiding opinion on launching an urban residents' social pension insurance pilot," no. 18 (2011),[113] and the announcement for the combined plan was issued by the State Council in 2014 under the title "Urban-Rural Residents' Basic Pension Insurance."[114]

---

113. Zhongguo renmin gongheguo, Guowuyuan [State Council of the Chinese People's Republic], "Guowuyuan guanyu kaizhan chengzhen jumin shehui yanglao baoxian shidian de zhidao yijian" [Guiding opinion of the State Council on launching an urban residents' social pension insurance pilot], Guofa [2011] 18 hao [State Council issuance 2011, no. 18], www.gov.cn/zwgk/2011-06/13/content_1882801.htm, accessed February 20, 2020.

114. State Council of the People's Republic of China, "State Council Opinion on Establishing a Unified Urban and Rural Residents' Basic Pension Insurance System," No. 8 (2014) [Zhongguo

Once a "resident" had paid his/her contributions into an individual account for at least fifteen years, the person would be eligible to receive this pension, as well as a non-contributory, government (tax-based)-funded universal pension. Specific premium amounts vary by cities and there is no standard national monthly pension subsidy. The fifteen-year pay-in requirement held just for individuals aged forty-five and under; those sixty and above were automatically granted the pension; and an individual aged between forty-five and sixty must pay in for the number of years still remaining until reaching sixty.[115]

But the amount of the assistance was miniscule. The initial governmental subsidy for a pensioner was 55 yuan per month, equivalent at the time to about US$8.50. That amount did increase, a bit, to at least 70 yuan per month in early 2015 (the exact amount to be decided locally),[116] and in 2018, it was upped once again, to 88 yuan per month.[117] Despite the subsidy, the actual benefit for the "resident"-pension-holder was thus quite low. And, like an employee pensioner, the former would have to make a contribution. Whereas the worker's contribution amounted to 8 percent of the person's wage, "residents" could choose to pay in at extremely minimal rates, ranging from as little as 100 yuan per year (as of 2020) up to 1000 yuan per year; the benefit the person received would be correspondingly variable.[118]

Several striking comparisons: in 2012, the monthly pension for retirees who had been employed by functioning state-owned firms came to more

renmin gongheguo, Guowuyuan, Guowuyuan guanyu jianli tongyi de chengxiang jumin jiben yanglao baoxian zhidu de yijian, Guofa (2014) 8 hao, www.gov.cn.zhengce/content/2014-02/26/content_8656.htm, accessed February 20, 2020. I thank Randong Yuan for bringing these documents to my attention.

115. Armin Muller, "Functional Integration of China's Social Protection: Recent and Long-term Trends of Institutional Change in Health and Pension Insurance," *Asian Survey* 57, no. 6 (2017): 1110–34.

116. Yang Lixiong, "The Social Assistance Reform in China; Towards a Fair and Inclusive Social Safety Net," prepared for "Addressing Inequalities and Challenges to Social Inclusion through Fiscal, Wage and Social Protection Policies," United National Headquarters, New York, June 25–27, 2018 (unpaginated), http://www.un.org/development/.../The-Social-Assistance-Reform-in-China.pdf.

117. Ministry of Finance, "Report on the Execution of the Central and Local Budgets for 2018 and on the Draft Central and Local Budgets for 2019," Second Session of the 13th National People's Congress of the People's Republic of China, March 5, 2019, 13. However, Ministry of Human Resources and Social Security of the People's Republic of China, "Interpretation of the Policy on 'Guiding Opinions on Establishing the Basic Pension Insurance for Urban and Rural Residents and the Basic Adjustment Mechanism of Basic Pensions,'" released March 29, 2019, http://www.mohrss.gov.cn/SYrlzyhshbzb/dongtaixinwen/buneiyaowen/201803/t20180329_291013.html, accessed January 2019, stated that as of the end of 2017, the monthly per capita payment amount was 125 yuan, as cited in Yang, "The Social Assistance." This is still a terribly small amount, equivalent at the time to about US$21.

118. As an example, a resident choosing to pay a contribution of 150 yuan per year could hope to receive 150 x 12 months x 15 (the number of years that the resident must pay in) divided by 139 (the number of months the pensioner was expected to draw on the pension) plus the 88 yuan subsidy, or a total of about 282 yuan per month (US$40) beginning in 2018.

than 1,700 yuan. But at this time, a retired "resident" was getting an average subsidy of 73 yuan (US$11.60) and, perhaps, 194 yuan (as in the example above), coming to 267 yuan per month, which amounted to less than 16 percent of the state workers' pension that year. The situation only deteriorated with time. In 2016, about one hundred million retired Chinese covered by the unified basic urban pension system, to which most full-time urban workers contribute, were awarded average benefits of 2,600 yuan (about US$369) per month, while those receiving the "residents'" pension got an average of 117 yuan per month (under US$17), or 4.5 percent of the state-owned workers' pension.[119]

Secondly, in 2013, the government was putting into this pension plan only 24 percent of its expenditure on the *dibao* (a non-contributory program) nationally. And third, even if the amount that came from the "residents'" own contribution were added onto the governmental subsidy, the total average benefit nationwide from the "residents'" pension (at 231 yuan per month) would have been just 64 percent of the average country-wide *dibao* payment that year, then 362 yuan monthly. So, if a person subscribed to this pension after losing or not obtaining the *dibao* his/her living standard would have dropped severely.

A fourth point is a catch: the regulations held that the insurance paid the household was not to be included in its income. Critically, this meant that getting this pension was not to impact the family's receipt of the *dibao*. And yet the claim has been advanced that one reason some people were removed from the *dibao* rolls is that they had reached retirement age and received a pension. But surely the amount disbursed by the insurance was by itself far below what would have been needed to provide adequate sustenance. And, like the *dibao*, it amounts more to a financial transfer than to an insurance. Another issue is that despite these very trifling contribution rates, participation in this scheme has been sparse among the poor, whether because people still could not afford to pay for it or because they believed its receipt would not be worth its cost.[120] All told, one definitely cannot count this new pension arrangement as capable of substituting for the *dibao*. Accordingly, its disbursal cannot justify eliminating a person's *dibao* allowance.[121]

---

119. N. a., "Chaguan: Heroic, expendable," *The Economist*, November 30, 2019, 41, citing the *China Labour Bulletin*.

120. Qin Gao, Sui Yang, and Fuhua Zhai, "Social Policy and Income Inequality during the Hu-Wen Era: A Progressive Legacy?" *CQ* no. 237 (March 2019): 86; thanks also to email from Tao Liu, January 18, 2020.

121. Thanks to Yujeong Yang for help concerning this plan. Her information came from Mark C. Dorfman, Dewen Wang, Philip O'Keefe, and Jie Cheng, "China's Pension Schemes for Rural and Urban Residents," in *Matching Contributions for Pensions: A Review of International Experience*, eds. Richard Hinz, Robert Holzmann, David Tuesta, and Noriyuki Takayama (Washington, DC: The World Bank, 2012): 217–41.

State Pension Funds in Deficit

One last, vital angle from which to dispute the notion that laid-off workers were granted their pensions—thus no longer qualifying for the *dibao*—is the perilous financial state of Chinese pension funds. This is not a new development, as pension funds saw a rising deficit as long ago as the mid-1990s.[122] By 1998, the capital needed to cover workers' pensions nationally had ballooned forty-one-fold as compared to the amount required less than twenty years earlier, in 1980. Two issues explain this: the number of firms and people paying into the funds had declined while the number of retirees grew steadily; and many retired workers had not made contributions while working.[123] By the end of 1999, only about 50 percent of eligible workers in twenty-eight cities were participating in pension insurance.[124]

Another decade on, in 2009, the Ministry of Finance announced that thirteen provinces were experiencing shortfalls in their pension funds.[125] By 2011, the total had climbed to fourteen provinces sustaining indebted funds, the debt amounting to 76.7 billion yuan.[126] Thereafter, the situation deteriorated further: by 2014, nearly three-quarters of the provinces (twenty-two, or 70 percent) were running deficits. Ominously, in addition, between 2009 and 2014, the earnings rate of the pension insurance funds, at an annual average under 2.5 percent, was below that of banks' interest rate. Besides, the coverage rate was very low, at just under 36 percent of the labor force, owing to a rise in the numbers of people not paying into the fund. All this led to an annual loss of 35 billion yuan nationwide.[127] In the most egregious case, in 2018, Heilongjiang's pension fund alone was short by about 21 billion yuan.[128]

The question is whether, during the period following 2009, this fund in serious deficit was really drawn upon to support long-since-retrenched workers. And, in the unlikely case that it was, did this constitute grounds to force these people's removal from the *dibao*? Much more probable is that diminishing holdings were used to reward more recently retired, formal state-sector work-

---

122. Leung and Xu, *China's Social Welfare*, 76.

123. Zhao and Wei, *"Yanglao baoxian"*; email from Andrew Watson, September 22, 2011.

124. N.a., "Zhongdian lianxi chengshi yanglaojin shehuihua fafang jindu" [Focus on the process of the socialized issuance of urban pensions], *Laodong baozhang tongxun* (Labor security bulletin) no. 6 (2000): 23.

125. Liu, "Zhongguo yanglao."

126. Leung and Xu, *China's Social Welfare*, 76.

127. Liu, "Zhongguo yanglao."

128. Crothall, email, February 4, 2019. Pensions expert Randong Yuan explained that, "If we define deficit as the shortfall between revenues excluding subsidies and expenditures, the pension funds have been in deficit in recent years nationally . . . the same is true for most provinces." He continued, "The annual revenues excluding government subsidies started to be insufficient to cover the annual expenditures for both the Basic Residents' Scheme (since 2015) and the Urban Employees' Scheme (since 2011)" (email, March 22, 2020).

ers. So, this data drives the final nail into the coffin of the story that so many *dibaohu* (and *xiagang*) were deprived of their *dibao* allowances after 2009 because they instead could depend on a pension.

CONCLUSION

Given all these considerations, it seems safe to conclude the following: that neither the receipt of pensions, nor the achievement of well-paid employment—the two justifications often put forward in recent years for the *dibao* cutbacks—accounts for the truly massive slashes in the numbers of *dibao* beneficiaries over the decade 2009 to 2019. We need to attribute this outcome chiefly to the major switches in policy explicated in Chapter Nine, that, following the year 2009, gradually converted the program from one directed at protesting past-proletarians. The bulk of this paring was implemented under the administration of Xi Jinping, which claimed—probably falsely—that (in addition to having acquired pensions or jobs) perhaps as many as two-thirds of the prior targets of the program were found unqualified to receive its allowance (but had done so, either because of cadres' mis-targeting or bribery) and were, rather, the arrogates of crooked dispensations, corruptly enjoying it.

So, my analysis resolves to this: with a new fund having been created to serve those without pensions but whose assistance is clearly too scant; with the pension funds in deficit; and with protests having died away, it seems most probable that the number of recipients dropped drastically because of a definite, intentional modification of *dibao* policy, as its initial motive faded in significance for the political elite. The alteration was made in order to leave laid-off workers to their own devices, while reverting back to pre-*dibao* days of succoring principally the fully desperate, that is, the disabled, the aged with no recourse, and orphans, the old *sanwu*.

Conclusion

"Q" is the interviewer; "R" is Ms. Xiao, a Changsha City, Tianxin District, cadre from the Bureau of Civil Affairs, 2008:

Q: What do you think is the reason for conflict [between *dibao* cadres and recipients]?

R: First it's the application; we go through the in-home inspection, you find they don't fit the norm, so want to take them off [the *dibao*]; in this kind of situation, very easy to produce acute conflicts. Sometimes, the conflict is rather severe; they strike someone; some make trouble without any reason. . . . But the residents' quality is only so high, the poorer they are, the more [they're] like that.

About their understanding of the norm, some enjoy a high allowance and some low, some want 400 yuan [per month], but according to regulations should get only 200 yuan . . . then they argue and make disturbance, make demands of work personnel.

The quality of the residents you have contact with is rather low, it's a kind of vicious circle. They don't have money to go to school because they're poor, then they act like barbarians.[1]

LESSONS

The cadre's reflections offer an apt closure to this text; they resonate ringingly with several of the volume's chief lessons. There is the frustrated

---

1. Han Keqing, ed., *Zhongguo chengshi dibao fangtanlu* [Interviews with Minimum Livelihood Guarantee Recipients in Urban China] (Jinan: Shandong renmin chubanshe [Shandong people's publishing], 2012), 366.

local official, exasperated with what she/he (probably often as not unfairly) experience as her/his bothersome, quarrelsome charges, pitted against the aggrieved, perhaps uninformed, welfare target, who is either feigning or imagining—or perhaps just hoping—that s/he ought to be accorded a larger monthly allowance. In other words, from this functionary's viewpoint, with their abysmal "quality," the *dibaohu* simply lack understanding. And, perhaps most centrally, in the midst of her griping, this bureaucrat has hit on a fundamental truth: the poverty into which these subjects have been thrust by the state itself is set to perpetuate itself: their families too poor to arrange proper schooling, the progeny remaining impoverished and, therefore, plunged into the plight of their parents; "it's a kind of vicious circle," just as the official contends.

The program under examination in this book, especially in its urban variant, may appear small-scale, servicing at its pinnacle just 23.6 million city residents in 2009, and even then, at the peak, amounting to a mere 3.65 percent of the municipal populace nationwide.[2] But its saga is pregnant with meanings for the Chinese state's journey from socialism to its present formation, best labeled harsh state capitalism. Indeed, one can study the *dibao* and the *dibaohu* to read much about the state and its decisions over the years from the time of the December 1978 Third Plenum of the Communist Party's Eleventh Central Committee to the convening of the party's Sixteenth Congress in autumn 2002.

For in the party's leaders' choice, following 1978, gradually to shift the motor of the economy from their plans to markets, they felt compelled to jettison their prior partner, the old proletariat, consigning its members—who for decades had symbolically stood at the helm of society—to a space where they would turn into an absent, invisible fragment of the populace. Three big queries arise here: Did these rulers truly have a choice? Were there realistic alternatives to the judgments they made and the course they adopted? And what, precisely, were their intentions when they called for the cashiering of millions?[3] Some of the answers—about leaders' precise intentions, for instance—must remain unknowable, in the absence of any available documentation. What is certain, however, is the reply to the queries about choice and alternatives: definitely a more attractive outcome should have been possible. Thus, a more generous welfare project could have been imagined and implemented. Clearly, for instance, the conditional cash transfers programs executed in many countries that are detailed in Chapter Seven, whereby the schooling and health care of the children of the poor must be assured in order

---

2. https://www.statista.com/statistics/278566/urban-and-rural-population-of-china/, accessed January 11, 2021.

3. Thanks to Thomas Bernstein for raising these issues.

to obtain an allowance, would go some way to help forestall the "vicious circle" depicted above.

But consider what happened instead to Chinese urban society: even as new economic forces propelled large numbers of the city residents to find their material lives elevated immensely, the authorities at the same time converted a scene (that existed before 1980) in which more or less universal low living standards obtained within urban society into one (after 1995) where the indigent were rejected, relegated to the margins of the polity. There, on the brink, hardship became concentrated in one unfortunate, isolated segment of the people, a cohort whose abjection had been forged by the governors themselves. This research has uncovered the story of the creation and, as time will show, the reproduction of privation, and of a permanent welfare class.[4]

Even long after the laborers of Mao's era became redundant—a cohort to whom the state owed a great debt for decades of grinding labor, and certainly not the treatment they were shown—in 2018, a Chinese scholar noted that, "Social assistance can only solve the problem of *wenbao* (温饱, dressed and fed); it cannot address the question of relative poverty and multidimensional poverty. It will keep them [the *dibaohu*] in poverty for the long term."[5] The fallout for society—not just for individuals and families—was expressed plaintively by junior-high-school-educated, fifty-year-old Mr. Wang of Xuanwu District, Beijing, a *dibao* beneficiary and the father of a sixth grader:

Adults like me at my age, whether I eat well or not isn't of importance, it's enough if I can eat my fill. But a child uses money in a lot of ways. Like now the child wants to go to school, expenses are high, if we can't meet the need, [the] child's study, physique, various aspects will all be influenced, in this way each generation, isn't society's burden getting heavier? If policy would have a slight tilt, let them get good education, if my child can go to college, society's *suzhi* (素质, quality) no matter from what angle, isn't it raised up?[6]

The account laid out in these pages also stands as a history of the regime's responsibility, intended or not, for a stunning rise in state-made, severe inequality. In this case, the state has chosen not violence or overt repression, and not so much propaganda (though there has been some of that as well), to handle this externality of market reform and global entry. No, chiefly, the

---

4. Claus Offe, "Advanced Capitalism and the Welfare State," *Politics & Society* (Summer 1972): 487, argues that the state supports this growing body of the population on a level close to subsistence; "thus a new class is generated, consisting mostly of the unskilled unemployed who have lost their competitive link to the labor market and who consist of a permanent welfare class."

5. Lan Jian, "Zhongguo shehui jiuzhu zhengce de yanjin, tuchu wenti ji qi fanpinkun tupo luxiang" [The evolution of China's social assistance policy, outstanding problems and the path toward breakthrough in fighting poverty], *Yunnan shehui kexue* [Yunnan social science] no. 4 (2018), 36.

6. Han, *Zhongguo chengshi*, 123.

leadership has dealt with its new urban poor via miniscule handouts, decked out in the garb of "social assistance." Yet, as I have argued, since the aim of the allowances has chiefly been placation and pacification, it could even be claimed that at least a portion of the *dibao*'s effect (again, whether intentional or not) has been to put aside the displaced workers, to make them vanish from sight, and quietly and stably so. And since the vision of their official allocators does not include facilitating the grantees' climb out from penury—the program's official classification as "social assistance" (which, as Chapter Seven pointed out, should entail the aim of facilitating recipients' permanent exit from poverty) could be interrogated.

Another thematic thread that weaves through the analysis of the book is the prod the program's parsimoniousness got from China's century-plus push for modernity, and also from the tight connection in the minds of the educated and the political elite between China and its people's modernization, cosmopolitanism, and sophistication on the one side, and citizens' "quality," on the other. Here one can deduce that these dislocated drudges were—and are—seen by the more educated and more skilled among the people as not deserving of much in the way of material aid.

The relevant view here was neatly conveyed in this statement from the 2015 Central Urban Work Conference, which called promoting the modernization of the citizenry's "quality" a necessity and bemoaned that "the quality of our urban citizens has lagged behind . . . Urban citizens," the proclamation continued, "should be educated to establish their consciousness as modern citizens, establish the behavioral norms of a modern citizen, and propel the modernization of people's relationships in a modern society."[7] Party leader Xi Jinping seconded this sentiment at the Party's Nineteenth Congress in October 2017 with his exhortation that, "People with talent are a strategic resource for China as it endeavors to achieve national rejuvenation and to stay ahead in international competition."[8] For the laid-off (*xiagang*) and the livelihood guarantee recipients (*dibaohu*), the crucial bond between what the larger society perceives as their lower "quality" and the size of their rations is this: "Economists think the *dibaohu* don't have *suzhi*, so why waste money on them?"[9]

Susan Greenhalgh's pertinent comments, similarly, link a "high quality, competitive workforce" with China's goal "to boost [its] global influence,

---

7. As cited in Peng Guohua and Ouyang Hui, "Chengshi shi xiandaihua 'huochetou'" [The city is the locomotive of modernization] *Renmin ribao* [People's Daily], February 21, 2016.

8. Xi Jinping, "Secure a Decisive Victory in Building a Moderately Prosperous Society in All Respects and Strive for the Great Success of Socialism with Chinese Characteristics for a New Era," delivered at the Nineteenth National Congress of the Communist Party of China, October 18, 2017, http://www.xinhuanet.com/english/download/Xi_Jinping's_report_at_19th_CPC_National_Congress.pdf.

9. Interview with social policy specialist, August 22, 2008, Beijing.

standing, and power."[10] Jean-Louis Rocca concurs with this appraisal in referring to official discourse, where he finds that, "Behind the propaganda for promoting 'civilization' rests the idea that the quality of the population must be improved in order to allow China to enter modernity."[11] Greenhalgh also refers to "a category of people deemed 'low in quality,'" which, in her telling, comprises rural residents, rural migrants, women, minorities and those with substandard bodies," whom she conceives as having been "abandoned as useless."[12] Surely, as two scholars of politics and law from the Zhengzhou Institute of Technology remarked in 2014, the urban low-income masses must include as well "the original urban laid-off and unemployed."[13] The self-same notion that undereducated persons without much of an income lack value appears in a skilled worker's characterization of a once vibrant neighborhood in Tiexi District, Shenyang: "The people with ability have all moved away: those left are useless, five or six people squeezed into a room,"[14] bolstering the claim above that these people are not just without any value but are also isolated.

THE SEQUEL

Besides the steady plunge in numbers of *dibao* beneficiaries after 2009 detailed in Chapter Ten, what else has happened in the realm of the laid-off workers, the *xiagang,* and in the arena of the welfare targeted at them, the *dibao*, in the decade following the start of that decline in the numbers of grantees? The answer is that both the recipients and their program seem to have vanished (or to be in the midst of vanishing) if one reads the Chinese press. So have the old laid-off workers totally lost their presence, now that they have aged and been muzzled? And what about the *dibao*? Word of that has also ebbed away.

These are questions worth considering. Two issues appear relevant, one concerning what seems to be an end to officialdom's resort to the *dibao* to counter potential protesting; the second is about the total disappearance of

10. Susan Greenhalgh, *Cultivating Global Citizens: Population in the Rise of China* (Cambridge, MA: Harvard University Press, 2010), x, xiv, 25.

11. Jean-Louis Rocca, "Governing from the Middle? Understanding the Making of China's Middle Classes," in *To Govern China: Evolving Practices of Power*, eds. Vivienne Shue and Patricia M. Thornton (New York: Cambridge University Press, 2017), 238.

12. Greenhalgh, *Cultivating,* 74.

13. Jiao Yazhuan and He Huijiang, "Chengshi dishou qunti jiuye zhengce de lunli xuanze" [The ethical choice of urban low-income masses' employment policy], *Zhengzhou hankong gongye guanli xueyuan xuebao* [Journal of Zhengzhou Institute of the Management of the Aeronautical Industry] 32, no. 2 (2014): 101.

14. Zhou Shoujing, "Xiagang shiwunian: ronghui yi cheng wangshi" [Laid off for 15 years: the glory is already in the past], *Juece tanso* [Policy explorations] 4 (2014): 50.

the old proletariat, the *xiagang*, from the worries of the rulers. First of all, references can be found repeatedly in later years (during the global economic crisis of 2008–2009, again in 2012, and in the years that followed) to ongoing massive layoffs and the installation of programs and policies to deal with them.[15] Indeed, the layoffs do go on: as a matter of fact, in early 2020, one observer noted news from the National Bureau of Statistics that, "Nearly 17 million jobs in industry and construction were lost since 2014."[16]

Along with the layoffs, there is routinely a listing of programmatic efforts to mollify the suddenly redundant, attempts that hark back to the reemployment "campaign" of 1998 to 2002 reviewed in Chapter Five. On all the different occasions when pronouncements were broadcast and directives released, the government always exhibited concern, even emitting a tone of stress and tension, as it called for succoring the newly laid-off in a range of ways. But in no case were these targeted people the old *xiagang.*

Thus, instructions the central authorities gave the localities to fend off anger from the newly displaced included supporting mergers among failing firms, whose regrouped component firms were to absorb the staff and workers from floundering enterprises; providing subsidies for training and professional introduction to new jobs for those sacked; and commanding bankrupted firms to terminate labor contracts, but still to submit delayed

---

15. John Giles, Albert Park, Fang Cai, and Yang Du, "Weathering a Storm: Survey-Based Perspectives on Employment in China in the Aftermath of the Global Financial Crisis," Washington, DC, The World Bank, Development Research Group, Human Development and Public Services Team, March 2012, for the 2009 financial crisis; "Taotai luohou channeng dui jiuye de yingxiang" [The influence on employment of eliminating backward production capacity], *Zhongguo jiuye* [China employment] no. 5 (2014): 54–55 for 2012, 2013, and 2014 (which states that 93.4 percent of those laid off had no skills); Liang Fengfang, "Guanyu xiagang zhigong zaijiuye shuishou zhengce de jidian xikao" [Several points of deliberations on tax collection policy about the laid-off staff and workers' reemployment], *Shidai jinrong* [Times finance] no. 2 (2014): 166 for 2014; Li Tao, "Jiaqiang fuwu zhongxin guanli, cujin xiagang zhigong zaijiuye" [Strengthen service center management, promote laid-off staff and workers' reemployment," *Sheke luntan* [Social science forum] no. 8 (2014): 165–66 for 2014; for 2015, Qi Yue, "Danyou di'er bo xiagangchao: xian lai suansuan chuqing 'jianghu qiye' yingxiang duoda" (Concern about the second wave of layoffs, first calculate how great the influence of clearing out the" "zombie factories" is), December 29, 2015, http://m.wallstreetcn.com/node/228035. For 2016, Nicholas Loubere, "Laying off Responsibility: Microcredit, Entrepreneurship, and China's Industrial retrenchment," *Made in China* 2 (2016): 20–23; Zhonghua renmin gongheguo renli caiyuan he shehui baozhangbu (Chinese People's Republic Human Resources and Social Security Ministry), "Renli caiyuan shehui baozhangbu, guojia fazhan gaigewei deng qi bumen guanyu zai huajie gangtie meitan hangye guosheng channeng shixian tuokun fazhan guochengzhong zuohao zhigong anzhi gongzuo de yijian" (Opinion of the Ministry of Human Resources and Social Security, State Development and Reform Commission, Seven Ministries on Arranging Well Staff and Workers Staff and Workers in Dissolving Steel and Coal Industries' Excess Capacity and Realizing Throwing off Difficulty), April 17, 2016, https://www.mohrss.gov.cn/gkml/xxgk/20160413_238000.html.

For 2019, Renli ziyuan he shehui baozhangbu dangzu [Party group of the Ministry of Personnel Rescourses and Social Security], "Ruhe kandai woguo jiuye xingshi" [How to view the situation of employment in our country], *Qiushi* [Seeking truth], January 3, 2020. This piece, about "the masses' employment work," explicitly proclaimed that "college graduates are the keypoint masses."

16. George Magnus, "Opinion: Beijing's Delicate Balancing Act Relies on Job Creation," *Financial Times*, January 2, 2020.

social insurance fees and back wages (but with what funds?). Other familiar exhortations were to encourage the retrenched to retire early or to create new firms of their own, backed up by no-interest loans and tax relief, and to offer subsidies and preferential tax policies for employers and companies that hire dislodged workers. Above all, orders went out to handle "sudden outbursts" in a timely manner; to strengthen monitoring of those ejected from their jobs, in order to guard against risk; and to prepare contingency plans for possible disruptive action. The regime in addition publicized a promise of hundreds of millions of yuan in assistance of various kinds for the newly unemployed. What is remarkable is that never was there any mention of the *dibao*. One could read this as a sign that the *dibao* was no longer seen as a tool to be put into the service of mollifying and quelling potential disorder caused by laid-off workers. As earlier chapters have shown, in time, that scheme was turned away from assisting dislocated employees and was switched to ministering only to the very most needy, the old *sanwu* poor, as under the rule of Mao Zedong.

The second issue, as just suggested, goes beyond sidelining the *dibao* program; it underlines a shift in the attention of the authorities as to who should be the proper subjects of employment and unemployment policy, and about whose jobs should be protected, whose miffs and antagonisms mitigated. Perhaps the most significant symbol of change, as Mencius—who emphasized the "rectification of names"—would have it, has been the abolition of the very name "*xiagang*." It is notable that after the year 2006, *xiagang* was no longer tabulated among the classifications of *dibao* recipients (see Table 9.3). Two interviewees in 2014 reported that the term had by then gone out of use: the concept is "outdated, no longer an outstanding social problem," explained an official at the Ministry of Civil Affairs. Could the erasure of the designation itself be intended to signal the public demise, indeed, the very nonexistence of these once-proud members of the old proletariat?

Redundant workers—especially (perhaps only!) at the time when they are dismissed—continue to be tended to, of course, because, for the regime, their proven capacity for unleashing unrest must be contained. But the gaze of the watchful eye of the leadership has been repositioned, as the workers of what now must seem the distant past (i.e., the proletariat of some twenty-plus years ago) have mostly retreated to their homes, as attested to by the same civil affairs official.[17] Indeed, rather than placing their primary focus on the socialist-era working class, top politicians demonstrate that what has been exercising their anxieties in recent years has been the plight of frustrated unemployed college graduates and the antagonism displayed by terminated migrant

17. Interview, October 9, 2014, Beijing. A social policy scholar, interviewed October 7, 2014, also in Beijing, concurred.

workers. This new angst was broadcast as early as 2003 and 2004;[18] in 2009;[19] in late 2018,[20] at the Fourth Plenum of the Nineteenth Party Congress in October 2019 (where ensuring stability in the arena of employment was the number one priority among "six stabilities");[21] and in mid-2020, as an offshoot of the coronavirus pandemic, to give a few examples.[22]

Thus, just as other campaigns in the past, the late 1990s/early 2000s movement to stem the tumult on the streets (or any imagined future disturbance there) occasioned by the discharge of tens of millions as China joined the global market—those under-skilled, barely educated emblems of the past—this one too, dressed up as "social assistance"—was short-lived and petered out rather quickly. That short life is evident not only in the huge cuts in the numbers of *dibaohu* on the rolls and, very likely, in a fall in the percentage of recipients who are physically fit to work (though who are of no interest to any prospective employers). It is also clear in the evanescence of the *dibao* itself (at least) in the form in which it was originally tailored, and, at least in public mention, of its initial target. As then-forty-seven-year-old Mr. Zhang of Xuanwu District, Beijing, lamented already quite some years ago, "We're all people, why can't we exist?"[23]

18. Sidney Leng, "After Coronavirus Pandemic, Chinese Students Grapple with First Economic Downturn of Their Lives," *South China Morning Post (SCMP)*, May 14, 2020.

19. Giles et al., "Weathering."

20. Zhongyang jingji gongzuo huiyi zai Beijing juxing, Xi Jinping, Li Keqiang zuo zhongyao jianghua [The Central Economic Work Conference was held in Beijing, Xi Jinping, Li Keqiang gave important speeches], Xinhuawang, December 21, 2018.

21. Renli ziyuan he shehui baozhangbu, "Ruhe kandai."

22. Sidney Leng, "Coronavirus: China Faces Historic Test as Pandemic Stokes Fears of Looming Unemployment Crisis," *SCMP*, May 11, 2020; Sun Yu, "China's Retraining Campaign Offers Scant Prospects for the Unemployed," *Financial Times,* September 15, 2020, https://www.ft.com/content/51caf358-1058-4ee7-834a-c5b5cb8bf205.

23. Han, *Zhongguo chengshi*, 54.

Glossary of Chinese Terms

bao'an	保安	security protection
baojie	保洁	sanitary worker
baozhangjin lingquzheng	保障金 领取证	certificate for collecting *dibao* funds
benqian	本钱	start-up capital
biao ti, liang jiang	标 提 量 减	raise standards, cut amounts
buxing	不行	no good
buzhu	补助	subsidy, (income) supplement
chengguan	城管	urban management police
chengshi hukou	城市 户口	urban household registration
chi dibao	吃 低保	rely on the *dibao*
dagong	打工	do odd jobs
dagongzhe	打工者	workers who do low-paid, low-skill, informal labor
danwei	单位	work unit
diaomin	刁民	wicked person
dibao	低保	short for Minimum Livelihood Guarantee
dibao biaozhun	低保 标准	*dibao* norm or standard, a given city's poverty line
dibao duixiang	低保 对象	targets of the *dibao* program
dibaohu	低保户	*dibao* households (recipients of the *dibao*)
dibaozu	低保族	disparagingly, the *dibaohu* tribe

difang zhengci	地方 政策	local policies
dingxinwan	定心丸	tranquilizer
fenliu	分流	channel elsewhere
fuwuyuan	服务员	service worker
gei duoshao,	给 多少, 就是 多少	give [us] a certain amount,
jiushi duoshao		that's all there is
gaizhi	改制	restructure (used
		with enterprises)
gongshilan	公示栏	public notice board
gongyixing	公益性	public interest
Gouwu daobao	购务 导报	shopping guide
guangcai	光彩	honorable
guanting bingzhuan	关停 并转	close, stop, merge, transform
hukou	戶口	household registration
huo yitian, suan yitian	活 一天, 算 一天	live a day and write it off
jianyuan, zengxiao	减员增效	reduce staff, increase
		efficiency
jiazheng	家政	housework
jiben shenghuofei	基本 生活费	basic living stipends
jiedao	街道	street
jin	斤	a bit more than a pound
Jingji ribao	经济日报	Economic Daily
juweihui	居委会	residents' committee
kang	炕	brick Chinese bed common
		in north China
kuale	垮了	collapsed, failed totally
laobaixing	老百姓	ordinary people
linghuo jiuye	灵活 就业	flexible employment
luohoude	落后的	backward, behind
ma	骂	curse
mafan	麻烦	nuisance
maiduan gongling	买断工龄	lump-sum severance
		payment
mei banfa de shiqing	没 办法 的 事情	no-way affair
mei banfa	没 办法	there's no way
mei chi ku	没 吃 苦	didn't eat bitterness,
		didn't suffer
mei suoweide	没所谓的	doesn't matter
Ming bao	明 报	Bright News
mingong	民工	casual labor
nao	闹	stir up trouble
ni ming	匿名	anonymity
ningjuli gongcheng	凝聚力工程	cohesion project

pubian xingde	普遍 行的,	
zaiyede hen shao	在业的很少	prevailing everywhere, very few are at work
qingbao	情保	favoring (undeserving) friends and relatives
qiye gaizao	企业 改造	enterprise restructuring
qu	区	district (the administrative level below the city)
quanyi	权益	right
renci	人次	people-times
renqingbao, guanxibao	人情保, 关系保	giving grants owing to personal relations
ridz jiang jiu hai neng guo	日子将就还 能过	put up with things
ruoshi qunti	弱势 群体	weak/vulnerable masses
sanwu	三无	three withouts
shangfang	上访	petition
shei jia haizi shei jia bao	谁 家 孩子 谁 家 保	whoever's child it is should pay, that is, enterprises should pay for allowances for their poverty-stricken employees
shequ	社区	community
shiqu	市区	city district
shuobuqing . . . xiangduide . . . meibanfa tongji	说不清 . . . 相对的 . . . 没办法 统计	can't say clearly, relative, no way to count
suzhi	素质	quality
Ta buguan ni; ni yao zhao ren, zhaobudao	他 不管 你；你 要 找 人， 找不到	they don't take care of you, if you look for anyone they can't be found
tekun renyuan	特困 人员	persons in extreme poverty
tekun	特困	especially difficult
tile ye shi baiti	提了是白提	raising it is useless
waidi	外地	other places (outside a given locality)
weiwen	维稳	stability maintenance
wenbao	温饱	dressed and fed, live comfortably
wending gongcheng	稳定 工程	stability project
xiagang	下岗	laid off
xiagang zhigong	下岗 职工	laid-off staff and workers

xiaokang	小康	moderately well off
xieguanyuan	协管员	assistant management personnel
xuni shouru	虚拟 收入	assumed (or notional) income
ying bao jin bao	应保尽保	protect as much as possible those who should be protected
ying tui jin tui	应 退尽退	as much as possible withdraw those who should be withdrawn
yiwu laodong	义务 劳动	either voluntary labor or obligatory labor
youhui zhengce	优惠 政策	preferential policies
yu jian ru she yi, yu she ru jian nan	由 俭入奢易, 由奢入俭難	it's easy to go from frugality to extravagance, hard to go from extravagance to frugality
yundong	运动	mass movement, campaign
zaogao	糟糕	awful, what a mess
zhongzhuan xuexiao	中专 学校	vocational school
zhuada, fangxiao	抓大, 放小	the central government grasps the large, strategically significant firms, releases (to the market) locally-owned, smaller firms
zuidi shenghuo baozhang	最低生活保障 (for short, *dibao* 低保)	Minimum Livelihood Guarantee

Works Cited

I list here only the works that I have cited in the text. This list is only a small portion of the materials I read in creating this book.

ABBREVIATED JOURNAL TITLES

I referenced these journals a number of times in the cited works:

AS	*Asian Survey*
CER	*China Economic Review*
CJ	*The China Journal*
CLB	*China Labour Bulletin*
CJSW	*China Journal of Social Welfare*
CP	*Comparative Politics*
CQ	*The China Quarterly*
CR	*The China Review*
GSP	*Global Social Policy*
IJSW	*International Journal of Social Welfare*
IJURR	*International Journal of Urban and Regional Research*
LDBZTX	*Laodong baozhang tongxun* (Labor security bulletin)
NBCY	*Neibu canyue* (Internal consultations)
NYT	*New York Times*
RMRB	*Renmin ribao* (People's Daily)
SCMP	*South China Morning Post*
SWB	*Summary of World Broadcasts*
ZGLD	*Zhongguo laodong* (Chinese Labor)
ZGMZ	*Zhongguo minzheng* (Chinese Civil Affairs)

Adler, Michael, "Conditionality, Sanctions, and the Weakness of Redress Mechanisms in the British 'New Deal." In Brodkin and Marston, *Work and the Welfare State*, 229–248.

An, Jin, "Ruoshi qunti jiuye cujin yanjiu" [Promote research on the employment of the vulnerable groups]. *Caijing lilun yanjiu* [Finance and economics theoretical research], no. 1 (2014): 48–57.

Anagnost, Ann. *National Past-Times: Narrative, Representation, and Power in Modern China*. Durham: Duke University Press, 1997.

Andreas, Joel. *Disenfranchised: The Rise and Fall of Industrial Citizenship in China*. NY: Oxford University Press, 2019.

Appleton, Simon, John Knight, Lina Song, and Qingjie Xia. "Labor retrenchment in China: Determinants and consequences." *CER* no. 13 (2002): 252–75.

Aspalter, Christian, "The East Asian welfare model." *IJSW* no. *15* (2006): 290–301.

Bakken, Borge. *The Exemplary Society: Human Improvement, Social Control, and the Dangers of Modernity in China*. Oxford: Oxford University Press, 2000.

Bane, Mary Jo, "Poverty Politics and Policy." In Cancian and Danziger, *Changing Poverty,* 367–86.

Barrientos, Armando. "Introducing Basic Social Protection in Low-Income Countries: Lessons from Existing Programmes." In *Building Decent Societies: Rethinking the Role of Social Security in Development*, edited by Peter Townsend, 253–73. Houndmills: Palgrave Macmillan 2009.

Barrientos, Armando. *Social Assistance in Developing Countries*. Cambridge, U.K.: Cambridge University Press, 2013.

Beijing chengxiang dibao biaozhun tongyi zhi meiyue 710 yuan [Beijing's urban and rural dibao norm unified at 710 yuan per month]. *Xin jing bao* [New capital paper], June 27, 2015.

Benkan jizhe/xinwen, benkan tongxunyuan/Liu Jing. [This paper's news, this paper's correspondent/Liu Jing]. "Guanzhu chengshi dishouru qunti: Wuhanshi Qiaokouqu chengshi jumin zuidi shenghuo baozhang gongzuo toushi" [Pay close attention to urban low-income masses: Perspective on the work of Wuhan's Qiaokou District's urban residents' minimum livelihood guarantee]. *Hubei caishui* [Hubei finance and taxes] 2, no.4 (2002): 4–5.

Bennett, Gordon. *Yundong: Mass Campaigns in Chinese Communist Leadership*. China Research Monograph, no. 12. Berkeley: Institute of East Asian Studies, University of California, Berkeley, 1976.

Berkowitz, Edward D., and Larry DeWitt. *The Other Welfare: Supplemental Security Income and U.S. Social Policy*. Ithaca: Cornell University Press, 2013.

Bian, Yanjie. "The Prevalence and the Increasing Significance of *Guanxi*." *CQ,* no. 235 (Sept. 2018): 597–621.

"Bian yingde shouru wei shiji shouru; dibao shouru keshi zhengce zuochu tiaozheng" [Change the income owed into real income; readjust the verification policy of the minimum livelihood guarantee]. Xinhuanet, October 24, 2002. http://news.xinhin net.com/newscenter/2002-10/24/content_607113.htm.

Blyth, Mark. *Great Transformations: Economic Ideas and Institutional Change in the Twentieth Century*. Cambridge: Cambridge University Press, 2002.

Bonoli, Giuliano, and David Natali, "Multidimensional Transformations in the Early 21st Century Welfare States." In *The Politics of the New Welfare State*, edited by Giuliano Bonoli & David Natali, 287–306. Oxford, UK: Oxford University Press, 2012.

Bonoli, Giuliano, and David Natali, "The Politics of the 'New' Welfare States: Analysing Reforms in Western Europe." In Bonoli & Natali, *The Politics,* 3–17.

Brodkin, Evelyn Z., and Flemming Larsen. "The Policies of Workfare: at the Boundaries between Work and the Welfare State." In Brodkin and Marston, *Work and the Welfare State*, 57–67.

Bruun, Ole. *Business and Bureaucracy in a Chinese City: An Ethnography of Private Business Households in Contemporary China.* Research Monograph 43. Berkeley: Institute for East Asian Studies, University of California, 1993.

Caizhengbu, minzhengbu tongzhi [Ministry of Finance, Ministry of Civil Affairs Circular]. "Guanyu yinfa 'chengxiang zuidi shenghuo baozhang zijin guanli banfa' de tongzhi'" [On the issuance of the circular on management of urban and rural minimum livelihood funds]. *Caishe* [Finance and society], 171 *hao* [no. 171] 2012. https://baike.baidu.com/view/9452029.htm accessed October 2012.

Campbell, Andrea Louise. *Trapped in America's Safety Net: One Family's Struggle.* Chicago: University of Chicago Press, 2014.

Canetti, Elias, *Crowds and Power*. Carol Stewart, trans. New York: Viking, 1963.

Cao, Yanchun. "Woguo chengshi 'dibao' zhidu de ba xiang jingzhundu shizheng yanjiu" [An empirical study on the targeting accuracy of minimum living security system for urban residents in China]. *Zhongyang caijing daxue xuebao* [Journal of the Central University of Finance and Economics] no. 7 (2016): 3–12.

Chak, Kwan Chan. "Re-thinking the Incrementalist Thesis in China: A Reflection on the Development of the Minimum Standard of Living Scheme in Urban and Rural Areas." *Journal of Social Policy* 39, no. 4 (2010): 627–45.

Chan, Kam Wing. "Fundamentals of China's Urbanization and Policy," *CR* 10, no.1 (2010): 63–93.

Chan, Kam Wing. "Urbanization in China: What is the True Urban Population of China? Which is the Largest City in China?" Unpublished ms., January, 2009.

Chen, Feng. "Industrial Restructuring and Workers' Resistance in China." *MC* 29, no. 2 (2003): 237–62.

Chen, Feng. "Subsistence Crises, Managerial Corruption and Labour Protests in China." *CJ*, no. 44 (July 2000): 41–63.

Chen, Feng, and Mengxiao Tang. "Labor Conflicts in China: Typologies and Their Implications." *AS* 53, no. 3 (2013): 559–583.

Chen, Honglin, Wong Yu-cheung, Zeng Qun, and Juha Hamalainen. "Trapped in poverty? A study of the *dibao* programme in Shanghai." *CJSW* 6, no. 3 (2013): 327–43.

Chen, Janet Y. *Guilty of Indigence: The Urban Poor in China, 1900–1953.* Princeton: Princeton University Press, 2012.

Chen, Shaohua, Martin Ravallion, and Youjuan Wang. "*Di bao:* A Guaranteed Minimum Income in China's Cities?" World Bank Policy Research Working Paper 3805, January 2006.

Chen, Xi. "The Logic of Fragmented Activism among Chinese State-Owned Enterprise Workers." *CJ,* no. 81 (January 2019): 58–80.

Chen, Xi. *Social Protest and Authoritarianism in China.* NY: Cambridge University Press, 2012.

Chen, Xiangming. "China's City Hierarachy, Urban Policy and Spatial Development in the 1980s." *Urban Studies* 28, no. 3 (1991): 341–67.

Chen, Xiaohong. "Dibao gongzuozhong de 'zuobi' xianxiang ji duice" [The phenomenon of 'fraud' in *dibao* work and measures to deal with it]. *ZGMZ,* no. 5 (2004): 48.

Cheng, Hang-Sheng. "A Mid-Course Assessment of China's Economic Reform." In *China's Economic Future: Challenges to U.S. Policy,* edited by Joint Economic Committee, Congress of the United States, 24–33. NY: Routledge, 1997.

Cheng, Zhiming. "Layoffs and urban poverty in the state-owned enterprise communities in Shaanxi Province, China." University of Wollongong Research Outline, 2012. Presented at 13th Annual Global Development Conference 'Urbanization and Development: Delving Deeper into the Nexus.' New Delhi, India: Global Development Network.

Cheng, Zhiming. "Poverty in China's Urban Communities: Profile and Correlates." *China Report* 46, no. 2 (2010): 143–73.

Chengshi shiye xiagang yu zaijiuye yanjiu ketizu [Research task force on urban unemployment, layoffs, and reemployment]. "Wo guo chengshizhong de shiye xiagang wenti ji qi duice" [The issue of our country's urban unemployment and layoffs and measures to handle it]. *Shehuixue* [Sociology], 3 (2000): 80–86.

'Chengzhen qiye xiagang zhigong zaijiuye zhuangkuang diaocha' ketizu [Task force on 'the investigation of the employment situation of urban enterprise laid-off staff and workers']. "Kunjing yu chulu" [A difficult pass and the way out]. In *Shehuixue yanjiu* [Sociology research] no. 6 (1997) [reprinted in *Xinhua wengao, shehui* [New China manuscript, society] no. 3 (1998)]: 21–28.

Chidambram, Soundarya. "The 'Right' Kind of Welfare in South India's Urban Slums: *Seva* vs. Patronage and the Success of Hindu Nationalist Organizations." *AS* 52, no. 2 (2012): 298–320.

China Institute for Reform and Development. "China Human Development Report 2007/08: Access for all, Basic public services for 1.3 billion people." Beijing: China Translation and Publishing Corporation, 2008.

China Labour Bulletin. "China's Social Security System." October 15, 2019. https://clb.org.hk/content/china's-social-security-system.

China Labour Bulletin. "Workers fight for social security as government cracks down on malpractice." October 8, 2018.

China Power. CSIS. "Is China's Health Care Meeting the Needs of its People." https://chinapower.csis.org/china-health-care-quality, accessed October 2, 2020.

Cho, Mun Young, *The Specter of "The People": Urban Poverty in Northeast China.* Ithaca: Cornell University Press, 2013.

Christiansen, Flemming. "The Legacy of the Mock Dual Economy: Chinese Labour in Transition, 1978–1992." *Economy & Society* 22, no. 4 (1993): 411–36.

Chutian jinbao [Golden News of *Chutian*, referring to Wuhan]. August 3, 2015, from *Dongfangwang* [Eastern network], August 4, 2015; http://hulunbeier.mca.gov.cn /article/jcxx/201507/20150700857842.shtml, accessed August 5, 2015.

Coady, D., M. E. Grosh, and J. Hoddinott. "Targeting of transfers in developing countries: Review of lessons and experience. Volume I. Washington, D.C.: World Bank and International Food Policy Research Institute, 2004.

Cohen, Myron L. "Developmental Process in the Chinese Domestic Group." In *Family and Kinship in Chinese Society*, edited by Maurice Freedman, 21–36. Stanford: Stanford University Press, 1970.

Connolly, P. "The Politics of the Informal Sector: A Critique." In *Beyond Employment: Household, Gender and Subsistence*, edited by N. Redclift and E. Mingione, 55–91. Oxford: Blackwell, 1985.

Cook, Linda J., *Postcommunist Welfare States*. Ithaca: Cornell University Press, 2007.

Cook, Linda J. *The Soviet Social Contract and Why it Failed.* Cambridge, MA: Harvard University Press, 1993.

Cook, S., N. Kabeer, and G, Suwannarat, eds. *Social Protection in Asia.* Delhi; Har-Anand Publications, 2003.

Cook, Sarah. "The Challenge of Informality: Perspectives on China's changing labour market." Paper for IDS Bulletin, 2008.

Cornelius, Wayne A., Ann L. Craig, and Jonathan Fox. "Mexico's National Solidarity Program: An Overview." In *Transforming State-Society Relations in Mexico: the National Solidarity Strategy*, edited by Wayne Cornelius, Ann L. Craig, and Jonathan Fox, 3–26. San Diego, CA: Center for US-Mexico Studies, 1994.

Crepaz, Markus M. L. "Global, Constitutional and Partisan Determinants of Redistribution in Fifteen OECD Countries." *CP* 34, no. 2 (2002): 169–88.

Cumings, Bruce. "The Political Economy of China's Turn Outward." In *China and the World*, edited by Samuel S. Kim, 235–65. Boulder: Westview Press, 1984.

Dang, Chunyan, and Ci Qinying. "Chengshi xin pinkun jiating zinu jiaoyu de shehui paichi." [Social discrimination in education against the children of the new urban poor]. *Qing nian yanjiu* [Youth Research], no. 12 (2008): 15–19.

Deng, Baoshan. "Zhengfu, qiye, he xiagang zhigong zai zaijiuye gongcuozhong de cuoyong" [The role of government, enterprise, and laid-off staff and workers in reemployment work]. *ZGLD* no. 3, 1999: 11–13.

Deng, Quheng, and Bjorn Gustafsson. "A New Episode of Increased Urban Income Inequality in China." In *Rising Inequality in China: Challenges to a Harmonious Society*, edited by Li Shi, Hiroshi Sato, and Terry Sicular, 255–88. Cambridge: Cambridge University Press, 2015.

Dickson, Bruce J. *Red Capitalists in China: The Party, Private Entrepreneurs, and Prospects for Political Change.* NY: Cambridge University Press, 2003.

Dickson, Bruce J. *Wealth into Power; The Communist Party's Embrace of China's Private Sector.* New York: Cambridge University Press, 2008.

Dickson, Bruce, J. Pierre F. Landry, Mingming Shen, and Jie Yan. "Public Goods and Regime Support in Urban China." *CQ*, no. 228 (2016): 859–880.

Dillon, Nara. "China's Welfare State in Comparative Perspective: A Preliminary Assessment after Twenty Years of Reform." Paper presented at the annual meeting of the American Political Science Convention, Seattle, September 3, 2011.

Ding, Langfu. "Cong danwei fuli dao shehui baozhang—ji zhongguo chengshi jumin zuidi shenghuo baozhang zhidu de dansheng" [From unit welfare to social security—recording the emergence of Chinese urban residents' minimum livelihood guarantee system]. *ZGMZ* no. 11 (1999): 6–7.

Dion, Michelle L. *Workers and Welfare: Comparative Institutional Change in Twentieth-Century Mexico.* Pittsburgh: University of Pittsburgh Press, 2010.

Dittmer, Lowell, and Xiaobo Lu. "Personal Politics in the Chinese Danwei under Reform." *AS* 36, no. 3 (March 1996): 246–67.

Dorfman, Mark C., Dewen Wang, Philip O'Keefe, and Jie Cheng. "China's Pension Schemes for Rural and Urban Residents." In *Matching Contributions for Pensions: A Review of International Experience,* edited by Richard Hinz, Robert Holzmann, David Tuesta, and Noriyuki Takayama, 217–41. Washington, D.C.: The World Bank, 2012.

Dou, Ding. "China's Ambitious Path to Poverty Eradication." *Global Asia* 11, no. 2 (Summer 2016): 22–26.

Dresser, Denise. "Bringing the Poor Back In: National Solidarity as a Strategy of Regime Legitimation." In Cornelius, Craig, and Fox, *Transforming State-Society,* 143–65.

Du, Yang, and Albert Park. "Social Assistance Programs and their Effects on Poverty Reduction in Urban China." *Economic Research* 12 (2007): 24–33.

Du, Yang, and Albert Park. "The Effects of Social Assistance on Poverty Reduction." The International Conference on Policy Perspectives on Growth, Economic Structures and Poverty Reduction, Beijing, China, June 2007.

Duckett, Jane. "Debate: Neoliberalism, Authoritarian Politics and Social Policy in China." *Development and Change* 52, no. 2 (2020): 523–39.

Duckett, Jane, and Guohui Wang. "Poverty and Inequality," In *China's Challenges,* edited by Jacques deLisle and Avery Goldstein, 24–41. Philadelphia: University of Pennsylvania Press, 2015.

Duckett, Jane, & Guohui Wang. "Why do Authoritarian Regimes Provide Public Goods? Policy Communities, External Shocks and Ideas in China's Rural Social Policy Making." *Europe-Asia Studies* 69, no. 1 (2017): 92–109.

Duoji, Cairang, et al. *Urban Poverty and Minimum Living Security: Main Report of China Urban Anti-Poverty Forum.* Beijing: Ministry of Civil Affairs, 2002.

Easterlin, Richard A., Fei Wang, and Shun Wang. "Growth and happiness in China, 1990–2015." In *World Happiness Report 2017,* edited by John Helliwell, Richard Layard, and Jeffrey Sachs, 48–83. http://worldhappiness.report/ed/2017, accessed 1 September 2017.

Esping-Andersen, Gosta. *The Three Worlds of Welfare Capitalism.* Princeton: Princeton University Press, 1990.

Evans, Harriet. *Beijing From Below: Stories of Marginal Lives in the Capital's Center.* Durham, NC: Duke University Press, 2020.

Evans, Harriet. "Patriarchal Investments: Expectations of Male Authority and Support in a Poor Beijing." In *Transforming Patriarchy: Chinese Families in the Twenty-first Century*, edited by Goncalo Santos and Stevan Harrell, 182–98. Seattle: University of Washington Press, 2017.

Fang, Cheng, Xiaobo Zhang, and Shenggen Fan. "Emergence of Urban Poverty and Inequality in China: Evidence from a Household Survey." *CER* 13 (2002): 430–43.

Feinerman, James V. "The Past—and Future—of Labor Law in China." in Schoepfle, *Changes in China's Labor*, 119–34.

Feng, Jie, and Zheng Hong. "'Yinfa langchao' shiyuxia chengshi 'dibao' de kunjing ji fazhan lujing" [On the Dilemma and Development of 'Minimum Livelihood Guarantee System' in urban areas in view of the 'grey-hair wave']. *Guangxi shifan xueyuan xuebao* [Journal of Guangxi Teachers Education University] 39, no. 5 (September 2018): 126–34.

Fewsmith, Joseph. *China Since Tiananmen*. New York: Cambridge University Press, 2001.

Fewsmith, Joseph. *Dilemmas of Reform in China: Political Conflict and Economic Debate* Armonk, NY: M.E. Sharpe, 1994.

Fleckenstein, Timo, and Soohyun Christine Lee. "Democratization, post-industrialization, and East Asian welfare capitalism: the politics of welfare state reform in Japan, South Korea, and Taiwan." *Journal of International and Comparative Social Policy* 33, no. 1 (2017): 36–54. https://doi.org/10.1080/21699763.2017.1288158

Flock, Ryane. "Panhandling and the Contestation of Public Space in Guangzhou." *China Perspectives* 2 (2014): 37–44.

Franzoni, Juliana Martinez, and Koen Voorend. "Actors and ideas behind CCTs in Chile, Costa Rica and El Salvador." *GSP,* no. 2 (2011):1–20.

Frazier, Mark W. *Socialist Insecurity: Pensions and the Politics of Uneven Development in China.* Ithaca: Cornell University Press, 2010.

Friedman, Barry L. "Employment and Social Protection Policies in China: Big Reforms and Limited Outcomes," in Schoepfle, *Changes in China's Labor*, 151–66.

Friedman, Eli. *Insurgency Trap: Labor Politics in Postsocialist China.* Ithaca, NY: Cornell University Press, 2014.

Gallagher, Mary E. "China's Older Workers: Between Law and Policy, Between Laid-Off and Unemployed." In *Laid-off Workers in a Workers' State: Unemployment with Chinese Characteristics,* edited by Thomas B. Gold, William J. Hurst, Jaeyoun Won, and Li Qiang, 135–58. NY: Palgrave, 2009.

Gang, Chen, and Xiao Yan. "Demand for voluntary basic medical insurance in urban China: panel evidence from the Urban Resident Basic Medical Insurance Scheme." *Health Policy and Planning* 27, no. 8 (Dec. 2012): 658–668. https://doi.org/10.1093/heapol/czs014.

"Gansusheng renmin zhengfu bangongting. "Guanyu zhuanfa 'Gansusheng chengshi jumin zuidi shenghuo baozhang banfa' de tongzhi.'" [Gansu Province people's government office. Notice on transmitting 'Gansu Province urban residents' minimum livelihood guarantee method']. *Caikuai yanjiu* [Finance and accounting research] no. 5 (2002): 58–60.

Gao, Qin. "Public Assistance and Poverty Reduction: The Case of Shanghai." *GSP* 13, no. 2 (2013): 193–215.

Gao, Qin. "The Social Benefit System in Urban China: Reforms and Trends from 1988 to 2002." *Journal of East Asian Studies,* no. 6 (2006): 31–67.

Gao, Qin. *Welfare, Work and Poverty: China's Social Assistance 20 Years After.* NY: Oxford University Press, 2017.

Gao, Qin, and Carl Riskin. "Generosity and participation: Variations in Urban China's Minimum Livelihood Guarantee Policy." In *Law and Economics with Chinese Characteristics*, edited by David Kennedy, and Joseph E. Stiglitz, 393–422. NY: Oxford University Press, 2013.

Gao, Qin, Shiyou Wu, and Fuhua Zhai. "Welfare Participation and Times Use in China." *Social Indicators Research* no. 124 (2015), 863–887.

Gao, Qin, Sui Yang, Yalu Zhang, and Shi Li. "The Divided Chinese Welfare System: Do Health and Education Change the Picture?" *Social Policy & Society* 17, no. 2 (2018): 227–44.

Gao, Qin, Sui Yang, and Fuhua Zhai. "Social Policy and Income Inequality during the Hu-Wen Era: A Progressive Legacy?" *CQ* no. 237 (March 2019): 82–107.

Gao, Qin, Sui Yang, Yalu Zhang, and Shi Li. "Three Worlds of the Chinese Welfare State: Do Health and Education Change the Picture?" Paper Prepared for the IARIW 33rd General Conference, Rotterdam, The Netherlands, August 24–30, 2014.

Gao, Qin, Sui Yang, and Shi Li. "Welfare, targeting, and anti-poverty effectiveness: The case of Urban China." *The Quarterly Review of Economics and Finance* 56 (2015): 30–42.

Gao, Qin, Jiyoung Yoo, Sooko-Mee Yang, and Fuhua Zhai. "Welfare Residualism: a Comparative Study of the Basic Livelihood Security Systems in China and South Korea." *IJSW no.* 20 (2011): 1113–24.

Gao, Qin, Fuhua Zhai, Sui Yang, and Shi Li. "Does Welfare Enable Family Expenditures on Human Capital? Evidence from China." *World Development* 64 (2014): 219–31.

Gao, Qin, and Fuhua Zhai. "Public Assistance, Economic Prospect, and Happiness in Urban China." *Social Indicators Research* 132, no. 1 (2017); 451–73.

Garnaut, Ross, Ligang Song, and Yang Yao. "The Impact and Significance of State-owned Enterprise Restructuring in China." *CJ,* no. 55 (January 2006): 35–62.

Garrett, Geoffrey. "Globalization and government spending around the world." *Studies in Comparative International Development* 35, no. 4 (2001): 3–29.

Garrett, Geoffrey, and Peter Lange. "Political responses to interdependence: what's 'left' for the left?" *International Organization* 5, no. 4 (1991): 539–64.

Gilbert, Alan. "Neoliberalism and the Urban Poor: A View from Latin America." In *Marginalization in Urban China: Comparative Perspectives*, edited by Fulong Wu, and Chris Webster, 29–56. Houndmills, Basingstoke: Palgrave/Macmillan, 2010.

Giles, J., F. Cai, and A. Park. "How has economic restructuring affected China's urban workers?" Unpublished paper, 2003. http://www.msu.edu/~gilesj/gilesparkcai.pdf.

Giles, John, Albert Park, and Feng Cai. "Reemployment of dislocated workers in urban China: the roles of information and incentives." *Journal of Comparative Economics* 34, no. 3 (2006): 582–607.

Giles, John, Albert Park, Fang Cai, and Yang Du. "Weathering a Storm: Survey-Based Perspectives on Employment in China in the Aftermath of the Global Financial Crisis." Washington, D.C., The World Bank, Development Research Group, Human Development and Public Services Team, March 2012.

Gladstone, Rick. "Brazil to Keep Allowances for the Poor." *NYT*, September 19, 2015.

Goel, Vindu, and Hari Kumar. "India Wants to Give a Half-Billion People Free Health Care." *NYT*, February 2, 2018, A6.

Gong, Li. *Kuashiji nanti: jiuye yu shehui baozhang* [A difficult issue straddling the century: employment and social security]. Kunming: Yunnan renmin chubanshe [Yunnan people's publishing], 2000.

Greenhalgh, Susan. *Cultivating Global Citizens: Population in the Rise of China.* Cambridge: Harvard University Press, 2010.

Guan, Xinping. "Poverty and anti-poverty measures in China." *CJSW* 7, no. 3 (2014): 270–87.

Guo, Jun. "Guoyou qiye xiagang yu fenliu you he butong?" [What's the difference between laid-off and diverted workers in state firms?]. *Zhongguo gongyun* [Chinese workers' movement] 3 (1999), 32.

Guojia jiwei hongguan jingji yanjiuyuan ketizu [State Planning Commission, Macroeconomic Research Institute Task Force]. "Jianli shehui baohu tixi shi wo guo shehui wending de guanjian" [Establishing a social protection system is the key to our country's social stability]. *NBCY* 511 (May 5, 2000), 10–11.

Guojia tongjiju, shehui tongjisi, bian [National Bureau of Statistics, Office of Social Statistics, ed.]. *1990 Zhongguo shehui tongji ziliao* [1990 Chinese social statistics materials]. Beijing: Zhongguo tongji chubanshe [China Statistics Press], 1990.

Gustafsson, Bjorn A., and Deng Quheng. "Di Bao Receipt and Its Importance for Combating Poverty in Urban China." *Poverty & Public Policy* 3, no. 1 (2011): 1–32.

Gustafsson, Bjorn A., and Quheng Deng. "Social Assistance Receipt and its Importance for Combating Poverty in Urban China." Bonn: Institute for the Study of Labor, Discussion paper Series, No. 2758, 2007.

Gustafsson, Bjorn, and Gang Shuge. "A comparison of social assistance in China and Sweden." *CJSW* 6, no. 3 (2013): 292–310.

Gustafsson, Bjorn, and Sai Ding. "Unequal Growth: Long-Term Trends in Household Incomes and Poverty in Urban China." In *Changing Trends in China's Inequality: Evidence, Analysis, and Prospects,* edited by Terry Sicular, Shi Li, Ximing Yue, and Hiroshi Sato, 241–65. NY: Oxford University Press, 2020.

Haggard, Stephan, and Robert R. Kaufman. *Development, Democracy, and Welfare States: Latin America, East Asia, and Eastern Europe.* Princeton: Princeton University Press, 2008.

Hall, Peter A. "Policy Paradigms, Social Learning and the State: The Case of Economic Policy-Making in Britain." *CP* 25, no. 3 (1993): 275–96.

Hall, Peter A. "Social Policy-Making for the Long Term," *PS* (April 2015): 289–91.

Hammond, Daniel Robert. "Explaining Policy Making in the People's Republic of China: The Case of the Urban Resident Minimum Livelihood Guarantee System, 1992–2003." Ph. D. dissertation, Department of Politics, University of Glasgow, 2010.

Hammond, Daniel R. *Politics and Policy in China's Social Assistance Reform: Providing for the Poor?* Edinburgh: Edinburgh University Press, 2019.

Hammond, Daniel. "Social Assistance in China, 1993–2002: Institutions, feedback, and policy actors in the Chinese policy process." *Asian Politics & Policy* 3, no. 1 (2011): 69–93.

Han, Keqing, et al, eds. *Chengshi zuidi shenghuo baozhang zhidu yanjiu* [Study of China's Urban Minimum Livelihood Guarantee System]. Beijing: Zhongguo shehui kexue chubanshe [Chinese Social Sciences Publishing Co.], 2015.

Han, Keqing, ed. *Zhongguo chengshi dibao fangtanlu* [Interviews with Minimum Livelihood Guarantee Recipients in Urban China]. Ji'nan: Shandong renmin chubanshe [Shandong people's publishing company], 2012.

Han Keqing, and Guo Yu. "Fuli yilan" shi fu cunzai?—Zhongguo chengshi dibao zhidu de yige shizheng yanjiu" [Does "welfare reliance" exist or not?—concrete evidence on China's urban minimum livelihood system]. *Shehuixue yanjiu* [Sociological studies] no. 2 (2012): 162–63.

Hanlon, Joseph, Armando Barrientos, and David Hulme. *Just Give Money to the Poor: The Development Revolution from the Global South.* Sterling, VA: Kumarian Press, 2010.

Harris, Gardiner. "With Deposits, India Aims to Keep Money for the Poor from Others' Pockets." *NYT,* January 6, 2013.

Hausman, Leonard J., and Barry J. Friedman. "Employment Creation: New and Old Methods." Unpublished ms. N.p., n.d. [1996 or 1997].

He, Shenjing, Fulong Wu, Chris Webster, and Yuting Liu. "Poverty Concentration and Determinants in China's Urban Low-income Neighbourhoods and Social Groups." *IJURR* no. 34, 2 (2010): 328–49.

Heberer, Thomas. "Relegitimation through New Patterns of Social Security." *CR* 9, no. 2 (Fall 2009): 99–128.

Heilmann, Sebastian, and Elizabeth J. Perry, eds. *Mao's Invisible hand: The Political Foundations of Adaptive Governance in China.* Cambridge, MA: Harvard University Asia Center, 2011.

Hemerijck, Anton. *Changing Welfare States.* Oxford, UK: Oxford University Press, 2012.

Hemerijck, Anton, and Martin Schludi. "Sequences of Policy Failures and Effective Policy Responses." In *Welfare and Work in the Open Economy: From Vulnerability to Competitiveness.* Volume 1. Edited by Fritz W. Scharpf, and Vivien A. Schmidt, 125–228. Oxford: Oxford University Press, 2ooo.

Hernandez, Javier C. "'We Couldn't Be Poorer': Pandemic Hinders China's Antipoverty Efforts." *NYT,* October 26, 2020.

Hicks, Alexander. *Social Democracy and Welfare Capitalism: A Century of Income Security Politics.* Ithaca, NY: Cornell University Press, 1999.

Hill, Michael, and Alan Walker. "What were the lasting effects of Thatcher's legacy for social security? The burial of Beveridge?" In *The Legacy of Thatcherism: Assessing and Exploring Thatcherite Social and Economic Policies,* edited by Stephen Farrall, and Colin Hay, 77–107. Oxford: Oxford University Press for The British Academy, 2014.

Holliday, I. P., and P. Wilding. "Welfare Capitalism in the Tiger Economies of East and Southeast Asia. In *Welfare Capitalism in East Asia,* edited by I. P. Holliday, and P. Wilding, 1–17. London: Palgrave/MacMillan, 2003.

Holzer, Harry J. "Workforce Development as an Antipoverty Strategy: What Do We Know? What Should We Do?" In Cancian and Danziger, *Changing Poverty*, 301–29.

Hong, Dayong. "Chengshi jumin zuidi shenghuo baozhang zhidu de zuixin jinzhan" [Recent progress in the minimum livelihood system]. In Hong Dayong, *Zhongguo de chengshi pinkun yu zuidi shenghuo baozhang* [Poverty and the Minimum Livelihood Standard Assistance Policy in Urban China]. Disan zhang [Chapter Three]. Beijing: Zhongguo shehui kexueyuan, shehui zhengce zhongxin [Social Policy Research Center, Chinese Academy of Social Sciences], 2005.

Hong, D. Y. *China's social assistance during the period of transition.* Shenyang: Liaoning Educational Press, 2004. [in Chinese]

Hong, Jun, SungYoung, Sook Kim, NaYoun Lee, and Ji Woong Ha. "Understanding Social Welfare in South Korea." In *Social Welfare in East Asia and the Pacific*, edited by Sharlene B. C. L. Furuto, 41–66. NY: Columbia University Press, 2013.

Hong, Zhaohui. "Lun shehui quanli de 'pinkun'—Zhongguo chengshi pinkun wenti de genyuan yu zhili lujing" ["On the 'poverty' of social rights: the roots and path of managing the problem of urban poverty in China"]. *Xiandai Zhongguo yanjiu* [*Modern China Studies*] 79, no. 4 (2002): 9–10.

Hsing, You-tien. *The Great Urban Transformation: Politics of Land and Property in China*. Oxford: Oxford University Press, 2010.

Hu, Angang. "China's Present Economic Situation and its Macro-Economic Policies." RAND-CHINA REFORMFORUM CONFERENCE, N. p. November 29–30, 2001.

Hu, Angang. "Employment and Development: China's Employment Problem and Employment Strategy." National Conditions Report, no. 6 April 30, 1998.

Hu, Angang. *Jingmao daokan* [Economic and trade guide], December 30, 1999. In *SWB*, FE/3750, G/10, January 29, 2000.

Hu, Angang. "Shishi jiuye youxian zhanlue, wei renmin tigong gengduode gongzuo gangwei" [Realize the employment preferential strategy and supply more jobs for people]. Zhongguo kexueyuan, Qinghua daxue, guoqing yanjiu zhongxin [Chinese Academy of Science and Tsinghua University National Conditions Research Centre], Report no. 78. Speech delivered at a specialists' forum directed by State Planning Commission Vice-Chairman Wang Chunzheng. Beijing, September 29, 2000.

Hu, Xinhua. "Woguo qiye zhigong duiwu de yuce bianhua ji baozhang duice" [Expected changes and security policies for the ranks of our enterprise staff and workers]. Unpublished ms., 2001.

Huang, Youqin. "Low-income Housing in Chinese Cities: Policies and Practices." *CQ*, no.212 (2012): 941–64.

Hubeisheng zonggonghui shenghuo baozhangbu [Hubei province general trade union livelihood guarantee department]. "Yunyong zhengce he falu shoujian, quanli tuijin zaijiuye gongcheng xiang zongshen fazhan" [Utilize policy and legal methods, fully promote the reemployment project to develop in depth]. *Lilun yuekan* [Theory monthly] 2 (1998): 18–20.

Huber, Evelyne, and John D. Stephens. *Development and Crisis of the Welfare State: Parties and Policies in Global Markets.* Chicago: University of Chicago Press, 2001.

Hung, Eva P. W., and Stephen W. K. Chiu. "The Lost Generation: Life Course Dynamics and *Xiagang* in China." *MC* 29, no. 2 (2003): 204–36.

Hung, Ho-fung. *Protest with Chinese Characteristics: Demonstrations, Riots, and Petitions in the Mid-Qing Dynasty.* NY: Columbia University Press, 2011.

Hunter, Wendy. Review of Ana Lorena De La O. *Crafting Policies to End Poverty in Latin America: The Quiet Transformation.* NY: Cambridge University Press, 2015. *Perspectives on Politics* 13, no. 4 (2015): 1178–79.

Hurst, William J. *The Chinese Worker After Socialism.* NY: Cambridge University Press, 2009.

Hurst, William, and Kevin O'Brien. "China's Contentious Pensioners." *CQ* no. 170 (2002): 345–60.

Hussain, Athar. "Urban Poverty in China: Measurement, Patterns and Policies." Ms. Geneva: International Labour Office, January 2003.

Imai, Hiroshi. Special Report: "China's Growing Unemployment Problem." *Pacific Business and Industries RIM* (Tokyo) II, no. 6 (2002).

Ishikawa, Shigeru. "Sino-Japanese Economic Cooperation." *CQ*, no. 109 (1987): 1–21.

Ji, Guangxu, and Youqin Huang. "Mobile Phone Culture among the Information Have-Less: A Case Study of Laid-Off Workers in Shenyang City, China." In *The Emergence of a New Urban China: Insiders' Perspectives*, edited by Zai Liang, Steven Messner, Cheng Chen, and Youqin Huang, 141–61. Plymouth, UK: Lexington Books, 2012.

Jiang, Zemin, "Political report." *SWB* FE/3023 (September 13, 1997), S1/1-S1/10.

Jiang, Zemin, "Report at 16th Party Congress," November 8, 2002, http://english .peopledaily.com.cn/200211/18/eng20021118_106983.shtml, and https://www .fmprc.gov.cn/mfa_eng/topics_665678/3698_665962/t18872.shtml (accessed January 2, 2020).

Jiao, Yazhuan, and He Huijiang, "Chengshi dishou qunti jiuye zhengce de lunli xuance" [The ethical choice of urban low-income masses' employment policy]. *Zhengzhou hankong gongye guanli xueyuan xuebao* [Journal of Zhengzhou Institute of the Management of the Aeronautical Industry] 32, no. 2 (2014): 101–15.

Jingji ribao [Economic daily]*,* May 18, 1998, 1. In *Gongyun cankao ziliao* [Workers' movement reference materials], March 1998, 9, http://data.people.com.cn/rmrb/19 980518/1/0ac9229cca77440781ef920...,accessed January 30, 2020.

Johnson, Chalmers. *MITI and the Japanese Miracle.* Stanford: Stanford University Press, 1982.

Josephs, Hilary K. "Labor Law Reflects New Realities." *China Rights Forum* (Fall 1996): 24–27.

Junior, Sergio Simoni. "How Bolsa Familia really impacts Brazilian elections." *The Brazilian Report*, October 26, 2018.

Kasza, Gregory J. *One World of Welfare: Japan in Comparative Perspective.* Ithaca, NY: Cornell University Press, 2006.

Kath, Elizabeth. *Social Relations and* the *Cuban Health Miracle.* Milton Park, Abingdon: Routledge Press, 2017.

Katz, Michael B. *The Undeserving Poor: America's Enduring Confrontation with Poverty.* 2nd edition. NY: Oxford University Press, 2013.

Kaufman, Robert R., and Alex Segura-Ubiergo. "Globalization, Domestic Politics, and Social Spending in Latin America: A Time-Series Cross-Section Analysis, 1973–1997." *World Politics* 53 (2001), 553–87.

Kernen, Antoine. "Surviving Reform in Shenyang—New Poverty in Pioneer City." *China Rights Forum* (Summer 1997): 8–11.

Kim, Taekyoon, Huck-Ju Kwon, Jooha Lee, and Ilcheong Yi. "'Mixed Governance' and Welfare in South Korea." *Journal of Democracy* 22, no. 3 (July 2011): 120–34.

Knight, John, and Shi Li. "Unemployment duration and earnings of re-employed workers in urban China." *CER* 17 (2006): 103–119.

Kohli, Atul. *Poverty amid Plenty in the New India.* NY: Cambridge University Press, 2012.

Korzec, Michael. "Contract Labor, the 'Right to Work' and New Labor Laws in the People's Republic of China." *Comparative Economic Studies* 30, no. 2 (1988): 117–49.

Lambert, Susan, and Julia Henly. "Double Jeopardy: The Misfit between Welfare-to-Work Requirements and Job Realities." In *Work and the Welfare State: Street-Level Organizations and Workfare Politics*, edited by Evelyn Z. Brodkin and Gregory Marston, 69–84. Washington, D.C.: Georgetown University Press, 2013.

Lan, Jian. "Zhongguo shehui jiuzhu zhengce de yanjin, tuchu wenti ji qi fanpinkun tupo luxiang" [The evolution of China's social assistance policy, outstanding problems and the path toward breakthrough in fighting poverty]. *Yunnan shehui kexue* [Yunnan social science] no. 4 (2018): 32–38.

Lardy, Nicholas R. *China in the World Economy.* Washington, D.C., Institute for International Economics, 1994 .

Lardy, Nicholas R. *Foreign Trade and Economic Reform in China, 1978*–1990. NY: Cambridge University Press, 1992.

Lawrence, Susan V. "Three Cheers for the Party." *Far Eastern Economic Review*, October 26, 2000, 32.

Lee, Ching Kwan. "The Labor Politics of Market Socialism: Collective Inaction and Class Experiences Among State Workers in Guangzhou." *MC* 24, 1 (January 1998): 3–33.

Lee, Ching Kwan. "Pathways of Labor Insurgency." In *Chinese Society: Change, Conflict and Resistance*, edited by Elizabeth J. Perry and Mark Selden, 41–61. New York: Routledge, 2000.

Lee, Ching Kwan. "Three Patterns of Working-Class Transitions in China." In *Chinese Politics: Moving Frontiers*, edited by Francoise Mengin and Jean-Louis Rocca, 62–91. New York: Palgrave, 2002.

Lee, Ching Kwan, and Guobin Yang, eds. *Re-envisioning the Chinese Revolution: Politics and Poetics of Collective Memories in Reform China.* Washington, D.C.: The Woodrow Wilson Center Press and Stanford: Stanford University Press, 2007.

Lee, Ming-kwan. "The Decline of Status in China's Transition from Socialism." *Hong Kong Journal of Sociology* 1 (2000): 53–82.

Lee, Yih-Jiunn, and Yeun-wen Ku. "East Asian Welfare Regimes: Testing the Hypothesis of the Developmental Welfare State." *Social Policy and Administration* 41, no. 2 (2007), 197–212.

Lei, Jiek and Chak Kwan Chan. "Does China's public assistance scheme create welfare dependency? An assessment of the welfare of the urban Minimum Living Standard Guarantee." *International Social Work* 62, no. 2 (2019): 487–501. https://doi.org/10.1177/0020872817731142.

Lei, Peng. "Zhigong peixun yu jiuye cujin—chengshi fupin de zhongyao lujing" [Staff and workers' training and the promotion of reemployment—the important path in urban poverty]. *Lingdao neican (LDNC)* [Leadership internal reference] no. 11 (1998): 30–31.

Leisering, Lutz. "Extending Social Security to the Excluded." *GSP* 9, no. 2 (2009): 246–72.

Leng, Sidney. "After coronavirus pandemic, Chinese students grapple with first economic downturn of their lives." *SCMP,* May 14, 2020.

Leng, Sidney. "Coronavirus: China faces historic test as pandemic stokes fears of looming unemployment crisis." *SCMP*, May 11, 2020.

Leung, Joe. "The Development of Social Assistance in Urban China." Paper presented at Provincial China Workshop 2008, Nankai University, Tianjin (PRC), October 27–30, 2008.

Leung, Joe C. B. "The emergence of social assistance in China." *IJSW* 15 (2006): 88–98.

Leung, Joe C. B., & Yuebin Xu. *China's Social Welfare.* Cambridge, UK: Polity, 2015.

Li, Bingqin. "Social Pension Unification in an Urbanising China: Paths and Constraints." *Public Administration and Development* 34 (2014): 281–93.

Li, Chunyan, and Ding Jianding. "Wuhanshi dibao guanlizhong cunzai de wenti yu gaijin duice fenxi—yi Wuchangqu weili" [Existing problems and analysis of measures for improvement in Wuhan's *dibao* management—Wuchang district as an example]. *Changjiang luntan* [Yangtze Forum] 1, no. 76 (2006): 25–29.

Li, Keqiang. "Report on the Work of the Government." Delivered at the Third Session of the 12th National People's Congress on March 5, 2015, 2–6. http://blogs.wsj.com/chinarealtime/2015/03/05/china-npc-2015-the-reports, accessed March 6, 2015.

Li, Keqiang. "Report on the Work of the Government." Delivered at the Fourth Session of the 12th National People's Congress of the People's Republic of China, March 5, 2016. http://en.people.cn/n3/2016/0305/c90000-9025486-2.html.

Li, Peilin. "Quanmian jianshe xiaokang shehui de sige guanjian wenti" [Four key issues in completely establishing a well- off society], *Lingdao canyue* [Leadership internal reference] no. 10 (2003), (April 5), 10.

Li, Tao. "Jiaqiang fuwu zhongxin guanli, cujin xiagang zhigong zaijiuye." [Strengthen service center management, promote laid-off staff and workers' reemployment]. *Sheke luntan* [Social science forum] no. 8 (2014): 165–66.

Li Zhengang. "2018 nian chengxiang shehui jiuzhu fazhan zhuangkuang fenxi baogao' [2018 report on analysis of the development of urban and rural social assistance]. In *2019 nian Zhongguo shehui xingshi fenxi yu yuce* [2019 Analysis and prediction of Chinese society], eds. Li Peilin, Chen Guangjin, and Zhang Yi, 77–90. (Beijing: shehui kexue wenxuan chubanshe [social science documents publishing company], 77–90.

Li, Peng. Speech. *SWB*, FE/3168, March 6, 1998, from Xinhua, March 5, 1998.

Li, Yuan. "China's Street Vendor Push Ignites a Debate: How Rich is It?" *NYT,* June 11, 2020.

Li, Yu-wai, Bo Miao, and Graeme Lang. "The Local Environmental State in China: A Study of County-level Cities in Suzhou." *CQ,* no. 205 (2011): 115–132.

Li, Zhu, Chen Li, and Wu Wei. "Chengshi dibao qunti shengcun zhuangtai diaocha baogao—ji yu Jiangsusheng de wenjuan diaocha" [Report on an investigation of the livelihood situation of the urban *dibao* group—based on a questionnaire investigation in Jiangsu province]. 4th International Conference on Chinese Society and China Studies, Nanjing University, Nanjing, October 27–28, 2012.

Liang, Fengfang. "Guanyu xiagang zhigong zaijiuye shuishou zhengce de jidian xikao" [Several points of deliberations on tax collection policy on laid-off staff and workers' reemployment]. *Shidai jinrong* [Times finance] no. 2 (2014): 166.

Lieberthal, Kenneth. *Governing China: From Revolution Through Reform.* 2nd edition. NY: W.W. Norton & Co., 2004.

Lim, Lin Lean, and Gyorgy Sziraczki. "Employment, Social Security, and Enterprise Reforms in China." In *Changes in China's Labor Market: Implications for the Future*, edited by Gregory K. Schoepfle, 45–87. (Washington, D.C.: U.S. Department of Labor, Bureau of International Labor Affairs, 1996.

Lin, Kevin. "Recomposing Chinese Migrant and State-Sector Workers." In *Chinese Workers in Comparative Perspective*, edited by Anita Chan, 69–84. Ithaca, NY: Cornell University Press, 2015.

Lipkin, Zwia. *Useless to the State: "Social Problems" and Social Engineering in Nationalist Nanjing.* Stanford: Stanford University Press, 2006.

Liu, Binyan. "The Working Class Speaks Out." *China Focus* 5, no. 8 (August 1997), 1.

Liu, Hong, and Zhong Zhao. "Impact of China's Urban Resident Basic Medical Insurance on Health Care Utilization and Expenditure." IZA DP No. 6768. Forschungsinstitut zur Zukunft der Arbeit [Institute for the Study of Labor], Bonn, Germany, July 2012.

Liu, Jieyu, "Life Goes On: Redundant Women Workers in Nanjing." In *China's Changing Welfare Mix*, edited by Beatriz Carrillo and Jane Duckett, 82–103. London: Routledge, 2011.

Liu, Jing, and Deng Jingyuan. "Gaishan woguo shiye xianzhuang de shixian fangshi" [A real method to improve our country's unemployment situation]. *Juece cankao* [Policy reference] 11 (2005): 61–62.

Liu, Tao. "Epistemological globalization and the shaping of social policy in China." *Journal of Chinese Governance*, 3, no. 4 (2018): 461–76.

Liu, Tao, and Li Sun. "Urban Social Assistance in China: Transnational Diffusion and National Interpretation." *Journal of Current Chinese Affairs* 45, no. 2 (2016): 29–51. https://doi.org.10.1177/186810261604500202, accessed November 11, 2020.

Liu, Wenhai. "Guanyu wanshan chengzhen jumin 'dibao' zhidu de jianyi" [Suggestions on perfecting the urban residents' 'minimum income' system]. *Canyue* [Consultations], no. 37 (September 26, 2003): 20–25.

Liu, Yunying. "Zhongguo yanglao baoxian tizhi de xianzhuang he nanti" [China's pension insurance system's present condition and difficult issues]. *Caixinwang* [Financial news network], May 16, 2016. http://opinion.caixin.com/2016-05-16/100943804.html, accessed December 6, 2017.

Liu, Yuting, Fulong Wu, & Shenjing He. "The Making of the New Urban Poor in Transitional China: Market Versus Institutionally Based Exclusion." *Urban Geography* 2, no. 8 (2008): 811–34.

London, Jonathan Daniel. *Welfare and Inequality in Marketizing East Asia.* London: Palgrave/Macmillan, 2018.

Looney, Kristen E. *Mobilizing for Development: the Modernization of Rural East Asia.* Ithaca, NY: Cornell University Press, 2020.

Loubere, Nicholas. "Laying off Responsibility: Microcredit, Entrepreneurship, and China's Industrial Retrenchment." *Made in China* 2 (2016): 20–23.

Lu, Y. "Shishi zuidi shenghuo baozhang zhidu de sikao" [Reflections on implementing the minimum livelihood guarantee system]. ZGMZ 4 (1998), 20.

Lu, Xueyi. *Dangdai zhongguo shehui jieceng yanjiu bao* [A research report on China's current social structure]. Beijng: shehui kexue wenxian chubanshe [Social science documents publisher], 2002.

Luo, Wenjian, and Wang Wen. "Chengshi dibao de jianpin xiaoying fenxi—ji yu zhongguo jiating zhuicong diaocha (CFPS) de shizheng yanjiu" [Analysis of the urban dibao's effect in reducing poverty—an empirical study based on China Family Panel Survey (CFPS)]. *Jiangsu caijing daxue xuebao* [Journal of Jiangsu University of Finance and Economics] no. 5 (2018): 62–70.

Lustig, Nora. "Solidarity as a Strategy of Poverty Alleviation." In *Transforming State-Society,* edited by Cornelius, Craig, and Fox, 79–96.

Ma, Hong. *Jingji jiegou yu jingji guanli* [Economic structure and economic management]. Beijing: Renmin chubanshe [People's publishing company], 1982.

Ma, Hong, and Sun Shangqing, eds. *Zhongguo jingji jiegou wenti yanjiu* [Investigations into problems of China's economic structure]. Beijing: Renmin chubanshe [People's publishing company], n.d.

Magnus, George. "Opinion: Beijing's delicate balancing act relies on job creation." *Financial Times*, January 2, 2020.

Mao, Jiansheng. "Liguo limin de ningjuli gongcheng—Fan Baojun fubuzhang jiu chengshi jumin zuidi shenghuo baozhang zhidu jianshe hui benkan jizhe wen" [A cohesive project benefiting the nation and the people—Vice Minister Fan Baojun answers this journal's reporter's questions about the minimum livelihood guarantee system's construction], *ZGMZ* no. 4 (1997): 4–6.

Mares, Isabela, and Matthew E. Carnes. "Social Policy in Developing Countries." *Annual Review of Political Science* 12 (2009): 93–113.

Meng, Jiawu, and Tan Zhilin. "Wuhan chengshi zuidi shenghuo baozhang zhidu de sige tedian" [Four characteristics of Wuhan city's minimum livelihood guarantee system]. *ZGMZ* no. 7 (1996): 19.

Meng, Xin, Robert Gregory, and Youjuan Wang. "Inequality and Growth in Urban China, 1986–2000." IZA Discussion paper series, no. 1452.

Miller, Tom. "Case Studies: I. Wuhan." *China Economic Quarterly* (March 2009): 32–35.

Ministry of Finance. "Report on the Execution of the Central and Local Budgets for 2018 and on the Draft Central and Local Budgets for 2019. Second Session of the 13th National People's Congress of the People's Republic of China, March 5, 2019.

Ministry of Human Resources and Social Security of the People's Republic of China. "Interpretation of the Policy on 'Guiding Opinions on Establishing the Basic Pension Insurance for Urban and Rural Residents and the Basic Adjustment Mechanism of Basic Pensions.'" March 29, 2019. http://www.mohrss.gov.cn/SYrlzyhshbzb/dongtaixinwen/buneiyaowen/201803/t20180329_291013.html, accessed January 2019.

Minzhengbu [Ministry of Civil Affairs]. "Minzhengbu guanyu jinyibu jiaqiang chengshi dibao duixiang rending gongzuo de tongzhi" [Ministry of Civil Affairs Circular on progressively strengthening the work of identifying urban minimum livelihood guarantee targets]. Minzhengbu tongzhi 140 hao [Ministry of Civil Affairs Missive no. 140], 2010. http://www.mca.gov.cn/article/zwgk/fvfg/zdshbz/201008/20100800096408.shtml .

Minzner, Carl. *End of an Era: How China's Authoritarian Revival is Undermining its Rise.* NY: Oxford University Press, 2018.

Mitchell, Don. "The Annihilation of Space by Law: the Roots and Implications of Anti-Homeless Laws in the United States." *Antipode* 29, no. 3 (1997): 303–35.

Miura, Mari. *Welfare through Work: Conservative Ideas, Partisan Dynamics, and Social Protection in Japan.* Ithaca: Cornell University Press, 2012.

Mo, Rong. "*Dui guoyou qiye zhigong xiagang yu zaijiuye wenti de renshi*" [Thoughts about state enterprises' staff and workers' layoffs and the question of reemployment]. *ZGLD* 2 (1998): 11–14.

Mo, Rong. "Jiaru WTO yu woguo de jiuye" [Entering the WTO and our country's employment]. *LDBZTX* no. 4 (2000): 18–21.

Mo, Rong. "Jiuye: xin shiji mianlin de tiaozhan yu juece" [Employment: the challenge and decision that the new century is facing]. In *2001 nian: Zhongguo shehui xingshi fenxi yu yuce* [2001: Analysis and forecast of China's social situation], edited by Li Peilin, Huang Ping, and Lu Jianhua, 217–33. Beijing: Shehui kexue wenxuan chubanshe [Social science documents publisher], 2001.

Mo, Rong. "Jiuye: zai tiaozhanzhong guanzhu kunnan qunti" [Employment: Under challenge, pay close attention to the masses in difficulty]. In *Shehui lanpishu: 2003 nian: Zhongguo shehui xingshi fenxi yu yuce* [Social blue book: 2003 Analysis and predictions of China's social situation], edited by Ru Xin, Lu Xueyi, and Li Peilin, 35–44. Beijing: shehui kexue wenxian chubanshe [social science documents company], 2003.

Mo, Rong, Zhao Liwei, and Chen Lan. "Guoji jinrong weijixia de jiuye xingshi he zhengce" [The employment situation and relevant policies under international financial crisis]. In *2010 nian: Zhongguo shehui xingshi fenxi yu yuce* [2010: Chinese society analysis and forecast], edited by Ru Xin, Lu Xueyi, and Li Peilin, 31–48. Beijing: shehui kexue wenxian chubanshe [Social Sciences Academic Press], 2010.

Muller, Armin. "Functional Integration of China's Social Protection: Recent and Long-term Trends of Institutional Change in Health and Pension Insurance." *AS* 57, no. 6 (2017): 1110–34.

N.a. "1998 nian qiye xiagang zhigong jiben qingkuang" [The basic situation of the laid-off enterprise staff and workers in 1998]. *LDBZTX* no. 1 (1999): 10–11.

N.a. "1998–1999 laodong baozhang tongji baogao" [Report on no. 1998–1999 labor insurance statistics]. *LDBZTX* no. 3 (2000): 35–36.

N.a. "Chaguan: Heroic, expendable." *The Economist*, November 30, 2019, 41.

N.a., "China's Resident Disposable Income Rises 6.5% in 2018." *China Daily*, January 21, 2019. https://www.chinadaily.com.cn/a/201901/21/WS5c4569fla3106c65c34e5a1f.html, accessed November 5, 2021.

N.a. "China's subsistence allowance system benefits urban, rural poor equally." http://english.people.com.con/90001/90776/6344770.html, accessed January 24, 2008.

N.a. "China's urban population 2010." https://www.google.com/search?q=china's+urban+population+2010&sxsrf=ACYBGNSYxCJd8zB9s1WBWaICiuNaWUlGhg:1577939887121&tbm=isch&source=iu&ictx=1&fir=4fGPwus92zdfOM%253A%252Cpqi1wgQexzDRRM%252C_&vet=1&usg=AI4-kRRwvt4A7GlLHdvpn5ssNUxoYl19g&sa=X&ved=2ahUKEwjlpMuTjOTmAhXYvp4KHZjcD0YQ9QEwAHoECAYQAw&biw=1536&bih=601#imgrc=Ys3a4o_fsLCGQM:&vet=1, accessed January 1, 2020.

N.a. "Deng Xiaoping: Rang yibufenren xian fuqilai." [Deng Xiaoping: First allow one group of people to get rich]. *Zhongguo gongchandang xinwenwang* [News of the Communist Party of China]. http://cpc.people.com.cn/GB/34136/2569304.html, accessed June 25, 2016.

N.a. "Duodi shixian chengxiang dibao biaozhun binggui, Nanjing biaozhun chao 700 yuan" [Many places are implementing a merger of their urban and rural *dibao* norms, Nanjing's norm has surpassed 700 yuan]. http://www.chinanews.com/gn/2015/07-8/7390743.shtml, accessed July 10, 2015.

N.a. "Guanyu 2016 niandu jumin jiben yiliao baoxian chouzi biaozhun tiaozheng" [On adjusting the norm for the 2016 residents' basic medical insurance premium]. http://www.cpic.com.cn/c/2018-04-19/1425447.shtml, accessed December 9, 2019.

N.a. "Jianli zuidi shenghuo baozhang zhidu de jige wenti" [Several issues in establishing the minimum livelihood guarantee system]. *ZGMZ* no. 9 (1996): 14.

N.a. "Ji'nan guiding mai diannao jingchang yong shoujizhe buneng xiangshou dibao" [Ji'nan regulates that those who bought a computer or often use a cell phone can't enjoy the *dibao*]. Zhongguowang, October 9, 2006. http: china.com.cn, accessed August 17, 2007.

N.a. Laodong baozhangbu buzhang Zeng Silin zai quanguo laodong baozhang tingjuzhang zuotanhuishang de jianghua [Minister of Labor and Social Security Zeng Silin's speech at the national labor and social security bureau and office heads' forum]. "Jiakuai tuijin zaijiuye gongzuo, quanmian wancheng jinnian gexiang laodong baozhang gongzuo renwu" [Speed up the work of promoting reemployment work, fully complete this year's various tasks in labor and social security work]. *LDBZTX* no. 9 (2003): 8–14.

N.a. "Low-income subsidy fraud in China." *Jiancha [Investigation] Daily*, June 23, 2014.

N.a. "Minzhengbu jiang jianli dibao jiating caichan hedui jizhi." [The Ministry of civil affairs will establish a mechanism for checking the figures on *dibao* households' assets]. www.21.cbh.com/HTML/2012-9-27/ONNjUxXZuZmduona.html, accessed October 16, 2012.

N.a. "Quanguo 36ge chengshi zuidi baozhang biaozhun yilan" [General survey of 36 cities' minimum livelihood guarantee norm]. http://china.com.cn/city/txt/2006 -11/25/content_740675\hich\af0\dbch\af13\loch\f0 8_2.htm, accessed August 17, 2007.

N.a., "Searching for the Union: The workers' movement in China, 2011–2013." *China Labour Bulletin,* February 2014, 15–16.

N.a. "Taotai luohou channeng dui jiuye de yingxiang" [The influence of eliminating backward production capacity on employment]. *Zhongguo jiuye* [China employment] no. 5 (2014): 54–55.

N.a. "Urban and rural population of China." https://www.statista.com/statistics /278566/urban-and-rural-population-of-china/, accessed January 11, 2021.

N.a. "Wuhan Shi fangzhi zaijiuye fuwu zhongxin yuncuo qingkuang huibao" [A Summary report on the situation of operations in the Wuhan City Textile Reemployment Service Center]. Prepared by the center, March 18, 1998.

N.a. "Xiao ziliao: quanguo gechengshi jumin zuidi shenghuo baozhang biaozhun" [Small material: Nationwide various cities' residents' minimum livelihood guarantee norms]. *Shehui* [Society], 6 (1999), 26.

N.a. "Zhongdian lianxi chengshi yanglaojin shehuihua fafang jindu" [Focus on the process of the socialized issuance of urban pensions]. *LDBZTX,* no. 6 (2000), 23.

N.a. "Zhongguo chengshi jumin zuidi shenghuo baozhang biaozhun de xiangguan fenxi, jingji qita xiangguan lunwen" [Relevant analysis of Chinese urban residents' dibao norm; economic and other related treatises]. Unpaged. http://www.ynexam .cn/html/jingjixue/jingjixiangguan/2006/1105/zhonggochengshijimin . . ., accessed August 18, 2007.

N.a. "Zhongguo jianli chengxiang shehui jiuzhu tixi, 7 qianwan kunnan qunzhong ganshou wennuan yangguang" [China constructs an urban-rural social relief system, seventy million masses in difficulty feel warm sunshine]. http://china.com.cn /txt/2006-11/30/content_7429928.htm.

Nathan, Andrew J., and Bruce Gilley. *China's New Rulers: The Secret Files.* New York: New York Review Books, 2002.

National Development and Reform Commission. "Report on the Implementation of the 2014 Plan for National Economic and Social Development and on the 2015 Draft Plan for National Economic and Social Development." Delivered at the Third Session of the Twelfth National People's Congress, March 5, 2015.

National Development and Reform Commission. "Report on the Implementation of the 2016 Plan for National Economic and Social Development and on the 2017 Draft Plan for National Economic and Social Development." Delivered at the Fifth Session of the Twelfth National People's Congress on March 5, 2017.

Naughton, Barry. *The Chinese Economy: Adaptation and Growth.* Second edition. Cambridge, MA: The MIT Press, 2018.

Naughton, Barry. "China's Emergence and Prospects as a Trading Nation." *Brookings Papers on Economic Activity*. The Brookings Institute no. 2 (1996): 273–344.

Naughton, Barry. "Danwei: The Economic Foundations of a Unique Institution." In *Danwei: The Changing Chinese Workplace in Historical and Comparative Perspective*. Xiaobo Lü and Elizabeth J. Perry, 169–82. Armonk, NY: M.E. Sharpe, 1997.

Naughton, Barry. *Growing Out of the Plan: Chinese Economic Reform, 1978–1995*. New York: Cambridge University Press, 1995.

Naughton, Barry. "Implications of the State Monopoly over Industry and its Relaxation." *MC* 18, no. 1 (1992): 14–41.

Ngok, King-lun. "Social assistance policy and its impact on social development in China: the case of the Minimum Living Standard Scheme (MLSS). *CJ SW* 3, no. 1 (2010): 35–52.

Odgaard, Ole. "Entrepreneurs and Elite Formation in Rural China." *Australian Journal of Chinese Affairs* 28 (1992): 89–108.

O'Donnell, Guillermo. *Modernization and Bureaucratic Authoritarianism*. Berkeley: University of California Press, 1979.

OECD. "Education in China: A Snapshot." (Paris: OECD, 2016), 15–16. https://www.oecd.org/china/Education-in-China-a-snapshot.pdf.

Offe, Claus. "Advanced Capitalism and the Welfare State." *Politics & Society* 2 (Summer) 1972: 479–88.

O'Keefe, Philip. "Social Assistance in China: An Evolving System." Draft. For ANU conference, August 27, 2004.

Oksenberg, Michel, and James Tong. "The evolution of central-provincial fiscal relations in China, 1971–1984." *CQ*, no. 25 (1991): 1–32.

Ong, Lynette H. "Reports of social unrest: basic characteristics, trends and patterns, 2003–2012." In *Handbook of the Politics of China*, edited by David S. G. Goodman, 345–59. Cheltenham, UK: Edward Elgar Publishing, 2015.

Orenstein, Mitchell. *Out of the Red: Building Capitalism and Democracy in Postcommunist Europe*. Ann Arbor, MI: University of Michigan Press, 2001.

Overholt, William H. "China in the Balance." Nomura Strategy Paper. Hong Kong, May 12, 1999.

Pan, Fu. "Minzheng xitong fucha jin jiu cheng dibao duixiang; 25.7 wan ren tuichu 'renqingbao' 'cuobao,'" [The civil affairs system rechecked *dibao* recipients; 257,000 people withdraw from the *dibao* because of having received it based on human relations or mistakes]. *RMRB*, December 9, 2014.

Pan, Jennifer. "Buying Inertia: Preempting Social Disorder with Selective Welfare Provision in Urban China." Ph.D. dissertation, Harvard University, 2015.

Pan, Jennifer. *Welfare for Autocrats: How Social Assistance in China Cares for its Rulers*. NY: Oxford University Press, 2020.

Park, Albert, Sangui Wang, and Guobao Wu. "Regional Poverty Targeting in China." *Journal of Public Economics* 86, no. 1 (2002): 123–53.

Pear, Robert. "Thousands Could Lose Food Stamps as States Restore Requirements." *NYT,* April 2, 2016.

Pearson, Margaret. *Joint Ventures in the People's Republic of China*. Princeton: Princeton University Press, 1991.

Peng, Guohua, and Ouyang Hui. "Chengshi shi xiandaihua 'huochetou'" [The city is the locomotive of modernization]. *RMRB*, February 21, 2016.

Perkins, Dwight H. *China: Asia's Next Economic Giant?* Seattle: University of Washington Press, 1986.

Perkins, Dwight. "Prospects for China's Integration into the Global Economy." In Joint Economic Committee, *China's Economic Future*. 34–40.

Perry, Elizabeth J. "From Mass Campaigns to Managed Campaigns: 'Constructing a New Socialist Countryside.'" In *Mao's Invisible Hand*, edited by Heilmann and Perry, 30–61.

Perry, Elizabeth J. "Masters of the Country? Shanghai Workers in the Early People's Republic." In *Dilemmas of Victory: The Early Years of the People's Republic of China*, edited by Jeremy Brown and Paul G. Pickowicz, 59–69. Cambridge, MA: Harvard University Press, 2007.

Perry, Elizabeth J., and Li Xun. *Proletarian Power.* Boulder, CO: Westview Press, 1997.

Pieke, Frank N. "Marketization, Centralization and Globalization of Cadre Training in Contemporary China," *CQ* no. 200 (Dec. 2009): 953–71.

Pierson, Paul. *Dismantling the Welfare State? Reagan, Thatcher and the Politics of Retrenchment.* Cambridge, U.K.: Cambridge University Press, 1994.

Pinches, Michael. "'All that we have is our muscle and sweat': The Rise of Wage Labour in a Manila Squatter Community." In *Wage Labour and Social Change: The Proletariat in Asia and the Pacific,* edited by M. Pinches and S. Lakha, 105–44. Clayton: Centre of Southeast Asian Studies, Monash University, 1987.

Piore, Michael J. *Birds of Passage: Migrant Labor and Industrial Societies.* Cambridge: Cambridge University Press, 1979.

Portes, Alejandro, and John Walton. *Labour, Class and the International System.* New York: Academic Press, 1981.

Premier Li Peng's address to the Ninth National People's Congress. *SWB*, FE/3168, March 6, 1998/98, S1/9, from Xinhua, March 5, 1998.

Putterman, Louis. "Dualism and Reform in China." *Economic Development and Cultural Change* no. 40 (1992): 467–69.

Qi, Yue. "Danyou di'er bo xiagangchao: xian lai suansuan chuqing 'jianghu qiye' yingxiang duoda" [Concern about the second wave of layoffs, first calculate how great the influence of clearing out the "zombie factories" is]. December 29, 2015. http://m.wallstreetcn.com/node/228035.

Qian, Jiwei, and Ka Ho Mok. "Dual decentralization and fragmented authoritarianism in governance: crowding out among social programmes in China." *Public Administration and Development* 36, no. 3 (2016): 185–97.

Qian, Zhihong, and Tai-chee Wong. "The Rising Urban Poverty: a dilemma of market reforms in China." *Journal of Contemporary China* 9, no. 23 (2000): 113–25.

Qin, Zhou, Gordon G. Liu, Yankun Sun, and Sam A. Vortherms. "The impact of health insurance cost-sharing method on healthcare utilization in China." *CJSW* 9, nos. 1–3 (2016): 38–61.

Qinghaisheng minzhengting jiuzai jiujichu [Qinghai province Civil Affairs Bureau, Disaster and Economic Relief Office]. "Wanshan chengshi jumin zuidi shenghuo baozhang zhidu" [Perfect the urban residents' minimum livelihood guarantee system]. *ZGMZ* no. 10 (1999): 24–25.

Quanguo zongtonghui baozhang gongzuobu [All-China General Trade Union Security Work Department]. "Guanyu xiagang zhigong laodong guanxi chuli ji shehui baozhang jiexu wenti de diaocha" [Investigation on handling laid-off staff and workers' labor relations and the issue of the continuation of social security]. *ZGGY* 5 (2001): 14–16.

Ravallion, Martin. "A Guaranteed Minimum Income? China's Di Bao Program." ppt. (n.p., n.d.).

Ravallion, Martin, and Shaohua Chen. "Benefit Incidence with Incentive Effects, Measurement Errors and Latent Heterogeneity." Policy Working Paper No. 6573. Washington, D.C.: The World Bank, Development Research Group, Poverty and Inequality Team, August 2013.

Ravallion, Martin, Shaohua Chen, and Youjuan Wang. "Does the Di Bao Program Guarantee a Minimum Income in China's Cities?" In *Public Finance in China: Reform and Growth for a Harmonious Society*, edited by Jiwei Lou and Shuilin Wang, 317–34. Washington, D.C.: World Bank, 2006.

Rawski, Thomas G. "Is China's success transferable?" In *Reform and Development in China: What can China offer the developing woirld?* edited by Ho-Mou Wu and Yang Yao, 320–48. London: Routledge, 2011.

Rawski, Thomas G. "Reforming China's Economy: What Have We Learned?" *CJ* no. 41 (1999): 139–56.

Renli ziyuan he shehui baozhangbu dangzu [The party group in the Ministry of Human Resources and Social Security]. "Ruhe kandai woguo jiuye xingshi" [How to regard the employment situation in our country]. *Qiushi* [Seeking truth], January 3, 2020.

Rocca, Jean-Louis. "Governing from the Middle? Understanding the Making of China's Middle Classes." In *To Govern China: Evolving Practices of Power*, edited by Vivienne Shue and Patricia M. Thornton, 231–55. NY: Cambridge University Press, 2017.

Rocca, Jean-Louis. "Three at Once: The Multidimensional Scope of Labor Crisis in China." In Mengin and Rocca, *Chinese Politics,* 3–30.

Rofel, Lisa. *Other Modernities: Gendered Yearnings in China after Socialism.* Berkeley: University of California Press, 1999.

Ru, Xin, Lu Xueyi, and Shan Tianlun, eds. *1998 nian: Zhongguo shehui xingshi fenxi yu yuce* [1998: Analysis and prediction of China's social situation]. Beijing: shehui kexue wenxian chubanshe [Social science documents publishers], 1998.

Rudra, Nita. "Globalization and the Decline of the Welfare State in Less-Developed Countries."*International Organization* 56, no. 2 (2002): 411–45.

Rueda, David. "The State of the Welfare State: Unemployment, Labor Market Policy, and Inequality in the Age of Workfare." *CP* (April 2015): 296–314.

Sabin, Lora. "New Bosses in the Workers' State: The Growth of Non-State Sector Employment in China." *CQ* gldno. 140 (1994): 944–970.

Sadanandan, Anoop. "Patronage and Decentralization: The Politics of Poverty in India." *CP* (January 2012): 211–28.

Saich, Anthony. *Providing Public Goods in Transitional China.* London: Palgrave/ Macmillan, 2008.

Scholz, John Karl, Robert Moffitt, and Benjamin Cowan. "Trends in Income Support." In *Changing Poverty, Changing Policies*, edited by Maria Cancian and Sheldon Danziger, 203–41. NY: Russell Sage Foundation, 2009.

Schoppa. Leonard J. *Race for the Exits: The Unraveling of Japan's System of Social Protection.* Ithaca: Cornell University Press, 2006.

Schram, Stanford F. *The Return of Ordinary Capitalism: Neoliberalism, Precarity, Occupy.* Oxford and NY: Oxford University Press, 2015.

Segura-Ubiergo, Alex. *The Political Economy of the Welfare State in Latin America: Globalization, Democracy, and Development.* NY: Cambridge University Press, 2007.

Shang, Xiaoyuan, and Xiaoming Wu. "Changing Approaches of Social Protection: Social Assistance Reform in Urban China." *Social Policy and Society* 3, no. 3 (2004): 259–71.

Shen, Wenming, and Ma Runlai. "Zaijiuyezhong de zhengfu xingwei" [The government's behavior in reemployment]. *ZGLD* no. 2 (1999), 19.

Shi, Xianmin. "Beijing's Privately-Owned Small Businesses: A Decade's Development." *Social Sciences in China* 14, no. 1 (Spring 1993): 153–64.

Shoudu jingji maoyi daxue, laodong jingji xueyuan shequ jiuye ketizu [Capital University of Economics and Trade, Labor Economics Institute, Community Employment Task Force]. "Shequ jiuye fuwu tixi jianshe de lilun yu shijian" [Theory and Practice in the construction of the community employment service system]. *Renkou yu jingji* [Population & Economics] no. 5 (2001): 59–64.

Sicular, Terry. "Will China Eliminate Poverty in 2020?" *China Leadership Monitor*, December 1, 2020, https://www.prcleader.org/sicular?utm_source =so&cid=181f57b0-7589-4ba6-b97c-2032dc9bab59, accessed December 18, 2020.

Smith, Joanna Handlin. *The Art of Doing Good: Charity in Late Ming China.* Berkeley: University of California Press, 2009.

Smith, Noah. "China Steps Up Health Care Spending Just in Time." *Bloomberg Opinion,* October 27, 2019. https://www.bloomberg.com/opinion/articles/2019-10-27 /china- steps-up-health-care-spending-just-in-time.

Solinger, Dorothy J. "Banish the Impoverished Past: The Predicament of the Abandoned Urban Poor." In *Polarized Cities: Portraits of Rich and Poor in Urban China*, edited by Dorothy J. Solinger, 59–84. Lanham, MD: Rowman & Littlefield, 2019.

Solinger, Dorothy J. "Capitalist Measures with Chinese Characteristics." *Problems of Communism* no. 38 (Jan.–Feb. 1989): 19-33.

Solinger, Dorothy J. *China's Transition from Socialism.* Armonk, NY: M.E. Sharpe, 1993.

Solinger, Dorothy J. "China's Urban Workers and the WTO." *CJ* no. 49 (January 2003): 61–87.

Solinger, Dorothy J. *Chinese Business under Socialism: The Politics of Domestic Commerce.* Berkeley: University of California Press, 1984.

Solinger, Dorothy J. "Commercial Reform and State Control: Structural Changes in ChineseTrade, 1981–1983." *Pacific Affairs* (Summer 1985): 197-215.

Solinger, Dorothy J. "Dibaohu in Distress: The Meager Minimum Livelihood Guarantee System in Wuhan." In *China's Changing Welfare Mix: Local Perspectives*, edited by Jane Duckett and Beatriz Carillo, 36–63. London: Routledge, 2011.

Solinger, Dorothy J. *From Lathes to Looms: China's Industrial Policy in Comparative Perspective, 1979–1982*. Stanford: Stanford University Press, 1991.

Solinger, Dorothy J. "Labor Market Reform and the Plight of the Laid-Off Proletariat." *CQ* no. 170 (June 2002): 304–326.

Solinger, Dorothy J. "A Question of Confidence: State Legitimacy and the New Urban Poor." In *Chinese Politics: State, Society, and the Market*, edited by Peter H. Gries, and Stanley Rosen, 243–56. London and NY: Routledge/Curzon, 2010.

Solinger, Dorothy J. *States' Gains, Labor's Losses: China, France and Mexico Choose Global Liaisons.* Ithaca: Cornell University Press, 2009.

Solinger, Dorothy J. "The Urban Dibao: Guarantee for Minimum Livelihood or for Minimal Turmoil?" In *Marginalization,* edited by Wu and Webster, 253–77. Houndmills, Basingstoke: Palgrave/Macmillan, 2010.

Solinger, Dorothy J. "Urban Entrepreneurs and the State: The Merger of State and Society." In *State and Society in China: The Consequences of Reform*, edited by Arthur Lewis Rosenbaum, 121–41. Boulder: Westview Press, 1992.

Solinger, Dorothy J. "Why We Cannot Count the 'Unemployed.'" *CQ* no.167 (2001): 671–88.

Song, Xiaowu. *Zhongguo shehui baozhang zhidu gaige* [The reform of China's social security system]. Beijing: *Qinghua daxue chubanshe* [Qinghua University Press], 2001.

Sorace, Christian, and William Hurst. "China's Phantom Urbanization and the Pathology of Ghost Cities." *Journal of Contemporary Asia* 46, no. 2 (2016): 304–322. http://dx.doi.org/10.1080/00472336.2015.1115532.

Soss, Joe, Richard C. Fording, & Sanford F. Schram. *Disciplining the Poor: Neoliberal Paternalism and the Persistent Power of Race.* Chicago: University of Chicago Press, 2011.

Stark, David. "Bending the Bars of the Iron Cage: Bureaucratization and Informalization in Capitalism and Socialism." *Sociological Forum* 4, no. 4 (1989): 637–64.

State Council of the People's Republic of China. "Compulsory Education Law of the People's Republic of China," June 26, 2006. http://english.www.gov.cn/archive /laws_regulations/2014/08/23/content_2814749830421 54.htm#:~:text=The%20 Compulsory%20Education%20Law%20of%20the%20People%E2%80%99s%20 Republic,go%20into%20effect%20as%20of%20September%201%2C%202006.

Stepan, Alfred. "State Power and the Strength of Civil Society in the Southern Cone of Latin America." In *Bringing the State Back In*, edited by Peter B. Evans, Dietrich Rueschemeyer, and Theda Skocpol, 317–43. Cambridge: Cambridge University Press, 1985.

Sun, Yu. "China's retraining campaign offers scant prospects for the unemployed." *Financial Times,* September 15, 2020, https://www.ft.com/content/51caf358-1058 -4ee7-834a-c5b5cb8bf205

Tan, Terence. "China's Jobless Can't Get New Work." *The Straits' Times*, September 27, 2002.

Tang, Jun. "Dibao zhiduzhong de shehui paichi" [Social discrimination in the minimum living guarantee system]. Paper presented at the Conference on Social Exclusion and Marginality in Chinese Societies, sponsored by the Centre for Social Policy Studies of the Department of Applied Social Sciences, the Hong Kong Polytechnic University and the Social Policy Research Centre, Institute of Sociology, the Chinese Academy of Social Sciences, Hong Kong, November 16–17, 2001.

Tang, Jun. "Jiasu zuidi shenghuo baozhang zhidu de guanfanhua yunzuo" [Speed up the dibao's normalized operation]. In *2004 nian: Zhongguo shehui xingshi fenxi yu yuce* [2004: Analysis and forecast of China's social situation], edited by Ru Xin, Lu Xuejin, and Li Peilin, 117–28. Beijing: shehui kexue wenxian chubanshe [Social science documents publishing company], 2004.

Tang, Jun. "The New Situation of Poverty and Antipoverty." in *2002 nian: Zhongguo shehui xingshi yu yuce (shehui lanpishu)* [2002: Analysis and Forecast of China's Social Situation (social blue book)], edited by Ru Xin, Lu Xueyi, Li Peilin, et al. January 1, 2002. [FBIS Translated Text].

Tang, Jun. "The Report of Poverty and Anti-Poverty in Urban China—The Poverty Problems in Urban China and the Program of Minimum Living Standard." Ms. N.p., 2002.

Tang, Jun. "Tiaozhengzhong de chengxiang zuidi shenghuo baozhang zhidu" [The urban and rural minimum livelihood guarantee system in adjustment]. In *Shehui lanpishu: 2006 nian: Zhongguo shehui xingshi fenxi yu yuce* [Social blue book: 2006 Analysis and predictions of China's social situation], edited by Ru Xin, Lu Xueyi, and Li Peilin, 165–75. Beijing: shehui kexue wenxian chubanshe [Social science documents publishing company], 2006.

Tang Jun. "2012: Zhongguo xinxing shehui jiuzhu tixi jiben jiancheng." [2012: China's new-style social assistance system is basically constructed]. In *2013 nian: Zhongguo shehui xingshi fenxi yu yuce* [2013: Analysis of China's social situation and forecast], edited by Lu Xueyi, Li Peilin, and Chen Guangjin, 213–25. Beijing: shehui kexue wenxuan chubanshe [Social science academic press], 2013.

Tang, Jun, and Xiu Hongfang. "2010–2011: Chengxiang shehui jiuzhu zhidu de wenti ji duice" [2010–2011: Urban and rural social assistance system's problems and their management], In *2011 nian: Zhongguo shehui xingshi fenxi yu yuce* [2011: Analysis of China's social situation and forecast], edited by Ru Xin, Lu Xueyi, and Li Peilin, 208–17. Beijing: shehui kexue wenxuan chubanshe [Social Sciences Academic Press], 2011.

Taylor, John G. "Poverty and vulnerability." In *China Urbanizes,* edited by Shahid Yusuf and Tony Saich, 91–104. Washington, D.C.: The World Bank, 2008.

Teichman, Judith A. *Social Forces and States: Poverty and Distributional Outcomes in South Korea, Chile, and Mexico.* Stanford: Stanford University Press, 2012.

Thompson, E. P. "The Moral Economy of the English Crowd in the Eighteenth Century." *Past and Present* no. 50 (February 1971): 76–136.

Thornton, Patricia M. "A New Urban Underclass? Making and Managing 'Vulnerable Groups' in Contemporary China." In *To Govern China: Evolving Practices of Power*, edited by Vivienne Shue and Patricia M. Thornton, 257–81. NY: Cambridge University Press, 2017.

Works Cited

Townsend, Peter. "Social Security in Developing Countries: a Brief Overview." In *Building Decent Societies: Rethinking the Role of Social Security in Development*, edited by Peter Townsend, 245–52. Houndmills: Palgrave Macmillan 2009.

Tsui, Ming. "Managing Transition: Unemployment and Job Hunting in Urban China." *Pacific Affairs* 75, no. 4 (Winter 2002–2003): 515–34.

Turkewitz, Julie, and Juliet Linderman. "The Disability Trap." *NYT*, October 21, 2012.

2015 nian Guangzhou Tianhenanjie chengguan xieguanyuan zhaopinwang [2015 advertisement for Guangzhou Tianhenan street *chengguan* assistant]. http://gd.huatu.com/sydw/2015/0922/1327898.html.

Vogel, Ezra F. *Deng Xiaoping and the Transformation of China.* Cambridge, MA: Belknap Press of Harvard University Press, 2011.

Wacquant, Loic. *Punishing the Poor: The Neoliberal Government of Social Insecurity.* Durham: Duke University Press, 2009.

Walder, Andrew G. *Communist Neo-Traditionalism.* Berkeley: University of California Press, 1986.

Walder, Andrew G. "The Remaking of the Chinese Working Class, 1949–1981." *MC* 10, no. 1 (1984): 3–48.

Waldfogel, Jane. *Britain's War on Poverty.* NY: Russell Sage Foundation, 2010.

Walker, Carol. "'Don't cut down the tall poppies': Thatcherism and the strategy of inequality." In Farrall and Hay, *The Legacy of Thatcher*, 282–305.

Wallace, Jeremy. *Cities and Stability: Urbanization, Redistribution, & Regime Survival in China.* NY: Oxford University Press, 2014.

Wang, D. "Director General of Economics Faculty at the Party School of the Chinese Communist Party Central Committee. Comments at the invitation of the "21st Century Business Herald," November 19, 2007. www.wsichina.org/morningchina/archive/20071120.html

Wang, Depei. "'San min' yu 'erci gaige'" ['Three people' and 'The Second Reform']. *Gaige neican* [Reform internal reference] no. 7 (2001): 2–26.

Wang, Dongjin. "Jianchi zhengque fangxiang, fahui xuehui gongneng wei jianshe you Zhongguo tese de laodong he shehui baozhang shiye fuwu" [Persist in an accurate direction, foster competence in studying, to build a labor and social security service with Chinese characteristics]. *ZGLD* no. 4 (2000): 4–8.

Wang, Hui. "Chengshi zuidi shenghuo baozhang gongzuo zhi wo jian" [My opinion on the urban minimum livelihood guarantee work]. *ZGMZ* 10 (1996): 34.

Wang, Jasmine. "Poor Attitudes towards the Poor: Conceptions of Poverty among the Rich and Powerful in China. *Made in China* (April–June 2019), 60–63. https://madeinchinajournal.com/2019/07/23/poor-attitudes-towards-the-poor-conceptions-of-poverty-among-the-rich-and-powerful-in-china/

Wang, Jinxian, and Yanfeng Bai. "Development of minimum livelihood guarantee programmes in urban China: an empirical analysis based on 31 regions over 2003–2013." *CJSW* 9, nos. 1–3 (2016): 155–75.

Wang, Meiyan. "Emerging Urban Poverty and Effects of the *Dibao* Program on Alleviating Poverty in China." *China & World Economy* 15, no. 2 (2007): 74–88.

Wang Shaoguang. "Shunying minxin de bianhua: cong caizheng zijin liuxiang Zhongguo zhengfu jinqi de zhengce tiaozheng" [A change that complies with popular sentiments: recent policy readjustment in the flow of financial funds toward the Chinese government]. Paper presented to the Center for Strategic and International Studies, Washington, D.C. Unpublished manuscript, January 16, 2004.

Wang, Tianxing. "Kunjing yu chulou" [Difficult straits and the way out]. *Shehuixue yanjiu* [Sociology research] 6 (1997). In *Xinhua wengao* [New China documents] no. 3 (1998): 21–28.

Wang, Ya Ping. *Urban Poverty, Housing and Social Change in China.* London and New York: Routledge, 2004.

Wang, Yanzhong. "Jiaru WTO hou wo guo jingji fazhan wenti yu zhanwang" [Looking back and forward at our country's economic development after entering WTO]. *Lingdao canyue* [Leadership consultations] no. 3 (January 25, 2003): 3–6.

Wang, Z. and Wang, H. "Luoshi chengshi jumin zuidi shenghuo baozhang zijin ying chuli hao wuge guanxi" [In order to implement urban residents' minimun livelihood guarantee funds we need to handle five relationships well]. *ZGMZ*, 3 (1998): 18, 19.

Wang, Zhikun. "Chengshi jumin zuidi shenghuo baozhang: buru fazhihua guanli guidao" [Urban residents' minimum livelihood guarantee: Step into the orbit of legalized managment]. *ZGMZ* no. 11 (1999): 18–19.

Wank, David L. *Commodifying Communism: Business, Trust, and Politics in a Chinese City.* New York, Cambridge University Press, 1999.

Weaver, R. Kent. *Ending Welfare as We Know It.* Washington, DC: The Brookings Institution, 2000.

Wei, Wei. "Chengshi dibao: tashang xin zhengcheng" [The urban dibao: step onto a new journey]. *ZGMZ* no. 1 (2000), 22–27.

Wen, Jiabao. "Report on the Work of the Government." Delivered at the First Session of the Eleventh National People's Congress, March 5, 2008. http://www .chinadaily.com.cn/china/2008npc/200803/19/content_6549177.htm, accessed May 26, 2008.

Wen, Jiabao. "Report on the Work of the Government." Delivered at the First Session of the Twelfth National People's Congress, March 5, 2013.

Wen, Zhuoyi. and Kinglun Ngok. "Governing the Poor in Guangzhou: Marginalization and the Neoliberal Paternalist Construction of Deservedness." *China Information* 33, no. 2 (2019), 210–33.

West, Loraine A. "The Changing Effects of Economic Reform on Rural and Urban Employment." Draft. Paper [to be] presented at "Unintended Social Consequences of Chinese Economic Reform" conference, Harvard School of Public Health and The Fairbank Center for East Asian Studies, Harvard University, May 23–24, 1997.

Westmore, Ben. "Do government transfers reduce poverty in China? Micro Evidence from Five Regions." OECD Economics Department Working Papers No. 1415. Paris: OECD Publishing, 2017. Also published in *CER* 51 (2018): 59–69.

Westmore, Ben. "Sharing the Benefits of China's Growth by Providing Opportunities to All." *Journal of International Commerce, Economics and Policy* 8, no. 3 (2017): 1–33.

Will, Pierre-Etienne Will, and R. Bin Wong, with James Lee. *Nourish the People: The State Civilian Granary System in China, 1650–1850.* Ann Arbor: University of Michigan Press, 1991.

Wilson, William Julius. *The Truly Disadvantaged.* Chicago: University of Chicago Press, 1987.

Won, Jaeyoun. "The Making of the Post-Proletariat in China." *Development and Society* 34, no. 2 (2005): 191–215.

Wong, Christine. "Central-local relations in an era of fiscal decline." *CQ* no. 128 (1991): 691–715.

Wong, Christine P. "Rebuilding Government for the 21st Century." *CQ* no. 200 (2009): 929–952.

Wong, Christine P. W., Christopher Heady, and Wing T. Woo. *Fiscal Management and Economic Reform in the People's Republic of China.* Hong Kong: Oxford University Press, l995.

Wong, R. Bin. *China Transformed: Historical Change and the Limits of European Experience.* Ithaca, NY: Cornell University Press, 1997.

Wong, Linda. *Marginalization and Social Welfare in China.* London: Routledge, 1998.

Wong, Linda. "Mending the Chinese Welfare Net: Tool for Social Harmony or Regime Stability?" Presented at conference on "Authoritarianism in East Asia: Viet Nam, China, North Korea," June 29–30, 2010, City University of Hong Kong,

Wong, Yu-Cheung, Honglin Chen, and Qun Zeng. "Social assistance in Shanghai: Dynamics between social protection and informal employment." *IJSW* 23 (2014): 333–41.

Woo, Jung-en. *Race to the Swift: State and Finance in Korean Industrialization.* NY: Columbia University Press, 1991.

Woo, Wing Thye. "Crises and Institutional Evolution in China's Industrial Sector." In *China's Economic Future,* edited by Joint Economic Committee, Congress of the United States, 162–75.

Woo, Wing Thye, Li Shi, Yue Ximing, Harry Wu Xiaoying, and Xu Xingpeng. "The Poverty Challenge for China in the New Millenium." Report to the Poverty Reduction Taskforce of the Millennium Development Goals Project of the United Nations, October 2, 2004.

The World Bank. *China 2020: China Engaged, Integration with the Global Economy.* Washington, D.C.: The World Bank, 1997.

The World Bank, Poverty Reduction and Economic Management Department, East Asia and Pacific Region. "From poor areas to poor people: China's evolving poverty reduction agenda: an assessment of poverty and inequality in China." Washington, D.C.: The World Bank, 2009.

Wu, Fulong. "Debates and Developments: The State and Marginality: Reflections on Urban Outcasts from China's Urban Transition.*" IJURR 33,* no. 2 (2009): 1–6.

Wu, Fulong. "Urban Poverty and Marginalization under Market Transition: The Case of Chinese Cities." *IJURR* 28, no. 2 (June 2004): 401–23.

Wu, Fulong, and Ningying Huang. "New urban poverty in China." *Asia Pacific Viewpoint* 48, no. 2 (2007): 168–85.

Wu, Fulong, and Chris Webster. "What Has Been Marginalized? Marginalization as the Constrained 'Right to the City' in Urban China." In Wu and Webster, *Marginalization.* 301–06.

Wu, Fulong, Chris Webster, Shenjing He, and Yuting Liu. *Urban Poverty in China.* Cheltenham, UK: Edward Elgar, 2010.

Wuhan shi tongjiju, bian [Wuhan statistical bureau, ed.]. *Wuhan tongji nianjian* [Wuhan Statistical Yearbook]. Wuhan: Wuhan chubanshe [Wuhan publishing company]. Selected years.

Wuxi Statistical Yearbook 2005, China data online, accessed May 29. 2008.

Xi Jinping, "Secure a Decisive Victory in Building a Moderately Prosperous Society in All Respects and Strive for the Great Success of Socialism with Chinese Characteristics for a New Era." Delivered at the 19th National Congress of the Communist Party of China, October 18, 2017, http://www.xinhuanet.com/english/download /Xi_Jinping's_report_at_19th_CPC_National_Congress.pdf

Xiang, Yunhua, and Zhao Lingya. "Jiyu kuozhan xianxing zhichu moshi de chengshi dibao biaozhun yanjiu: yi Wuhanshi weili" [Research on urban dibao norm based on the extension line expenditure model: taking Wuhan as example]. *Diaoyan shijie* [Investigation world] no. 10, 2018: 42–47.

Xin, Sun. "Campaign-Style Implementation and Affordable Housing Provision in China." *CJ* no. 84 (July 2020): 76–101.

Xing, Zhaohui. "Fenlei shibao ruhe fenlei" [How to make distinctions in executing the *dibao*]. *ZGMZ* 4 (2004): 41.

Xinhua, "China regulates social assistance." February 28, 2014.

Xinwen zhongxin jiuye fuwu, peixun jianding laodong guanxi yu gongzi shehui baozhang zhengce cixun shuju fenxi dushu pindao [News center employment service training appraisal, labor relations and wages, social security policy consultation, statistical analysis readers' frequency channel]. May 11, 2005. There is no further citation information on this and I could not find it online.

Xiong, Yang. "Guizhou qiye xiagang zhigong zaijiuye wenti fenxi" [Analysis of the issue of the reemployment of Guizhou's staff and workers laid off from enterprises]. *Xueshu tantao* [Academic Inquiry] no. 5 (2011): 389.

Xu, D. "Jiada gongzuo lidu, chengxiang quanmian tuijin—Guangdong sheng jianli chengxiang hu (cun) min zuidi shenghuo baozhang zhidu de zuofa" [Strengthen work, carry out fully in the cities and rural areas—Guangdong province establishes a method for an urban and rural (village) residents' minimun livelihood guarantee system]. *ZGMZ* 3 (1998): 9–10, 15.

Xu, Liqi. "Xiagang zhigong xintai diaocha fenxi" [An analysis of research on laid-off staff and worker's psychological state]. *LDBZTX* no. 5 (2001): 29.

Xu, Yuebin, and Ludovico Carraro. "Minimum income programme and welfare dependency in China." *IJSW* 26, no. 2 (2017): 141–150.

Xue, Zhaoyun. "Dui xiagang zhigong zaijiuye xianzhuang de diaocha, sikao yu jianyi" [Research, reflections, and suggestions about the reemployment situation of laid-off staff and workers]. *Gonghui gongzuo tongxun* [Bulletin of trade union work] no. 7 (2000): 8–10.

Yang, Dali L. "China in 2002: Leadership Transition and the Political Economy of Governance." *AS* 43, no.1 (2003): 25–40.

Yang, Jae-Jin. "The Korean Welfare State in Economic Hard Times: Democracy, Partisanship, and Social Learning." *Taiwan Journal of Democracy* 8, no. 1 (July 2012): 51–68.

Yang, Jae-Jin. "Parochial Welfare Politics and the Small Welfare State in South Korea." *CP* 45, no. 4 (2013): 457–75.

Yang, Lixiong. "The Social Assistance Reform in China; Towards a Fair and Inclusive Social Safety Net." Prepared for "Addressing Inequalities and Challenges to Social Inclusion through Fiscal, Wage and Social Protection Policies." United National Headquarters, New York, 25–27 June 2018 (unpaginated). http://www.un.org/development/.../The-Social-Assistance-Reform-in-China.pdf.

Yang, Mungji. *From Miracle to Mirage: The Making and Unmaking of the Korean Middle Class, 1960–2015.* Ithaca: Cornell University Press, 2018.

Yang, Yiyong. "2000 nian wo guo jiuye xingshi fenxi" [An analysis of the employment situation in our country in the year 2000]. *NBCY* no. 4 (2000): 10–14.

Yang, Yiyong, et al. *Shiye chongji bo* [The shock wave of unemployment]. Beijing: Jinri Zhongguo chubanshe [China today publishing company], 1997.

Yang, Zongchuan, and Zhang Qilin. "Wuhanshi chengshi jumin zuidi shenghuo baozhang zhidu shishi zhuangkuang de diaocha fenxi" [Analysis of an investigation of the true situation of Wuhan's urban residents' minimum livelihood guarantee system]. *Jingji pinglun* [Economic review] 4 (1999): 99–103.

Yao, Jianping. "Zhongguo chengshi dibao miaozhun kunjing: zige zhang'ai, jishu nanti, hai shi zhengzhi yingxiang?" [Chinese urban dibao targeting predicament: qualifications obstacles, technical difficulty, or political influence?]. *Shehui kexue* [Social science] no. 3 (2018): 61–72.

Yao, Jianping. "Zhongguo chengshi zuidi shenghuo baozhang biaozhun shuiping fenxi" [An Analysis of the Level of Minimum Livelihood Standard in Urban China]. *Keji yu shehui* [Technology and society] no. 11 (2012): 57–67.

You, Jong-sung. "State Intervention Can Cut Inequality, But the Current Approach is Wrong." *Global Asia* 14, no. 1 (March 2019): 56–57.

Young, Susan. *Private Business and Economic Reform in China.* Armonk, N.Y.: M.E. Sharpe, 1995.

Yuan, Lanhua, and Lin Chengmei. "Ai ru chao yong—Qingdaoshi chengxiang zuidi shenghuo baozhang zhidu shishi jishi" [Love like a rising tide—a true reporting of the Qingdao city urban and rural minimum livelihood guarantee system]. *ZGMZ* no. 7 (1998): 10–11.

Yuan, Shaohua. "Chongqing jianli chengshi zuidi shenghuo baozhang zhidu de zuofa" [Chongqing's method of establishing an urban minimum livelihood guarantee system]. *ZGMZ* no. 5 (1997): 22–23, 12.

Yuan, Yang, and Nian Liu. "Inside China's race to beat poverty." *Financial Times,* June 25, 2020.

Yuan, Yuan, and Fulong Wu. "Multiple Deprivations in Urban China: An Analysis of Individual Survey Data." in Wu and Webster, *Marginalization*, 226–50.

Yuriko, Takahashi. "The Political Economy of Conditional Cash Transfers in Latin America." Prepared for delivery at the 2013 Annual Meeting of the American Political Science Association, Chicago, August 29–September 1, 2013.

Zhang, Chunni, Qi Xu, Xiang Zhou, Xiaobo Zhang, and Yu Xie. "Are poverty rates underestimated in China? New evidence from four recent surveys." *CER* no. 31 (2014): 410–425.

Zhang, Handong. "Dangqian zaijiuye gongchengde qi da wuqu" [Seven big misunderstandings in the present reemployment project]. *LDNC* no. 7 (1998): 27–28.

Zhang, Haomiao. "China's social assistance policy: experiences and future directions." *CJSW* 7, no. 3 (2014): 219–236.

Zhang, Haomiao. "Frustration, Shame, and Gratitude: The meaning of social assistance for women recipients in China." *Asian Women* 32, no. 1 (2016): 53–75.

Zhang, Laosheng. "Quanmian tuijin guifan guanli—Hubeisheng jianli chengshi jumin zuidi shenghuo baozhang zhidu de jingyan" [Fully promote standardized management—Hubei province's experience in establishing urban residents' minimum livelihood guarantee system]. *ZGMZ* no. 9 (1998), 24.

Zhang, Ruli, and Peng Qing. "Zhongguo chengshi gaigezhong pinkun qunti zhengce de zhuanxing ji qi tedian" [In China's urban reform, the transformation of policy for the poor masses and its characteristics]. S*hehui kexue jikan* [Social science journal] no. 4 (2014): 44–50.

Zhang Shifei, and Tang Jun. "Chengxiang zuidi shenghuo baozhang zhidu jiben xingcheng" [Urban and rural minimum livelihood guarantee system has basically taken form]. In *2008 nian: Zhongguo shehui xingshi fenxi yu yuce* [2008: Analysis and forecast of China's social situation], edited by Ru Xin, Lu Xueyi, and Li Peilin, 57–73. Beijing: Social Sciences Academic Press, 2008.

Zhang, Xiaoyi. "Wanshan shehui jiuzhu zhidu, shixian gongping gongzheng" [Perfect the social relief system, realize fairness and impartiality]. In 2013 *Shanghai lanpishu: Shanghai shehui fazhan baogao* [2013 Shanghai bluebook: Report on Shanghai's social development], edited by Lu Hanlong and Zhou Haiwang, 262–81. Beijing: shehui kexue wenxuan chubanshe, 2013.

Zhang, Yuanchao. "Guoyou qiye tekun zhigong shenghuo de zhuangkuang ying yinqi gaodu zhongshi" [The livelihood situation of state-owned firms' especially difficult staff and workers ought to promote taking it seriously]. *Zhongguo gongren* [Chinese worker] 7 (2000): 4–7.

Zhao, Yuezhi. "The Rich, the Laid-off, and the Criminals in Tabloid Tales: Read All About Them!" In *Popular China: Unofficial Culture in a Globalizing Society*, edited by Perry Link, Richard P. Madsen, and Paul G. Pickowicz, 111–35. Lanham, MD: Rowman & Littlefield, 2002.

Zhao, Zhongheng and Wei Zhikui. "Yanglao baoxian zhidu chuangxin yunxingzhong de san da nanti" [Three big difficulties in blazing a trail in running a pension insurance system]. *ZGLD* no. 1 (2000): 12–15.

Zhong, Renyao. *Shehui jiuzhu yu shehui fuli* [Social assistance and social welfare]. Shanghai: Shanghai University of Finance and Economics Press, 2005.

Zhongguo qiye lianhehui "qiye yingdui 'rushi' celue" ketizu [Task force for Chinese enterprise union's 'enterprise response toward the strategy of entering the WTO']. "Jiaru WTO hou wo guo qiye mianlin de xingshi ji duice" [The situation and response measures facing our enterprises after our country enters the WTO]. *NBCY no.* 561 (April 27, 2001): 12–19.

Zhongguo renmin gongheguo, Guowuyuan. "Guowuyuan guanyu jianli tongyi de chengxiang jumin jiben yanglao baoxian zhidu de yijian" [State Council of the People's Republic of China. "State Council opinion on establishing a unified urban and rural residents' basic pension insurance system]. Guofa (2014) 8 hao [State Council Document (2014) No. 8], www.gov.cn.zhengce/content/2014- 02/26/con tent_8656.htm, accessed 20 February 2020.

Zhongguo renmin gongheguo [People's Republic of China], Guowuyuan [State Council] (2012), "Guowuyuan guanyu jinyibu jiaqiang he gaijin zuidi shenghuo baozhang gongcuo de yijian" [State Council's Opinion on progressively strengthening and improving the Minimum Livelihood Guarantee work], Guofa {2012} 45 *hao* [issuance no. 45], www.gov.cn/zwgk/2012-09/26/content_2233209.htm, accessed September 2012.

Zhongguo renmin gongheguo, Guowuyuan [State Council of the People's Republic of China]. "Guowuyuan guanyu kaizhan chengzhen jumin shehui yanglao baoxian shidian de zhidao yijian," [State Council Guiding opinion on launching an urban residents' social pension insurance pilot]. Guofa [2011] 18 hao [State Council issuance [2011], no. 18. www.gov.cn/zwgk/200116/13/content_1882801.htm, accessed 20 February 2020.

Zhongguo tongjiju, chengshi shehui jingji diaochasi, bian. [China Statistical Bureau, urban social and economic investigation office, ed.]. *Zhongguo chengshi tongji nianjian* [China city statistical yearbook]. Beijing: China Statistics Press. Multiple years.

Zhongguo tongjiju renkou he shehui keji tongjisi, Laodong he shehui baozhangbu guihua caiwusi, bian [China Statistical Bureau Population and Social, Science, and Technology Statistics Department, and Ministry of Labour and Social Security, Planning, and Finance Department, ed.]. [*Zhongguo laodong tongji nianjian* [China Labour Statistical Yearbook]. Beijing: Zhongguo tongji chubanshe [China Statistics Press]. Multiple years.

Zhonghua renmin gongheguo Guowuyuan [State Council of the People's Republic of China], "Chengshi jumin zuidi shenghuo baozhang tiaoli" [Regulations on the urban residents' minimum livelihood guarantee] (1999), *ZGMZ* no. 11 (1999): 16–17. dbs.mca.gov.cn/article/csdb/cvfg/200711/20071100003522.shtml, accessed August 13, 2013.

Zhonghua renmin gongheguo guojia tongjiju, bian [Chinese People's Republic State Statistical Bureau, ed.]. *Zhongguo tongji nianjian. [China Statistical Yearbook]*. Beijing: Zhongguo tongji chubanshe [China Statistics Press]. Multiple years.

Zhonghua renmin gongheguo minzhengbu [Ministry of Civil Affairs of the People's Republic of China]. "Minzhengbu fabu 2012 nian shehui fuwu fazhan tongji gongbao" [Ministry of Civil Affairs announces 2012's social services development statistical bulletin]. Renminwang. June 19, 2013. http://jnjd.mca.gov.cn/article/zyjd /bzjzx/201306/20130600476925.shtml, accessed February18, 2021.

Zhonghua renmin gongheguo minzhengbu, bian [Civil Affairs Ministry of the People's Republic of China, ed.]. *Zhongguo minzheng tongji nianjian* [China Civil Affairs Statistical Yearbook]. Beijing: China Society Publishing Co. Multiple years.

Zhonghua renmin gongheguo renli caiyuan he shehui baozhangbu [Chinese People's Republic Ministry of Human Resources and Social Security Ministry]. "Renli caiyuan shehui baozhangbu guojia fazhan gaigewei deng qi bumen guanyu zai huajie gangtie meitan hangye guosheng channeng shixian tuokun fazhan guochengzhong zuohao zhigong anzhi gongzuo de yijian" [Opinion of the Ministry of Human Resources and Social Security, State Development and Reform Commission, seven ministries on arranging well staff and workers in dissolving Steel and Coal Industries Excess Capacity and Realizing throwing off difficulty]. April 17, 2016, https://www.mohrss.gov.cn/gkml/xxgk/20160413_238000.html.

Zhonghua renmin gongheguo shehui baoxianfa [The Social Insurance Law of the People's Republic of China], October 28, 2010. http://www.gov.cn/zxft/ft209 /content_1748773.htm, accessed March 2020.

Zhonghua renmin gongheguo zhongyang renmin zhengfu [Central Government of the People' Republic of China]. "Guowuyuan guanyu jinyibu jiaqiang he gaijin zuidi shehui baozhang gongzuo de yijian" [Strengthening and Improving the Minimum Livelihood Guarantee Work]. *Guofa* [2012] 45 *hao* [State Council Document [2012] no. 45]. www.gov.cn/zwgk/2012-09/26/content_2233209.htm, accessed September 15, 2012.

Zhongyang jingji gongzuo huiyi zai Beijing juxing, Xi Jinping, Li Keqiang zuo zhongyao jianghua [Central Economic Work Conference was held in Beijing, Xi Jinping, Li Keqiang gave important speeches]. Xinhuawang, December 21, 2018.

Zhou, Shoujing. "Xiagang shiwunian: ronghui yi cheng wangshi" [Laid off for 15 years: the glory is already in the past]. *Juece tanso* [Policy explorations] no. 4 (2014): 50–53.

Zhou, Sophie Fenghua. "Selectivity, Welfare Stigma, and the Take-up of Social Welfare—How Do Chinese People Manage Welfare Stigma." Prepared for "Social Welfare Development and Governance Transformation in East Asia," sponsored by the Harvard-Yenching Institute and the Central China Normal University, 17–18 May 2012, Central China Normal University, Wuhan, China.

Zhu, Qingfan. "Jiexu chengzhen pinkun qunti" [The ongoing urban poor masses]. *Gaige neican* [Reform internal reference] no.8 (2002): 30–31.

Zhu, Rongji. "Zaijiuye gongcheng guanxi guoqi gaige chengbai" [The reemployment project relates to the success or failure of the reform of state enterprises]. From *Jingji guanli wengao* [Drafts on economic management]. In *Gongyun cankao ziliao* [Workers' movement reference materials] no. 3 (1998): 5–6.

Index

This listing contains only terms and proper nouns that appear in the text, not those that are in the notes. All nouns that are not names of persons, places, or events pertain to China, unless otherwise noted.